BUILD A BETTER BUDDHA

BUILD
A BETTER
BUDDHA

the guide to remaking yourself

exactly as you are

JAMES ROBBINS

NICOLAS-HAYS, INC.

Berwick, Maine

First published in 2003 by
NICOLAS-HAYS, INC.
P. O. Box 1126
Berwick, ME 03901-1126
www.nicolashays.com

Distributed to the trade by
Red Wheel/Weiser, LLC
P. O. Box 612
York Beach, ME 03910-0612
www.redwheelweiser.com

Excerpts from *Be as You Are* by Sri Ramana Maharshi edited by David Godman copyright © 1988 Sri Ramana Maharshi. Reprinted by kind permission of Penguin Books.

Excerpts from *The Dhammapada*, translated by Eknath Easwaran, founder of the Blue Mountain Center of Meditation, copyright © 1985, reprinted by kind permission of Nilgiri Press, P. O. Box 256, Tomales, California, www.nilgiri.org.

Excerpts from *The Freud Reader* by Sigmund Freud, edited by Peter Gay, copyright © 1989 by W. W. Norton & Company. Used by kind permission.

Excerpts from *The Tao Te Ching* by Lao Tsu, translated by Gia-Fu Feng and Jane English copyright © 1997 by Jane English. Copyright © 1972 by Gia-Fu Feng and Jane English. Used by permission of Alfred A. Knopf, a division of Random House, Inc.

Library of Congress Cataloging-in-Publication Data
Robbins, James.
    Build a better Buddha : the guide to remaking yourself exactly as you are
    / James Robbins.-- 1st American paperback ed.
       p. cm.
    Includes bibliographical references.
    ISBN 0-89254-065-6 (alk. paper)
    1. Spiritual life. 2. Conduct of life. I. Title.
BL624.R617 2003
291.4'4--dc21   2003004157

Cover and text design by Kathryn Sky-Peck
Typeset in 9.5/13 Berkeley Book
BJ
Printed in the United States of America

09   08   07   06   05   04   03
7   6   5   4   3   2   1

The paper used in this publication meets the minimum requirements of the American National Standard for Information Sciences—Permanence of Paper for Printed Library Materials Z39.48–1992 (R1997).

For Maharaj-ji—
and for Heather,
my impossibly kind, brilliant,
and beautiful wife, whose generous support has helped to birth this work.

CONTENTS

A GOOSE IN A BOTTLE

A high-ranking officer in the T'ang dynasty presented a famous Ch'an (Chinese Zen) master the following riddle: "A long time ago, a man kept a goose in a bottle. The goose grew larger and larger until it couldn't get out of the bottle anymore. He didn't want to break the bottle, nor did he wish to harm the goose. How would you get it out?"

The Ch'an master was silent for a few moments, then suddenly shouted, "Oh, Officer!"

"Yes?"

"It's out!"

When it comes to the tricky business of living our daily lives, most of us can easily identify with the dilemma of this goose. We frequently feel trapped, bottled up by this or that circumstance. It seems that the more we try to force our way out, the more we find ourselves stuck in tighter and tighter spaces. We don't want to harm ourselves, but we also don't want to break the bottle; it's our own bottle after all, our own life, with all its familiar routines and relationships, so we want to keep it intact without being imprisoned by it.

So it goes with the paradoxical buddha construction project suggested by this book's title. We all want to improve ourselves, remake ourselves into someone more relaxed, more giving—someone more spiritual. At the same time, we feel quite attached, albeit unconsciously so, to our old habits of worrying and complaining, acting selfishly and impulsively, etc. To complicate things further, all the spiritual paths emphasize the same core solution to this riddle: Be yourself. Each of us is already perfect, the wisdom traditions tell us, a spontaneous manifestation of the divine, the One Self. Consequently, to try to improve our situation, we are told, is to fundamentally misunderstand that situation; to fail to recognize the innate, effortless perfection of every moment. Most of us, however, feel neither perfect, nor do we experience life's many difficulties as perfection itself. Like our goose, then, we seem to be stuck in an impossible paradox of struggling and relaxing, improving and accepting.

In the following pages, I'll approach this predicament in a couple of different ways. First, we'll look at the practical and logical escape plan described by the world's spiritual belief systems. I will show you a cross section of traditions such as Zen, Taoism, Christianity, and Hinduism, highlighting the fundamental teachings common to all, rather than each of their particular differences. Similarly, I will add the viewpoints of younger traditions such as science, psychology, and philosophy into the mix, suggesting that we are all after the same ultimate goal—liberating that goose—even those of us who profess no "official" spiritual belief whatsoever. I will share with you numerous practices and techniques designed toward this end, such as meditation, guru yoga, and dream work, using an inclusive, rather than exclusive, focus. In doing so, we will trace the basic self-improvement blueprint described by all paths of spiritual inquiry and self-realization, asserting that—impossible as our predicament may seem—ultimate liberation can be achieved by following an incredibly simple, self-evident, step-by-step plan of escape.

Second, I am going to approach this predicament from the "as you already are" perspective. Ironically, the more skill you gain in spiritual practices of any sort, and the further you proceed along your path toward total freedom, the clearer you become regarding the most fundamental existential truth: There is nothing to escape. Properly understood, this simple realization is both the end and the means for all authentic projects of "self-improvement." We have been trying so desperately to free the goose, we have failed to notice that, like the Zen master said, it's already out. You will learn to recognize that your ordinary, daily life, exactly as it already is, has always been the most direct path to complete liberation. Spiritual practice ultimately means simply living, "being ourselves."

This book—like life itself—has necessarily been booby trapped with contradictions. One wrong step and you are likely to lose parts of yourself. Stray too far to the left and you will likely trigger the "Quick: Do Nothing!" landmine. Stray too far to the right and you may encounter the "Spontaneous Spiritual Practice is Mandatory" pit, filled with starving "self-improvement" crocodiles. Consequently, I would suggest you stay strictly to the middle path, which has been clearly marked throughout the following pages. Then again, if you keep always to the middle, you may never have the opportunity of experiencing all those interesting booby traps. . .

The Confines of the Bottle

Freud sums up our confusing predicament as human beings quite nicely: "[B]esides the instinct to preserve living substance and join it into ever larger units, there must exist another, contrary instinct seeking to dissolve those units and to bring them back to their primaeval, inorganic state. That is to say, as well as Eros there was an instinct of death. The phenomena of life could be explained from the concurrent or mutually opposing action of these two instincts."[1] From the very beginning, Freud is suggesting, the experience of life has been fueled by an ongoing struggle of opposites. Love and aggression, merger and separation, even life and death, have been playing in opposition to one another longer than we—deeply imbedded in this process as we necessarily are—can possibly know. On the one hand, this instinctual clash is the source of all of daily life's frustrating dilemmas and injustices, the original mold of our inevitable human suffering. On the other hand, this perpetual wrestling match between good and evil, positive and negative, male and female—Taoism's yang and yin—seems to provide the essential life spark, the fundamental flame of consciousness itself. Without this difficult struggle, you may ask, could there even exist such a strange creature as this "phenomenon of life?"

Before we start up the slippery slope of this ancient paradox, we can try to better define the apparent causes and effects surrounding this relentless play of opposites. Let's take a look at our "bottle" from a few differing, although necessarily intersecting, perspectives.

ME VS. YOU

Each of us has our personal villains, of course, the various bad guys who stand in the way of our various good guys. The fact that life can be conceptualized in terms of Me versus You, Us versus Them, is obviously nothing new. More interesting in our current context, however, is how even our favorite good guys can quickly become stunt doubles for the bad guys. To put it simply: All human relationships, whether friendly or hostile, involve a large degree of emotional ambivalence and uncertain alliance. This being the case, you can read Freud's view of the human dilemma simply as a wordier version of the "can't live with 'em, can't live without 'em" quip. Part of the problem of being, Freud is suggesting, is that it necessarily involves a kind of tug-of-war with all other human beings. We all experience this ancient struggle between Eros and the death instinct, or love and aggression, on a day-to-day basis. To confirm this, you need only take a long, intimate vacation with someone close to you. No doubt, by the vacation's end, you will remember how your best friends are sometimes your worst enemies. Strange as it may seem, to be truly close to someone necessarily involves—at one level at least—an ongoing, continually unfolding skirmish between love *and* aggression. It's a crazy dance you have simply got to do if you are going to have a dance partner at all.

I remember playing Pee Wee football as a kid. At age seven, I would be out there on the gridiron chanting this little ditty our coach had taught us: "Kill, Kill, Blood makes the grass grow!" I would be chanting this ditty over and over, wishing the opposing team much damage. Yet, I would have this other, anxious little prayer going on the whole while. Between each play, I would ask God to protect us all from injury—my team and the opposing team, alike. There's that crazy dance again. But how does this bizarre struggle between God thirst and blood thirst, between Eros and death, get going in the first place?

"This conflict is set going," says Freud, "as soon as [we] are faced with the task of living together."[2] Wherever we find people living together, we are going to find two opposite drives. On the one hand, we are going to be driven by Eros, "whose purpose is to combine single human individuals, and after that families, then races, peoples and nations, into one great unity."[3] We are all deeply motivated by a feeling of love, a desire to integrate ourselves into larger and larger groups. On the other hand, we also want to individuate. From the very start, each of us wants, rather desperately, to separate from the whole. We want to clutch our own goodies tightly so we don't have to share—a strategic maneuver Darwin called "competition for resources."[4] Love is great, we all recognize, but how about survival? How about the harsh facts of reality? There are only so many goodies to go around, after all, so I've got to scavenge as many as possible before the other guy gets his grubby hands on them.

According to Freud, the roots of this struggle are originally present in the Oedipus complex. Imagine a male child, for instance, and the curious relationship he forms with his parents. From the very start, says Freud, the male child is going to have two opposing feelings toward his father. He wants to love him, of course, be accepted and nurtured by him. He wants to form an alliance, or union with him. At the same time, however, he has an opposing feeling of aggression toward him from the very start. Why? Simple: He doesn't want to share his mother's attention. Very early on, the male child learns that Mommy has only so much attention to go around, so the more Daddy "steals," the less he gets for himself. Consequently, the child also has a strong, unconscious urge for his father to go away—or worse.

We don't need to look far to see this same ambivalence playing out in our adult relationships. Aside from the very familiar tug-of-war of Who Gets What, we also find ourselves continually battling with loved ones for subtler reasons. We have learned, in fact, to fear no one so much as those closest to us. This curious phenomenon is similar to the love-hate relationship the addict develops with his or her addiction of choice. To the degree that we have become "addicted" to someone, or dependent on the love that person offers us, we become angry with him or her in advance should that love be withdrawn sometime in the future. After all, at the very least, that person is going to die sooner or later, and what are we supposed to do then? This unconscious fear of loss, or separation anxiety, compels us to draw a boundary around ourselves, a nervous little line in the sand that we feel we must defend if we are to secure our long-term individuality, our sense of personal stability and identity. Paradoxically, then, the closer we become to someone, the fiercer the battle becomes and the more urgently we feel the need to separate, to protect this individual self. It's the same sort of anxiety the guilt-ridden alcoholic feels after a night of drunkenness—the frustrating, although ever-alluring, push/pull surrounding the desirable/repulsive object. Round and round we go, dancing the crazy dance, becoming "addicted" to our loved ones, and then going cold turkey. I love you . . . I hate you . . . I can't live without you . . . I can't live with you. And all the while we feel pulled in two directions at once.

ME VS. ME

The individual's innate feeling of aggression, or desire to separate, says Freud, is expressed in two essential ways. In the first, we simply act it out, direct it at some external object. Someone gets in the way of my individual wants, I get angry with him, bundle my toys up securely, and set up camp, ready to fire the cannons at the first sight of invasion. This is essentially the Me versus You strategy as described above. Civilization, however, tends to frown on this particular method. Rather than firing the cannons, civilization much prefers that we introject our aggression, or simply swallow the cannon balls. This is where the Me versus Me phenomenon comes in. We see this sort of backfired anger, what Friedrich Nietzsche calls "re-sentiment," happening all the time. We do something "bad"—according to contemporary mores, usually—so we feel guilty, anxious, ashamed, etc. We are really angry with someone else, of course, typically some powerful figure whom we feel is keeping us from something we want. I want a raise, for instance. My boss doesn't give me one, so what do I do? Well, to the degree that I am properly "civilized," I turn this anger inward, begin to question myself, begin to feel guilty or anxious about my job performance, etc. Or maybe I punish myself through other self-defeating means. Maybe I tell myself I am stuck with such and such a person and simply have no other choice but to endure—and likely to complain, as such is the way of life, etc. In short, I turn me against me.

Despite what society may want us to believe, things are no better when we simply swallow the cannon balls whole, or direct our aggression back on ourselves. Through this process of introjection, I learn to cultivate a me that I am proud of, a "good me," which I carefully display to the external world. This is the me with whom I consciously identify, the part of the personality Freud associated with the superego. Then I have got the shameful, "lights off" me who is weathering all the heavy artillery, the guilty me who is dealing with all the repressed anger and resentment. Anger, after all, doesn't go anywhere on its own momentum. If not aired, it simply festers, eventually infecting the good me along with the bad me. Although society may pat us on the back and congratulate us on our benevolence, the conflict remains essentially the same. I remain split right down the middle, and in no hurry to heal this fundamental wound because I'm afraid the rotten me, if given half a chance to express itself, would spread like a cancer and take over my entire personality. Instead, I diligently cultivate this split personality, determinedly remain half of an organic whole, so that I can always "put my best face forward." And all the while, of course, I feel like a fake, a phony. If the world only knew what sort of ugliness was lurking just beneath bad me's smiling face.

Truth be told, even when we pursue the seemingly more direct Me versus You strategy, we rarely get by without a good dose of Me versus Me. In those situations where we are so "uncivilized" as to direct our anger outwardly, we later feel divided into Dr. Jekyll and Mr. Hyde, because our anger most likely has yet to be fully processed and/or satisfyingly expressed. To whatever degree I feel the need to "hold back"—due to fear of retribution, the desire to be labeled "civilized," "kind," and so on—I have to section out a portion of myself that functions as a kind of receptacle, or container of this unresolved anger. All of a sudden, I've got a good me and a bad me all over again who hardly know each other. The angry, drunken rants of Mr. Hyde— the secret keeper of good me's unresolved anger—are merely the vaguest of recollections for our lovable Dr. Jekyll. And what, inevitably, is the first thing we say when we apologize for Mr. Hyde's behavior? Sorry, I just *wasn't myself* the other night. . .

ME VS. NOT-ME

In a larger sense, this same struggle between Eros and death, integration and disintegration, is present from the moment we are living organisms. On one level, of course, every biological organism seeks to improve itself, better its circumstances. It wants to protect its body, nurture itself, pass along its genetic material and so forth. Well, what better way to do so than to join up with a biological community? Cells hook up with other cells that share common interests, and so on down the line, forming increasingly complex organisms, because, as the saying goes, there is strength in numbers. This is the conscious level of biological motivation, more or less—the way nature, at various levels, expresses love.

Then there is the part of our biology that we do our best to ignore—the aggressive manifestations of nature. From the moment we are born, we are also headed toward biological destruction, albeit unconsciously. From this perspective, the organism's process of maturing, or growing up, is really a process of getting forever closer to its final destination, which is death. With every success we achieve in life, every milestone we reach in our career, family development, and personal aspirations, comes the quiet reminder that we are one milestone closer to our ultimate biological disintegration. In this context, the ultimate biological merger of the individual happens when that individual finally gives up its body and rejoins the universe. "Ashes to ashes," as we say, "dust to dust." Interestingly, whereas the Eros instinct often seems to fail us, the death instinct never does. Obviously, not everyone expresses the pull toward love all that well, but everyone expresses the pull toward death perfectly. In the end, no single obstacle can keep us from this ultimate biological goal; as Emily Dickinson wrote, "Because I could not stop for Death/He kindly stopped for me."[5]

Rather strangely, although most of us profess a considerable fear and feeling of regret regarding the inevitable fact of our own death, our behaviors sometimes express otherwise. Despite our professed love of life, we often engage in risky behaviors and habits that significantly compromise our physical health. Why do we do this? To feel more alive, we say. It is as if our capacity for life is measured by our willingness, or need to, embrace Freud's relatively hidden death instinct. We cheat death time and again, in both small and large ways, in order to test the limits of our personal Eros, or instincts of abundant, communal preservation—which is the stuff of love itself.

Going Two Ways at Once

This constant struggle between love and aggression, between life and death, is the primary force that brings each of us to a book like this. Naturally, we want to resolve this emotional and instinctual civil war somehow, find a bit of peace. Eastern wisdom, as evidenced in the following passage from the early Taoist, Chuang Tzu, is full of instructions for just such a resolution:

> To exhaust the spirit and the mind by laboring to make things One, never realizing they are all the same—I call this "Three in the Morning." Why "Three in the Morning?" There was a monkey keeper who fed his monkeys nuts. When he said, "I'll feed you three in the morning and four in the afternoon," the monkeys were furious. So he suggested, "Four in the morning and three in the afternoon," much to the monkeys' delight. The words say the same thing, and yet one phrasing produced anger, another delight. The keeper simply made use of this knowledge. The sage brings what is into harmony with right-and-wrong and rests under the tree of balance of nature. This is called going two ways at once.[6]

This passage seems to suggest that Eros and aggression are somehow one and the same, simply two different phrasings of the same drive. Whether my body is in its current form—which my acquaintances recognize as "James Robbins"—or reorganized back into its original elements, what's the difference? A body is a body is a body, right? Well, this may be so, but such an intellectual realization falls way short of a genuine solution for the majority of us. Regardless what Chuang Tzu may have to say, we generally don't *feel* like we are in harmony while going two ways at once. We are certainly not all that comforted by the fact that—in this very moment—each of us is dying at exactly the same rate we are living! Each of us wants, like Chuang Tzu, to enjoy a peaceful rest under the tree of balance of nature, but how can we rest when every breath we breathe brings us one closer to our last? "I've got to get out of this bottle—and quick," we tell ourselves, "because this bottle is a sinking ship!"

This same struggle between the drive to merge and the drive to separate typically plays out in another highly frustrating way. To illustrate this version of the struggle, I'll borrow a metaphor from the Western scholar and Zen philosopher, Alan Watts. Let's imagine a man looking through a hole in a fence. On the other side of this fence is a cat, which keeps walking back and forth. The perspective of the man is such that he can never see the whole cat at once. Over and over again, he sees a head go by, soon followed by a tail. If this man has never seen a whole cat before, he might describe this cat as a dynamic process in which a head consistently *happens* just before the event of a tail—much like one marching soldier happens after the next. Obviously, the problem here is that the man fails to realize he is observing things from a very limited perspective. He doesn't understand that he's not really watching separate and distinct "parts" related to one another—he's watching a whole cat!

At present, our situation as sentient creatures is very much like the man at the fence. Because we each, due to a limited perspective, think we are watching all these separate parts march back and forth in the field of our daily life-vision, we assume that our own self is also a separate, "individual" part. This sort of assumption, says Watts, is one of many "social fictions, arising from commonly accepted or traditional ways of thinking about the world."[7] Addressing this same social fiction, Lao Tzu, one of the founders of Taoism, says:

> Once the whole is divided, the parts need names.
> There are already enough names.
> One must know when to stop.
> Knowing when to stop averts trouble.
> Tao in the world is like a river flowing home to the sea.[8]

Not that the Eastern traditions have a monopoly on this sort of wisdom. In fact, this same message is, quite literally, all over the place. Consider, for instance, the self-evident, yet famously "non-sensical" lyric of John Lennon: "I am he as you are he and you are me and we are altogether."[9] It is obviously all one big Walrus, Lennon is reminding us, one infinitely large Egg Man, so what's all the fuss and bother about?

We can get the point of oneness, intellectually speaking, but still feel very isolated, like a haphazard collection of separate parts randomly bumping into other collections of separate parts. To say it differently: Each of us feels like something is missing—he or she couldn't say what exactly, just something. No doubt, this pervasive feeling of "something missing" brings us to books like this time and again. It brings us to psychotherapists, bars, love affairs, creative endeavors, Las Vegas, and just about anywhere else we can imagine. The world's religions—not to mention countless pop songs, highway billboards, and magazine ads—clearly answer this question of "What's missing?" over and over. The answer is simple: *I'm* missing— parts of me, anyway. I go around thinking I am a cat head, naming myself "cat head," and wondering why I can't move myself around like I would like to. There is a whole cat body out there, of course, right behind me in fact, but I can't see it because I don't know when to stop dividing the whole into parts. According to Lao Tzu, I simply don't know how to stop naming things. Be that as it may, if I can't see it, I *can't* see it, so what am I supposed to do?

The basic riddle of human awareness, then, is this: Being lost at present, a stranger in a strange land, how can I reconnect with the One, the Whole? How can I re-member the rest of my body when I am clearly suffering from cosmic amnesia? How can I first join together my own seemingly opposing parts and then go on to join my individual whole to the larger whole? To sum it up: How can I be myself when I'm *not* myself?

The Great Escape

A man who has at length found something to do will not need a new suit to do it in.
—Henry David Thoreau[10]

A quick stroll along the aisles of our local bookstore will remind us just how many different versions and detailed elaborations there are of "The Answer." We will find half a dozen different translations of the *Tao Te Ching* and *I Ching*, a few pocket-size collections of Zen koans and, of course, the ever-popular, fully-illustrated guide to Tantric sex practices. A few aisles over, we will wander onto a Feng Shui encyclopedia, meditations we can do with our cat, an astral travel kit with foldout chakra map and . . . Hey! Put that fully-illustrated guide to Tantric sex practices down for just one minute! My point is simply this: There are a lot of ways, these days, of looking into whatever spiritual question we might happen to ask. So many ways, in fact, we may feel a little overwhelmed, and who could blame us?

In one way, of course, we are very lucky. For the Westerner, until the mid-1950s or thereabouts, when the Beatniks and the psychoanalysts began to "discover" Zen, all these alternative approaches to spirituality were not so easily found. Since then, of course, alternative spirituality of every sort has turned into a booming business. Whether we want to sample traditional Eastern wisdom these days, or try our hand at tarot according to Aleister Crowley, we needn't go any further than the corner bookstore.

In another way, however, maybe we are not all that lucky. When it comes to Westerners, one thing is for certain: We love to shop. New suits? Great! We'll take 'em! New spiritual systems? Fantastic! Add them to the cart! Unfortunately, at the end of the day, many Western seekers are left dizzily panting in the corner of the spiritual shopping mall, trying to catch their breath after their latest shopping frenzy. They have tried on suit after suit, many of which have fit quite nicely, but have yet to find something to do in them. Although there is obviously merit in this recent spiritual "boom," we might wonder if all this "stuff" is really necessary. Are we really getting anywhere, we might wonder, or are we mostly just bargain shopping?

When we study a variety of metaphysical belief systems in earnest, from the ancient *Upanishads* to contemporary New Age works, we begin to notice that they all emphasize the same essential messages over and over: direct perception and compassion. Although all genuine spiritual paths necessitate a healthy balance of both these elements, most traditions tend to emphasize one more than the other. Hinduism, Buddhism, and Taoism, for example, tend to emphasize direct perception as the "highest" path to self-liberation. Similarly, contemporary science, psychology, philosophy, and Native American belief systems typically center on this approach. Christianity, Judaism, and Islam, on the other hand, tend to place more emphasis on the path of compassion and selfless service, as do contemporary humanitarian movements and secular charitable organizations. Unfortunately, these seemingly different approaches to the universally shared goal of total enlightenment or Christ consciousness often lead to considerable confusion and misunderstanding among followers of the various disciplines. Properly understood, direct perception and compassion, however contrasting they may appear at various stages along their respective paths, are in no ways mutually exclusive. Rather, when viewed from a larger perspective, perfect, direct perception *is* compassion. Perfect compassion *is* direct perception.

Philosophical intricacies and metaphysical details aside, the key to all paths of genuine self-knowledge and freedom is contained in a few, incredibly simple words—the most basic, self-evident teachings of the historical Buddha and Christ. Contained therein is the original well, the purest, crystal-clear source, from which all other metaphysical streams continue to bubble and gurgle to this day. We will begin our search for The Answer here, then, slipping back into that familiar old suit at the back of the utility closet. . .

The Buddha

5 00 years or so before Jesus of Nazareth walked the earth, a young prince named Siddhartha Gautama snuck out of his father's palace in the wee hours of morning, leaving his royal family and luxurious life behind. Dissatisfied with life's passing pleasures, Siddhartha headed for the forest to study with the sages of his day. He stayed there several years, mastering even the most rigorous disciplines of asceticism, living at one point—so legend has it—on a single grain of rice daily. Still thoroughly dissatisfied, Siddhartha sat down beneath a sacred fig tree near the city of Gaya and said, "Come what may—let my body rot, let my bones be reduced to ashes—I will not get up from here until I have found the way beyond decay and death."[11] The rest is, as they say, history.

When Siddhartha left his fig tree behind—which is now known as the Bodhi Tree—and stepped back out into the Himalayan foothills, having finally found "the way," the people were dazzled by his radiant appearance. "Are you a god?" they asked. "Are you an angel?" The former prince and ascetic smiled and said, "I am awake." From this point on, Siddhartha was no longer Siddhartha—he was the Buddha, the "one who has awoken." On this day, Buddha "set in motion the wheel of the *dharma* [spiritual teaching, the way]"[12] with his teaching of the Four Noble Truths. These truths are the pillars of Buddhist thought, the fundamental supports that hold up the complex structure and intricate ornaments of all the ensuing sutras and tantras. To truly understand these four truths is to directly perceive the way itself.

THE FOUR NOBLE TRUTHS

"The First Truth," said Buddha, "is the fact of suffering. All desire happiness. . . . Yet all find that life brings . . . frustration, dissatisfaction, incompleteness. . . . Life is change, and change can never satisfy desire. Therefore everything that changes brings suffering."[13] We all see this simple truth playing out in our lives over and over again. I finally get that big vacation and it's great. I'm sipping drinks by the pool, sleeping in late, reading that book I've been meaning to get to . . . then what? Well, then the vacation is over and I'm back in the daily grind, waiting for that *next* Big Vacation in the Sky. But it is somehow never the Big Vacation, right? It always ends sooner or later, because life is change. Everything we love, life and all its varied pleasures, are, by definition, impermanent. No matter how much security we carve out for ourselves, how much money we save, how much food we stuff in the refrigerator, it is never going to be enough. That's just the way life works, Buddha said. We all carry this tangled knot of fear deep inside our gut because we know that life itself is a temporary vacation. We sip our drinks awhile, take in some sun and then, suddenly, it's over.

"The Second Truth is the cause of suffering. It is not life that brings sorrow, but the demands we make on life. . . . Thinking life can make them happy by bringing what they want, people run after satisfaction of their desires . . . [demanding] what experience cannot give: permanent pleasure unmixed with anything unpleasant. But there is no end to such desire; that is the nature of the mind. Suffering because life cannot satisfy selfish desire is like suffering because a banana tree will not bear mangoes."[14] This last point is particularly important. There is nothing wrong with expecting a banana tree to bear bananas; it just won't work if we keep looking to it for mangoes. I point this out because this truth is often misunderstood. People sometimes say, "Okay, Buddha, I can see that I suffer because I want stuff. Therefore, I will simply quit wanting stuff." Some seekers shut themselves up in caves and eat insects or, less dramatically, they avoid the natural pleasures of sex, food, and drink. But this strategy—especially when pursued from a place of fear and defensiveness— can never work. Why not? Because that's simply replacing one desire with another, exchanging desire to drink with desire to not drink. True, we're not asking the banana tree for mangoes anymore—now we're asking for oranges. So what are we supposed to do? If wanting stuff doesn't work, and wanting to *not* want stuff is the same problem, how are we ever going to cure ourselves of suffering?

"There is a Third Truth. . . . Any ailment that can be understood can be cured, and suffering that has a cause also has an end. When the fires of selfishness have been extinguished, when the mind is free of selfish desire, what remains is the state of wakefulness, of peace, of joy, of perfect health, called 'that which is extinguished': *nirvana*."[15] Okay, so there is a way to quit asking the banana tree for mangoes and oranges, but what is this way?

"The Fourth Truth . . . is that selfishness can be extinguished by following an eightfold path: right understanding, right purpose, right speech, right conduct, right occupation, right effort, right attention, and right meditation. If dharma is a wheel, these eight are its spokes." The first spoke on the wheel, "right understanding," is the key to all the others. In fact, if we truly and fully comprehend this one, which is the very essence of direct perception, we automatically comprehend all the others. What exactly is right understanding? "Right understanding," said Buddha, "is seeing life as it is."[16] Once again, we encounter the frustratingly slippery, fortune-cookie elusiveness of Eastern wisdom. It's as if we've asked an Olympic sprinter for advice on sprinting and she says, "Wait until the whistle blows, then run as fast as you can!"

When we really stop, look, and begin to see life as it is, we begin to notice something very interesting: Wanting stuff isn't the problem—it is expecting to get it, expecting to be satisfied by the getting that's confusing. That's just not the way life is. The word *dukkha*, which is usually translated as "selfish desire" as in the Third Truth, is used in the Pali language to refer to wheels whose axles are off center, or "that which is hard to bear." Our desire, then, which is "selfish" in that it tends to preoccupy us with our own wants, somehow keeps us from rolling along smoothly. We are wobbling along from tree to tree, deeply absorbed in our limited individual perspectives, angrily shaking branch after branch, waiting for the sky itself to fall. The Buddhists call this foolish, yet amazingly persistent, expectation "attachment." When we begin to really "see life as it is," however, the never-ending dramas of our daily lives take on a richly artistic, or at least cosmically comedic, atmosphere. It is still a rather bumpy ride—still not so easy to bear—but what's wrong with bumpy rides? I'm still shaking the banana tree waiting on mangoes, only now I know the whole time there are no mangoes on the way! I'm still *wanting* mangoes, you see, but I am not really *expecting* them. I am no longer so attached to the outcome, no longer so identified with the predicament of my one, very tiny self within the infinitely vast universe. I am still wobbling along slightly off center, licking my lips for that Big Vacation in the Sky, only now I'm aware there is never, ever going to be a Big Vacation in the Sky.

Freud said, "When any situation desired . . . is prolonged, it only produces a feeling of mild contentment. We are so made that we can derive intense enjoyment only from a contrast and very little from a state of things."[17] If we ever really achieved that Big Vacation, Freud is saying, all of a sudden it would no longer feel like the Big Vacation. Sipping drinks by the pool would start to seem like work. Sleeping in would become tedious and boring. We have all seen people who spend their whole lives dreaming of retiring. Well, what happens when they finally retire? Do they spend their final days in bliss, weeping tears of joy? Maybe—for the first month or two. Then, like Freud said, they are wanting something else, a "contrast." It is not a dirty trick being played on us, this fact that we can never fully satisfy our desires. It's a gift, really, in that it keeps things from stagnating, keeps things rolling along, however bumpily. In short, our constant frustration compels us to keep searching for the one, true, ultimate meaning—the authentic spiritual heart of existence. I know it certainly doesn't feel like a gift sometimes, but that's just it: If it always felt like a gift, it wouldn't be a gift anymore! We are on our way to that damn banana tree again, shaking our heads because we know the whole thing is absolutely ridiculous. Still, what an incredibly beautiful dance it is, what a poignant, artistic journey! When we can step outside the habitual "rat race" of desire, outside the compelling drama of our tiny, individual selves long enough to directly perceive this beauty, this is when we experience the true meat of experience, the essential, permanent satisfaction behind the seeming dissatisfaction. Oh, and I just *can't wait* to sink my teeth into one of those mangoes. . . .

THE GATE TO ALL MYSTERY

As Buddha neared death, his body began to deteriorate. He was making the very same absurdly poetic journey that all of us are making, you see—albeit from a place of perfect artistry, or direct perception. One day he asked his beloved follower, Ananda, to prepare him a bed in a grove of trees, "for I am *suffering*, Ananda, and *desire* to lie down."[18] From a certain perspective—the perspective of those of us still "on the path"—we can just feel what a beautifully sad moment that must have been. Here is this incredibly wise being who knows all about desire and suffering, he certainly understands that lying down isn't going to stop his bodily suffering, but he asks anyway because what else is he going to do? Some of the most familiar statues of the Buddha depict him lying down in the "lion posture," on his side propped up on an elbow. These were made to celebrate the Buddha's last hours, symbolic reminders of his total humanity right until the very end. The Buddha's last words were: "Remember, all things that come into being must pass away. Strive earnestly!"[19] No mangoes at the banana tree, he was saying, but don't let that keep you from shaking it with total and complete sincerity. It is a message that comes from a place, not of detached cynicism or lack of fulfillment, but of perfectly compassionate, direct artistic experience. At that moment, Buddha—like everything else that comes into being—passed on.

A passage from the *Tao Te Ching* comments on the elusive beauty of our bizarrely human predicament of desire:

Ever desireless, one can see the mystery.
Ever desiring, one can see the manifestations.

These two spring from the same source but differ in name;
This appears as darkness.
Darkness within darkness.
The gate to all mystery.[20]

We might ask: How can one be "ever desireless?" Desire seems to be the very stuff of life itself, the very fuel that propels the creative journey onward, so how can we imagine a being that is truly free from desire? Such a question arises from a common misunderstanding of the Buddha's teachings. Once we have gone to the banana tree enough times to see how the whole thing works, once we appreciate that our normal human desires, by definition, simply are not going to be satisfied, we could be said to be "desireless." We have finally accepted how things are, and we wouldn't want them to be any different. Paradoxically, we are somehow satisfied with our necessary dissatisfaction. We're still a goose in a bottle, only now we have settled into our favorite chair and propped our feet up.

At the same time, then, we are still "ever desiring." We are still fully human, waiting for those banana tree mangoes to fall simply because that's what physical beings do. For that matter, the *Tao Te Ching* reminds us, it is desire that lets us "see the manifestations" in the first place—the banana tree and all other aspects of the material world, according to Taoism, being such manifestations. This is Taoism's way of celebrating desire, honoring the profane within the sacred, a statement similar to the Buddha's symbolic "indulgence" in bodily suffering. Viewed from this perspective, my individual desire is no longer "selfish"—nor is it exactly individual any longer. I have seen the bigger picture and my only true desire is that the universe go on exactly as the universe needs to go on. Such is the essence of harmony, a "river flowing home to the sea." This harmonious desire, which comes from a place of wholeness, a place of deep calm and security, is a very different sort of desire altogether. It is more like your desire to breathe your next breath than it is your desire to win the lottery, for instance—it grows from a wide-open space of total confidence rather than the cramped, claustrophobic space of anxiety. Ironically, the minute we let go of our desperate, bottled-up urge to escape life's bizarre predicaments, we are free.

To confuse things further, these two ways of seeing are somehow the same. Like love and aggression, desire and desirelessness "spring from the same source"—a situation which Chuang Tzu would describe as "Three in the Morning." This darkness within darkness is in no way bleak or cynical. Rather, it is a state of profound, yet transient, beauty—a state that, like a dynamic moment of music or a wave in the ocean, we can never truly grasp. Like a fleeting vision in our periphery, the minute we turn to look directly at this mysterious source of all life and love, of all wanting and doing and being, it is gone, a ghost on the stairs. And unlike our physical bodies, which seem to belong to us, what can never be had, can never be un-had. Chuang Tzu's elusive "source" is eternal, forever beyond both desire and desirelessness. The original "gate to all mystery," then, can only be experienced through direct perception, a state at once free from, and fully participating in, ordinary human concerns.

Christ

As for those radical "new" teachings of Jesus that stirred up so much trouble, were they any less self-evident than those of Buddha? It has been said that if all the New Testament had been lost—everything but the Sermon on the Mount, that is—we would still have the essential message of Christ. I will go one step further and say all we really need are a few verses from the Gospel of Mark. In this passage, a teacher of the law approaches Jesus and asks, "Of all the commandments, which is the most important?" Jesus responds, "The most important one . . . is this: 'Hear, O Israel, the Lord our God, the Lord is one. Love the Lord your God with all your heart and with all your soul and with all your mind and with all your strength.' The second is this: Love your neighbor as yourself. There is no commandment greater than these" (Mark 12: 28–31).[21] The first scripture Jesus quotes is known as the *Shema* by the Jews. In Hebrew, *shema* means "hear." In the same way Buddha's whole cure comes down to seeing life as it is, Jesus' message is simply one of: Listen up—"He who has an ear, let him hear" (Rev. 2:7). If you listen closely enough, Jesus was saying, you will notice that the Lord is one, God is whole, undivided, everywhere and everything.

The emphasis of Christ's message is, however, different from that of Buddha's. Although all spiritual seekers share the goal of perfect self-knowledge and liberation, the methods taught by Buddha and Christ describe unique paths. Typically, the Buddhist cultivates direct perception, or bare awareness, through meditation and other solitary, inwardly-directed acts of focus and contemplation. The Christian path, by contrast, tends to be more externalized; the follower of Christ's teachings makes acts of service and unconditional love his or her meditation. In striving to love one another with perfect, Christ-like compassion and understanding, we naturally grow to know one another as we really are, begin to encounter the divine presence the Christians call the "Holy Spirit" living deep within every being. As we merge with one another in love, we begin to see past our own desires, to directly experience the spontaneously perfected "other" person that once was hidden behind our own projections of prejudice, envy, and judgment. Consequently, in following Christ's teaching of love, we begin to perceive our own, divine nature reflected back to us everywhere we look—in Buddhist terms, an act of direct perception of Chuang Tzu's mysterious "source."

John the Baptist said of Jesus, "From the fullness of his grace we have *all* [my italics] received one blessing after another" (John 1:16). Look around, as Buddha said, and see if it's not true. Everywhere we look, if we can truly "see life as it is," we will see we are being given one blessing after another. We are dissatisfied, sure, we suffer, but that's not a lack of blessing—that's an integral part, remember, of the blessing itself! In working with our individual desires, it is essential that we honor our own suffering, and that of others, as holy, for suffering is an integral part of what makes the whole creative journey serious and meaningful. Without it, life would be a slapstick cartoon rather than a moving Beethoven sonata. "Blessed are you who hunger now," Jesus said, "for you will be satisfied" (Matt. 5:6). Our hungering now, however uncomfortable it may be, is a necessary stage of the process of satisfaction. It is not exactly that mangoes are going to eventually fall from the banana tree, it's more that we begin to wake up to the fact that the whole ridiculous, yet indescribably beautiful, journey of shaking the tree is already perfect, has always been perfect from the very beginning. That is the real satisfaction Jesus is talking about. That is the path of true compassion, the recognition that the Lord is one. If we can truly hear and see our neighbor as he or she is, we realize our neighbor is none other than the one God shaking the one God, waiting for the one God to fall.

ENOUGH IS ENOUGH

We can return to the *Tao Te Ching* for the same message:

> *There is no greater sin than desire,*
> *No greater curse than discontent,*
> *No greater misfortune than wanting something for oneself.*
> *Therefore he who knows enough is enough will always have enough.*[22]

Since "sin" has a nasty connotation for most Westerners, let's clarify what it means in this passage. For the Taoist, it is not like we are really sinning in the biblical sense when we want something, it is just that we are failing to hear the name of the one God, the Tao, or way. Our curse is not a punishment from God, that is to say—it is a punishment from our own, temporarily deluded selves. Our own confused expectations of life and other people lead to our discontent and misfortune. Open our eyes and ears, see and hear the one God everywhere, let go all our judgments, envy, and resentment, and we will suddenly realize enough is enough. Things are already just as they should be. You are already just as you should be. Go ahead and shake that tree, not because you need something else, but *just because*. We dance, not to earn our keep, but simply because we are dancers.

Once we see that we already have everything because God is everywhere and everything, how could we not love God with all our heart, mind, soul, and strength? God is my very own body—my very own heart, mind, soul, and strength—so every action I perform, every action you perform, is necessarily a perfect act of worship. It is so simple a truth, so incredibly obvious, that we keep overlooking it, time and again. It's like looking through a window so perfectly clean and clear that we fail to realize we are looking through a window. As Jesus said, when speaking of the Holy Spirit, "[Y]ou will realize that I am in my Father, and you are in me, and I am in you"

(John 14:20). *I am he as you are he and you are me and we are all together!* If aggression and internal struggle arise from our fundamental competition for resources, what happens when we realize, through perfect compassion and direct perception, there are forever unlimited, infinitely available resources stretched out before each of us in all directions? How could we not love our neighbor as ourselves? Our neighbor is God, too, of course—the Great Egg Man, the Grand Walrus in the Sky—and he has got his own banana trees to shake, but wow! Look at him go!

A Better Buddha

The Indian sage, Sri Ramana Maharshi, was spontaneously enlightened at the age of sixteen. He had undergone no previous spiritual training, engaged in no formal study or practice whatsoever. Ramana's essential message: "Remain as you are. That is the aim."[23] Look around, listen up, and you will see that you are, quite literally, a divine being among other divine beings, so just do what you do and things will be just fine. Banana trees will be banana trees, mangoes will be mangoes, neighbors will be neighbors. So relax: buddhas, with no renovation whatsoever required, will continue to be better and better buddhas.

Well, come on, Ramana, how could I not do what I do? How could I ever, for one single moment, fail to remain myself, fail to be exactly as I am?

Precisely. Now, how about some mangoes?

SEEING PAST
THE OPTICAL DELUSION

A human being is part of the whole, called by us "Universe," a part limited in time and space. He experiences himself, his thoughts and feelings, as something separate from the rest—a kind of optical delusion of his consciousness. This delusion is a kind of prison for us, restricting us to our personal desires and to affection for a few persons nearest to us.
—ALBERT EINSTEIN[1]

The Rorschach test is probably the most infamous of tools used in psychological evaluations. We laypeople know this test as the dreaded "inkblot test." The way it works is pretty simple. The test subject is presented with a standard set of inkblots. Of particular significance to our context, these inkblots were originally generated randomly by dropping some ink on paper and folding the paper in half. In and of themselves, these inkblots aren't infused with any meaning. The test subject takes a look at these blobs of ink and describes what he or she sees, along with any associations that come to mind. The basic idea, then, is that whatever the subject sees in these random blots is a psychological projection of her own mental state.

Another important criterion in evaluating the Rorschach test subject's responses is that of reality testing. In this case, reality testing simply means that the subject bases his or her imaginings and associations on the actual, objective features of the inkblots. If he is seeing his mother in card III, then he should be able to point at that inkblot directly to indicate specific features which somehow remind him of his mother. This is a vastly oversimplified description of how the Rorschach is actually scored, but it gives you a basic idea of how this test might be used to reflect various tendencies and idiosyncrasies of the subject's own mind.

In *Transformations of Consciousness: Conventional and Contemplative Perspectives on Development*, Daniel Brown and Jack Engler describe a study in which the Rorschach was administered to a population of meditators at various levels of skill and development. One of these meditators was reportedly an enlightened master from Southeast Asia. The master's responses were highly unusual in a couple of ways. First, the master used what Brown and Engler call an "integrative style" throughout the responses. Whereas Rorschach test subjects typically treat each ink blot as a separate event, the master treated all ten cards as parts of a single whole, hooking them together in a kind of parable or story. Second, the content of this story itself is very interesting. In the first few cards, the master describes the inkblots as suffering creatures. "Inside," the master says, "there is envy, disease, sorrow and hatred in the form of black shapes." In the next few cards, the inkblots begin to engage in spiritual practice, resulting in the elimination of suffering. "After conquering truth, the mind has become clean and white," the master says. The remainder of the cards describes, from the master's perspective, the continuing enjoyment of total self-realization, or enlightenment. We should add that the master's responses tell this story of spiritual progress "without any significant departure from reality testing and without ignoring the realistic features of the inkblot(s.)"[2] For the master, these "random" inkblots, *just as they are*, clearly describe the very same path of self-knowing contained in the countless spiritual and metaphysical books in your local bookstore.

The Optical Delusion

The relevance of the above experiment is simply this: It's not so much what we are looking at that is important, but how we are looking. The same message—Buddha's Four Noble Truths, Jesus' One Lord—is literally everywhere, if we only know how to see it. All too often, however, our eyes aren't so good. According to Einstein, our "eyes" tend to play tricks on us.

As Alan Watts suggested in his cat metaphor, we can't see the whole when our perception is limited. Although we tend to forget it, we are peering through a small hole in a very big fence. Due to this "optical delusion," we feel stranded, isolated, cut off—both from parts of our own personalities as well as parts of the whole, the One. Consequently, we may feel that Buddha's teaching of direct perception, as well as Christ's message of total compassion or "oneness" with our neighbors, is virtually impossible.

"What exactly is causing this delusion?" you might ask. "How did this big fence get put up in the first place?" Let's look at four different factors or distractions, that tend to play tricks on our spiritual vision: the lures of self-consciousness and safety, and the myths of better and worse and one thing leading to another.

The Lure of Self-Consciousness

Krishnamurti said, "The moment you are aware that you are happy, you cease to be happy. . . . You want to be consciously happy: the moment you are consciously happy, happiness is gone."³ If you have ever tried to stand beneath a rainbow, you've noticed a peculiar phenomenon: The faster you chase it, the faster it retreats. So it goes with self-consciousness. This is one of the most logically incomprehensible ironies of the human predicament: The harder we try to be ourselves, the further we stray from our true nature. To chase happiness—which is what we are doing when we try so desperately to be ourselves—is to make ourselves unhappy. Why? Well, as the wisdom traditions tell us again and again, happiness is our natural, God-given state of being. We can't find it because we never lost it!

There is a Zen story in which a caterpillar is happily walking along, not a care in its caterpillar world. Then it happens on a frog, and the frog says, "Hey, I was wondering how you manage to keep all those legs going just so? Is there a plan I should know about, a general strategy for caterpillar walking?" This, of course, stops the caterpillar dead in its tracks. "How *do* I keep all these legs working?" it wonders. Needless to say, the caterpillar becomes paralyzed, unable to move a single leg, and the frog eats it.

Unfortunately, most of us spend a good deal of time getting gobbled up by the self-consciousness frog. Have you ever wondered how you know when to blink? How about yawning? Think about those instinctive processes for a minute and see if blinking and yawning don't become very cumbersome affairs. Self-consciousness is more cumbersome still at the interpersonal level. You go to a party, for instance, and you are wandering from room to room, a strategic smile pressed on your face, casual poses carefully planned. You're very polite, of course, choosing just the right words, careful to select just the right number of Sally's cheese blobs versus Uncle Mark's sausage wraps. There is absolutely no way, obviously, you are simply going to relax, loosen the grip on your quality control filtering mechanism, and say—much less do—whatever comes to mind. No one gets to know who you really are, and you miss out on the real meat of life while that frog is gobbling and gobbling. . .

In a 1969 interview with *Life Magazine*, rock legend Jimi Hendrix said that, "A musician, if he's a messenger, is like a child who hasn't been handled too many times, hasn't had too many fingerprints across his brain."⁴ From the perspective of my own career as a professional musician, it seems to me that these "fingerprints" Hendrix is talking about are often the smudges of self-consciousness. Being a true "messenger" requires, first and foremost, letting go of all this anxious self-monitoring. When you see a really amazing musician or athlete doing his or her thing, you almost get the feeling that no one is home. There is no separate chief executive running things in such an instance, no captain manning the ship—there is just automatic, unplanned *being*. That is what the Taoists call being one with the Tao. In one way or another, that's really what we are looking for in a star athlete or a musician. We want to be reminded of what it is to be truly natural, free and clear from the restricting barbs of self-consciousness. These athletes and artists carry the message of the Tao to us to the degree that they can just let go and "go with the flow." Unlike our caterpillar, they have learned to trust the instinctive process of walking to take care of, or understand itself.

Another frog story comes to mind. Remember the Warner Brothers' cartoon where the guy finds the singing frog? He is understandably enthused at his discovery, so he seeks out audience after audience, wanting someone else to get a look at this amazing frog. The frog, of course, will have none of it. It's nothing but croaks and tongue so long as it is being forced into the limelight. The moment it is alone with the one guy, however, it's Fred Astaire and Frank Sinatra all over again. Angelus Silesius, a Christian mystic, once wrote: "God, whose boundless love and joy/Are present everywhere;/He cannot come to visit you/Unless you are not there.[5] This singing frog, like God, is only there when the audience isn't.

Strange as it may sound, we all have moments in which we are "not there." It's not that we literally disappear, of course, or slip into unconsciousness—it's simply that we temporarily merge with the whole natural process of being, trust that process enough so that we allow the imaginary boundary we stake out as "I" to momentarily dissolve. This is what the Buddhists call "entering the stream." In such moments, we quit filtering our actions and thoughts and just sort of . . . float . . . along. We've merged our two halves. We are so totally immersed in whatever task we're doing that there is simply no room for some other detached part of ourselves to sit up on the observation tower and calmly score our performance. To be totally natural like this, to be completely one whole being acting without self-consciousness is, quite simply, to be God—one without a second.

Much of the cure of psychoanalysis relies on a powerful technique known as free association, the use of which Freud describes as follows: "Instead of urging the patient to say something upon some particular subject, I now asked him to *abandon himself* to a process of *free association*—that is, to say whatever came into his head, while ceasing to give any conscious direction to his thoughts."[6] Saying whatever comes to mind sounds easy, I know, but I suggest you try to implement this technique for even half a day. You will soon find yourself censoring this or that thought as inappropriate, irrelevant, etc. The psychoanalytic cure is built around this same idea of self-conscious censorship. In observing how the patient repeatedly gets stuck, or tangled up in him or herself, the analyst works closely with the patient to understand the various tendencies of repression and obsessive self-monitoring that habitually restrain natural speech and actions. The problem, Freud is suggesting, isn't so much what we do or say as it is what we don't do or say.

This Flax Weighs Three Pounds

Zen's "cure" is very similar. It is more concerned with spontaneous rather than proper speech and action, with the natural result of a relaxed, effortless state of being, which Zen calls no-mind. The following famous koan (a logically unsolvable riddle used in Zen training) from the *Mumonkan* (Gateless Gate) provides a perfect example of such letting go:

> A monk asked Tozan when he was weighing some flax: "What is Buddha?"
> Tozan said: "This flax weighs three pounds."

We could go round and round analyzing Tozan's response, no doubt, attaching all sorts of significance to it, but this isn't the point of Zen at all. It's not so much what Tozan said as how he said it. He answered spontaneously, without deliberating or philosophizing, and simply said whatever came into his head. Like the skilled athlete or musician, Tozan simply reacted to the situation as an automatic messenger, a relaxed communicator of Zen's no-mind.

Ironically, whenever we authentically enter into such an effortlessly spontaneous place, all those details we normally worry so much about sort themselves out. Remember the guy with the frog? Having finally given up his hopes for vicarious stardom, he is suddenly so into this frog's incredible performance he doesn't even notice the large crowd that has gathered. . . .

For whatever reason, most of us don't trust the process of entering the stream enough to hop in the raft and say, "Let's go!" Instead, we like to keep one foot securely planted on the shore so we can abandon ship if we hit whitewater. No wonder, then, we feel so isolated and disconnected. We want to be happy, of course, but we also want to be able to watch ourselves *being* happy. We want to be able to say, in the middle of our most intense happiness, "Wow! Would you look at me go!" It's like trying to take a picture of ourselves by standing in front of a mirror. No matter how we arrange things, there is still going to be a camera obscuring our face in the photo. Many of us have trouble sleeping for this very reason. We simply don't trust the natural process of letting go. "Can I really count on my body and my lower brain to take care of things," we ask ourselves, "if my higher brain wanders off for a while?" Similarly, we don't easily lose ourselves in a spontaneous act of sexuality, for instance. We wonder: If I just let it happen, how can I be sure I won't come out looking like an idiot? How can I be sure I will be able to "perform" properly?

Like the caterpillar, we have become so distrustful of our body's most natural processes, believing that our body won't work just right without some detached CEO looking over things, that we have become paralyzed. For that matter, notice how we speak possessively about our body and our brain, as if there is some separate "real" owner who is sitting inside our head somewhere working the controls. Through this imagined real controller, we try to suspend the expression of our spontaneous emotions, bodily actions and so forth until we have put the proper market-ing spin on them. We step out the front door each morning, imaginary CEO already scrambling around in our head, crunching numbers, rehearsing speeches, trying to plot our day's most efficient "strategy"—and all the while that flax still weighs three pounds. . . .

The Lure of Safety

"The secret for harvesting from existence the greatest fruitfulness and the great-est enjoyment from life is," said Friedrich Nietzsche, "to *live dangerously!*"[7] You could say that Nietzsche means simply letting go and entering the stream—being without a life jacket, without some conceptual system or set of rules. As Henry David Thoreau pointed out, however, dangerous living also tends to involve that much-feared human commodity: originality. "If a man does not keep pace with his companions," said Thoreau, "perhaps it is because he hears a different drummer. Let him step to the music which he hears, however measured or far away."[8] Most of us, however, prefer to follow the "music" of the most popular leader, even when that leader turns out to be the Pied Piper of Hamlin. We like the cozy safety of crowds, so we march behind the other mesmerized followers, right over the edge of a cliff, if that's where they're going. This idea of originality and non-conformity is talked about a lot in the West, but is it really practiced that often? How many of us have truly original tastes in clothes, music, or art, for example? How many of us have the courage to be radically different from our co-workers and peers when necessary? How many of us are authentically prepared to part with our family's most cherished values when we feel they are constricting our own lives?

In one of my favorite biblical stories, the teachers of Hebrew law bring to Jesus a woman caught in adultery. They ask Jesus what he thinks they should do with this woman. This is a sneaky little question. Hebrew law, descending from Moses, required that such a woman be stoned to death. Roman law, however, didn't allow the Jews to carry out death sentences. Either way Jesus (a Jew) answered, then, the teachers of the law were planning to use his response to get him in trouble with one side or the other. Jesus gets out of this trap by saying, "If any one of you is without sin, let him be the first to throw a stone at her" (John 8:7).

There is a little, often-overlooked detail in this story, however, which has always interested me. When Jesus is first questioned, before he says a word, what does he do? He bends down, the Bible tells us, and writes on the ground with his finger. What does he write? We can only guess—the Bible never says. Interestingly, this is the only biblical account of Jesus writing anything. This is a very Zen-like lesson Jesus is providing. He doesn't exactly write with a pen and paper, notice, but with his finger on the floor. Why is this significant? Well, we are probably not going to be able to read anything written on a sandy floor for very long. The law of Moses, however, was the exact opposite; after all, we're talking stone tablets, here. Jesus was reminding his questioners of the inevitable limits of concrete rules and regulations. Apart from this one instance of sand writing, his own teachings were oral, often varying from situation to situation. He might forgive a dishonest tax collector in one instance, but overturn the money-lenders' tables in the temple, the next. Forget about all these rules and regulations, Jesus was saying, and see what is really going on in your heart of hearts. "The kingdom of God does not come with careful observation, nor will people say, 'Here it is,' or 'There it is,' because the kingdom of God is within you" (Luke 17:22).

Thoreau's "far away" music isn't outside—it's inside. True originality comes from listening to our own deepest heartbeat, feeling the authentic rhythm of our own spiritual center. No set of fixed ideas—whether they belong to Jesus, Buddha, or the guy who wrote that Tantric sex book—can ever really capture the essence of who we are. Stop and think about that one for a minute. Who you are changes from day to day, hour to hour, moment to moment, like words drawn on sand. Not only are you not who you were five years ago, you're not even who you were five minutes ago! If spiritual teachings are to speak to each of us from moment to moment, they have to be infinitely flexible, unattached to any one doctrine, so that they are free to float along down the stream of awareness, wherever that stream may take us.

At the same time, however, Jesus and Buddha did lay out many a concrete rule, many a "Thou shall not." But these were just the exoteric teachings—the teachings comprehensible or suited to the public, the teachings pertaining to the outside. To really understand Jesus and Buddha, we have to ferret out the esoteric teachings—those subtle teachings which are confined to a small group, those teachings which were not publicly disclosed. If you really want to understand the rules, you have to understand who was doing the rule giving. Ironically, to follow the deeper message of these individuals, their radical life message, is to decide for ourselves. Although Jesus made it clear—from the Christian standpoint, at least—that he was very much a part of Hebrew tradition in that he came to fulfill the Old Testament prophecies of the chosen messiah, he also made it clear he aimed to do so by turning the existing establishment on its head. "You suppose," said Jesus, "that I have come to bring peace on earth? I tell you, No. I have come to bring division. The father will be divided against the son, and the son against the father" (Luke 12:51).

This sort of violent upheaval is likewise evident in a story told by the Zen master Shen-ting:

> When I set out on my journey, I didn't have the right intention to study Zen and learn the way; I just wanted to go to the eastern capital and listen to one or two scriptures and treatises to sustain me for everyday life. I didn't expect that I'd end up traveling around until I happened to meet the Zen master Shou-san. Getting stuck by him, I simply ran with sweat. At

that time, I unconsciously bowed, but I've never gotten over my regret.

What do I regret? I regret not having dragged him off his Zen chair and given him a thrashing.[9]

The Zen master I-Hsüan puts it a little more succinctly: "Kill the Buddha if you happen to meet him."[10]

You might think that Buddhism—Zen, in particular—is a very violent affair. And it is, in a way. Zen demands rigorous self-exploration without the reassuring guardrails of this or that fixed system, without the training wheels of this or that practice. Consequently, in Zen they say that the best Zen practitioner has forgotten all about Zen and other such nonsense. He or she has become the very essence of Zen itself.

Toward the end of Buddha's life, his disciple, Ananda, became concerned that his teacher would die without leaving proper instruction as to his followers' spiritual advancement. "Why should I leave instructions?" Buddha said. "Be a refuge unto yourselves, Ananda. Be a lamp unto yourselves. Rely on yourselves and nothing else."[11] When I-Hsüan speaks of killing the Buddha, he is reminding us that the surest way to Buddhahood is not through following the Buddha. Rather, it is by being the Buddha. Ironically, each and every one of us reading these words right now is already the Buddha. This is not some metaphor, this is literally true. The Hindus like to say *Tat Twami Asi*—"That Thou Art." We can never find the Buddha simply because we *are* the Buddha. Looking for our own Buddha nature is like getting lost driving in the country and looking for ourselves in the glove compartment. I like to think of the historical Buddha, Siddhartha, as a kind of stunt double or stand in. He is sort of filling in for each of us until we can recognize our very own, ordinary self as the true Buddha. As Apostle Paul says to the Corinthians, "Don't you know that you yourselves are God's temple and that God's Spirit lives in you?" (I Cor. 3:16) Since our bodies are God's temple, every action we perform, every thought we think, is an act of worship.

In the early 1900's, the Theosophical Society declared Krishnamurti as the much-anticipated World Teacher and made him the head of their Order of the Star. Soon thereafter, Krishnamurti officially dissolved the Order of the Star, proclaiming that "truth is a pathless land."[12] Groucho Marx put it a little differently: "I don't want to belong to any club that will accept me as a member"[13]—or, in Krishnamurti's case, its leader. People don't need guidance, Krishnamurti was saying. They need simply to look at their own selves, be fully present in their daily lives. "Don't agree," he said. "Find out."[14]

THE FORM OF THE FORMLESS

The Lure of Safety, as it turns out, is a lot like a fishing lure. If you chomp down on it too hard, you are going to get hooked and dragged somewhere you don't want to go. For this reason, Christ consciousness, Buddha nature, the Tao—whatever you want to call it—can never be securely possessed or obtained. Trying to capture "the way" or "The Answer" is like trying to capture a handful of water. The moment you have it, it is already slipping away from you. To get distracted by one of the many, temporary forms the divine takes, is, well, to get distracted. The Buddha said, "Every form or quality of phenomenon is transitory and illusive. When the mind realises that the phenomena of life are not real, the Lord Buddha may then be perceived."[15]

We can never truly know Jesus or Buddha by form because they are *beyond* form. They represent pure, dynamic change that does not cling to any one idea or doctrine, any one teaching or philosophy. And it is not just Jesus and Buddha who are beyond form, but every living thing. From the moment we become physical beings, we are changing, growing, dying. This is what the Hindus mean by their mantra, "*Gate, gate, paragate, parasamgate, Bodhiswaha*" ("Gone beyond! Gone beyond! Gone beyond beyond! Hail the goer!") That's you: the goer. As such, you're beyond everything—all rules or codes of conduct, all spiritual teachings, all appropriate or inappropriate actions you might ever perform. You are beyond it all because you *are* it all. Job says of his own search for God:

> But if I go to the east, he is not there;
> If I go to the west, I do not find him.
> When he is at work in the north, I do not see him;
> When he turns to the south, I catch no glimpse of him.
> But he knows the way that I take. (Job: 23:8–10)

The location of God is forever unclear, as are his actions. The only thing that is clearly known is the way that Job takes. Well, *that* is God. That's where God resides—in Job's very own nature, or way.

To seek safety is to seek something other than the Divine. The Divine is perfect but it isn't secure. Because, as Jesus said, the Lord is one, God is necessarily the seeker as well as the sought, the profane as well as the sacred, the doubter and the doubt. The *Tao Te Ching* echoes Job's words:

> Look, it cannot be seen—it is beyond form.
> Listen, it cannot be heard—it is beyond sound.
> Grasp, it cannot be held—it is intangible ...
> The form of the formless,
> The image of the imageless,
> It is called indefinable and beyond imagination.
> Stand before it and there is no beginning.
> Follow it and there is no end.
> Stay with the ancient Tao,
> Move with the present.[16]

How do we find the ancient Tao? We simply move with the present. I challenge you to try something other than that. Even when you are reminiscing about the past, even when you are thinking about the future, you can only do those things in one place: the present. In each moment, one thing always holds true: Wherever you go, there you are. There God is. You need no teacher or guide that exists outside of yourself. For that matter, what use is a guide when you are already where you want to go? When you are courageous, determined, and original enough to fully embrace life's many seeming dangers, you realize you are forever free to wander wherever you would like—however pleasant or unpleasant, however holy or profane—because God always knows the way that you take.

How do you build a better Buddha?

By taking your next breath.

The Myth of Better and Worse

Imagine three fellows taking a journey. All three are setting out from Texas and heading for Alaska. One of our travelers—Ram, we will call him, that being one of the Hindu names for God—goes straight for the gold. He's in Alaska before our other two travelers could eat his dust. Another of our travelers—Ned, we will say—has gotten waylaid in Arizona. He has decided to stop awhile and shop for authentic Native American headdresses. As for Willy, our third traveler, he has barely made it across state lines before he realizes he has a passion for beef jerky. Before proceeding to Alaska, Willy has decided he will make a pilgrimage to each and every convenience store in Arkansas, searching for the Beef Jerky to End All Beef Jerky.

When it comes to physical travel, we can all recognize that there are simply different ways of going about it. Personally, and much to the annoyance of my fellow travelers, I prefer to travel full-steam-ahead, not stopping to eat or take rest stops. Some of us, like Ned and Willy, like to pause for various diversions along the way. Only they are not really diversions, Ned and Willy would say, they are very much an integral part of the trip itself. After all, what's a road trip without beef jerky and Native American headdresses?

When it comes to the spiritual journey, however, many of us fail to appreciate the countless, often bizarre, infinitely varied "traveling" approaches. Spiritually speaking, some of us are already in Alaska and some of us are, admittedly, just now creeping into Arkansas. But why is it that we tend to assume that the individual who is already in Alaska is somehow better, is somehow winning? Who says we were ever racing in the first place? Is the whole point of the trip the destination, or is it also the journey itself? We tend to get confused regarding this matter of spiritual travel because—let's face it—we love to be ahead of the other guy, love to look over our shoulder and congratulate ourselves. I can see that I am in Arizona, and I have to admit that's not nearly as good as Alaska, but come on: I sure am outclassing that idiot in Arkansas!

Part of what makes our traveler Ram, Ram, however, is the fact that he doesn't really think of things as a race. He's in Alaska right now, not because he wanted to win, but because he just happens to be less interested in beef jerky and headdresses. For that matter, Ram understands that Alaska isn't really a place, it is a state of mind. What each of our travelers was after when he set out for "Alaska" was really a certain feeling of belonging. Willy, it just so happens, found out he belongs—for the time being, at least—in Arkansas, as Ned belongs in Arizona. Each of them will move on to Alaska when, and if, he is ready. To berate himself into doing so before he has had his satisfactory fill of Arkansas and Arizona isn't going to get him to Alaska any quicker. In fact, just the opposite is true. Like we said, Ram knows that Alaska is a state of mind, a state of total peace and acceptance. The more guilty Willy feels about being stuck in Arkansas, then, and the more pride Ned takes in clobbering him, the further each of them feels from Alaska. In this context, guilt and pride are simply two different ways of not fully appreciating wherever we happen to find ourselves along the way.

Let's consider a slightly different example. We all recognize a certain developmental hierarchy among a cat, a child, and an adult. Obviously, a cat is less intelligent than a child, but is it worse? Likewise, an adult is more mature than a child, but is he or she better? Needless to say, these terms don't really apply here. Even though the child is eventually heading for adulthood (and, as the Hindus would suggest, so is the cat throughout countless reincarnations), this doesn't exactly imply the adult has won some sort of race. Rather, part of what makes an adult an adult is his or her ability to appreciate the beauty and necessity of various developmental stages.

So it goes with Ram. Ironically, unlike Willy and Ned, Ram doesn't feel so desperately attached to his particular method of traveling. Because he's not so busy defending his place in the hierarchy of better and worse, holy and unholy, moral and immoral, he can really enjoy the richness that Ned and Willy bring to the journey. Like Jesus, Ram is not interested in throwing stones at the adultress because he is always examining his own nature, always enjoying his own unique journey. Truth be told, Ram so fully accepts Ned and Willy that he *is* Ned and Willy, in addition to being Ram. He is content to sit in his igloo because a certain part of his infinitely large self is also enjoying beef jerky and headdresses at this moment, through Ned and Willy. He has relaxed and broadened his individual boundaries to the point where he has become the whole process of journeying itself, all travelers and destinations along the way included. He hasn't exactly given up the "lower," or worldly, aspects of the path, and he hasn't exactly moved past them—he has simply learned to trust others to experience and participate in that level of the Divine Drama.

Spiritually speaking, each of us knows someone who is winning and someone who is losing in comparison to our own, individual selves. One of the ways we can recognize the so-called losing party is a certain feeling of guilt, inadequacy, or anger he or she habitually manifests. Such a person has yet to accept his or her place in life, and feels life has somehow been a raw deal. Consequently, he or she resents others who seem to be coming out ahead. By contrast, the so-called winning party is just happy to be where he or she is. Complaints will probably be minimal because this person feels, generally, that he or she is in just the right place at just the right time. Rather than resenting other's places in their own spiritual evolution, such a person genuinely appreciates the richness and diversity of the journey, and can enjoy the lower along with the higher, in much the same way the human adult can enjoy children and cats without competitive resentment. The authentically spiritual adult is in no particular hurry for each of us to grow up because he or she enjoys us just the way we are—not despite our imperfections but because of them.

To reject any individual, however personally upsetting you may find his or her actions, is necessarily to limit your own experience of the whole. When you are judging another, you are at once distracted from your ultimate goal, yet behaving in a way that is absolutely appropriate to your current place on your path. Like the essence of the entire path itself, this paradoxical truth is beyond language and logic—the indefinable way of things which Chuang Tzu calls "going in two directions at once."

THE HOLE MAKES THE DONUT

My own incredibly simple strategy when it comes to the spiritual journey is this: Whatever situation I find myself in, I assume it must be just the right situation, however difficult or unpleasant it may be. This is the path of surrender, which we will examine in more detail in the next chapter. Does this mean that every leg of the journey is equally comfortable, or that I enjoy all phases of the journey equally? Not at all—not for me, not yet. Still, I am learning all the while, gradually, step by step, to appreciate more fully the necessity of all phases of the journey. Consequently, I am no longer in such a hurry to get to that next place—the place of more money, more recognition, more stuff—that next Big Shiny Vacation Place in the Sky.

You can compare the path of self-realization to the journey of an ongoing process like self-nourishment. This particular journey has three phases: hunger, eating, satisfaction. If you reject the first two phases and try to rush through them, what fun is the last one? You are on your way to your favorite restaurant and you are absolutely starving. "Boy, I can't wait until I sink my teeth into that burger!" you think, your mouth watering. Obviously, a distinct kind of joy goes along with this kind of situation, this kind of wanting or lack. Is it really better, for example, to have a little snack when you are just vaguely hungry? Is it better to not be hungry at all? All three phases, hunger, eating, and satisfaction, are simply part of the same process—in the same way that all individuals, wherever they find themselves spiritually at present, are part of the One.

It is nonetheless important for each of us to accurately recognize where he or she is along the path. If I am in Arizona, it's just going to confuse me to pretend I am in Alaska. I am probably going to deprive myself of the much-needed developmental pleasures of beef jerky and headdresses for one thing. In the words of Chuang Tzu: "Therefore: he who knows enough to stop at what he does not know is *there*. . . . Just take advantage of things as they are. Let your heart and mind roam free. Accept what you can't get and nourish your center on that acceptance. Then you're there. That's all. What else is required? Nothing but that you be willing to act in accord with your own destiny, even if that means going to your death. This is the only difficulty."17

One thing the wisdom traditions definitively promise each of us is: Like it or not, we *will* act in accord with our own destiny. This is not meant to sound fatalistic. Rather, this is a simple reminder of a very Zen-like existential truth: Slice it how you want to, you are always going to do what you are going to do. Like Ramana Maharshi said, no matter what you do, no matter how you may happen to feel about it afterward, you are always being who you are. The trick, says Chuang Tzu, is accepting what you do willingly. If you are in Arizona, then you should accept the inadequacies of Arizona, accept what you can't get. To the degree that each of us can do this honestly, to the degree that we can truly accept all the inadequacies of daily life—we're there. All of a sudden, these inadequacies aren't distractions or diversions from our enjoyment of life—they simply offer additional character. They begin to appear somehow quaint and pleasantly mysterious like the flaws of an antique. The very things that are missing, or seem to be missing, from our individual lives become the nourishing center. More and more we begin to appreciate the true meaning of a familiar saying: The hole makes the donut.

The Myth of One Thing Leads to Another

When God spoke to Moses from the burning bush, telling him to lead the Israelites out of Egypt, Moses wanted more information. "Suppose," Moses said to God, "I go to the Israelites and say to them, 'The God of your fathers has sent me to you,' and they ask me, 'What is his name?' Then what shall I tell them?" (Ex. 3:13). If he goes to the Israelites and says, "I am sent by Holy Mel, The Mediocre Angel!" the Israelites are going to be unimpressed. Why? Well, no one has ever heard of Holy Mel doing anything—his work history is sketchy. Moses wants a name, a business card he can flash, that will immediately reference Yahweh's past accomplishments.

This is how we tend to think of all beings, divine or otherwise. We habitually categorize someone based on what he or she does. According to the French philosopher, René Descartes, what a being does defines its formal reality. Formal reality is simply a measure of how much a being can affect form. The person who has the most formal reality, or power, then, is the person who has done the most, has amassed the largest resume of effects. In this sense, we tend to think of people as things that lead to other things. The people who do or accomplish the most, we tend to rank the highest or most important. In the language of philosophy, we often think of people in terms of causality. For Descartes, God is the being with the most formal reality, the most power of causality. It is interesting, in this context, to note Yahweh's answer to Moses' question. He doesn't say, "I'm the guy that makes it all happen." Instead, God says, "I AM WHO I AM. This is what you are to say to the Israelites: 'I AM has sent me to you'" (Ex. 3:14).

On the one hand, the Bible makes it very clear that God causes everything—it's an essential part of his job description. At the same time, however, God seems reluctant to define himself in terms of causality. We see this same ambivalence about causality even more clearly in Buddhism. One of the Buddha's core teachings was that of karma, the law of cause and effect. Apostle Paul summarized this law perfectly when he said, "Do not be deceived: God cannot be mocked. A man reaps what he sows" (Gal. 6:7). What goes around comes around. For the Buddhists especially, karmic law doesn't require an old man in the sky dealing out punishments to the wicked, and rewards to the good. It is a natural law more in the way of, say, gravity. You drop a stone, it falls. The law of gravity works automatically, without requiring divine intervention in the usual sense of the phrase. Buddha said, "The immature are their own enemies, doing selfish deeds which will bring them sorrow."[18] Our actions are their own judges. If I am a real hothead, God doesn't exactly need to step in and zap me. I am likely, based on my own temperament, to lose my temper often and treat people unkindly. It is perfectly natural, then, that people will respond to me in a similar manner, providing an equal and opposite reaction to my original action. I am my own worst enemy—or greatest savior. That's how karma works.

On one level, then, the Buddhist strategy for working with karma is pretty simple. Do more good things so that more good consequences will follow. Do less bad things so that less bad consequences will follow. That is only part of the story, however. The ultimate goal is to be done with, or at least unattached to, *all* karma—good and bad. As Satguru Sivaya Subramuniyaswami writes in *Merging with Śiva: Hinduism's Contemporary Metaphysics*, "One does not have the experience of realizing the Self until all of his karma is in a state of resolve."[19] Our goal, the Satguru asserts, is to release ourselves from all karmic bonds, ultimately becoming "timeless, formless, spaceless."[20] At such a point, presumably, each of us could also say simply, "I AM WHO I AM." But as long as we are doing anything at all, how could we ever possibly quit causing things to happen?

We find this very same goal in Taoism. If a thing has a use, say the Taoists—if it causes effects, that is—it is doomed from the start, because that which has a use can always be used up. Chuang Tzu tells a parable about an ancient, gnarled old tree. Since the tree's wood was useless in a practical sense—no good for carpentry and so forth—it managed to outlive the surrounding trees. Its longevity comes from the fact that it doesn't do anything—it just is. Its only real function is simply to be a gnarled old tree. How is it a person can possibly avoid doing, become truly and perfectly useless in Taoism's positive sense of the word? How is it any being can ever step outside of the laws of cause and effect? In answering this question, it might be helpful to examine some less paradoxical objections to causality.

INDUCTION AND INFINITE REGRESS

In the mid-1700s, the Scottish philosopher David Hume created quite a stir when he questioned one of our most basic assumptions—the idea that one thing leads to another. Hume attacked this assumption through two key concepts: induction and infinite regress. Induction is such an automatic process we probably don't even think of it as a process. It works like this: We see a certain something happen enough times in the past, we assume, or induce, that it will happen likewise in the future. For example, over the years, I stick my hand in a fire half a dozen times and notice that my hand hurts just after doing so. I then induce that sticking one's hand in the fire seems to happen just before a feeling of pain happens. My "logical" conclusion: Fire causes pain—in the past, as well as in the future. Obviously this induction process is useful and necessary when it comes to a lot of things. These small assumptions we make every day are usually harmless enough. Some pretty huge errors, however, have resulted from this very same process of induction.

In the not-so-distant past, people believed in spontaneous generation. We noticed that shortly after we observed a hunk of rotting meat, we would then observe a swarm of maggots. Obviously, then, the rotting meat was causing the maggots. The more complex the events we are observing, the more incorrect our inductions tend to be. Let's say I grew up in a small community where I only encountered three or four black individuals, all of whom happened to be uneducated. I might go on to induce that being black is the cause of being ignorant. Time and again, we have learned that some of our most basic assumptions about the world have been simply, well, assumptions. Until the last hundred years or so, we were absolutely convinced of Newton's idea of gravity. We drop things, they fall. Why? There is a mysterious, unseen force called gravity, said Newton, that pulls them to Earth. Einstein came along, however, and said, Guess what? There is no such thing as gravity. In reality, things fall because space and time are this one thing that happens to be curved. And, of course, the half dozen people who really understood what Einstein was saying nodded their heads and now those of us who are properly educated know that apples fall, not because of gravity, but because of curved space-time.

Hume's point was simply that we can never be certain of true causes. Until we can observe an infinite number of rotting carcasses paired with an infinite number of maggot swarms, we can't really say with absolute certainty that rotting meat causes maggots. For that matter, until we have thoroughly examined an infinite number of falling objects, we can't really say curved space-time causes the appearance of gravity. How much more so, then, are people likely to make confused assumptions when it comes to spirituality? Okay, Buddha did this and this and became enlightened, we observe. Ghandi did this, Jesus did this . . . Logically, then, if I just do this, this, and this, then I will become enlightened, too. Well, maybe, but that's still a pretty huge assumption, especially when we consider what a small number of cases we have to work with. How are we supposed to know, then, the true cause of spiritual awakening? For that matter, can we ever know?

Before we attempt to answer the above question, let's move on to Hume's second objection to causality: the problem of infinite regress. Let's say I am stopped at a red light and someone hits me from behind. I then hit the guy in front of me, smashing his taillights. What is the cause of the guy's taillights getting smashed? That probably depends on whom you are talking to. The guy with smashed taillights is probably going to say my hitting him is what caused it. I'm probably going to say that the *real* cause of all this mess, the original cause, was the idiot that hit me. The idiot that hit me explains that he fell asleep behind the wheel. He wasn't able to sleep last night, you see, because his idiot neighbor's dog was barking all last night. The real cause of all this, then, is the idiot neighbor and/or his idiot dog. So on and so forth. That's infinite regress. According to the idea of causality, every cause is necessarily the effect of some other cause. That being the case, we can trace any given event all the way back to the Big Bang itself. At which point we have to ask ourselves, of course, "Now what exactly caused this whole Big Bang thing?"

This infinite regress problem can turn into a real mess when considering spiritual matters. What caused Jesus' perfect spiritual realization? Simple. He acted with perfect love and compassion in every situation. Okay, but he was the Son of God, after all, which gave him a kind of unfair advantage to no small degree. His divine origins, we might say, caused his ability to be so loving. Okay, then what about God himself? What caused God to share his divine son? For that matter, we might as well ask, what caused God to be God? Once again, we are brought back to a very difficult and important question: How are we to ever know the true cause of spiritual accomplishment? Where, exactly, does the causal buck stop?

"Because there is, monks, an unborn, not become, not made, uncompounded, therefore an escape can be shown for what is born, has become, is made, is compounded."[21] There is *something*, the Buddha was saying, that exists outside of causality, but what? As each of the wisdom traditions emphasizes over and over, we are that very something. God is that something, spiritual realization is that something, our ordinary, daily actions are that something. We can't do some magical act, we can't manufacture some divine cause to produce the effect of enlightenment, because we are *already* enlightened. We can't "fix what ain't broke." To say it more abstractly: There is no such thing as cause. That is the only way—to recognize how things really are, already "unborn," already "not become"—we can ever truly step outside of cause and effect. Things happen, sure, because that is what things do. To hook them together in a causal way, however, is always to make a huge, rather arrogant assumption. See for yourself—you are, at present, one of those things happening after all. Take a minute and try to feel what is causing you right now. Try to feel what is causing you to breathe, causing you to read these very words. Try to connect to that elusive something that has brought you to this very moment. Really, take a minute and try it out. . .

Of course, you didn't come up with anything—nothing concrete anyway. You didn't come up with anything because there isn't anything. You are "unborn, unbecome." Just like God, YOU ARE BECAUSE YOU ARE. You are the original rebel without a cause. End of story. This is the ultimate goal of all meditation practices, as I will discuss in a later chapter: to cultivate the experience of pure, logically "pointless" being. To the degree that the spiritual universe operates beyond cause and effect, even if you wanted to follow a kind of cooking recipe that would lead to self-realization, it would never work. You can't teach an apple pie how to be an apple pie. Rather, the best we could say would be what Ramana Maharshi was always saying: "Remain as you are."

Chuang Tzu puts this idea of the "unbecome" nicely: "Anger and delight; happiness and grief; anxiety and regret . . . music out of emptiness. Fungus sprouts in mustiness. Day and night follow each other. Who knows which came first or what are the sources of the sun and moon?

"Enough. Aren't they enough, sunrise and sunset? . . . Although this knowledge is clear to me, I do not know what's responsible for making it so. It's as if there were such a thing as a True Lord, but I find no evidence of such—I can go forward believing, and yet I find no such form."[22] Where is the True Lord? What is the way to him? He is right here, right now—closer than close. That Thou Art. There is no way to him other than the way you are already taking. Every word you read, every thought you think, every breath you breathe is bringing you one step closer to your very own self.

Letting Things Take Their Course

We are aware that we suffer from optical delusions, but we still suffer, nonetheless. We have more or less just shifted our dissatisfaction onto a new playing field, it might seem. Like Paul Simon sings, "breakdowns come/And breakdowns go/So what are you going to do about it?/That's what I'd like to know."[23] We can see that there has been a breakdown somewhere along the way, but by what practical means are we going to heal ourselves?

The answer to this all-important question—the comically simple message which recurs, in one form or another, anywhere we look—is summed up by Lao Tzu:

In the pursuit of learning, every day something is acquired.
In the pursuit of Tao, every day something is dropped.
Less and less is done
Until non-action is achieved.
When nothing is done, nothing is left undone.
The world is ruled by letting things take their course.
It cannot be ruled by interfering.[24]

How are we going to build a better buddha for ourselves? Not by assembling, it would seem. According to Lao Tzu, we are going to build a better buddha by, well, *not* building. We are simply going to "let things take their course"—what the Taoists call "non-action" or "work without doing." We will sit back, relax, and let the buddha do all the work—let the buddha build the better buddha.

Imagine a bowling ball rolling down a hill. Once this process has been set in motion, there is nothing for you to do. The ball, the hill, and natural physical forces take care of the rest of the journey. The best you can do to help the ball along toward its destination is simply avoid interfering. So it goes with the spiritual path. Each of us is already rolling down the hill just fine, already well on his or her way to perfect Christ consciousness or Buddha nature. Each of us has already received the necessary initial push the minute we started to wonder about God, death, morality, and the meaning of life. Just as the bowling ball automatically gains momentum as it rolls further and further down the hill, you also gain momentum as you tumble along your own explorative path. From that perspective, trying to speed yourself along is no more useful than the bowling ball trying to speed itself along.

In the same way the many spiritual paths differ in their relative emphasis on direct perception versus compassion, they also tend to take different approaches to individual effort. The traditional Hindu path, for example, tends to encourage vigorous individual effort, which, over millions and millions of lifetimes, finally results in liberation. Zen, on the other hand, ultimately encourages the process of "sudden awakening," an event that sometimes occurs after a single unexpected word, or startling bamboo strike, from the Zen master. Properly understood, however, these are not two entirely different paths. Let's go back to the metaphor of the bowling ball. The bowling ball receives a single push and it is on its way. The ensuing spontaneous, effortless journey down the hill may take moments or even days depending on the size and slope of the hill. Even so, the moment when the bowling ball finally reaches the bottom of the hill, it is suddenly there. In the same way, as individual seekers, we receive that initial push at various places along various paths. At present, you may think you are making this and that effort—and to the degree you need to think of it this way, this is true—but you are actually just rolling along, having received some unplanned for push somewhere in the past. Even so, the day will inevitably come when you reach your destination and—all of a sudden—you realize you have been there the whole time.

A VISION UNFOLDS

My own path illustrates how this paradoxical course of effort/effortlessness can run. I grew up Christian. Being a rather anxious child, I tended to fixate on certain elements of the Christian faith that stress the need for constant effort and struggle, a kind of perpetual "work" on the seeker's part. Entirely unfamiliar at this stage with the paradoxical idea of "work without doing," I instead internalized Apostle James' assertion that "faith without works is dead" (James 2:26). Whereas the *Tao Te Ching* encourages the "no fight: no blame"[25] attitude toward spiritual evolution, Paul admonishes Timothy to "Fight the good fight" (1 Tim. 6:12). Throughout both the Old and New Testaments, in fact, military imagery pervades. Although Taoism certainly isn't without its own military metaphors, its writings typically favor the image of a stream, an effortless flow that, like the bowling ball in the previous example, tumbles along without resisting the natural currents. Taoism, in fact, is often called the "Watercourse Way":

> The highest good is like water.
> Water gives life to the ten thousand things and does not strive.
> It flows in places men reject and so is like the Tao.[26]

This is not to suggest, of course, that all Christians necessarily get distracted by the unrelenting spiritual "fight." As I said in chapter 1, when viewed from the highest, broadest perspective, the teachings of Christ likewise encourage total peace and acceptance, both of oneself and of others. My personal temperament, however, mingled with certain biblical teachings in such a way as to cultivate a rather workaholic approach to the spiritual path. Not surprisingly, then, despite my regular church attendance and earnest Bible study, I felt quite distant from God and all things sacred. I had a feeling that something holy was sort of "out there," but I certainly hadn't encountered it. There was a lot of work and military maneuvers going on, but very many things left undone.

Due to this chronic spiritual dissatisfaction, I grew up in the Church with a feeling that I was waiting on something—some kind of call from God. I remember being very affected by one story about the Old Testament prophet, Samuel. "In those days," the story starts, "the word of the Lord was rare; there were not many visions" (1 Sam. 3:1). This was a beginning I could relate to. Despite my continued efforts, there were most certainly not many visions. Here enters Samuel, a boy who gets called by God in the middle of the night. Samuel goes on to do many great things because "The Lord was with Samuel as he grew up, and he let none of his words fall to the ground" (1 Sam. 3:19). So I would wake up every night, thinking maybe *this* was the night. I was ready to do something dramatic and holy, as long as it meant connecting with something genuinely sacred. After much angst and metaphysical contemplation, I arrived, nonetheless, in late adolescence having never received the call. Frustrated and painfully disappointed, I gave up on all things spiritual, dismissing them as fearful superstition, and became a rather militant atheist. So how did I end up here, then, writing this book?

We will need to backtrack a bit to when I was about ten or so. At this time, I'd happened—through my martial arts study—on some books about meditation. Having a general interest in all things metaphysical, I began to experiment with meditation a bit. I had no concept, however, of meditation as something people did for spiritual advancement. My church hadn't made the connection between prayer and meditation evident for me. I simply thought of it as a hobby, something I did out of curiosity. Within the first week or two of experimenting with some very simple mindfulness meditations, I began to experience states of heightened mystical awareness—states that, I came to discover years later, are well-documented in the Eastern traditions and are considered highly significant. My meditation books didn't mention anything like these experiences, nor did the Bible, so I lacked a solid context in which to understand what was going on. I found these experiences pleasant and interesting, but I didn't recognize them as hugely significant at that time.

I thought of these "visions" as being similar to what happens when you stare at a bright light too long. When you look away, the afterimage follows you wherever you look. In the same way, I intuitively understood, these colors and sounds I was experiencing in deep meditative states were a kind of perceptual foundation that was always there—a kind of subtle, organizing grid lying beneath any experience I would encounter. When I saw this so-called grid in meditation, I was just seeing it more directly, looking straight into the framework of my own perception.

I remember playing with a toy called an Etch-a-Sketch as a kid. If you sketched away all the magnetic filaments, or whatever formed the drawing surface, you could see right down into the mechanics of the machine. This meditative experience was very much like that. I was using the process of my mind to sketch away all the other surface stuff so that I could look directly into my mind's mechanics. These experiences began to occur at night, throughout the various sleeping and dreaming states. Sometimes, I would wake up out of a dream into these experiences, which were very relaxing and familiar somehow. In a way that is difficult to put into language, I realized these experiences represented the me that continued even when I lost my normal, waking consciousness. Such occurrences continued for a few months, gradually tapering off as I lost interest in formal meditation practice.

In my early 20s, however, in the middle of my roaring atheist phase, these experiences began again. This time they were entirely spontaneous. As in childhood, I was reading a bit of everything around this time, so soon thereafter, I inadvertently encountered descriptions of the *mandala* (Sanskrit for "magic circle") in the writings of the psychologist, Carl Jung. His account of the mandala as an archetype of the collective unconscious really resonated with me, as it seemed to perfectly describe my own mystical experiences. One thing led to another and, via Jung, I eventually discovered the writings of Eastern mysticism.

NOWHERE TO GO, NOTHING TO DO

After exploring a variety of Eastern spiritual systems including Buddhism, Hinduism, Taoism, and many others, I came across the Tibetans. I was amazed to find an incredibly detailed account in Tibetan literature describing the clear light experience. The literature spoke of the sound, rays, and light manifesting as one cohesive experience of flowing mandalas and so forth—the exact phenomenon I had first witnessed as a child. According to the Tibetans, such experiences, which can arise both in meditation and in sleeping states, were a kind of direct peek into the natural mind. The experience is typically illustrated as a cloudy sky clearing so that we can see the sun, which has been shining the whole time; which brings us to the moral of the story: the complete *naturalness* of the individual's relation to the whole, or One Self.

Although I do not currently identify myself within any one metaphysical system or practice, my present beliefs are perhaps best described through the teachings of Dzogchen, which is a form of Tibetan Buddhism. The Dzogchen "motto," much like the Taoist motto, is often expressed like this: "There is nothing to do. There is nowhere to go." This is in no way a negative or nihilistic statement, but simply an expression of profound peace and appreciation of the universe's innate wholeness. The essence of Dzogchen is that of spontaneous self-perfection. The bowling ball is already rolling down the hill, says Dzogchen, so what else is there to do but sit back and watch as it reaches its ultimate, perfectly harmonious destination? Imagine a caterpillar gradually transforming into a butterfly. Does the caterpillar work to make this happen? Not exactly—not unless you want to consider a caterpillar just *being* a caterpillar work. Such is the paradoxical "method" of Dzogchen. If you simply be who you are, do what you do, then you are already well on the way to realizing your caterpillar self as a butterfly.

Dzogchen is already so close to us, it is said, that we tend to overlook it. The best meditation, according to Dzogchen, is no meditation. Here is where a lot of us are likely to get confused. Dzogchen, like Zen and Taoism—and all other spiritual paths at their most genuine, esoteric core—tends to be so elusive because it sounds too good to be true. The idea of "practice makes perfect" is so deeply ingrained in our collective psyches that we are very suspicious when someone comes along and says, "Hey! Guess what! *Being* makes perfect, not practice." It is amazingly simple. Want to discover what your most effective "meditation" or "practice" is? You need only look to those things in your life that you already enjoy. Look to those things you do *just because*. You also have to look to those things we don't enjoy, look to those things we do because it seems like we have no other choice. Pleasant or unpleasant, desirable or undesirable, it's all living, all being. There is only one possible direction along the spiritual path, that is to say: onward, forever closer to total Christ consciousness or complete self-liberation.

We have all experienced what the Tibetans call the clear light time and again throughout our lives. It may not take the exotic form I'm describing, but the essence of the experience is the same. Ironically, such an experience of the natural mind is so natural that we tend to overlook it altogether. It might be as simple as sitting on the porch having a glass of lemonade, or taking the dog for a walk. The form it takes isn't nearly so important as the feeling, the essence of the experience. If we are looking for something "big," something strangely mystical, we are going to overlook those perfectly small, quiet moments in which we experience Zen's effortless no-mind.

Goo-Goo G'Joob

I am the eggman
They are the eggmen
I am the walrus
—JOHN LENNON AND PAUL MCCARTNEY[27]

As long as the Dzogchen approach to self-realization sounds too good to be true, it probably is—for you. Maybe you are still busy "improving" yourself. That's one of the darkest clouds in the sky of authentic self-perception to be sure, so take your time. The various paths of spontaneous perfection aren't going anywhere. For the time being, you have simply yet to realize a caterpillar, just as it is, is already just as good as a butterfly. Since this state of non-acceptance of caterpillar-ness describes the vast majority of us, I will later outline some specific means of self-improvement. Ironically, as you commit more and more energy to your practices of meditation and dream yoga, etc., they begin to "undo" themselves, somehow replacing effort with non-effort, or acceptance. There are no accidents along the spiritual journey, you begin to realize, no tangents or distractions, only one experience of the True Self after another. As you reach this point, the point where you actually begin to enjoy being a caterpillar, suddenly you're popping out of your cocoon, unfolding your beautiful new wings.

THE EGGMAN DANCES THE COSMIC DANCE

At this point, I think it is fair to ask an obvious question: If you are already perfect, if you are already heading full steam down the path of spontaneous self-perfection, why are you reading this book? For that matter, why am I writing it? Alan Watts considers this same dilemma when he writes: "People appear to be under the fixed impression that one speaks or writes of these things in order to improve them or do them some good, assuming, too, that the speaker has himself been improved and is able to speak with authority."[28]

For the record, let me just make it clear: I am not out to "improve" anyone, myself included. I have got a dance to do, you see, so I do it. This is what the Hindus call karma yoga. Your dance, which is no better or worse, no higher or lower, than my own, seems to involve reading this book just now. We have got a dance to do *together*, that is, so here we go—round and round until we are dizzy. In *The World's Religions*, Huston Smith describes this Cosmic Dance beautifully:

> If we ask why Reality, which is in fact one and perfect, is seen by us as many and marred; why the soul, which is really united with God throughout, sees itself as sundered; why the rope appears to be a snake—if we ask these questions we are up against the question that has no answer, any more than the comparable Christian question of why God created the world has an answer. The best we can say is that the world is *lila*, God's play. Children playing hide and seek assume various roles that have no validity outside the game. They place themselves in jeopardy and in conditions from which they must escape. Why do they do so when in a twinkling they could free themselves by simply stepping out of the game? The only answer is that the game is its own point and reward. It is fun in itself, a spontaneous overflow of creative, imaginative energy. So too in some mysterious way it must be with the world. Like a child playing alone, God is the Cosmic Dancer, whose routine is all creatures and all worlds. From the tireless stream of God's energy the cosmos flows in endless, graceful reenactement.[29]

This dance doesn't *mean* anything, that is to say. We dance for the sake of the dance alone. As Shakespeare wrote about life in *Macbeth*, "it is a tale told by an idiot, full of sound and fury, signifying nothing." Put in the right context, this is far from a gloomy statement. If life "signified" something, someone would require us to write a book report at the end, right? We would have to tease out the moral or the message from its drama if we were to pass the final exam. As it is, life is non-sense— there is no final exam! Still, there is so much in it, so much sound and fury, like a beautiful Beethoven Sonata or a ridiculous Beatles song, this bizarre dance of life means nothing in particular—nothing other than, well, a Beethoven Sonata or a Beatles song—which is no small thing to mean.

To summarize everything we have examined so far, to succinctly address any questions that might have so far arisen, or will likely arise throughout the many pages that follow, I would like to offer a wise chunk of non-sense told by a fellow "idiot," Chuang Tzu:

Now I want to say a few words. Whether they are the right or wrong kind of words, they are at least some kind of words, and are no different than the words of others, so they're just okay. But please permit me to say them. There is a beginning. And there is a not-yet-beginning-to-be-a-beginning. There is a not-yet-beginning-to-be-a-not-yet-beginning-to-be-a-beginning. There is being. There is not beginning to be being. There is not yet beginning to be not yet beginning to be being. Oh, suddenly there's being and not being. Now I just had my say. But I don't know whether my saying has said anything or nothing. . . .

To use a finger to make the point that a finger is not a finger is not as good as using a nonfinger to make the same point. To use a horse to prove that a horse is not a horse is not as good as to use a nonhorse to prove that a horse is not a horse. Heaven-and-earth is one finger. All ten thousand things are one horse. Okay? Not okay. Okay? Okay.[30]

Huh?

Exactly.

It's like the story where the philosophy professor puts up the single question of the class final on the blackboard. As it turns out, that question consists of just one character: a question mark. One student turns his test in a few seconds later—the only student who ends up making an A on the final. His equally elegant answer: an exclamation point. That's the whole crazy dance, nicely summed up—Question? Exclamation! How do you get that damned goose out of the bottle? I don't know, but it's out!

GRAVITY AND THE GURU:
AN INEVITABLE JOURNEY

Sometimes in his life a man becomes dissatisfied and, not content with what he has, he seeks the satisfaction of his desires through prayer to God. His mind is gradually purified until he longs to know God, more to obtain his grace than to satisfy his worldly desires. Then, God's grace begins to manifest. God takes the form of a Guru and appears to the devotee, teaches him the truth and, moreover, purifies his mind by association. The devotee's mind gains strength and is then able to turn inward. By meditation it is further purified and it remains still without the least ripple. That calm expanse is the Self.

The Guru is both external and internal. From the exterior he gives a push to the mind to turn it inwards. From the interior he pulls the mind towards the Self and helps in the quieting of the mind. That is the Guru's grace. There is no difference between God, Guru and the Self.

—RAMANA MAHARSHI[1]

The spiritual path can be utterly bewildering and frustrating. Most of us feel, from time to time, that our lives would be much simpler, run much more smoothly, if only someone with impeccable wisdom and integrity were to sit us down and tell us what to do. We want a reliable teacher, a guide—what the Eastern traditions call a guru. Oddly enough, given my previous emphasis on genuine originality, individuality, and courageous self-inquiry on the spiritual path, there really is such an ideal being. In many ways, any and all of life's ultimate undertakings, be they spiritual, philosophical, psychological, or artistic, necessarily start with a search for this sacred being. Ramana Maharshi describes this peculiar search, known as *guru yoga* by the Eastern traditions, in the book *Be as You Are*.

According to Ramana, each of us reaches a certain critical point in life when we realize our same old routine just isn't working any longer. We will experience that pervasive and painful feeling of "something missing," and recognize, with a sudden, existential panic, we are out of parlor tricks. No matter how much money we collect, or how much prestige we gain, we have begun to realize it's never going to be enough. We begin to look for something else at such a juncture, something higher than the deeply-ingrained habits of our daily rat race. At this point, says Ramana, once we begin to seek this higher something authentically—with all our hearts, souls and minds—once this transcendental something begins to truly take precedence over our various worldly ambitions and so forth, the guru will appear to us to lead us along our ultimate path. As for the particular form the guru takes, it need not be a luminous being knocking on our front door. In fact, as we shall see, this sort of appearance is quite unlikely. Ramana tells us that the guru is as much internal as external. Even so, the guru is a very real being. And at that very moment when we truly and whole-heartedly yearn for the divine, this very real being will, without fail, make itself known to us.

Belief in the guru does not require a belief in any god or deity, nor need it conflict with any of your theistic beliefs. Although it is true that Christians often connect to the guru through the form of Jesus of Nazareth and the various Christian saints, and Buddhists often honor the guru through the form of the historical Buddha and other revered teachers, these particular methods are by no means necessary, or even preferable. The atheist, in fact, can perform guru yoga just as effectively, and with just as much sincere devotion, as the monk. To search for the guru, to devote yourself deeply to this search, is simply to recognize there is more to the world than self-serving greed and brute functionality. To sincerely yearn for goodness, love, beauty, even romance—this is to yearn for the guru in one of its many forms. Whatever name you call your deepest, most genuinely human needs, dreams, and desires, is simply one of many ways of referring to the one guru, the all-important form of original being.

Not surprisingly, because this yearning for something higher, something transcendental, is as old as the material world itself, numerous practices and systems have been developed to help each of us along in our journey of guru yoga. *Yoga* means "to yoke, harness, unite." Guru yoga, then, is the process by which each of us discovers his or her own self as the one divine being, re-members his or her own self as an infinite body of pure love, beauty and awareness.

The Purpose of Guru Yoga

Upon hearing that a certain individual was a man of good principles, the English dandy Topham Beauclerk responded, "Then he does not wear them out in practice."[2] This quip comes in particularly handy when considering the much-debated topic of spiritual practice. Whenever I hear this highfalutin phrase, "spiritual practice"—usually declared more in the manner of "SPIRITUAL PRAC-

TICE!"—I am reminded of the old joke where the man goes to see the doctor with a prostate problem. The doctor asks him, "Do you practice masturbation?" The man responds, "What's there to practice?" As I have emphasized in the previous chapters, the more we think there is something specific to practice, some particular method of self-improvement, the more we tend to entangle ourselves in our old webs of obsessive behaviors and patterns. The practice of guru yoga has this same catch-22 built in from the very start. If, as Ramana Maharshi says, "God, Guru and the Self" are all the same thing, aren't I confusing myself when I go looking for, well, myself? Aren't I simply exhausting my innately good principles by wearing them out in practice?

The wisdom of Zen, in particular, is built around this infamous paradox of disciplined non-discipline, looking without seeking, the practice of non-practice. Although Zen masters typically encourage their students in relentless sitting meditation, often to the point of striking them with bamboo sticks when their concentration fails, they simultaneously denounce such formal practices. The Zen master Pao-chi said, "Seekers clinging to method . . . are like silkworms spitting out thread binding themselves."[3] To the degree that guru yoga is a method, how do we know it is not simply another tempting morsel laid out on the cosmic booby trap?

For the time being, we will let sleeping dogs lie, and allow this riddle of effortless effort, this paradox of "work without doing" remain as it is. Be confident, however, that the very practice of guru yoga will likely go a long way toward solving this riddle for you. For now, all catch-22's aside, rest assured that if you choose to go on this particular journey, you'll engage in some of the highest, most authentic acts of kindness and devotion an individual may perform. Done with a pure heart and concentrated mind, guru yoga quite literally changes the external world as well as the individual seeker. Each time you perform one of the devotional practices, however imperfectly, you are engaging in a genuine act of service, offering up your very own self for the ultimate good. At the same time, it's important to understand that you do nothing through your own accord. The very act of guru yoga belongs, first and foremost, to the guru.

Many spiritual systems consider guru yoga an essential, preparatory practice that the devotee must regularly perform before undertaking other meditations. At the same time, many highly-realized teachers still perform guru yoga on a daily basis. Wherever the course of your individual path may lead you, you are never too "impure" or too "holy" to benefit from guru yoga. It is simply one of the most flexible and most connecting practices along any given spiritual journey. It is a proven way of planting your spiritual roots, cultivating the selfless and compassionate attitude that lends meaning to all other artistic, psychological, or metaphysical pursuits. It has been said that if you are going to perform only one spiritual practice, either formal or informal, guru yoga is that one.

The Weighty One—Who or What Is the Guru?

*G*uru is often translated as "weighty one," as the guru necessarily has a very weighty effect on the devotee's life and path. According to Ramana Maharshi, "Guru only means *guri*, or concentration."[4] What is the guru concentrated on? Like a black hole, the guru is concentrated solely on the guru—a dense, one-pointed mass of perfect self-awareness which, paradoxically, also contains the whole universe, material and immaterial. To perform guru yoga, then, is to concentrate your own, individual mind on the incredibly dense love and wisdom of the entire universe, the Divine Self.

The Hindus recognize two distinct categories of gurus: *upadesa* and *sat*. Upadesa gurus are individuals who give spiritual instruction. They are not usually fully-realized beings. If you're a Christian, your pastor or youth minister could be considered an upadesa guru. If you're a Buddhist, your meditation teacher or the author of your favorite discourse on Buddhism would be an upadesa guru. From a practical perspective, these teachers still have work to do, karma to fulfill. Every individual has many, many upadesa gurus along the path, each with something very specific to teach. By contrast, each individual has only one sat guru. The sat guru is the "truly weighty one," a fully-realized manifestation of your particular path, a reflection of your highest self. A sat guru is with you strictly out of love. His or her work has already been accomplished, and karma fulfilled. The sat guru tends to teach strictly by being. His or her very presence is the way itself.

In Hinduism and Christianity, as well as many forms of Buddhism, the sat guru is, or once was, embodied in a specific, physical form. In Christianity, for example, Jesus is a concrete manifestation of a sat guru, as is the historical Buddha in Buddhism. In teachings such as Zen and Taoism, however, the sat guru is an abstract being. It is an infinite, intelligent presence much more similar to *Star Wars'* elusive "force" than it is to a specific, physically embodied individual. For the Taoist, the sat guru represented by the Tao is "nameless," beyond form, the ancient "gate to all mystery." Likewise, for the Zen practitioner, the sat guru is embodied in the unadorned Self—a pervasive sort of perfectly transparent energy vibrating throughout all creation. For the artist, the sat guru might be pure beauty itself, the source of all artistic creation. Similarly, the sat guru might be pure idea and understanding for the scientist, the source of inspiration for all intuitive, scientific knowing. Whether your sat guru takes the form of the concrete or the abstract, sincere devotion and surrender to this divine aspect both within yourself and outside yourself allows for a process of opening up, your individual boundaries becoming increasingly transparent so that the pure love of the sat guru can flow freely through you. As you cultivate an ever-deepening love for the sat guru, you see more of this love reflected back to you, more of the sat guru present in everything around and within you.

How Do You Find Your Guru?

For those of you who don't already feel connected to a particular form of the sat guru, you may be asking yourself, "How do I go about finding my guru? How will I know my guru when I encounter him, her or it? What if I meet this being or experience along the way somewhere but fail to recognize it?" First, you need not encounter the sat guru in the physical form. Most of us, in fact, won't meet the sat guru on the physical plane, in much the same way that the Christian never expects to meet Jesus in this concrete sense. Second, *finding* the sat guru is impossible. Rather, the sat guru finds you. As Ramana suggested in his description of the guru, you can only prepare yourself by going deeper and deeper within, and when you are ready, the guru will manifest. There is no such thing as "missing" the guru.

How I Encountered My Sat Guru, Neem Karoli Baba (Maharaj-ji)

AFTER I BEGAN HAVING SPONTANEOUS mystical experiences as a young adult, I began looking into various spiritual systems, trying to sort out some of life's most fundamental existential truths. My music studio quickly became cluttered with texts from a variety of disciplines. One day, one of my voice students unexpectedly showed up with a handful of books for me. Although I didn't know it until that time, this student was a teacher of kundalini yoga and had noticed all my spirituality books lying around. One of the books he brought me was Ram Dass' *Be Here Now*. I didn't read it immediately, as it seemed a little kooky to me. I was pretty snobby at the time, preferring only the "cleanest," most intellectually respected of systems such as Zen and Taoism. The predominantly Hindu teachings Ram Dass was conveying seemed gaudy to me—all counterculture flash and ignorant superstition. A month or two later, however, I browsed this book a bit and something strange, albeit very subtle and gradual, began to unfold. Although the sat guru described in Ram Dass' book, Neem Karoli Baba or Maharaj-ji, seemed mostly nutty to me, I found that I kept replaying various photos of him in my mind's eye. For those of you who have never read *Be Here Now*, you should know that Maharaj-ji looks like someone's pudgy grandfather wrapped in a blanket, and undergoing early-onset Alzheimer's. Not a very austere figure, to be sure. As my meditative practice continued to deepen, I began to encounter Maharaj-ji in lucid, or wakeful dreams—what the Hindus would describe as encountering the guru on inner planes, or an astral encounter with the guru. These encounters had a profound effect on me, raising my practice to another level almost overnight. Recognizing Maharaj-ji as the guru I'd been unknowingly waiting for since I was a child, I began to perform formal guru yoga practices using him as my focus. As a result of his grace, I began to encounter him more frequently on the astral planes, receiving very deep teaching and instruction.

Sometime later, I encountered—very much by accident—a woman whose husband had recently died, suddenly and unexpectedly. This woman and her husband were also devotees of Maharaj-ji. We developed an intimate friendship as we worked through her grief together. She told me that at a prior meditation retreat, both she and her husband had been given mala beads (similar to rosary beads) made by Ram Dass from strands of Maharaj-ji's blanket. At the time of her husband's death, however, his beads had been lost for some time. After he died, she had looked for them rather desperately but with no luck. One night soon after we met, she had a dream in which Maharaj-ji and I were massaging her feet. The next morning—taking this dream as some sort of sign—she renewed her search and found her husband's mala beads. She took this as an indication that I was meant to have them, and sent them to me soon thereafter. Maharaj-ji had left his body (the Hindus refer to the act of conscious, bodily death as *mahasamadhi*) more than 20 years earlier, so I had never imagined I would ever possess a physical artifact of my guru, some object that had actually been in physical contact with him. Upon receiving these beads, which I placed in my teaching studio, my business prospered unexpectedly. My life and relationships became much richer and fulfilling. My practice continued to grow by leaps and bounds.

About this time, I had an astral encounter with Maharaj-ji in which I was instructed to write this book—a project which I had been aware of, on one level or another, as forthcoming since early childhood. I began the next day, a work which has since flowed easily and readily, continuing to have a profound impact on all aspects of my life. Consequently, in each word of this book, I am directed back toward my sat guru, reminded of his subtle and peculiar grace. This book is a direct manifestation of his love for each of us. If you have a strong karmic connection to Neem Karoli Baba, or another guru, somewhere in the deepest layers of your unconscious something will begin to stir, gradually working its way into your daily consciousness. Such is the inescapable gravity of the guru, which is always, in each and every moment, pulling you and pulling you. As my own tale illustrates, your encounter with the sat guru need not be a dramatic one. In fact, it is much more likely to sneak up on you, quietly, inch by inch by inch. For those of you interested in learning more about Maharaj-ji and his many documented miracles, I have provided a Reading List on page 315.

Reading List on page 315.

༄

In reality, the sat guru is nothing new. Whatever form he, she, or it may assume in the lives of individual seekers, it has been with us from the very beginning, beyond time. It is at that most crucial moment in our spiritual awakening that the eternal Self presents itself to us in a particular form which we then identify as the sat guru. You, as the devotee, don't need to do anything in particular other than go about your daily business, follow the unpredictable twists and turns of your own unfolding path. When the time comes, the guru will manifest. It's important to remember that your connection with the guru, however it may seem to you, is absolutely permanent and unshakable. As Maharaj-ji said, "You can leave me. I won't leave you. Once I catch hold of you, I don't let go."[5]

In what follows, I describe two different methods of guru yoga, one formal, one informal. Formal, in our context, does not mean more serious or more advanced—it simply means more structured. Whichever of these methods appeals to you is the method for you. If you are uncertain, try them both out—see which practice most deeply, or most comfortably, connects you.

Guru yoga is not for everyone, of course. If you are uncomfortable with the idea of devotion, or if you simply don't feel drawn to these exercises, a different form of meditation or concentration (many of which are described in later chapters) is probably best for you. As with everything else along the path, it is important to engage only in those practices that give you joy and a sense of connectedness. To engage in a certain practice because you have to, or because this or that teacher said you should, is to mistake spiritual practice with going to the dentist. Remember, any practice is allowed, but no practice is *required*. Anyone who suggests otherwise is probably stuck at that flypaper level of guilty obligation. Most importantly, understand that it is not really you or I doing guru yoga in the first place. It's the *guru* doing guru yoga. Ironically, once you really experience this state of heightened awareness directly, there is no such thing as guru yoga anymore. Instead, your entire life becomes your guru yoga.

Prayer to the Divine Self

THIS IS A PRAYER THAT A DEVOTEE offered Maharaj-ji. It's a beautiful prayer to begin any guru yoga practice.

O my God, O my Guru,
I do not know how to worship you.
I do not have the power to worship you.
Whatever I am,
Every bit of my self and my being,
I am offering you,
Sitting next to you at your feet.
And I request you,
To make me an instrument of yours.
And all actions done by me,
Let it be your offer of worship.[6]

Informal Guru Yoga

Informal guru yoga offers a way to connect with the guru without radically changing your lifestyle. Through it, you learn to remember the divine in your life, to have compassion for others, and walk the paths of surrender and simplicity. You may want to start with this form of practice to prepare for more structured formal guru yoga.

SELECT AND PREPARE A SPECIAL PLACE

For any spiritual practice, it's a good idea to set aside a certain area of your home or office, some area in which you feel particularly relaxed and positive. Think of this area as a place of direct connection to the guru. You might want to post images of the guru here, as well as passages from scripture or spiritual texts that inspire you. Many practitioners find it helpful to set up a small *puja* (devotion) table on which they place any objects that make them feel connected to their chosen teaching.

Placing incense on your puja can be an easy way to remind you of your connection to the guru. As you wander by your puja table in the course of the day, you might light some incense from time to time. As the fragrance drifts throughout the area, you might imagine it as your guru's presence blessing the room with positive energy.

The items you collect for your special area need not be overtly spiritual objects. A photo of your family members, closest friends, or pets can be the most effective way to connect to the all-pervasive love and goodness manifest in the guru. If you don't feel you have encountered some specific, highly significant spiritual teacher as of yet, or if you seem drawn to a more abstract representation of the guru such as the Tao, you might place a few beautiful pieces of art in this area, reminding you that the same creative force that made the realization of this artwork possible is also making your own self-realization possible, as well as that of others.

You might find it helpful to listen to a piece of beautiful music during the day as a means to focus your energy on the infinitely positive and creative aspects of the universe. This abstract creative force, present in objects of art, ordinary human relationships, and even those quirky little things that just happen from day to day, is consciousness, is love and life itself, the breath within the breath.

From this perspective, the practice of guru yoga is essentially a practice of stopping to smell the roses, a way of slowing life's hustle and bustle down long enough to appreciate and honor the elusive, indefinably beautiful mystery of being. When you earnestly open yourself to this eternal energy, you will feel it communicating with you, flowing through and around you. This presence is the guru. The guru is none other than this boundless life force itself. For this reason, every time you engage in guru yoga, you are engaging in a highly creative act, a beautiful celebration of all that ever is, was, or will be.

SPIRITUAL OBJECTS

I think Westerners are easily confused about what constitutes a spiritual object. The Protestants and Catholics have been heatedly debating this topic for a very long time. For the Protestant, any sort of icon is essentially an idol, a kind of "false god." The third commandment says, "You shall not make for yourself an idol in the form of anything in heaven above or on the earth beneath or in the waters below" (Ex. 20:4). Even for the non-Protestant, using icons in worship may simply seem too primitive or superstitious—not necessarily a sin so much as a waste of time. For the Catholic, however, religious icons need not be idols or superstition. In their view, icons have essentially the same function as a church hymnal. Although not holy in and of themselves, they are aids for directing the devotee's attention toward the real God, who is necessarily beyond concrete form. Given these two contrasting views, then, what should our attitude be toward our puja table and these spiritual reminders we place upon it?

Arresting the Stone Buddha

THERE IS A ZEN STORY ABOUT A STONE BUDDHA. One day, a traveling cotton merchant stops to rest beneath this stone Buddha. He falls asleep and his roll of cotton goods is stolen. He reports the matter to the local authorities, and a judge decides to take action against the stone Buddha. "That stone Buddha must have stolen the goods," he says. "He is supposed to care for the welfare of the people, but he has failed to perform his holy duty. Arrest him." The stone Buddha is arrested, and a large crowd gathers, laughing and joking about the ridiculous sentence. The judge rebukes the crowd, declaring that they are in contempt of court and will be imprisoned. The people quickly apologize. The judge says, "I shall have to impose a fine on you, but I will remit it provided each one of you brings one roll of cotton goods to the court within three days. Anyone failing to do this will be arrested." As the rolls of cotton are brought in, the merchant recognizes one of them as his own, thereby discovering the thief. The cotton rolls are returned to the people and the stone Buddha is freed from prison.[7]

Ironically, the stone Buddha *does* ultimately care for the welfare of the people. We might object, saying it was obviously the judge's wisdom and not the power of the stone Buddha which brings justice, and we would be right. Still, this Zen story is titled "Arresting the Stone Buddha," not "The Wisdom of the Judge." The stone Buddha is simply a focusing device. It is not the Buddha himself, of course, just an ordinary image chiseled from stone. Like they say in Zen, it is important not to confuse a finger pointing at the moon with the moon itself.

ॐ

The objects on your table are not to be worshipped as some holy artifacts, anymore than you should bow down before your car every morning, honoring it as "The God of Sacred Commuting." On the other hand, certain objects are, in fact, particularly useful "pointers at the moon." Everything is necessarily a part of buddha-nature. Those objects on your puja are much more than just "any old" objects. To the degree that they remind you of the divine, they are truly sacred. Your puja, along with the objects you place on it, is a genuine shrine. If you use it as an authentic means to connect with the guru, it can become as holy a place as any temple in India or Israel.

REMEMBERING

In addition to setting aside a specific physical place of connection, you can perform many other informal practices throughout the day. By simply focusing on the guru as you drift off to sleep at night, as well as when waking the next morning, you can establish a deep bond of connection. Such loosely scheduled acts of remembering can help you frame your day with the guru's presence, reminding you that all actions you perform are, in reality, fruits of the guru's understanding. You might want to read stories about the guru, carry an image with you, or wear some piece of jewelry that reminds you of your connection. When you feel anxious or stressed during the day, you can pause for a moment to call on the guru or Tao, feel the nurturing presence that is always surrounding you, protecting you. When your awareness shrinks and you feel intense anger or frustration toward others, you can open up into the boundless space of the guru, remembering the relationships you have cultivated throughout life with those closest to you. Negative emotions tend to be a kind of energetic tightening or constriction, a protective curling inward. When you can see that you are totally safe, surrounded by infinite love and light, however strange some of its forms may seem, you can more easily expand once again to your fullest awareness. In this state, your anger and frustrations naturally dissolve, leaving you more relaxed and open.

COMPASSION AND SURRENDER

More important than the specific practices you perform in informal guru yoga is the attitude with which you perform them and go about your daily tasks. Two qualities are necessarily cultivated by these exercises: compassion and surrender. Not only are these qualities cultivated, they are also the very fuel that drives the practices themselves. These qualities, in their most boundless forms, *are* the guru. The more you connect to them in yourself, the more you connect to the guru.

The Guru Is Everyone

I REMEMBER A DREAM in which I WAS searching all over for my guru, Maharaj-ji. I was walking from street to street, asking passers-by if they knew his whereabouts, but having no luck. When I was just about to give up my search, a little man walked by me and I thought, well, he's not Maharaj-ji but he sure does look like him. I looked up at that moment and, suddenly, every person I passed was Maharaj-ji.

ﻥ

See the guru in everyone because the guru is everyone. That's what compassion is all about. If you can't find the guru, can't recognize the abundance of love and goodness that threads together every aspect of your daily life, it is simply because you are failing to see what is already right in front of your very own face. The more you cultivate your compassion toward others, the more the guru connects to you, and the more you remember that every one of us, just as we already are, is the guru.

Sometimes it can be very useful to focus on one particular person, someone to whom you are very close, as a direct manifestation of the guru. When you are in a fight with your intimate other, try your best to see that person as God manifest. When he or she needs your help with something, even when you're deeply involved in this or that project, try to view it as an opportunity for an act of highest devotion, a direct opportunity to serve God. When you have sex, try to remember that it is a genuinely holy act, a beautiful performance of the simple, everyday song of reality. In this way, your most intimate, "worldly" relationship continually directs and redirects you toward the highest source itself.

The Beloved as Guru

I RECALL ANOTHER DREAM IN WHICH I was searching for the guru, this time accompanied by one of my inner plane teachers. I followed my teacher from place to place, encountering my parents, friends, and total strangers along the way. In each scenario, my teacher was directing me to be more compassionate, more understanding toward these individuals. Finally, we entered a very holy place, what I took to be some sacred temple. As we stood in the temple, clear white light exploded through the windows, enveloping us. A huge voice from within the white light said something to the effect of, "The clear white light entered Ezekiel's body. Though he closed his eyes and tried to hide himself from it, it poured itself through him, entering his every cell." At this point, the light began to retreat from the temple and my teacher and I were weeping, filled with great awe and devotion. We began to sing a very intense round of Hallelujah in beautiful harmony, offering our voices to God. The whole thing was quite dramatic, you understand, very Old Testament.

When the light had shrunk back into a single corner of the temple, my teacher and I came to understand this to be the very presence of God himself. We approached very timidly, much like Dorothy and her friends approaching the Wizard of Oz, performing continuous prostrations, and mantras. When we finally stood before the light, a beautiful young woman appeared within it, whose form we understood to be a direct manifestation of God. The woman said to us, "I have two favorite songs, one of which you just sang." My teacher and I began to discuss what the other favorite song of God might be, trying out several church hymns with no success. After several failed attempts, the woman spoke to us again. She said, "My other favorite song is the song of reality." She smiled when she said this and she was indescribably beautiful. I felt an incredible longing for her, a deep sexual yearning, and fell down on my knees, weeping and ashamed for wanting to have sex with God. At that moment, I woke up. I realized immediately that the woman in the light had been none other than my wife. The temple had been my very own house. I was looking for something so holy and otherworldly in this dream, I had failed to recognize these familiar reminders of my daily existence. God's other favorite song, the song of reality, was none other than my ordinary, daily life itself. My day-to-day relationship to my wife was holy, I was being reminded, already equal to the highest spiritual practices of devotion. My sexual desire toward my wife, rather than being sacrilege, was just another expression of my longing to return to the original state of the Self.

TRUSTING THE PROCESS

Along with developing compassion toward others, guru yoga helps us cultivate a state of selfless surrender. Surrender tends to be a particularly hard pill for most Westerners to swallow, as we wrongly believe it will somehow infringe upon our individuality. In fact, the exact opposite is true. What are we really surrendering to, after all, other than the highest version of our very own self? Regarding surrender, Ramana Maharshi said, "Surrender appears easy because people imagine that, once they say with their lips 'I surrender' and put their burdens on their Lord, they can be free and do what they like. But the fact is that you can have no likes or dislikes after your surrender; your will should become completely non-existent, the Lord's will taking its place."[8] Statements such as this make most Westerners pretty squirmy in their seats. Our discomfort with this idea results from a simple misunderstanding. In my developing path of surrender, I am continually discovering something very ironic: The more I sincerely give up my rights to have my own likes and dislikes, my own will, the more I understand that they were never really *my* likes and dislikes, never *my* will in the first place. Rather, they have belonged to

God the whole time. As you progress further along the path, you begin to dissolve your individuality into God and, amazingly, nothing changes; that's what is meant by total compassion. God wants you to be nothing other than exactly who you are. If you like to go fishing, the more you surrender this like to God, the more you realize God likes to go fishing through you.

The story of Christ is a very beautiful metaphor for this kind of surrender. Just before his arrest, we see Christ in the garden, weeping tears of blood, asking God to save him from his long-prophesied crucifixion. Even so, Christ ends his prayer with, "Yet not as I will, but as you will" (Matt. 26:39). As we know, Christ is crucified, nonetheless. God does, in fact, take Christ up on his offer to surrender his individual will. What happens next is the really amazing part. After Christ, through his attitude of total love and surrender, has been sincerely willing to die, God resurrects him. Jesus of Nazareth is still Jesus of Nazareth, only now he is also something else, something much bigger than Jesus of Nazareth, something perfectly secure and eternal.

The path of genuine surrender is, without a doubt, one of the fastest ways to God. I would like to emphasize, however, that we *do* give up everything along the way—even if only for a time. Our favorite music, our favorite food, our loved ones—our attachments to all of these will be tested one by one, eventually pried from our white-knuckled grip. This may sound terrifying and harsh but, rest assured, it is part of a very natural process. Sooner or later, whether each of us has chosen to consciously walk this or that spiritual path, he or she dies. No matter how hard we clutch at all our worldly stockpiles of material and immaterial things—human relationships not excluded—we have no choice but surrender these things at the moment of death. This being an inevitable existential fact, why not learn to give these things up willingly, consciously, while still in the midst of life? Why live our lives with that constant, nagging fear of death buried somewhere deeply within our guts?

I am an absolute Beatles nut, for instance. Like we said, the more I am able to give up my preference for the Beatles, the more I see that God happens to also be a big Beatles fan. It has really been God enjoying the Beatles the whole while. Once I have sincerely given up my so-called right to a kind of personal ownership of the Beatles, every time I listen to a Beatles song I am engaging in a very high act of devotion or guru yoga. Still, it doesn't quite work if I surrender just because I am pretty sure I won't really have to give up the Beatles. This isn't really surrender at all, but merely bargaining. We can't authentically trust in the perfection of the Tao or the sat guru until we are really ready to give everything up, even if it means losing ourselves in the process. It is a difficult path but an unavoidable, and ultimately perfect one. Like Christ, sooner or later we all have to be willing to die for the sake of love itself. Trust in the guru and the guru will cultivate this unshakeable courage and trust deep within you.

SIMPLICITY

One of the principal ideas of informal guru yoga is to keep it simple. Rather than getting lost in the details of this or that practice, simply find a few, quiet ways to connect to the guru throughout your ordinary day. You'll likely discover you have already been doing guru yoga without knowing it. Anything—and I do mean *anything*—done with the right attitude of compassion and surrender is already guru yoga. This is the highest lesson that guru yoga teaches. If you can truly honor the guru with a shot of tequila and a pack of cigarettes, then go ahead. There doesn't need to be—and ultimately, really can't be—anything especially holy to do. You are always the guru worshipping the guru, God honoring God. To forget this is essentially to make an idol out of your own self, a false god of your own life. It is to divide yourself into two parts—higher and lower, good and bad—and to worship the first from the viewpoint of the second. Ironically, even when we do seem to get confused, there is still only one whole, one total Self. As it is said, God is forever "one without a second." It's all God because God is all. However you choose to go about your journey of guru yoga, then, know that you are never truly separate from the One—not even for a single instant.

Ritual and Formal Guru Yoga

Some of the most traditional guru yoga practices rely heavily on the ancient concept of ritual, which tends to be rather foreign to many Westerners. Ritual is prevalent in most metaphysical systems, from the Christian's weekly partaking of communion, to the tantric practitioner's intricate mandala visualization practices. If ritual is to be effective, it is important that the practitioner understand its usefulness beyond the point of mere superstition. One way in which ritual works is as a focusing device, or a means of cultivating concentration. To perform any intricate ritual effectively, our mind has to be very sharp and alert, not distracted by stray thoughts and stimuli.

In the earlier stages of Carlos Castañeda's apprenticeship, don Juan has him perform numerous rituals, many of them ridiculously complex.[9] Later in the apprenticeship, don Juan explains to Castañeda that the specific rituals, in and of themselves, weren't all that important. Rather, by engaging Castañeda's rational mind in complicated concrete tasks, many of them arbitrary fictions of don Juan's fertile imagination, Castañeda's rigid intellect was less likely to interfere with his intuitive mind where the deeper, although hidden, teaching was being pointed. In this case, then, ritual was being used as a sort of decoy, a red herring to capture the energy of the structured, thinking mind.

You might think of the detailed, repetitive practices of formal guru yoga as simply concentration devices that engage your mind in structured activities so that you can make a deep, non-intellectual connection with the guru. Ramana Maharshi often said his highest teaching was one of mere silence. For mature devotees, the deepest lesson was simply to sit with Ramana in complete, non-distracted silence, absorbing his radiant, nameless knowledge. For most devotees, however, decoys were needed. For these individuals, Ramana would often prescribe very specific practices—a kind of spiritual sleight of hand to engage such devotees on a comparatively surface level of their intellect—so that they might be less distracted, or more open on a deeper, purely intuitive level to receive his teaching of silence.

At the same time, another benefit of ritual is that of authentic magic. For most Westerners, the idea of magic is simply an archaic and superstitious, pre-scientific notion. From studying more supposedly primitive cultures, however, we know that magic can be undeniably powerful in its effect. It is common knowledge these days that traditional faith healers and medicine men can often cure illnesses well beyond the scope of Western medicine. The Western psychologist tends to describe this well-documented effect as one of powerful belief and suggestion. If we believe in ritualistic practices, they work. If we don't, they don't. The problem here is that many of us think ourselves too "sophisticated" to believe in all this hocus-pocus: "Sure, all of these magic incantations may work wonders for a bunch of naked aborigines, but I'm not about to fall for such nonsense." For this sort of person, I would recommend engaging in these rituals *just because*. Think of them like a series of dance steps. You don't perform dance steps for any reason other than the dance itself, right? You can think of guru yoga in this way. If you feel ridiculous performing prostrations or chanting mantras, consider all the other individuals around the world who are doing the very same practices. These other individuals, like you, want some way to connect to God, the Tao, whatever. Ritual is often a kind of "YMCA" dance we engage in simply because we are not really sure what else to do.

Nevertheless, there really is something to magical practices. Although many of the specific rituals involved in formal guru yoga may seem arbitrary, there is a reason they have been around for thousands upon thousands of years. Slice it however you want to, a stone buddha is different from a stone giraffe.

To a certain degree, the only way to understand ritualistic practices is to try them out. Suspend disbelief for a time and make an earnest effort to open up and connect. After some time, if these practices still don't seem joyful and beautiful to you, but merely tedious errands, simply quit them.

Remember: Spiritual practice is an art form, a performance of an elaborately choreographed drama, and like all other art forms, its highest function is simply to express the beautiful peculiarity of humanity's predicament. When I think of the apparent absurdity of ritual, I am reminded of Samuel Beckett's dark, existential comedy, *Waiting for Godot*. In this play, two hobos wander aimlessly with the vague goal of waiting for the unseen figure of Godot. They spend their days in elaborate and seemingly meaningless slapstick routines. After one such routine in the play's first act, they exchange the following words:

VLADIMIR: That passed the time.
ESTRAGON: It would have passed in any case.
VLADIMIR: Yes, but not so rapidly.

In this context, we might think of ritual as a sort of comedic diversion. We do it simply because we might as well do something. In my experience, this attitude of absurdity lends ritual a very high, although easily overlooked, meaning. In such cases, ritual becomes the very essence of courage: taking a decisive and concrete course of action in the face of existential uncertainty.

Formal Guru Yoga Practices

The formal guru yoga practices I describe below represent a cross-section of various systems. I have included quite a bit of stuff here, hoping to provide a little something for everyone. I can't emphasize enough, however, that you keep only those practices that you find useful. To perform this or that list of instructions as if devotion and surrender were recipes in a cookbook is much worse than performing no practices at all. After all, you are always your own guru in the end. This being the case, you may very well come to discover the best form of guru yoga for you is to have a glass of wine and watch your favorite television program. Boring is just *boring*, that is to say, no matter how many realized beings instruct us otherwise. Be truly original and dangerous in your spiritual practices, using the following suggestions as springboards for your own individual and creative expression of celebration—sincerely artistic and loving acts of honoring your highest self and the sacred universe that flows through you.

POSTURE

Go to your special place you have set aside for guru yoga. Sit in a comfortable chair with a straight back. Various meditation postures such the half-lotus or full-lotus are also fine, although unnecessary. For most Westerners who, unlike Eastern practitioners, have not grown up their entire lives sitting in such postures on a daily basis, they can easily be more of a distraction than a support to practice. Still, to insure alertness, sit up in your chair with your spine straight, both feet on the floor, hands positioned comfortably in your lap. You may want to begin with the Prayer to the Divine Self on page 48.

NINE BREATHS

There are many forms of this exercise. I have chosen the method described in the

Tibetan *Ngondro*, or "something which precedes," practices. This exercise is a way of working with your breath in order to purify your body and mind, relaxing you and making you ready to receive the grace of the guru.

Begin by visualizing the three primary subtle energy channels in your body. (See pages 214–216 and 233–234 for more detail on the energy body.) The central channel is blue and runs just in front of the spine. It is about the thickness of a cane and rises from the anus straight out the crown of the head. The two side channels are thinner, about the thickness of a pencil. These channels enter through the nostrils and run along either side of the central channel. Near the bottom of the pelvis, they curve back into the central channel. In men, the right channel is white and the left is red. In women, the right channel is red and the left is white. As you visualize these channels, know that you are not simply imagining them. You are redirecting your attention to subtle energy currents that are just as real as your internal organs. With intense focus, you can begin to actually feel these channels circulating energy up and down your torso. When you feel you have adequately tuned in to these channels, you are ready to begin the nine breaths.

First Three Breaths:

If you're a man, close your right nostril with the ring finger of your right hand; if a woman, close the left nostril with the ring finger of your left hand. Inhale green light through the unblocked nostril and feel it being drawn down the red channel. Block the opposite nostril and exhale. As you do so, feel the energy moving back up the white channel, being expelled from that nostril as light blue air. Repeat this exercise for three inhalations and exhalations. With each exhalation, know that you are clearing your energy body of all obstacles associated with the past. Guilt, shame, and other painful emotions resulting from past actions and experiences are being released with each of these three breaths. When you perform this with your full concentration, you can actually feel your energy body relax and open up as it lets go of past wounds and painful memories.

Second Three Breaths:

Here, you will breath using your other hand and nostril. (Men should block their left nostril with their left hand. Women should block their right nostril with their right hand.) Perform three inhalations and exhalations in the manner described above. With each exhalation, expel light pink air from the nostril of the red channel. These exhalations are cleansing the energy body of all obstacles associated with the future. Whatever worries, expectations and emotional attachments you may have concerning the future, feel them untangling from deep within you and being expelled in the form of light pink energy.

Third Three Breaths:

Men and women, inhale green light through both nostrils. Feel this energy travel down the side channels and curl back into the central channel about two inches below the navel. As you exhale, feel the energy move up your central channel and out the crown of your head in the form of black smoke, clearing you of all obstacles associated with the present. Whatever your present concerns, physical pains, or negative emotions, be confident they are being expelled in the form of black smoke. At the end of these nine breaths, your body and mind should feel very relaxed and light. Your energy body is now open to receive the powerful healing energy of the guru.

MAKING AN OFFERING

You are now ready to make an offering. Visualize a being of pure white light seated about ten feet in and slightly above you, about 45 degrees. You are not merely imagining this being. This is the guru, a being of perfect light and love, manifesting to you right now in this subtle form. If you have a particular guru, you may find it useful to visualize that particular form. You can visualize Jesus, Buddha, your grandfather or grandmother—any being that you feel best represents pure love and understanding for you. Know that he or she is here right now because you have sincerely called for help along your path. The more sincere and intense your devotion, the more immediate the guru's presence. As you visualize the guru, you can make your offering. This offering might be a concrete physical act such as performing prostrations, lighting incense, or placing a flower on your puja table. (See the Reading List for books that describe these and other devotional practices in detail). You might say some formal prayer such as the Bodhisattva vows, the Lord's Prayer, or those offered in the Appendix (see page 306). You need not say anything formal at all. You may simply express, in whatever form you feel comfortable with, your deepest desire to devote yourself to the path. Try to connect to your highest feelings of unconditional love for your guru, yourself, and all other beings in the universe. Traditionally, such prayers are offered anywhere from three to 1,000 times per session. You may want to decide on a specific number of repetitions for each session, or you may simply want to make your offering until you feel you have sufficiently gathered your highest intentions for compassion and understanding. Remember, whatever words you say are authentically magic to the degree that you offer them from a place of sincere devotion and pure intention. Mindless repetition of words will accomplish nothing other than putting you to sleep.

RECEIVING BLESSINGS

You are now ready to receive the three rays, or blessings, from the guru. Take a deep breath. As you exhale, sound the mantra OM (AH-OOH-MM). As you sound the mantra, visualize a ray of intense white light traveling from the center of the guru's forehead to the center of your own. As this white light penetrates you, feel it cleansing your body of all tensions and sicknesses, as well as any wrong actions you feel you may have performed in the past. Repeat this process three times.

The next blessing will take the form of an intense red light traveling from the guru's throat to your own. Sound the mantra AH three times to receive this blessing. As this ray enters your throat, feel your energy body being cleared of all obstructions. As your speech is closely associated with your energy body, know that any harsh words you may have said, any lies you may have told, are being purified through this ray of red light.

To receive the last blessing, sound the mantra HUM (HOOM) three times. As you do so, visualize an intense ray of blue light traveling from the center of the guru's chest into your own. As this light penetrates you, your mind will be cleared of any angry thoughts and anxieties. Feel your mind becoming relaxed and open.

It is not important to have an intellectual understanding of these three mantras and colors of light. These words are used in an intuitive way similar to the Christians' use of "amen." The colors also invoke certain rates of vibration that allow the guru to send his three blessings. Be confident that these mantras, when joined with the rays of light, are the guru's blessing in manifest form.

RECEIVING THE GURU

You are now ready to receive the guru, in his entirety, into your very being. To do so, perform the following mantra three times:

OM AH HUM VAJRA GURU PADME SIDDHI HUM
(Pronounced *ah-ooh-mm ah hoom vahj-rah guru pahd-mah see-dee hoom*)

In a way, this mantra is one of the deepest names of the guru, which applies equally to Christ and Buddha. To say this mantra is to directly align your own energy body with that of the guru, to invite the guru to inhabit your own being. As you perform this mantra, visualize the body of the guru dissolving into beautiful rainbow light. Feel this light pouring into your spiritual heart through the center of your chest. As this light and warmth spreads throughout your body, feel the infinite love of the guru radiating throughout your every cell, healing you at the deepest level.

Upon the third recitation of this mantra, the guru now resides in you. *You are the guru.* The guru now looks out at the world through your eyes. Whatever thoughts you might have, whatever physical sensations you might have, these belong to the guru. Know that every part of you is made of perfect love and light. Every act you perform, however flawed it may seem at the time, is nothing less than the guru's perfect manifestation of grace. You can see yourself and the entire universe from a much broader understanding right now as you and the guru are one. Remember these words of Ramana Maharshi: "The Grace of the Guru is like an ocean. If one comes with a cup he will only get a cupful. It is no use complaining of the niggardliness of the ocean. The bigger the vessel the more one will be able to carry. It is entirely up to him."[10]

RETURNING LOVE

For the final practice of guru yoga, you will return the guru's love and compassion back to the external world. Feeling the guru residing deeply within you, feeling your presence residing deeply within the guru, visualize all the beings of the universe surrounding you. With every exhalation, pure love and compassion pours from your body in the form of white light. Picture your family and friends, your boss and neighbors, your worst enemies. You feel only love and understanding for each of these individuals as you bathe them in radiant white light. In this moment, you appreciate the perfect uniqueness of each individual without judgment or blame. You are love and awareness. You are the entire universe, spontaneously created from the infinite white light of your love. As you return to the world today, know that this white light travels with you, residing deep within your heart. Know that this same gift of love has been given equally to every individual being that you encounter. The grace of the guru, your grace, vibrates everywhere.

A Path of Grace

Ram Dass tells the story of his participation in an intense meditation seminar. The participants were given a particular koan to concentrate on—in this case, something like, "What was your original face before your parents were born?" This is Zen code, more or less, for "Show me the guru." Ram Dass describes how he goes in for several frustrating interviews with the Zen teacher in which each of his solutions to the riddle is curtly dismissed. More and more frustrated, he tries increasingly clever responses, all of which receive the same abrupt dismissal. Finally, Ram Dass goes for his interview one morning, thoroughly disgusted with the whole affair. He has decided to simply give up. The Zen teacher fires off the same question, but this time Ram Dass simply smiles and responds with "Good morning, Roshi."

Well, that's it. *That's* the solution—or at least a big step in the right direction. Through the very act of giving up his intense effort, Ram Dass came much closer to solving the riddle of the sat guru. This is what we mean when we say that the journey of guru yoga is an inevitable journey. We search and we search, we struggle and we struggle, and one day we simply throw in the towel. Enough is enough, we decide, and then something very peculiar happens to us: We get it—whatever "it" is. A little light goes off in our head somewhere and we can't help but chuckle to ourselves because we finally realize we have somehow "gotten" it the whole while. Ramana Maharshi said, "At one stage you will laugh at yourself for trying to discover the Self which is so self-evident."[11]

Guru yoga is always an inevitable journey because it doesn't depend on our own efforts. Rather than thinking of the spiritual journey as a difficult campaign of self-improvement, it might be helpful to compare the individual's progress along the spiritual path to the natural, or spontaneous, development of a fruit tree. The tree starts as a seed, of course, because that's just the way trees go about things. As it grows, the tree begins to unfold its branches—not in order to somehow improve itself, but simply because that's what a tree does. When the tree's development finally culminates in the bearing of fruit, we don't say, "Wow, that tree must have really worked hard to bear that fruit!" Neither do we say, "Wow, that tree's really superior to that young sapling over there!" We recognize the difference in development, sure, but we understand that both trees have been nourished by the same impersonal force.

Although you are certainly much more complicated than a fruit tree, your process of spiritual unfolding isn't so different. You may think you are the one pushing yourself to grow higher and higher, but in actuality, you are being pushed. This is the work of the guru, a being of immense spiritual gravity that is pulling you forever closer and closer. In the same way that a sapling doesn't need to struggle to become a tree—and certainly can't speed up its development by struggling to do so—your own development is also part of an automatic process. It may not look that way from where you are sitting at present, but that's just because of where you are sitting. The Christians call this fuel of spontaneous perfection "grace"—a divine gift freely given. Jesus reminds us of this in the Sermon on the Mount: "And why do you worry about clothes? See how the lilies of the field grow. They do not labor or spin" (Luke 12:27).

At the same time, however, your needless struggle is very much a part of the spontaneous process itself. It is all part of the same inevitable journey. Your struggle is no more or less beautiful, no more or less necessary or inevitable, than your spontaneous realization.

I had been performing formal guru yoga practices twice daily for several months when I had a very powerful experience on the astral plane. Such experiences, although they occur while your body sleeps, are very different from an ordinary dream. You remain perfectly conscious and aware in a kind of wakeful dreaming, often called "lucid dreaming." (I will describe such dreams in much more detail in chapters 10 and 11). In this encounter, I came upon a sort of astral ashram, or temple, of my guru, Maharaj-ji. His ashram was set in this incredibly beautiful landscape of lush green hills, sparkling rivers, and golden sunshine. There were Hindus of various descriptions lounging around by the river, eating, laughing, drinking wine. I had been admitted through the front gate only after some difficulty. The guard had initially turned me away, but after my relentless chanting of the guru yoga mantra presented above, I was let in. I spotted Maharaj-ji lounging around, wrapped in one of his infamous blankets and went sprinting toward him, yelling, "Neem Karoli Baba! Neem Karoli Baba!" at the top of my lungs, much to the amusement of onlookers. I fell down at his feet, weeping and performing prostrations, doing my mantra—the whole formal-guru-yoga nine yards.

At some point, Maharaj-ji put out his stubby little foot to block my enthusiastic prostrations, and told me, with a benevolent grin, to lay off on the guru yoga. I calmed down a bit and we stood there just looking at each other. I think it is fair to say Maharaj-ji is certainly not a physically attractive person—not in the typical sense at least—but as I looked at him, he seemed incredibly beautiful. His face was somehow swirling in and out of the landscape, the sunlight dancing with him somehow. The whole scene was pure liquid energy, everything swirling and melting into and out of everything else. The only things that remained at all "stable" in this dizzy kaleidoscope goo were Maharaj-ji's eyes, so I focused all of my energy there. As I looked deeply into his eyes, I began to realize I was looking into my own eyes. Maharaj-ji was somehow me, looking back at me, looking back at Maharaj-ji, and so on.

At that moment, my usual focal perspective sort of dislodged, my conceptual mind essentially short-circuiting, and I suddenly became everything—Maharaj-ji, myself, the sunlight, the green grass, the flowing streams . . . In that moment I understood Ramana Maharshi's statement that, God, guru, and the Self are one. I realized that I had been so worshipful in my devotional practices that I had lost sight of what I was really worshipping—myself, the Self, whatever you want to call it. Immediately thereafter, I discontinued my guru yoga practices as they seemed to be rather redundant from my new perspective. If I'm already all of that, I realized, the whole Self, why do anything other than just be my self?

Even now, as I write this very sentence, I am aware that this, too, is a direct manifestation of the guru. This is Maharaj-ji speaking directly to you. At the same time, of course, it is also James Robbins struggling along to try to describe things in some sensible manner. Moreover, it is also you, reminding yourself of your own deep spiritual knowledge, your own most authentic truths, manifesting just now as this very sentence. We are all in here somehow—me, you, the guru, God—meeting in this indescribable place of love, this beautiful, constantly swirling flow of awareness.

It's so easy to tune into it right now, at this very moment. Let your eyes relax a little, barely soft-focusing on the words on this page. Relax deeper and deeper into this page and you will notice the words start to wobble a little bit. Relax even further and you will begin to notice a very subtle play of rainbow light around the edges of the black ink. You're not imagining it. It's really there, if you want to see it. Melt into the white spaces on the page and you'll see they're not really white at all, but composed of tiny points and swirls of beautiful rainbow light. It's all you. This very subtle flow of energy is you.

To the degree that you can see the manifestations I am describing, you already understand this. If you can't see these things, it is of little importance. To see the flow of subtle energy in this particular way is little more than a parlor trick. Even so, guru yoga may be the very thing that helps you to connect to this aspect of yourself. It's all right there in front of you all the time, if you just relax and take a look. Of course, it doesn't have to be about mystical encounters with gurus and swirling rainbow light. For you, maybe it's nothing more than the next song you hear on the radio, the next phone call you get, the next cup of coffee you drink. These are all, by definition, reminders, billboards along the path reminding you who you really are. Know, in this very moment, that who you really are, always have been, always will be, is nothing other than pure, boundless love and awareness. That's the place you are reminding yourself of every time you perform guru yoga.

IN DEFENSE OF JUDAS:
HONORING THE ANTI-GURU

Two Zen practitioners, Tanzan and Ekido, were traveling down a muddy road.
A heavy rain was falling. Coming around a bend, they met a beautiful young
woman in a silk kimono and sash, unable to cross the intersection.

"Come on, you," Tanzan said to the woman, lifting her in his arms and
carrying her over the mud.

Ekido didn't speak again until that night when they reached a lodging
temple. Then he could no longer restrain himself. "We monks don't go near
women," he said to Tanzan, "especially not young and beautiful ones. It is
dangerous. Why did you do that?"

"I left the young woman there," said Tanzan. "Are you still carrying her?"[1]

I f the guru is all form that tends to connect each of us to the path, then the anti-guru—seemingly the opposite side of the same coin—is all form that tends to disconnect us from the path. In reality, of course, we are dealing with a one-sided coin. Properly perceived, there can be no true distinction between the guru and the anti-guru—the guru being *all* form, *all* means of overcoming obstacles to the path, as well as the one and only source of the obstacles themselves. For this reason, we need to honor all things that manifest as difficulty and struggle throughout the journey, things that many of us may consider negative, immoral, unjust, or—like the beautiful young woman in the above story—dangerously tempting.

I would like to be clear, however, that it is not my intention to encourage you to indulge in, or actively cultivate, such behaviors or desires, however you may define them. I mean only to facilitate your ability to accept all seeming obstacles to the path, to help you perceive the struggle, in whatever uncomfortable and disturbing form it may manifest, as a legitimate means to the solution itself. Before you can genuinely let go of such obstacles, you must first be confident enough to carry them.

Our habitual reluctance to take the bad along with the good, to accept the unpleasant that necessarily accompanies the pleasant, is possibly the single most difficult hurdle to clear along the spiritual path. As life is an ongoing struggle of polar opposites, however, there can be no other means to true wholeness, no other way to genuine integration, love, and abiding peace. For this reason, I encourage you to keep an open mind as you read ahead, and be always on the lookout for your ready-made judgments and moral assessments. As you proceed, keep the following passage from the *Tao Te Ching* in your heart and mind:

> Give up sainthood, renounce wisdom,
> And it will be a hundred times better for everyone.
> Give up kindness, renounce morality,
> And men will rediscover filial piety and love.
> Give up ingenuity, renounce profit,
> And bandits and thieves will disappear.
> These three are outward forms alone; they are not sufficient in themselves.
> It is more important
> To see the simplicity,
> To realize one's true nature,
> To cast off selfishness
> And temper desire.[2]

You honor the anti-guru, then, not to excuse your own aggression and self-centeredness, but to overcome it. So long as you are categorically rejecting this and that, ranking your various experiences in some sort of spiritual hierarchy, you will be unable to see the simplicity of the Tao, which is Oneness, love, itself. You can begin this difficult journey of integration by reconsidering one of the best-known struggles of good versus evil, sacred versus profane: the story of Jesus of Nazareth.

The Necessity of Judas

If Jesus of Nazareth is the most famous good guy in all of history, then Judas Iscariot is the most famous bad guy. We all know how this sort of drama has to play out. Good Guy meets Bad Guy. Good Guy is challenged by Bad Guy. It looks, for a minute, like Bad Guy is going to win. At the last precarious moment, Good Guy pulls an unexpected trick from his sleeve and Bad Guy loses. Bad Guy is punished for being the bad guy. Good Guy is rewarded for being the good guy. Everyone lives happily ever after—at least until the inevitable sequel, in which the whole familiar routine plays itself out once again.

On first glance, the story of Jesus and Judas seems to follow this same proven pattern. Jesus handpicks Judas to be one of his twelve disciples. Judas later betrays Jesus to the Roman authorities for a handful of silver coins. Jesus is condemned to death. Judas feels remorseful, hangs himself, and presumably falls straight into hell. Darkness settles over the land as Jesus cries out, "My God, my God, why have you forsaken me?" (Matt. 27:46). Jesus is crucified and buried, giving the appearance of defeat, and it is an unspeakably sad moment when we encounter Joseph of Arimathea rolling the stone in front of Jesus' tomb. Then, just when we are sure all is lost, Jesus arises, triumphing over death, and ascends into heaven. His last words: "And surely I am with you always, to the very end of the age" (Matt. 28:20).

It is a beautiful and compelling story, which continues to inspire countless believers and non-believers alike. At the merely dramatic level, however, this bread-and-butter story of the New Testament plays very much like a spaghetti Western. There is even the high noon showdown in the garden of Gethsemane, complete with the requisite tough guy one-liner in dire circumstances. "Friend," Jesus says to Judas, "do what you came for." (Matt. 26:50). Let me assure you, I mean no mockery of this treasured Gospel story whatsoever. Rather, I simply mean to suggest that perhaps something infinitely more complicated is going on behind the scenes, some very unexpected and non-routine plot twists and turns. After all, if the crucifixion drama was really this black and white, really this cut and dried, could it have so successfully etched itself into the deepest folds of the collective unconscious?

For me, the story of the betrayal of Jesus becomes much more interesting and complex when viewed from a less traditional perspective. A few things always bothered me about this story while growing up in the Church, for instance. The ostensible moral of the tale is a very clear one: Jesus made a good choice and was rewarded. Judas made a bad choice and was punished. This simple moral is immediately complicated, however, by the fact that Judas' betrayal was prophesied well in advance in the Old Testament. Given this context, we might likely wonder: Does someone who has been prophesied—by Yahweh himself—as the villain-to-be, ever really stand a chance at *not* ending up the villain? We will say it's highly unlikely—but possible. Similarly, Jesus' crucifixion was also prophesied well in advance.

Even so, despite the fact that he has known about his fate for quite some time, Jesus seems quite uneasy about it up until the very last minute. Just before his arrest, we find Jesus in the garden of Gethsemane, poignantly praying for release from the Old Testament prophecy. "Abba, Father," Jesus prays, "everything is possible for you. Take this cup from me. Yet not what I will, but what you will" (Matt. 26:39). Jesus makes it very clear here what his personal vote is. He recognizes, however, that it's not really his decision to make. One way or another, Jesus recognizes, God always does whatever God always does. If Jesus' surrender to the cross is an act of God's will, how about Judas' betrayal of Jesus? After all, if there is going to be a good guy who is willing to sacrifice himself for the salvation of all, there simply has to be a bad guy who is willing to do the sacrificing. Without a bad guy, we just don't have a story. If Jesus and Judas are equally necessary to the very crucial climax of the Gospel story, why does one of them get punished while the other gets exalted?

The Brazilian writer Jorge Luis Borges took this idea of the necessity of Judas a few steps further. In his essay, "Three Versions of Judas," Borges asserts that perhaps Judas was the real Christ, the Christ prophesied in the Old Testament, making Jesus of Nazareth a kind of decoy.[3] Borges cites an Old Testament description (Isaiah 53:2–3) of the coming Christ as evidence. "He hath no form nor comeliness; and when we shall see him, there is no beauty that we should desire him. He is despised and rejected of men; a man of sorrows, and acquainted with grief." Judas certainly fits this description as well as Jesus. Certainly Jesus was despised, rejected, and acquainted with grief, but how much more so was Judas? At least Jesus was ultimately viewed as a perfect martyr, but Judas, even to this day, is still despised and rejected.

Borges also cites the Gospel of John's description of Christ.[4] "He was in the world, and the world was made by him, and the world knew him not" (John 1:10). Well, what if Judas *was* the real Christ? We could definitely assert that "the world knew him not." And is there any humbler role for a divine being to play than that of the despised villain? At least Jesus was loved and cared for by his followers, but Judas was alone until the very end. No one comes to mourn for Judas at his death. In his anguished suicide, the point could be made that Judas also gave his life for the good of others. It could be logically argued, in one sense at least, that the necessary role of Judas in this scenario—the pivotal situation for the entire New Testament—required an even greater degree of selfless sacrifice than that of the cherished, officially-recognized Christ figure.

Obviously, the real point here is not to debate whether Jesus or Judas was the real Christ. I think very few of us, regardless of our personal relationship to other Christian views, would argue against the fact that Jesus is clearly meant to be the hero of our tale. Instead, Borges seems to be drawing our attention to the fact that *all* the roles played in this drama—by Jesus, by Peter, by Judas, by Pilate—were equally important. In this context, we could look at Jesus as simply a sort of focal point for this huge process going all the way back into Hebrew prehistory, all the way back, in fact, to the act of creation itself. The crucifixion, then, would be an elaborately choreographed dance in which all the participants cooperate for the ultimate goal: the fulfillment of God's will.

When I reconsider the drama in this way, even if just for the sake of argument, the little things that always bothered me as a child start to click into place. I had always wondered, for instance, why Jesus chose to single out Judas as the prophesied betrayer by breaking bread with him—a symbolic gesture which, according to Hebrew custom, implies intimate friendship. At the Lord's Supper, Jesus says to his disciples, "I tell you the truth, one of you is going to betray me. . . . It is the one to whom I will give this piece of bread when I have dipped it in the dish" (Matt. 26:21). So Jesus hands Judas the bread, and "as soon as Judas took the bread, Satan entered into him" (John 13:27). Viewed from a non-traditional perspective, this passage could be interpreted to suggest that Jesus was the primary instrument of his own crucifixion, giving, as he did, Judas the very bread that seemed to convey some Satanic force. If we consider Jesus and Judas to be collaborators, however, this act of the bread passing looks more like a secret code. "What you are about to do, do quickly" (John 13:27), Jesus tells Judas immediately thereafter, while the other disciples blunder on, ignorant of what has just transpired. This is the very stuff of spy novels.

And this cooperative perspective puts a completely new light on Judas' actions as well. *Why did the Romans bother to hire Judas to betray Jesus?* I had always wondered. Jesus was a highly visible figure, after all, always available to the public, preaching in the temples and so forth. So why take the considerable risk of hiring one of his own disciples to single him out for identification? And consider the manner in which Judas does signal Jesus out: with a kiss. Consider, just for a moment, what if Jesus and Judas really were the most intimate of friends, right up until the very end? What if, as Borges is suggesting, each simply had a necessary role to play in the divinely ordained drama? The last words Jesus speaks to Judas would now have a very different feel about them. "*Friend*," Jesus said, "do what you came for."

KEEPING THE BLACK

Taoism, among all the world's religions, seems to place the greatest, or at least most overt, emphasis on the necessary harmony of yin and yang and the polarity they represent. Passages such as the following abound throughout Taoist literature:

> Under heaven all can see beauty as beauty only because there is ugliness.
> All can know good as good only because there is evil.[5]

Elsewhere in the *Tao Te Ching*:

> Know the white,
> But keep the black![6]

Although Taoism encourages this sort of harmony of opposites as an integral part of its basic morality, Christianity seems to have a very similar message, albeit not quite so exoteric, at its core. As almost all sermons from the pulpit remind us, even the staunchest of Christians recognize that Jesus' goodness is best appreciated when contrasted with Judas' badness. In the same way, the Christian often defines God as all that is contrary to Satan, and vice versa. Even more interestingly, perhaps, the Bible tells us that both God and Satan have not always been around. It is just God and his angels at first, until Lucifer is cast out of heaven due to his arrogance, and given his own place to rule. Hell, then, it would appear, was created from a kind of cooperative effort between God and Satan. We might wonder why God would ever allow such a place as hell as part of his perfect creation. After all—as Jesus says in his final prayer to God, asking for relief from the burden of the crucifixion—all things are possible to God, so why allow all the burdensome bad guys? Why all the strife and trouble in the world? Perhaps, as the story of Judas' betrayal suggests, evil is just as necessary an instrument of Yahweh's will as is good.

This joining of opposites is repeated, time and again, throughout the Bible, Old and New Testaments alike. Take the story of Job, for instance. Job is, in God's words, blameless and upright. As a way of proving this fact, God agrees to allow Satan to test Job's faith. Satan—with God's permission—kills Job's children, covers him in painful sores, and takes his riches from him. Then, and only then, does Job seem to discover his true and unshakable faith. We might be inclined to be disturbed by God allowing Satan such free reign in this situation. Toward the end of his various tests, Job himself does a good bit of whining about this very fact. His friend, Elihu, reminds him, however, that God's justice is beyond man's understanding. "He brings the clouds to punish men," Elihu says, "or to water his earth and show his love" (Job 37:13). The exact same manifestations of God's will, then—which are necessarily perfect—can serve two very different functions, one seemingly moral, one seemingly immoral. When Job complains, bemoans his miserable fate, rages against God, etc., God chastises him very severely—despite the fact that Job, by God's own admission, has done absolutely nothing to deserve all this misery. "Will the one who contends with the Almighty correct him?" (Job 40:2) God asks Job, reminding him that God's workings are beyond his mortal comprehension and judgment.

If a man who is already deemed by God as blameless and upright still seems to benefit from a healthy does of difficulty and struggle, what does that say about each of us? When we judge Judas, or, more importantly, the various villains of our daily existence, aren't we making exactly the same mistake Job made? Aren't we also pretending, despite our very limited individual perspective, to understand the infinite mind of God? After all, as the Bible seems to imply, "evil" things happen only when God decides they are necessary.

Many of us are relatively comfortable accepting the immorality that necessarily underlies morality, the hell that underlies heaven—so long as it is at a safe distance. The *Tao Te Ching* and the Bible are one thing; our own lives, however, are quite another. How do we come to terms with the immediate, daily reality of serial killers, rapists, and child molesters? How do we make sense of war, disease, and famine? Do most of us truly accept these difficulties as equally necessary manifestations of the one Tao?

The Blame Game

My wife and I have four cats, which we spoil to no end. One of their favorite pastimes is to capture some small insect and play with it. In this case, "play with it" means something very much like "torture it." My wife and I like to use this polite euphemism because it makes us a little uncomfortable to see Mother Nature still so raw and present, even in our spoiled, highly domesticated pets. Still, we don't think of our cats as villains. They are not being malicious, they are just being cats, after all.

Thomas Robert Malthus, an English political economist, wrote about what he called "the perpetual struggle for room and food."[7] Because the population tends to increase much more rapidly than natural resources such as food and shelter, Malthus viewed certain "natural checks" of the population as necessary. War, disease, famine—all of these, said Malthus, however unpleasant, are nature's way of regulating the natural balance of things. Violent struggles for natural resources are commonplace in the animal kingdom. Cats eat insects. Insects eat smaller insects, and so on. Without this violence, the natural world would quickly outgrow itself. This, according to Malthus, is just the way things are. The same struggles for room and food likewise occur among the human animal, of course—which is where things start to get sticky. This is where most of us feel compelled to start playing the blame game.

This tendency to blame seems to be innate in humans. It doesn't seem to manifest equally in all difficult scenarios, however. We accept some unpleasant circumstances as more or less inevitable, whereas we blame others on some malevolent force, some sort of *intentional* wrongdoing. Whether we accept or blame depends on two key factors: (1) How close, emotionally speaking, is the victim to us? (2) How conscious is the villain? In the example of my cats, for instance, most of us are unlikely to lay blame. None of us are likely to be very close to the maimed cockroach in any significant emotional sense. Moreover, cats are obviously not very conscious of their actions—not in the same way people are, at least.

Let's consider another example, though. Suppose a small child is maimed by a rabid dog. Most of us wouldn't exactly blame the dog, would we? We might agree that, blame or no blame, the dog needs to be put out of its misery for the safety of others, but we wouldn't really feel angry or morally indignant toward the dog. What about the maimed child's mother, however? She understands, just as we do, that a dog is just a dog and has no capacity for moral reasoning. She can also see that this dog is itself a victim. This dog was bitten by another dog with rabies. The mother is aware of what I call "the chain of victims," then. Still, because it was *her* child that this dog maimed—now that's a different story. Maybe she wants to have this dog killed, not just for practical reasons, but because she is after revenge—she is pursuing a much more personal affair. Why? Because, unlike us, the mother is very close to the victim. So far as she is concerned, emotionally speaking, this dog is likely a real villain.

We can easily conjure up additional situations that bring up further moral sticking points. Consider, for instance, a situation involving a physically abusive father, his son, and a concerned social worker. In this drama, things quickly get messy. The idea of morality in this situation is a knee-jerk reaction for most of us. Our old habits aside, let's apply the first factor that determines to what degree we accept or blame: How close is the victim? The father is, of course, very close to the victim, in more ways than one. Aside from their biological and emotional closeness, father and son share a common circumstance. In the same way the rabid dog in our previous example was both villain and victim, our father and son are also strung together along the chain of victims. We know nowadays that the vast majority of abusive parents were also abused children. The very father whom many of us might want to point our finger at was, in all likelihood, once a helpless victim himself. Ironically, in sharing this common circumstance with his son, our father feels that his abusing his son is a decidedly moral action. *After all*, the father thinks, *I was beaten as a child and I ended up just fine. My father was right when he told me that hitting your kids is the only way they learn to behave.* So, because the father is very close to the victim, he tends to make a definite moral judgment. For him, this situation is good—exactly as it should be. The social worker also makes a pretty definite moral judgment. She identifies with the son in her own way, in that he reminds her of her own son. No matter how angry she has gotten at her son, *she's* never physically abused *him*. Why? Because she thinks of herself as a moral person, which must make the abusive father an immoral person. Her moral ruling: This situation is clearly bad—an unnecessary tragedy.

Now let's apply our second factor: How conscious is the villain? In this drama, both the villain, which is the father, and the hero, which is the social worker, happen to think the villain is perfectly conscious of his actions. The father pats himself on the back because he *knows* he is doing the right thing. He is perfectly aware that some would disagree with his behavior, but that's fine by him. He has a choice to make and he has made it. To the degree that the social worker also believes the father has made a conscious, reasonably informed decision, she thinks of him as a monster. After all, if we see the father as simply a passive notch on the chain of victims, another unconscious participant in Malthus' perpetual struggle for resources, we would be no more likely to morally blame him for his nature than we would our cats for torturing insects. So, from the perspectives of both the father and the social worker, the father has a choice to make and he has made it.

Let's see what happens when we further complicate things by introducing another participant into our drama: a Zen master. The Zen master reads all about this situation in the paper. He makes no moral judgment. He sees these difficult actions as neither good nor bad. How can he do this? For one thing, he's not nearly so close to the victim in the sense that he feels no need to either protect him, as does the social worker, or to discipline him, as does the father. It's not that our Zen master is a cold and heartless person, it's just that he has much more faith in the subtle harmony of the universe than have our other participants. There are no digressions from progress, says our Zen master, no single quantum of energy ever wasted on unnecessary evils. He neither accepts nor rejects, blames nor condones. He is abiding by Taoism's principle of spontaneous harmony, which says, "A great tailor cuts little."[8]

The Zen master also differs in his assessment of the father's level of consciousness, or awareness. From where the Zen master sits—much more aware of all aspects of his own mind and the universe than the villain *or* the hero—the father looks to be not much more conscious than a cat eating an insect, operating on animal instinct. This doesn't necessarily mean the Zen master wouldn't vote to have the father put away in prison, I should emphasize. Nor does it mean that he wouldn't go to great lengths to protect abused children or, in certain circumstances, possibly even be in favor of capital punishment or other violent means. I simply mean to assert that the Zen master would do whatever he did without moral judgment. Unlike both the father and the social worker, the Zen master is no longer interested in playing the blame game. If he were to send the father to prison, he would do so, not as a morally superior person punishing a morally inferior person, but rather as an empty vessel—a morally neutral check required by this environment. In this sense, the Zen master is more like an impersonal force of nature than he is a personally involved individual. He is simply at one with the Tao, which transcends all ideas of morality.

THE PRINCIPLE OF RELATIVITY

We have, then, three very different takes on the father and his actions. So which is right? Is he moral, immoral, or simply playing his role? Aside from all these individual perspectives, what is the real truth here?

A relatively recent revision of scientific thought might lend some insight into this moral dilemma. In 1905, Albert Einstein introduced the principle of relativity, an amazingly simple idea that turned our intuitive ideas of how the universe works on their heads. Complicated mathematics aside, Einstein simply asserted that different observers view the same happening from different perspectives. Any test that claims to determine which observer has the most accurate observation, Einstein said, is no test at all, but strictly an arbitrary opinion.

For example, imagine a transparent train rolling down the tracks. Inside it, a man is bouncing a basketball. Outside, standing alongside the tracks, another man is watching the train go by. The man inside the train sees the ball bouncing straight up and down. He would describe the motion of the ball as going up and coming down.

The man outside the train agrees with the man inside the train, but he also sees the ball moving down the track with the train. Consequently, he describes the ball as moving along in a series of arcs, more or less like a wave. So who's right? They both are, Einstein said. It simply depends on where you are standing. Neither perspective can claim to have an exclusive, insider's privilege on the real situation. No matter what sort of objective test we try to set up to determine the so-called true motion of the ball, we are still doing so from within the limits of a particular vantage point.

So let's apply the principle of relativity to the moral drama we've been considering. To the degree that I agree with the social worker, I am probably standing somewhere much closer to her vantage point. Maybe I am also a concerned and protective mother. If I agree with the father, I am probably nearer his observation tower. Maybe I was also an abused child and am now an abusive parent. The Zen master, however, knows the most important thing is to not get stuck inside his own vantage point. We can even feel indignant and offended if we want to, he might say, so long as we remember that our feelings don't *prove* we have somehow got the inside track on the way things really are.

Feelings of moral superiority, then, are nothing more than symptoms of our ignorance and self-importance—a result of our being stuck within, or attached to, our limited individual perspectives. "This isn't just another vantage point, after all, this is my vantage point!" we say—which is, of course, the vantage point. To be able to get outside our own personal views, to allow our perspective to float from point to point, is a feat that greatly reduces our defensiveness. Why waste time defending one particular perspective if we realize they are all equally valid? I choose not to abuse my own son, then, not because I believe such abuse to be immoral, but simply because I don't want to. I wouldn't be a lesser, immoral person if I beat my son, I just wouldn't be me. Rather than encouraging violent or anti-social behaviors, such a realization allows each individual the opportunity for genuine benevolence—a free, non-judgmental, artistic expression of kindness and respect, as opposed to mainstream society's guilty, constrictive compulsion to "do the right thing."

Similarly, when we are wronged somehow, or see those close to us wronged, it can be useful to try to adopt the perspective of the villain. We can do so only to the degree that we have learned to see past our own vantage point, given up our seeming moral superiority. If we can be agile enough to stand where the villain stands, we might see that what we thought was malice is really fear and a sense of helplessness. This doesn't mean we have to behave as the villain behaves, but simply that we are able to see that, from the villain's perspective, maybe *he's* the hero and *we're* the villain. Let's reconsider the biblical story of the adultress. When the "teachers of the law" brought the adulteress before Jesus, he neither condoned nor condemned her actions. He avoided the moral trap set for him by the Pharisees simply by not commenting on the morality or immorality of her actions. "If any one of you is without sin," Jesus said, "let him be the first to throw a stone at her" (John 8:7). He thus invited her accusers to make their own moral judgments, thereby reflecting them back on their own vantage points.

When a devotee asked Ramana Maharshi why the world was so full of suffering and evil, Ramana responded, "Who is it that raises the question?" Understand the limits of your own vantage point, he was saying, and the question will answer itself. "What is right and wrong?" asked Ramana Maharshi. "There is no [objective] standard by which to judge something to be right and another to be wrong. Opinions differ according to the nature of the individual and according to the surroundings."[9] Know your own nature, as well as that of your surroundings, and moral judgments will become unnecessary.

Be that as it may, we do get stuck clinging to the supposed superiority of our personal views. Let's take a more detailed look at two of the most compelling reasons for this tendency: herd morality and self-importance.

Herd Morality

Morality," said Friedrich Nietzsche, "is the herd instinct in the individual."[10] Nietzsche believed that most of us lack the existential courage necessary to forge our own systems of belief and value. We mistrust our own moral leanings due to a lack of self-confidence, so we join up with a herd, add ourselves to a social group and adopt their belief system. Whereas this much may seem obvious, the specifics of Nietzsche's ideas about morality are quite revolutionary.

In every group, Nietzsche said, there are going to be dominant and non-dominant factions, strong and weak. The strong are presumably strong because—for whatever reasons—they control more of the financial and political resources. According to Nietzsche, however, every individual has a will to power—not just the individuals belonging to the dominant group. For this reason, the weaker faction is not going to be satisfied with this situation. They will engage the dominant group in a struggle for power. If the dominant group controls more of the resources, however, how does the non-dominant group go about this struggle?

The weaker party has to wage a kind of underground or subversive war. To do so, they invent a morality—what Nietzsche called a "slave morality"—in opposition to that of the dominant party. They simply take a look at what the in-group has and categorize it as immoral. If the in-group is rich, material wealth becomes immoral. If the in-group is physically robust, meaning they enjoy healthy sexual desire and sensual gratification, the "slaves" decide that sex, food, drink, etc., are also immoral. The problem here, said Nietzsche, is that this isn't really morality at all—it is strategizing. These so-called moral decisions have very little to do with personal choice or authentic beliefs regarding right and wrong, good and bad. Instead, such decision arise out of feelings of repressed anger and envy, "re-sentiment," in Nietzsche's language.

The *Tao Te Ching* expresses a very similar idea:

Is there a difference between yes and no?
Is there a difference between good and evil?
Must I fear what others fear? What nonsense![11]

Both Nietzsche and Lao Tzu are equating a certain kind of moral judgment with fear. Both men would agree that it is a perfectly legitimate decision, a perfectly moral decision even, if I choose not to engage in pre-marital sex, for example. When I go on to decide that this—my personal choice—must be the best choice for everyone, pre-marital sex suddenly becomes immoral. This second step, which is always unnecessary, both men would agree, comes from a place of envy. I am secretly jealous of those strong individuals who enjoy healthy sexual satisfaction. Moreover, I feel I can't compete with them on their own turf, so I simply opt out of the game. Better yet, I go on to declare myself the moral winner. The presence, or lack thereof, of this secretive, poisonous feeling of envy and contempt, according to Nietzsche, is what determines the difference between mere strategizing and authentic morality. "All naturalism in morality, that is, all healthy morality, is ruled by an instinct of life. . . . some restriction and hostility on life's path is thereby shoved aside. Anti-natural morality—that is, almost every morality that has been taught, honored and preached up to now—turns, in contrast, precisely against the instinct of life; it is a sometimes stealthy, sometimes loud and bold condemnation of these instincts."[12]

If what has been suggested about moral judgment is true, it raises an interesting question: How can I know which of my decisions are natural manifestations of a healthy morality, and which come from a tense and fearful place of anti-natural morality? This dilemma actually has a rather simple answer: If we're running with the herd, we are probably tending toward the latter. Well, how can we recognize when we are running with the herd? Simple. When we are deeply unhappy, when we think we are being treated unfairly, when we think we have been short-changed somehow—these are all indications, or symptoms, of herd mentality. This is why anyone joins up with the herd in the first place: to struggle against the "powers that be," thinking them to be corrupt and unjust. The first step, then, in cultivating a truly natural morality, is simply learning to see the absolute fairness in all situations. As this is far from easy to do, I would like to examine this suggestion further by way of another relatively new scientific principle: chaos theory.

Chaos Theory and Sensitive Dependency

If we listen to an old jazz record produced in the 1930s, we will inevitably notice quite a bit of static or noise by today's recording standards. Some listeners might find this noise a very irritating distraction from the music. Other listeners might have the opposite reaction. They might believe that the noise adds a richness to the recording, allows for a certain quaintness missing from today's modern recordings. For the second group of listeners, the noise is a necessary part of their overall musical experience. In the *Tao Te Ching*, we find a reference to the "noise" that necessarily accompanies the Tao:

> The wise student hears of the Tao and practices it diligently.
> The average student hears of the Tao and gives it thought every now and again.
> The foolish student hears of the Tao and laughs aloud.
> If there were no laughter, the Tao would not be what it is.[13]

In this example, the noise of the Tao arises from the foolish student, who distracts with his laughter. Most of us would tend to call this person ignorant or, depending on the degree of his foolishness, immoral or evil. The *Tao Te Ching*, however, considers this noise to be an integral part of a larger process. Rather than being a distraction that should be eliminated, it is a necessary component of the Tao, a kind of quaint static that lends the overall recording its richness.

In a scientific sense, noise is often defined as that which gets added to the system through randomness or chance. Since the 1960's, however, scientists have begun to redefine their original definition of randomness. Edward Lorenz, a meteorologist, is often credited as the pioneer of what is now known as chaos theory. Through his study of weather back in the 60's, Lorenz began to discover that much of what we classified as random behavior wasn't really random. Certain "variations are not random but look random,"[14] Lorenz said. Traditionally, science defined as random anything that it could not predict fairly accurately. Consider this sequence of numbers, for instance: 2, 4, 6, 8. We wouldn't consider this to be a random sequence of numbers because we understand the ordering sequence behind the numbers. In a system such as weather, however, the ordering sequence is much more complicated—so much so that we can never fully comprehend the organizing structure behind it. One of the factors that makes weather prediction so difficult, claimed Lorenz, was a phenomenon called "sensitive dependency."

Sensitive dependency means that little causes often have big effects. To illustrate this idea, Lorenz uses the example of a pinball machine. Let's imagine two separate plays on the same pinball machine. On both plays, as the ball comes out of the chute, it strikes the same pin. Moreover, it strikes the same pin at *almost* exactly the same angle and at *almost* exactly the same speed. Even our most accurate measuring devices would record the balls traveling at nearly identical speeds, let's say, and striking at nearly identical angles. If we could freeze-frame both of our plays right here, we might predict that the balls would end up in almost the same place as they traveled down the board toward the flippers. In reality, however, this wouldn't necessarily be the case. The very slight differences in the initial pin strike tend to lead to bigger and bigger differences as the balls travel down the board.

Edward Lorenz wrote an article titled, "Does the Flap of a Butterfly's Wings in Brazil Set Off a Tornado in Texas?" Although he didn't answer this question directly, his point was clear: Even the most seemingly insignificant of happenings, the slightest trace of noise in the system, can dramatically alter the overall outcome. Because science cannot possibly measure all these minute variables that affect a huge process such as the weather, it cannot predict the weather with much accuracy.

More relevant to our discussion of morality, we can examine sensitive dependency from a less scientific perspective. Let's consider the effects of the Civil War. To a Southern plantation owner just after the Civil War, the war was unwanted noise in the system. He lost two sons to the war, not to mention his entire slave population. He suffered much personal grief and financial loss. Many decades later, however, the Southern person is likely to feel very differently. Why? Well, he's sitting much closer to the flipper end of the pinball machine. For me, personally, as a modern Southern person, I feel the Civil War had an overwhelmingly positive effect. After all, I didn't lose any family to the war, nor did I suffer financially. For me, the Civil War isn't all that personal of an affair. For that matter, the contemporary South as a whole would probably agree that, in the end, the Civil War has had mostly positive effects on every aspect of Southern life. The point is, due to the immeasurable intricacies of sensitive dependency, we are very likely to misunderstand situations if we jump to conclusions too soon, particularly if we feel very personally involved.

Centuries from now, even a tragedy such as the Holocaust may not look so tragic—a statement which is not at all intended to invalidate the unmistakable pain and misery many have suffered from this devastating event. This is just to say that personal pain and misery don't necessarily prove that some event—however traumatic or heart-wrenching—was strictly, or even mostly, distracting noise in the system. By definition, strong negative emotions suggest a personal closeness to the event—a state akin to predicting the pinball's path when it has just struck the first pin out of the chute. By contrast, now that we can observe even recent history with slightly less emotional involvement—a state of observation somewhat further down our pinball surface—we can already see some positive effects of the Holocaust. As a nation, not to mention as a world, we are all becoming more aware of our tendencies toward racism and ethnocentrism. These tendencies are such deeply-ingrained human habits that it seems very unlikely we could ever truly let them go without some terribly shocking evidence of their destructive potential. Whether such a feat of preemptive "letting go" is possible, recorded history would suggest cultural prejudices are surrendered only when there is no other choice. To honor such difficult events as the Holocaust or the Civil War—which is not at all the same thing as condoning them—is a simple act of humility. Just as the instruments of modern science are still inadequate to perfectly measure all factors that affect the weather, our own very slight errors of perception always have the potential to end up as much bigger misunderstandings somewhere down the line.

INFORMATION THEORY

You can think of information theory as a kind of subset of chaos theory. Information theory is generally considered the creation of an engineer, Claude Shannon. This theory simply states that in any communication, the message is made up of two parts: the intended message and the unintended message, or noise.[15] As an AT&T employee, Shannon was mostly concerned with eliminating as much noise as possible, as he believed it to interfere with the intended message. Shannon's most important commentator, however, a man named Warren Weaver, had a different take on noise. Weaver asserted that a noisy system necessarily contained more information than a quiet one.

Suppose your friend calls and leaves a message on your machine. His message says simply, "I'll try you again tomorrow." His consciously intended message is just that: He'll call you tomorrow. Suppose we add some noise to his message, however. Let's say, in addition to his spoken message, you hear loud talking and music in the background. Now you know your friend is probably calling from a party. Moreover, you notice sadness in your friend's voice, a slight tremor. From this added noise, you deduce that your friend ran into his ex-girlfriend at a party and is feeling depressed. In this case, more noise has led to more information. Similarly, the same effect is evident in the infamous Freudian slip. My wife *intends* to say to me, "The meal you prepared was truly awe-inspiring!" What she *actually* says is, "The meal you prepared was truly awful!" To her, perhaps this is a simple slip of the tongue, distracting noise from her intended message. I, the cook, however, might see this unconscious noise as a way of obtaining more information about what my wife really thinks. In one simple communication, my wife has simultaneously sent an intended and unintended message.

It is just this sort of noise or seeming accident that makes biological evolution possible. Without the unintended noise of genetic mutation, life would theoretically not have progressed from the simple to the complex. Incidents of noise resulting in spontaneous organization, such as biological mutations, are known as self-regulating systems. On a smaller scale, we can look into a famous chemical reaction, a BZ (Belousov-Zhabotinski) reaction. Chemists discovered that, when left undisturbed, these two particular chemicals remain in a sort of homogenous blob. When the Petri dish is shaken, however, the chemicals begin to organize into geometrical shapes. When the external disturbance is stopped, the geometric shapes soon dissipate back into a homogenous blob. And when the chemicals are sufficiently stirred, the reaction permanently organizes, flashing blue, red, blue, red at regular intervals.[16] Based on such phenomenon, the scientist Ilya Prigogine asserted that certain systems, when sufficiently disturbed, spontaneously self-regulate or organize.[17]

For the Buddhists, the very fact of our human existence offers each of us a unique opportunity within a self-regulating system. Multiple realms, believe the

Buddhists, exist alongside our own realm—the reality we know as ordinary, daily life. Some of these realms are heaven-like, whereas others are hell-like. The heaven-like realms, although incredibly beautiful and pleasant, don't offer the ideal conditions for spiritual advancement. They simply lack sufficient struggle and challenge to motivate the individual's desire for ultimate spiritual betterment or enlightenment. In the context of chaos theory, we would say these heaven realms lack sufficient noise or disturbance to motivate spontaneous organization. With the hell realms, the opposite is true. Existence here is pure misery, pure distraction. There is so much noise that whatever spiritual information there is gets lost in the disorder. Our own realm, however, the human realm, is by far the most desirable reality in which to be reborn, say the Buddhists. Although our world provides necessary basic resources, it also mixes in a good deal of pain and suffering. From the Buddhist perspective, to want to rid the world of all strife and suffering is simply to take for granted our unique opportunity for maximum information.

When we apply these various elements of chaos theory to a subject such as morality, then, we can gain a much larger, less egocentric perspective. Even if we view immorality as chaos and random noise, we can learn from nature that such disturbances are the very catalysts that motivate progress. As the Buddhist teachings assert, when we seek to eliminate all unwanted or unintended noise from our experience, we are unknowingly trying to stagnate, to lock ourselves inside of rigid systems that permit only limited expansion and flexibility. By learning to appreciate the necessity of all experience, be it pleasant or unpleasant, we are learning to be as the Zen master: A great tailor who cuts little.

Self-Importance

Self-importance has much the same effect on individual awareness as does Nietzsche's herd morality. It tends to limit our experience of the universe around us and within us, to get us stuck inside our own, egocentric vantage points. Two of the most deeply-ingrained means by which we cling to our self-importance for dear life are arrogance and guilt.

Arrogance

Arrogance is nothing other than the belief that my vantage point, my perspective, is somehow more important, more accurate than someone else's. Whereas everyone else seems to be confused and deluded, my arrogance claims, I can see things the way they *really* are. One of the most damaging things about arrogance is that it allows us to assume that we can understand someone else's life experience from the outside. We project our own qualities and experiences onto their unique situation and more or less guess the rest. We judge, for example, the heroin addict quite readily. I may be well aware that she grew up in poverty and came from a broken family. "Even so, *I* grew up poor and came from a broken family," I may say to myself, "and *I* didn't end up a heroin addict. Therefore, she must be somehow morally inferior to me—somehow not *trying hard enough*." My arrogance overlooks one obvious fact. If I truly had the heroin addict's exact life circumstances, I would have—by definition—ended up in the same place she is in. Sure, maybe she's less intelligent than me. Sure, maybe she has less willpower, but what does this really say? Even qualities such as intelligence and willpower are really nothing other than certain measures of how an individual's genetics interact with the environment—measures that have been tossed about so frequently, and so carelessly, as to have lost any essential meaning.

When we are perfectly honest with ourselves, tracing our various good and bad qualities back as far as we can throughout our experiential timeline, we have to admit that we, as individuals, deserve no special credit or special punishment. We are who we are because, well, that's who we are—that's what the world is. No one exists in a vacuum. In the same way that the flap of a butterfly's wings may influence global weather, my behaviors and personality qualities are part of a larger, intricately connected whole. This being the case, we could say that I am as personally responsible for the addict's addiction as she is personally responsible for my career success, for example. For that matter, we can't really get a clear idea of my so-called individual personality without understanding my parents, their individual backgrounds, their parents' backgrounds, ad infinitum. Like Hume said, this idea of cause and effect can be traced back and back and back. This, in one sense, is what is meant by oneness, by interrelatedness. Taoism reminds us:

> Everyone under heaven says my Tao is great and beyond compare.
> Because it is great, it seems different.
> If it were not different, it would have vanished long ago.
> I have three treasures which I hold and keep.
> The first is mercy; the second is economy;
> The third is daring not to be ahead of others.[18]

Without a doubt, my own vantage point is truly great and unique. So is the next guy's, however. However he may look to me from the outside, he also happens to think of his own vantage point as *the* vantage point. Whatever difficulties she may have, it is simply not the case that the heroin addict is sitting around truly wishing she was me. Once I begin to appreciate the greatness and uniqueness of the vantage point of each and every individual—despite widely varying opinions on morality, ethics, religion—I no longer feel the need to cling to my own so tightly. It's not that I give up all of my personal beliefs and convictions, and somehow melt into an undifferentiated goo of awareness. After all, as the above passage assures us, if my own Tao were not truly unique, it would have vanished long ago. Rather, as I begin to cultivate authentic respect for other belief systems and personality organizations—and this is extremely difficult, not at all the same thing as simply saying I respect other belief systems and personality organizations—I begin to loosen my ego boundary, bit by bit, and see more and more of the bigger picture.

Interestingly, our arrogance is often so great that we think we have outsmarted the very Tao itself. Supposedly unfair things happen to us and we get angry with life itself—assuming we can already see far into the future, certain that we are fully aware of the long-term consequences of some immediate difficulty. My wife, for example, is currently a clinical psychologist. Just after she graduated high school, however, she wasn't quite sure what career she wanted to pursue. She happened to meet a modeling agent who convinced her that modeling would be just the thing. She decided to postpone college in order to pursue a modeling career in Europe. Her stay in Europe proved to be confusing and painful. Just out of high school, the various modeling agencies tended to exploit her vulnerability and lack of experience for financial gain. Several months later, she came home, thoroughly disappointed with the whole industry. At this time, both of us were quite angry at the way she had been treated.

These days, however, my wife and I have a very different perspective on the whole fiasco. We are actually quite grateful for her disillusionment with this field. She quickly realized the modeling industry simply wasn't for her and—after one seemingly chance situation after another—found her true role as a psychologist. Had she pursued success as a model, it might have taken her much longer to realize that her core interests lie elsewhere. All of a sudden, then, the villains in this drama become heroes in disguise—Borges' secretly beneficent Judas. This isn't to say that these individuals were consciously doing my wife a favor. In fact, they had very little conscious interest in my wife beyond how she might be of use to them. Even so, despite—or, more accurately, *because of*—their shortsighted self-absorption, they proved to be very helpful to my wife, nonetheless. The error wasn't made by the Tao, that is to say, but by my wife and I. The only real problem in this situation was our own arrogant, nearsighted assumptions about the way things should be.

GUILT

Although we don't tend to think of it this way, guilt is really another form of arrogance, albeit more subtle, more socially acceptable. We feel guilty when we imagine we have done something bad, somehow wronged another person. Let's say I am angry at my boss, but have been repressing my anger for some time. The company Christmas party rolls around and, in a drunken rage, I dump a bowl of punch on his head. The next day I feel guilty. Why? Well, I'm being very self-important, for one thing, imagining that this incident was entirely my doing. I am viewing my boss as the passive victim in this scenario, a powerless innocent. I am simply failing to recognize that every act in every relationship is—due to the fact of ultimate interrelatedness, or oneness—necessarily a cooperative effort. Truth be told, I probably like to imagine my boss as a passive victim in this scenario because I like to fantasize that I have some sort of unassailable power over him. My boss is helpless to defend himself against my anger, my guilt reassures me, albeit in a rather self-punishing way. Moreover, similarly driving my guilt is the arrogant assumption that I must know what my boss needs from life just now. Despite the fact that my own experience tells me that, from time to time, I myself have needed an unexpected punchbowl or two dumped on my head—what we could think of as creative chaos or the maximum information of noise—I am guessing that this definitely doesn't apply to my boss. My poor boss—he's just too frail and delicate to recover from such a thing.

Another way our guilt causes problems for us is by tempting us to wrongly identify with the so-called villain in certain situations. One of the most cumbersome burdens when it comes to accepting all the evil in the world is our tendency to think we can know the mind of the evildoer. We hear about an act of violence and we imagine ourselves committing such an act, essentially feeling a kind of guilt by association. Our guilt is simply arrogance in disguise. If I am not a violent person myself, what makes me think I can know what it is to be a violent person? What makes me think I can imagine what that person's experience feels like from the inside?

> There is always an official executioner.
> If you try to take his place,
> It is like trying to be a master carpenter and cutting wood.
> If you try to cut wood like a master carpenter,
> You will only hurt your hand.[19]

The seeming villain, like Lao Tzu's "master carpenter," is a kind of expert at his own "vocation." Bizarre as it may sound, we can think of villainy as a kind of talent. As the story of Jesus and Judas implies, and as the natural world is continually reminding us, violence of all sorts seems to play an essential role in the universe. Even so, the vast majority of us can't even yell at our bosses, much less commit an act of primal violence—not that we would want to, of course. My point is simple enough: Leave the executions to the executioner. Don't go "borrowing" guilt, don't go confusing yourself when it comes to fundamental and necessary existential struggles, by attempting to imagine the unimaginable.

Ironically, accepting the harsh reality of the world we live in without indulging in moral judgment is the very key to true morality. To divide the world into good and bad, moral and immoral, is to split our own selves down the middle. Those difficult aspects of the universe, such as human power struggles and seemingly arbitrary injustices of every sort, can only be resolved through total acceptance and calm awareness. The Dhammapada says, "Not by enmity are enmities quelled. . . . By the absence of enmity are they quelled. This is an ancient truth."[20]

Anti-Guru Yoga

When Ramana Maharshi was asked whether the world was created for happiness or misery, he didn't say, "Do nice things and you will be happy." We have all done enough nice things to know that this is mostly a platitude—a useful learning tool, no doubt, but a strategy that ultimately falls way short of authentic liberation. Nor did Ramana Maharshi say, "Quit doing bad things and you will be happy." Instead, Ramana addressed the real root of the problem: the judging mind, the individual's need to be better than some and worse than others, somewhere between Jesus and Judas. Ramana said:

> Creation is neither good nor bad; it is as it is. It is the human mind which puts all sorts of constructions on it, seeing things from its own angle and interpreting them to suit its own interests. A woman is just a woman, but one mind calls her "mother," another "sister," and still another "aunt" and so on. Men love women, hate snakes, and are indifferent to the grass and stones by the roadside. These value-judgments are the cause of all the misery in the world. Creation is like a peepul tree: birds come to eat its fruit, or take shelter in its branches, men cool themselves in its shade, but some may hang themselves on it. Yet the tree continues to lead its quiet life, unconcerned with and unaware of all the uses it is put to. It is the human mind that creates its own difficulties and then cries for help. Is God so partial as to give peace to one person and sorrow to another? In creation there is room for everything, but man refuses to see the good, the healthy and the beautiful. Instead, he goes on whining, like the hungry man who sits beside the tasty dish and who, instead of stretching out his hand to satisfy his hunger, goes on lamenting, "Whose fault is it, God's or man's?"[21]

The problem, Ramana is suggesting, is not our own actions or the actions of others, but the judgmental way we tend to categorize those actions. Once we begin to let go of our habitual moralizing, we begin to appreciate that in creation there is room for everything—heroes and villains alike.

The following anti-guru yoga exercises, when properly understood, are not negative in their focus compared to the guru yoga practices presented in the previous chapter. Rather, the following are means for viewing the world from a much broader perspective, ways of seeing the good, the healthy, and the beautiful throughout the entirety of the one, whole Divine Self.

EXERCISE: FORGIVING OTHERS

■ Think of something someone has done to you in the past, some way in which you have felt wronged, an incident about which you still carry considerable anger. Recognize your anger—with all its delicious and tempting flavors—honor it, and put it aside for the time being. Being as objective as you possibly can, try to trace all the subtle consequences of that original offence. You are already aware, no doubt, of its various negative effects. Instead, try to focus your awareness on the many small or large ways in which you have benefited from this action, all the things you have been able to learn about how your own personality works. Whether or not the offending party intended for you to benefit from his or her behavior is not important. That person's problems are his or her problems, just as your problems belong strictly to you. If you are unable to see the ways in which you have benefited from this difficult behavior, consider one positive aspect of your current life situation. Since all things are interrelated, try to trace the subtle karmic currents that must connect some present blessing with some previous conflict.

EXERCISE: FORGIVING YOURSELF

■ Think of some offence you have given in the past. Recognize your guilt—with all its delicious and tempting flavors—honor it, but put it aside for now. Just as in the previous exercise, try to trace the positive consequences of this offensive behavior—many of them likely quite subtle. Don't get distracted by your conscious intention at the time you committed the offence. After all, when we begin to let go of our personal ownership of our actions, both good and bad, we begin to see that each of us is a perfect vessel of the Tao, a pure instrument of God's will. Notice how the ways in which you tend to get "stuck" in this exercise are similar to the obstacles you encountered in the "Forgiving Others" exercise. Try to see the ways in which anger and guilt are simply different manifestations of the same obstacle: self-importance.

EXERCISE: SEEING THE WHOLE PERSON

■ Think of someone for whom you have strong feeling—both positive and negative. Try to list what are, in your opinion, his or her most striking traits in both of these categories. Try to imagine this person without these negative traits. As you do so, notice the ways in which his or her positive and negative qualities are intricately intertwined. Imagining any given person minus this or that negative quality seems to diminish the overall richness of that person, to flatten out his or her personality. Be aware of the unavoidable fact that the very things you like about this person seem to necessitate those traits you don't like. Upon closer inspection, try to see the positive in the negative. If you are honest with yourself, you will notice that, in some very subtle and paradoxical way, you admire this person's negative traits as much as you admire his or her positive traits.

EXERCISE: SEEING THE WHOLE TAO

■ Think of some feature of life that is particularly precious to you—humor, for instance. Now think of some feature that is especially disturbing to you, such as violence. Notice the ways in which you continually seek out the first item, which should be obvious enough. Now notice the ways in which you continually seek out the second item, which will likely be much less overt, carefully hidden beneath the surface of your day-to-day personality. Despite the fact that you are disturbed by violence, you may notice that you are drawn to violent movies, news stories, fantasies, etc. Try to imagine life entirely devoid of this troublesome feature. Be aware that the feature you so love in life only has meaning when considered alongside that feature you so dislike. Try to notice the ways in which you habitually seek these seemingly opposing features out simultaneously. Maybe you often laugh during violent movie scenes, finding something inexplicably funny. Maybe you often tell jokes that—as most jokes do—contain a significant element of aggression. Recognize the interrelatedness of these seemingly opposing drives, the beauty and clarity the yin lends the yang, the yang lends the yin. Both are absolutely necessary, absolutely perfect in their unique way.

Know that all things in life, however sacred or profane, however moral or immoral, spontaneously spring from the same pure source: the ancient, perfectly harmonious Tao.

CONCENTRATION PRACTICE: THE WISDOM OF NARROW-MINDEDNESS

To restore the mind to its unfragmented origin, sit quietly and meditate. First count the breaths, then tune the breath until it is imperceptible. Sense the body as like the undifferentiated absolute, and you won't hear anything. Those who can regain their composure after a mountain crumbles before them are second best; not even being startled is expertise.

— ANCESTOR LU, *VITALITY, ENERGY, SPIRIT*[1]

omewhere along the path, all of us reach a place where we realize that some of our most cherished notions about The Way Things Are, some of our most deeply imbedded beliefs concerning Who I Am, simply don't hold water. We begin to recognize that the ways in which we have previously kept our feet on the ground are, ironically, the very roots of our most persistent struggles. Anger, arrogance, pride, fear, guilt, desire—we begin to realize that these have been our favorite placeholders, our preferred strategies for relating to the world so far. These things are beginning to fall away, however, and we very likely panic. We suddenly feel ungrounded, insecure, and helpless, our minds restless and fragmented. We need some new means of organizing ourselves, of keeping ourselves together in the wake of our crumbling ego mountains.

Then again, just as many of us have yet to reach this place. Our old habits of thinking and feeling are still reassuringly intact. Even so, we are beginning to get sick of dragging these restrictive tendencies around with us everywhere we go. We are tired of all the fear and anxiety, all the regret and resentment we carry around from moment to moment, and we are ready to let these exhausting habits go—however painful and scary the letting go may be. We want, quite simply, to be free at any cost. *Anything* would be better than this, we say. Bring on the avalanche. . .

Whatever your individual case may be, this is where concentration practice comes in. Concentration practice is a meditation technique that is absolutely essential for progress along any spiritual path. As the spiritual journey is an arduous and often terrifying one, you are going to need a solid pair of mountain climbing boots at some point, and concentration practice is just that. With just a few minutes of practice every day, this meditation technique allows you a firm hold in any situation. Once you are confident you have a truly reliable means of remaining calm, steadfast, and safe throughout any experience, you can open up to the spiritual path with newfound gusto and an ever-deepening respect for the cosmic adventure.

Some of you may feel you don't fall into either of the above categories. You are not suffering from existential panic at present, nor are you ready just yet to be free at any cost—not when that cost means surrendering even your most familiar, time-honored habits of feeling and cognition. Even so, you will find that concentration is also a highly effective means toward more practical improvements. With progress in concentration, your mind becomes a precise laser beam. You can willingly aim your single-pointed awareness at any task—be it small or large, short- or long-term—thereby beginning to achieve your most ambitious goals through sheer determination and focus. Similarly, concentration practice teaches you to relax at will, sleep more soundly, and relieve persistent physical pains and emotional stress. Whatever your individual goals, needs, and wants may be, concentration helps you satisfy them by improving your vision, lets you see more clearly into the innermost nature of The Way of Things, and launch yourself more freely into the incredibly rich and continually unfolding story of Who You Are.

Less Is More

Traditionally, concentration practice is known by many names—*zhiné* (pronounced "zi-náe"), *dhyana*, and single-pointed awareness among them. Various terminologies aside, concentration practice always comes down to one basic method: Pick an object of focus and concentrate on it. It's that simple. In his work, *A Map of Mental States*, British psychologist John H. Clark describes this form of meditation as a "method by which a person concentrates more and more upon less and less."[2] This is where you might ask, "Now, why would I possibly be interested in learning to concentrate more and more upon less and less?"

I first began formal concentration practice under the guidance of a meditation teacher. After I had been at it for a couple of weeks, he asked if I had noticed any recurring thoughts or experiences in my sessions. I told him I often found myself thinking, while sitting in the middle of my apartment, staring at a candle flame or whatever, "This is absolutely ridiculous!" My teacher was quite amused by my remark, chuckling somewhat cryptically. At the time, I assumed he was amused by such a remark that only a foolish beginner could make. Since then, after spending countless hours in all sorts of variations of such a practice, I see things very differently. Looking back, I think it much more likely my teacher was so amused because I was absolutely right: Concentration practice is absolutely ridiculous. Ironically, in many ways, this simple realization is probably the ultimate goal of all concentration practice. Even so, as is typical with the many paradoxes encountered in any spiritual practice, most of us simply have to engage in a good deal of focused meditation before this realization is at all useful to us.

For now, let me just suggest you try the following experiment: However you feel about concentration practice at present, commit to trying it out for two weeks. If it still seems ridiculous, like a total waste of time, then so be it. This is a perfectly valid response to the experiment. Unlike many aspects of organized religion, concentration practice doesn't require faith or belief in any particular spiritual system. In this context, learning to focus your mind has much more to do with applied science or artistic expression than it does religion or metaphysics. Without trying it out for at least a couple of weeks, however, you are simply making an uninformed guess, an assumption. Like all things along the path, concentration can only be understood from the inside out—deeply from within your own, subjective space. Maybe you suspect you are already quite an accomplished concentrator. Could be—many of us acquire the ability for heightened concentration throughout the ordinary tasks and responsibilities of our daily lives—but why not test it out and see? Either way, the ability to concentrate the mind in a very precise, highly energetic way is a prerequisite to each of the practices that we will examine in later chapters.

The Practice of Zhiné

Most systems recognize various stages of development in concentration, each of which emphasizes slightly different techniques for continuing progress. In the text that follows, I am loosely basing my descriptions of method on the Dzogchen view, which divides concentration, or zhiné, practice into three distinct phases: forceful zhiné, natural zhiné, and ultimate zhiné. Although I'll be using this particular view as a means to focus our discussion, these same essential techniques can be found in Zen, Christianity, Judaism, and any other spiritual practice. Although the particular terminologies, recommended postures, and so forth may differ somewhat from system to system, the ultimate goal of concentration is the same in each: to calm the mind, which is habitually distracted by this or that, so that it becomes an incredibly sharp and agile instrument of perception.

Preparation for Forceful Zhiné

*C*hoose a special place in which to perform concentration practice. This will help prepare your mind for focused self-inquiry. Whatever success in concentration you have over a period of time, your mind will automatically associate with this place of practice, allowing a kind of confidence or momentum to be stored in this place. The various sacred places and temples around the world, in fact, employ this same, self-evident mechanism. Such constructions and locations are highly-charged places, sites associated with some particularly energetic spiritual happening or continued practice that still resonates in that area long thereafter. Every time you perform a spiritual practice at your special site, you are building a distinct, physical connection to the sacred.

Set aside a special time of the day for your practice. To perform your practice at the same time every day—as is the case with the Moslem's precisely regulated daily prayers—builds the same sort of positive momentum that selecting a place for meditation does.

Set goals for your daily practice. Deciding on specific goals before you begin each day or week of sitting can be one of the most effective ways to lend structure to your practice. In the beginning, I suggest you decide on one to two sessions per day, for no more than five minutes. Five minutes doesn't sound like much, I realize, but it is much better to set a modest initial goal for yourself so that you can appreciate objective achievements from the very outset. Regardless of your internal experience, if you are able to sit for the length of time you have apportioned in advance, you should consider your session a decided success. Even if you can discipline yourself to sit in concentration for several hours daily, it does little good if the practice becomes drudgery. Remember: The goal here is cultivating a joyful and creative spiritual performance, not adding yet another errand to your busy day.

Keep in mind that the setting of the goal and the sticking to that goal is concentration practice. To get distracted in thinking, "Well, maybe I should sit for a couple of extra minutes this time . . . Maybe I should cut it a few minutes short today," is just that: getting *distracted.* Modify your goals as often as you like, but remember that meditation isn't a competition or a way to prove yourself. Neither is it exactly a practice of self-discipline. Rather, meditation is a simple questioning, a relaxed examination of yourself, a deep exploration into your own mind. Focus is both the means and the goal of this examination.

Choose a posture that is comfortable and allows you to maintain concentration. Meditation books often give very lengthy, detailed instructions regarding this or that posture. In my opinion, such specifics are not at all necessary. I recommend simply sitting up straight in a comfortable chair with a sturdy back, hands resting comfortably in your lap, head straight or tilted slightly down to relax your neck muscles.

Some systems insist on postures such as the lotus or the half-lotus. There are particular benefits to these postures in that they allow the body to remain very balanced and still—qualities which are, without a doubt, facilitators of concentration. If such a posture comes easily to you, then you may certainly use it to your advantage. If you have to work at it, however, you are probably better off with the chair.

Keep in mind, most of the traditional meditation instructions were intended for peoples of very different cultures who grow up sitting in such postures daily. For such individuals, these postures are very natural. To sit up straight, however, is very important, particularly when you are just getting started. If you relax your posture too much, you are likely to loose your intense focus and become drowsy.

As for clothing, I suggest you wear more or less what you normally wear—the obvious exceptions being unusually restrictive or uncomfortable clothing. If you get accustomed to sitting in a full lotus in a bathrobe, it creates an unnatural distance between meditation and your "normal" life. The idea is to create a very natural nook within your daily life, intentionally relaxed and supportive without being unnecessarily exotic or pretentious. The eventual goal is to dissolve formal meditation practices into your daily life so that no such external, or even internal, distinctions exist any longer.

Meditate with your eyes open. Different schools have varying views regarding this topic, but in my experience, since we spend most of our day with our eyes open, meditation seems less secluded from our waking life if we allow this simple consistency. Some spiritual traditions assert that closing the eyes is necessary in order to cut off impure karmic vision. I am more in agreement with the Dzogchen view, however, which asserts that there is simply nothing impure to cut off. What you see in the external world through your ordinary, physical eyes, you begin to learn, is merely a reflection of your own, internal, spontaneously perfected state.

WORKING WITH AN OBJECT OF FOCUS

There is a widely-held traditional belief that certain objects have an undeniable aspect of magic. The very fact that a rock is a rock and a leaf is a leaf is, in fact, the greatest magic of all. This is really the whole point behind magical thinking in the first place: a heightened appreciation of the unmistakable distinctness of all objects. That an object can be at once a part of The One, the unbounded cosmic goo, and yet somehow remain a distinct object is a deceptively simple, profound truth. However you feel about magic or such mystical ideas as energy storage, keep in mind that each of the objects of focus I suggest you try using has been used in spiritual practice for thousands of years. Although I recognize that a toaster or a wristwatch can theoretically be just as sacred an item of focus as a more traditional object, I think most of us find it easier to get started with some more overtly spiritual point of focus.

Breath

In Eastern thinking, the breath is closely associated with *prana*, or "vital energy." To work with the breath, then, is to work with the very fuel of the cosmos, the animating principal of the universe. With each breath, remember, a very ancient chemical interaction is taking place—an interaction which is directly traceable to the green plants around you, the sun above you, not to mention the most distant stars in the most distant galaxies. You don't need to think about all of this while you focus on your breath. In fact, the more you try to grasp the breath by thinking about it, the more you are going to lose it. Rather, as concentration practice teaches us over time, the vital energy of the universe will itself see to the unfathomable details. Simply attend to each breath with sufficient focus and this ancient, mystical connection will be automatic.

The breath is probably the most easily portable object of focus. Wherever you go, whatever you're doing, your breath is necessarily part of the process. There are many different methods for focusing on the breath. I suggest the following:

- Focus at the tip of your nostrils.

- Feel your breath passing through this place with every inhalation and exhalation.

- No matter how fast or slow your breaths, no matter how deep or shallow, attend to each one as it passes by the tip of your nostrils. Notice the bare moment in which your breath pauses after each inhalation and exhalation.

- "Thread" your breath through your nostrils as you would thread a needle. Try not to lose focus on the subtle physical sensation for even a microsecond.

- When you are first getting started, it may be useful to count the breaths. With the first exhalation, say to yourself, "One." With the next exhalation, say to yourself, "Two," and so on, all the way up to ten breaths, at which point you will start back at one.

Mantra

A mantra is any sound, or collection of sounds, repeated over and over to focus or relax the mind. Some of the most common mantras are:

> OM (pronounced *ah-uh-mm*)
> RAM (pronounced *rahm*)
> AH
> HUM (pronounced *hoom*)
> OM MANI PADME HUM (pronounced *ah-uh-mm mah-nay pahd-may hoom*)

Some might say that any sound will do as a mantra, that specific mantras are little more than arbitrarily chosen words, enforced by thousands of years of superstition. To a certain degree, no doubt, this is true. If you choose to practice in this way, you might as well say your own name over and over, or anything else that strikes you. I prefer another level of viewing mantra, however, one more in line with the beginning of the Gospel of John where it says, "In the beginning was the word." In this context, every time you sound a mantra with the proper attitude and focus, you are invoking that one original word, the ever elusive name of God, or creative aspect of the universe.

Moreover, to the degree that every mantra sounds different, every mantra connects you to this original word in a slightly different way. At the same time, it is not all that useful to go round and round about what certain mantras mean. Meditation upon mantras teaches you that their sound is their meaning—in the same way that to simply focus on each breath is to immediately and intuitively grasp the very mechanism of photosynthesis and the Big Bang. In his classic work, *Foundations of Tibetan Mysticism*, Lama Govinda discusses this elusive quality of mantra. He asserts that all words, including mantras, contain "qualities which are not translatable into concepts—just as a melody which, though it may be associated with a conceptual meaning, cannot be described by words or by any other medium of expression."[3] As a musician, I find this description very fitting. The true meaning of any mantra, you could say, can only be perceived by listening to its "music."

To work with mantra, simply choose one that catches your eye or ear and work with it for at least a couple of weeks.

- Breathe deeply. As you exhale, sound your mantra repeatedly, in rhythm.

- As you inhale, internally sound the mantra. The idea is that the mantra keeps going the whole time, whether or not it is externally sounded, as it is inextricably connected to the process of respiration.

- Know that the mantra is the energy of cosmic consciousness flowing through your uniquely personal focal point of awareness.

- When you feel the mantra has acquired a momentum of its own, I suggest you work with it internally, simply listening as it turns over and over in your subtle spiritual ear.

To the degree that different mantras represent different vibrations, they connect us to varying planes of consciousness, different astral planes. Work with a few mantras until one really seems to stick. You will know it when you find it. In many cases, the mantras choose us. I wasn't very interested in working with mantra, for instance, until one was transmitted to me while I was in a very deep state, having a certain variety of lucid dream experience—a clear light experience—when my guru appeared internally, sounding the mantra RAM over and over.

Many schools of thought assert that mantras must appear in such an extraordinary way if they are to be effective. The Hindu devotee, for example, is most typically given a certain mantra only after it has been invested by a highly-evolved being. Although I don't doubt the usefulness of this method, I haven't found it to be necessary. Due to the nature of all authentic mantras, they are already invested from the very beginning. This is part of what makes them mantras in the first place. No individual can truly add to their infinite energy, nor detract from it, in the same way that no one needs to invest your breath with the power to carry oxygen to your cells. Rather than consciously choosing your mantra, however, you may simply want to sit in a very quiet and calm state and listen for it. Be assured that whatever your mantra is to be at this time, it's already in there. If you can listen deeply enough, it will definitely surface into your conscious mind when the time is right.

Visual Focus

In this form of concentration, you fix your eyes upon a certain external object. This is the primary form of concentration in the Dzogchen tradition. One advantage to a visual focus is that the eyes interact with both the internal and external—by means of the spiritual heart center and energy body—in a way that is not so readily accessed by the other senses. I will explain this process in considerable detail in chapters 10 and 11. For now, understand that the visual focal point is particularly useful in developing awareness in dreams, as the visual aspects of the dream world tend to be the most striking. The Tibetans concentrate on the Tibetan letter AH which has great significance in the Dzogchen system. The Zen practitioner might choose to use a beautiful piece of calligraphy as an object of focus, whereas the Taoist might use the yin-yang symbol. Other traditions use a candle flame, a mandala, or a portrait of an enlightened being. In theory, you can choose any visual object on which to focus. In practice, however, you can increase concentration, particularly in the beginning stages, if you focus on an image that has some higher meaning to you. Whatever object you choose, it's important to stick with it from session to session to develop continuity.

- Place the object at eye level, four to ten feet in front of you.

- Select one small part or section of the object to focus on. Let your gaze center there, taking in the remainder of the object in your peripheral vision.

- You don't so much look *at* the object as *into* it, allowing your focus to slightly blur.

As with all other objects of concentration, the sensory information will quickly distort with intense concentration. The object will seem to wobble, change color, or shape. It is important to understand that this distortion is not an obstacle to the practice, but rather, the most direct means to the practice itself. You may say that the object distorts, but what you really mean is that your own perception, your own mind, is distorting. Paradoxically, such a distortion allows you a much clearer look into your normal process of sensory perception and awareness itself. After all, if you look through a perfectly clean window, you are likely to forget there is a pane of glass between the landscape and yourself. If you muddy the glass a bit, however, distorting the outside scenery, you are automatically reminded of the presence of the glass.

METHOD

Choose your object, relax, sit down for a scheduled length of time, and concentrate on it. All other description beyond this point may very well do more harm than good. The sole instruction the Zen master often gives the beginning meditator is simply to sit and watch the mind. Still, for those of you who would like more concrete guidelines, here are a few pointers:

1. *Concentrating on an object is not the same thing as thinking about an object or, really, even observing an object.* The goal is to merge with the object, a process in which all mental observations seem to cease. For the purposes of forceful zhiné, all thoughts are distractions. The thought of, "I just got distracted," is a distraction, as is the thought, "Wow! I'm really concentrating now!" Other distracting thoughts: "My back hurts . . . I need to blink now . . . I need to go the grocery store later." These distractions will come up almost constantly at first, but don't be discouraged. The real goal here is not to eliminate these distractions so much as learn how to work with them skillfully.

2. *In forceful zhiné, as soon as you recognize a distracting thought, you* forcefully *ignore it.* Even so, it just doesn't work to say to yourself, "I am forcefully ignoring the fact that I'm thinking about grocery shopping right now." Ironically, this sort of antidote only creates a kind of suffocating feedback loop, getting you stuck more and more deeply inside the labyrinth of your original distraction. The actual method is to simply return to your object of focus with more and more intensity. As soon as you become aware of a distracting thought, you allow the distraction to become the very fuel that points you back at your object. When you can concentrate on your object with a great enough intensity, such distracting thoughts—for all practical purposes—simply quit arising.

3. *It is probably much easier and simpler than you'll want to make it.* When you give up trying to understand how to do it and just do it, you are already there. Ramana Maharshi said, "There are no impediments to meditation. The very thought of such obstacles is the greatest impediment."[4] Simply fix your mind on a single point and leave it there. If you think you have gotten distracted, that's just because you are *thinking.* Get it? Practically speaking, however, you are probably going to have some problems at first. With that in mind, let's look at some methods for troubleshooting various difficulties that you are likely to experience.

Troubleshooting Your Zhiné Practice

*D*rowsiness can be one of the most formidable and persistent obstacles to progress for beginning meditators. Luckily, however, it is pretty simple to work through drowsiness:

- Check your posture. Make sure your back is straight. The slight but constant muscular effort it takes to hold your back straight is a great way to defend against drowsiness.

- Try changing the angle of your gaze a bit if your back is straight but drowsiness still persists. Point your eyes up at about a forty-five degree angle. The constant muscle tension necessary to maintain such a gaze will do much to lessen drowsiness.

- Change the time of day in which you practice. Choose a time of day when you feel particularly awake and alert. If drowsiness still persists, shorten your practice sessions to a minute or two. During this brief session, try to maintain perfect and intense concentration. Several very short sessions of this sort throughout the day will train your mind to associate concentration practice with a highly energetic awareness rather than a constant, groggy fight to fend off accidental napping.

- Reconsider your motivation. Do you really want to meditate right now? Is this something you are really committed to? Maybe take a few weeks off and try again.

If you are really ready to meditate, rest assured you won't meet a single obstacle that you can't overcome. If you are not really ready to meditate, however, no matter how much effort you apply, your results will probably be discouraging. Like every other spiritual practice, meditation isn't for every individual at every stage in his or her development. Perhaps there is something more urgently requiring your attention in your daily life right now. Don't abuse yourself if you are not ready to meditate. Paradoxically, by the time you are ready to meditate, you may very well discover that you no longer find formal practices of any sort necessary.

Like everything else along the path, even your apparent failures can be great successes. Whether you encounter persistent drowsiness or any other obstacle to meditation, if you are not ready to meditate just now, ask yourself, Why not? Is there something you are avoiding in your daily life, some relationship left unresolved? Ironically, as you look into this very question, you are still practicing a form of meditation. One of the most direct forms of meditation, which Ramana Maharshi called self-inquiry, is to repeatedly ask yourself the simple question: Now who is it, who is it really, that's having all these problems with meditation? The point here is not to find the "right" answer, some static label which you then apply to yourself. Rather, the goal is to watch how your desire to meditate dances alongside and within your seemingly conflicting desires to not meditate. As your inquiry goes deeper and deeper, you begin to realize that neither of these desires is higher than the other. Neither of these desires, in and of themselves, are the real you. In fact, you are this very *process* of struggle, a dynamic ongoing event of desire playing against desire. When you begin to see this, you're there. That's meditation—simply sitting back and watching yourself unfold gradually from moment to moment, simply *being yourself* from moment to moment.

Anxiety can arise when you first sit down to meditate, and are surprised by the "monkey mind" phenomenon. The more you try to hold your mind to a single point, the more it races around like an enraged monkey trapped in a cage. The smaller you make the cage, of course, the wilder the monkey gets. Maybe you have thought of yourself as a very calm person in the past. Now you begin to see that your mind is always racing, even in your calmest moments. This kind of identity crisis is nothing other than a growth pain. It is not that your mind is actually racing around in some new frenzy, remember. It's been doing this the whole time—you have just never settled down long enough to notice. With any boundary stretch, there are going to be some aches and pains. That said, if you are *not* experiencing some discomfort in the beginning, you have probably yet to ask the fundamental question: "Who am I, really?"

Still, it is important to stabilize your anxiety enough so that you can work with it. If you come out of a session feeling very uncomfortable and agitated, you are likely to build an unconscious association between spiritual practice and misery.

- Try relaxing your posture a bit during practice.

- Let your eyes gaze toward the floor.

- Try relaxing your concentration just a bit. Focus loosely on your object, but let your mind wander a bit if it wants to.

- Rethink concentration practice as *relaxation* practice. If you relax so much that you nod off a bit, then so be it. The very recognition of, "Wow, I relaxed so much that I fell asleep!" is still meditation.

Once you have built a more positive association with meditation sessions, once your mind has begun to calm down a bit, then you can go back in and attempt a more intense concentration.

For certain personality types, there tends to be a very fine line between skillful discipline and self-abuse. Between sessions, begin to ask yourself, *Now why am I doing this again? Am I mostly doing this out of guilt or out of an authentic desire to increase my capacity for love, enjoyment, and understanding in my daily life?* If you find yourself getting more and more tense as you continue your daily meditation, the best meditation may be just to quit practicing formally, but continue to ask yourself, *What's all this anxiety about? What's so scary about sitting still for five minutes and concentrating on my breath?*

Take a look at your daily life and maybe you will notice that you tend to surround yourself in noise and distraction. Maybe you come home from work and turn on the radio and TV, get on the phone and eat at the same time—one stimulus after another, one distraction after another, but what exactly are you avoiding? What are you so frightened of that you spend so much time and energy trying not to notice it?

If you continually encounter anxiety in formal or informal practice, the best practice for you right now might be to take one night per week to go out to dinner by yourself at a dimly lit restaurant. Have a glass of wine with your meal and just relax. Watch how your mind tries to agitate you, get you involved in this or that dilemma. Watch it all happening and then, very gently, just bring yourself back to your food, your wine, the music in the background. If you get distracted, so much the better. That just gives you the opportunity to consider and reconsider, *Now, what am I getting distracted from?* Let this be your meditation until you learn to not fight yourself so much, learn that there is nothing scary about relaxing into your own quiet, personal space. I can promise you: No matter how much you relax or how much you fight, you are not going to find anyone or anything inside your own mind other than yourself.

Do anything long enough—work, meditate, vacation, sleep—and you are bound to get bored with it. David Lee Roth sings, "Gotta keep things moving, 'til my personality starts improving."[5] Such is the exact mechanism of boredom. We feel—due to an experience of deep lack, a vague hole or gap in the story of Who I Am—we have to constantly keep things moving so as not to come head-to-head with such a "something missing."

In meditation, boredom tends to take the form of a fundamental questioning of the practice itself. "Is this really working?" you may ask. "Maybe I should go about this meditation business later," you may tell yourself, "once my personality starts improving." When you really look into it, boredom is nothing other than anxiety in disguise. It is your ego's way of saying, "Better stop now. You keep at this much longer, you're likely to learn something unpleasant about yourself."

If you can stick to your guns for just a little longer, this uncomfortable, fidgety feeling of boredom tends to break wide open into something very different. It might be some deep sadness or some very high mystical experience—something very different from boredom, either way. You might think of your feeling of boredom as a feeling of dissatisfaction. "This meditation stuff is okay," you may think during your session, "but still, there is something missing." Once again, you're right. There probably is something very important missing, at least on one level. Formal meditation practice aside, you can probably see this very same pattern of something missing playing out in the rest of your life. You go to dinner, you come home, you have some ice cream, you watch TV. . . . It's one thing after another just to avoid this feeling of boredom. You know that dinner wasn't perfect and you know that TV wasn't perfect, but isn't that just the way things work? Well, yes and no. The more you are able to look straight and deeply into your experience of boredom, the more satisfaction you start to enjoy in the simplest of tasks. All of a sudden, dinner isn't perfect, but it's getting there. Like every aspect of your daily life, every simple, mundane experience, it is simply getting more and more perfect in its imperfection. As your vision improves, your capacity for direct perception becoming increasingly refined, you begin to conceptualize these imperfections as colorful enrichments, much in the way antiques are considered valuable not despite of, but because of, their seeming imperfections.

As you begin to pay more attention to your mind, you start to discover there is a whole symphony of experience inside every moment of what you used to call boredom. Maybe it's still not very pleasant, but at least there is always a movie on after all. Boredom was just the name, as it turns out, you were accustomed to giving this particular feature. Pleasant or otherwise, it is still a movie worth watching. It's your own movie, after all, so there has to be some compelling reason you keep showing it, right?

Still, if boredom persists past a certain point, it probably is a sign that you are ready to move on, maybe to the next level of practice, maybe to something else entirely. Try a practice that's more "exciting" for a while. Dedicate your meditation sessions to visualizing your most taboo fantasies, maybe. You know what they are. If not, sit down and wait. They'll come. Now *this* is an exciting practice, no matter how you look at it. Love it, hate it—either way you are not going to be bored. But watch how your mind starts trying to trick you. You start saying to yourself, "Well, this isn't *really* meditation, after all. This is just daydreaming. Maybe I should get back to the real thing, the thing I started out with in the first place." So there you go, moving and moving, waiting on your personality to do something interesting. The best thing I can tell you about boredom is this: There's no such thing. It's a decoy, a red herring, saying, "He went that way!" Push just a little harder, hang on just a little longer, and you will start to see through your boredom. Rest assured, whatever is on the other side is never as scary, or as boring, as you thought it might be.

Take your pick—backache, neck ache, leg cramp, eyes burning—it won't be long until you run into some form of physical pain. In forceful zhiné, pain is nothing more than another distraction, another scarecrow guarding the fields of deeper awareness. It's that crazy monkey all over again, banging his knuckles on the bars, chewing his own tail—anything to avoid sitting still inside that damn cage. Stick to your object of focus with sufficient intensity and these physical distractions will disappear. If not, switch your object of focus to your very pain itself. Dive deeply, deeply into it. Go in way behind the hurt and what do you find? If there is going to be hurting, there has got to be someone who's hurting, right? Intensify your focus, become the hurt itself, dissolve into the very pain itself. When you do this with sufficient intensity, you discover a rather bizarre, closely guarded secret: The pain is nothing other than yourself. Which is not to say you are this bad thing, this negative thing that wishes pain and hurt on the world. Quite the opposite is true.

Let's pretend you are losing your memory very quickly, so every day you keep trying to leave yourself notes all around the house reminding you who you are, and what you are supposed to be doing that day. All too often, by the time you find these notes, you have already forgotten you were the one who wrote them so you simply discard them and go around confused all day. Something is missing, you vaguely realize, but what? Well, that's what pain is: a kind of reminder note your higher self has left behind for you. In this context, physical pain is a way of saying, "Hey! Remember me!" See past this little scarecrow called physical pain so you can remember who left you this note in the first place. *You did.* The Self did. However you may happen to feel about the various experiences you may encounter in concentration practice, you are the one making all this stuff happen—you just can't necessarily remember why you are experiencing these things just now. Properly understood, physical pain is nothing more than a pointer, a flashing red light meant to indicate some other kind of spiritual or emotional discomfort. The more you can relax into the pain, accept the pain rather than guard against it, the less pain there is, the less distracted you are.

Ironically, tensing, both mentally and physically, in an effort to avoid or lessen pain, is the very cause of pain itself. When perceived directly, while calmly watching from outside of the habitual mental box we all tend to get lost in, you observe that physical pain hurts to the degree that it divides the whole, splits you into two parts: the hurter and the hurt. Consequently, as you merge these two, dissolve the seemingly separate experiencer of the pain into the experience of pain itself, the hurting stops.

Remember that all of this requires a balancing act. Many of us are very blood-thirsty when it comes to improving ourselves, or reminding ourselves of our whole, organic nature. We may be tempted to bring so much physical pain to ourselves that it is no longer a helpful tool, but another means of inflicting guilt and misery. If you are not sure which variety of pain you are experiencing—the adaptive kind or the pathological kind (not that there is really a difference)—look into it and see. If you try and you try, but you fail to see through the pain, fail to merge with it, just give up. For a little while just try not hurting—an extremely useful meditation in its own right. Take some aspirin. Go get a massage. Take a day off from work. Do all this, but pay attention. I can promise you, whatever was causing the physical pain in the first place is still going to be there—it has just changed forms. One of the lessons meditation teaches us is that body and mind are one—*there can be no physical pain without mental pain and vice versa.* Even so, if you feel more comfortable recognizing yourself in nonphysical discomfort—stress about paying your bills, for example—than you do a physical discomfort such as a headache or a backache arising in con-centration practice, then go ahead, make this avoidance of physical pain your object of focus. The most important thing, whatever your individual means, is simply to recognize yourself, to remember the One Self that resides within your spiritual center. Find yourself out there enough times, recognize reflections of yourself over and over in the various problems that your daily life brings home, and you may start to find it a relief to just sit down and watch your breath. You are that, too, after all. You are your own, simple, day-to-day breathing process, but at least you know who is doing what in this scenario. Hurts will arise, both physical and mental, only now there are no bosses to blame, no spouses, no neighbors. For better or worse, it's all you in there, watching yourself watching yourself, time and again falling into the same old patterns of tension and avoidance, repeatedly getting stuck in deeply ingrained patterns of self-abuse. Unpleasant as such experiences may be, they can be highly useful tools—very effective reminder notes—only this time you remember who is writing a note to whom.

Signs of Progress

Beginning meditators might want to practice for a few weeks before reading the following list of signs of progress. Otherwise, you are likely to get distracted in your practice, spending too much energy on obtaining these specific results as opposed to simply sticking with your object of focus.

Remember: The following signs are not the goal, in and of themselves. They are simply reminders that you are on the right track, fruits of your labor. The deepest sign of positive results is always an improvement in the overall quality of your daily life. Do you feel more calm and at ease? Does your life make more sense? Are you able to relax and enjoy yourself more? Are you connecting with others around you more deeply? These are the real goals of any spiritual practice. Always shoot for these and the other signs will appear of their own accord when it is time for you to move on to another practice. When you begin to see some of the signs listed below on a regular basis, you are probably ready to move on to the next stage of concentration, natural zhiné:

- You can consistently sit for 20 minutes or more in intense concentration.

- Your breath becomes very slight, a bare trickle.

- Your body feels very relaxed and permeated by a kind of warm, electric tingle.

- You begin to shake, almost as if vibrating with a slight electric current. This is the result of increased kundalini, or life energy, beginning to rise up your spine.

- You feel almost paralyzed at the end of your session, having difficulty breaking your concentration from your object of focus.

- You begin to wake up in your dreams at night (a process known as lucid dreaming), or have dreams in which you are meditating.

- You feel a lightness in your head. You may feel a kind of dizzy light or fogginess between and slightly above your eyes or at the crown of your head.

- Your gaze "locks in" to your object so that you no longer need to blink or swallow.

- You have sudden bursts of intense emotion. You may feel like crying, screaming, or dancing with joy.

- You want to practice more and more.

- You accidentally fall into meditation at various times throughout the day.

- You can turn on a state of concentration almost automatically.

Various meditation systems have numerous objective standards that allow the student and the teacher to measure the student's progress. There is simply no foolproof means, however, to evaluate spiritual progress by objective measures of any sort. The only truly reliable indication of progress is your own growing feeling of confidence. Move on to the next stage when *you're* ready to move on. It's probably much simpler than you think.

Natural Zhiné

The practice of natural zhiné is not so much the application of a new method as it is a considerably deeper understanding of the concentrated state. By this point, you have begun to notice that even when you loosen the clamp of your focus a bit, it still tends to stick on its own. Easily able to sit in intense concentration for 20 minutes or more, you no longer have to struggle against various distractions such as external noise, thoughts, etc., as you are realizing they need not take you away from your object. If forceful concentration is a single point of light, natural concentration is a point of light surrounded by a loose haze. Through this haze, you notice more and more items passing through your awareness. You begin to realize that these distractions never really stopped in forceful concentration, you simply didn't attend to them. You will notice that the mind tends to work in waves. Swirls of thought may enter your awareness for a time, then subside into a very calm state without thoughts. Throughout these waves, however, your awareness remains loosely tethered to your object of focus. Stray thoughts and stimuli are now very much a part of the intended practice itself. In fact, if nothing other than your object of focus passes through your awareness, you are probably still using too much force. There is still a certain amount of effort involved in natural zhiné relative to forceful zhiné, but the former should feel more loose and peaceful, almost as if it is running on its own fuel while you simply sit back and watch.

CULTIVATING THE WITNESS

Since natural zhiné incorporates a much larger field of awareness into its method, it is much easier to integrate into your daily life. Let's say you are working with mantra, for instance. When you get up in the morning, you may want to do a brief formal session of five or ten minutes. At the end of the formal session, however, try to keep the mantra going as you go about your daily tasks. Cultivate a little place inside your mind that attends to your mantra all day, despite whatever intense emotional experiences or complicated tasks you may encounter. This steady point of awareness is often called "the witness." As your witness becomes stronger, you learn to rest more deeply inside of it, simultaneously experiencing your life from the point of a detached observer as well as active participant. With continued practice, the very distractions that formerly tended to disengage your hold on the witness—intense anger, for example—become automatic triggers that strengthen and deepen the witness.

I should point out, however, that the use of the witness is by no means your final goal. Many meditative systems place way too much emphasis on the cultivation and maintenance of the witness. Even when you can consistently maintain a single object of focus throughout your day, there is a certain degree of duality in this practice, a division of your self into two distinct parts—witness and witnessed—which necessarily perpetuates a slight, albeit calm, dissatisfaction. Although this division can be useful along the way, it gets discarded in the end. Think of the witness as training wheels right now. It is there for your safety so you can learn to ride without the fear of falling. As your confidence increases, however, it is much more satisfying to ride through life without your safety wheels. To sit around *watching* yourself eating ice cream simply isn't as deep, or satisfyingly "dangerous," an experience as just *eating* ice cream. It sounds simple, I know, but don't underestimate the profound beauty in the process of cultivating and, ultimately letting go of, the witness.

NO OBJECT OF FOCUS

As part of the process of developing natural zhiné, the Dzogchen teachings recommend meditation without an object. This is a slight mislabeling, because wherever you have meditation practice, you are going to have an object. Perhaps a better way to think of this practice is meditation with a very subtle object. The technique is very simple. Imagine a small sphere of white light about twelve feet in front of you. As you watch it, allow it to slowly dissolve into space. When it is completely dissolved, you will find yourself loosely focused on space itself. It's not that you should try to focus on the specific area of physical, external space itself, but rather, allow your awareness to turn inward, becoming fascinated by the vast internal space of your own mind. Somehow, your fluid process of focus has become the object of focus itself. You are beginning to point your awareness back onto itself. When I perform this practice, I feel as if my head is very light, almost dissolved into space itself. I feel a very relaxed kind of glow residing in the middle of my forehead or opening out of the top of my head. This feeling of open space will begin to "turn on" more and more, throughout various experiences, allowing you to feel much less constrained by your anxieties and troubling emotions. All of these difficult emotions are still there, but now they have got a lot more room to run around in. You have made the monkey's cage much bigger, and he was already starting to settle down quite a bit anyway. When you find that you can keep this spacious feeling the majority of the day—or, more accurately, when you begin to discover that spaciousness begins to maintain *itself* throughout the day—you are probably ready to proceed to ultimate zhiné.

Stalking—The Toltec Method Concentration

As a way of introducing ultimate zhiné, I would like to present a fascinating practice that the Toltecs (practitioners of ancient Native American shamanistic techniques) call "stalking." Much like ultimate zhiné, stalking lies somewhere in the twilight between concentration and contemplation. When you have begun to gain stability in both forceful and natural zhiné, you are likely ready to try stalking. One of the primary differences between stalking and the concentration practices we have examined so far is that stalking uses much more complex objects of focus. Let's consider, for instance, the act of driving to work every morning. If you were to make a concentration practice out of this task, you would need to apply a much looser focus than you would when following each breath, for example. Moreover, the quality of the focus itself would be a little different, as it would be "roving" constantly from one aspect of driving to another. If you allowed your awareness to focus too intently on the feel of the steering wheel in your hands, for instance, you might find your attention to the road lacking. If you attended too much to the other vehicles on the road, you might forget to take the proper exit, etc. The relatively broad, freely roving focus you apply in such a task is very similar to the focus you are refining in the practice of stalking.

Don Juan tells Castañeda about how his own mentor tricked him into an act of stalking when he was just beginning his own Toltec training.[6] He convinced don Juan that he was being pursued by a dangerous monster of sorts and that don Juan needed a disguise. So don Juan adopted the disguise of a woman and, over time, learned not only to dress like a woman, but also to walk, think, act, and feel like a woman. For all practical purposes, we might say don Juan *became* a woman in that time due to this intense focus.

In don Juan's language, such an act would be described as a shifting of the "assemblage point" (I will further discuss this idea in chapter 10) to the same *setting* as that of femaleness. To put it differently, consider all conscious beings as inhabiting one, jelly-like pool of awareness. One half of this pool tends toward a so-called feminine character or texture, whereas the other half tends toward the masculine. Women are simply those individual points of awareness within this shared, jelly-like consciousness that are mostly identified with those areas of that pool that we call "womanly." There is no intrinsic reason, then, that men, who necessarily share this jelly-like field of consciousness, can't also learn to shift their individual awareness into those womanly regions, thereby identifying with femaleness. In fact, don Juan claims that some Toltecs became so adept at the art of stalking that they could literally switch their gender at will, not to mention adopt the forms of certain animals and exotic astral manifestations.

Much less dramatically, each of us shifts our assemblage point to some degree whenever we empathize with another individual. In effect, we are moving our own point of awareness very near that of the other individual's so that we can temporarily share his or her unique perspective inside our communal pool of awareness. We are walking in his or her shoes, we commonly say. According to don Juan, such shifts, when performed with expert focus and precision, make extraordinary acts such as mind reading and telekinesis possible.

Of course, stalking need not be nearly so dramatic as gender switching, bodily transformation, mind reading, and so forth. Let's look into three everyday behaviors—or specific locales within the field of communal awareness—which are particularly useful to stalk: kindness, fearlessness, and absurdity.

STALKING KINDNESS

To stalk kindness, you apply a constant focus on the needs of others. Feelings of anger and irritation will continue to arise, as will other distractions such as your own anxiety. Such naturally arising energies should not be considered as obstacles to the practice, but rather as an essential part of the very practice itself. The goal of the practice, I should emphasize, is not to simply act kindly. Stalking is a very refined art of focus. To behave kindly when you have no other competing thoughts or feelings isn't exactly stalking. As you try consistently to manifest kind behaviors despite contrary feelings, you begin to notice something very interesting: To perfectly stalk kindness, you *have* to cultivate an authentic empathy and love for others. If you just "put on" kindness, when strong contrary feelings such as anger arise, if you lack sincere empathy, you are unlikely to maintain your kind disposition.

You are learning to become an expert actor of sorts, and when expert actors describe their art, they tend to emphasize an authentic accessing of the sought-after feeling, rather than a mere "acting" of it. This is what is known as method acting. You shouldn't be concerned, then, that your acts of kindness might be somehow degraded because they are a kind of performance. In fact, the exact opposite is true. To treat others with kindness from the stalking perspective is a much richer experience than giving to some charitable organization, for example, out of some social guilt. Unlike guilt, stalking always results from sober intention rather than compulsive fear. Unfortunately, society tends to cloak blind conformity and forced civility—which are two of the most fundamental tamers of humankind's innate and, at times, reckless individuality—in the guise of genuine kindness and beneficence. Although this process of socialization certainly has its practical benefits, it is important to be able to discern between genuine kindness or morality—which is always a liberated individual choice, never a guilty obligation—and the false, small-minded mores of mass social structures, which are driven by political and economic goals. The art of stalking, however contrived it may at first seem, goes a long way to highlighting the differences between true kindness and mere obedience or social strategizing.

As with any other practice, it is best to set specific goals when stalking. Rather than resolving to practice perfect kindness for the rest of your life—a lofty resolution which tends to fall by the wayside as soon as you become very angry with your spouse, stuck in rush-hour traffic, etc.—you might simply choose to intensely focus on stalking kindness for the next two hours, or every time you have to deal with your obnoxious boss for the next two weeks. Remember: To the degree that you set an unreasonable goal for yourself, you are much more likely to ignore your moments of distraction in a defensive way. The practice of stalking kindness gains its power from unflinching honesty and ruthless self-inquiry. To fully recognize and accept when, within the context of reasonable stalking goals, you fail to concentrate upon kind behaviors, is just as effective as the acting out of those same behaviors. The ultimate goal is total self-knowledge and individual freedom—a goal which is not won by following this or that set of rules or fixed ideas.

STALKING FEARLESSNESS

One of my wife's psychology professors used an interesting treatment for patients with anxiety disorders. The specific anxieties of these individuals manifested as intense fear of embarrassment in social situations. He had one socially anxious patient gawk at a pornographic magazine in a conspicuous public setting. He assigned another patient the task of riding the bus, standing and loudly announcing each stop to his fellow passengers. Believe it or not, treatments such as these have proven very effective in the management of specific phobias. In effect, such treatments are ways of stalking fearlessness.

Whether or not you have specific phobias, you probably have a certain set of rules, conscious or unconscious, that govern your behavior regarding sex, food, intoxicant usage, relationship boundaries, and so forth. Stalking fearlessness is really nothing other than learning to bend these boundaries skillfully, making your idea of yourself, your ego story of Who I Am, much more flexible. Notice, however, you are learning to *bend* your boundaries *skillfully*—not *break* them *violently*. This simply means that rethinking some limits would be more disruptive to your much-needed ego functioning than others. To start using cocaine every day and quit your job, for example, would probably not do much in the way of making your idea of yourself more flexible. Such extremes would make most of us panic as we feel like fish out of water, our old ego story being so radically dissolved that we feel very unstable.

It is very important, then, to start with small, reasonable ego stretches. Let's say that you always allow an extra 30 minutes when leaving for work every morning in case of traffic. Try cutting it a little closer, maybe leaving only 15 minutes. Preoccupied with financial security? Treat yourself to an overpriced meal at a fancy restaurant, leaving a 30 percent tip regardless of the quality of service. Terrified of snakes? Try spending some time in the reptile house at the local zoo, and so forth.

Stalking fearlessness is, by definition, not the same thing as *being* fearless. This means you are probably going to experience some discomfort as you begin to play with some of these behavioral boundaries that have probably been around quite awhile. As with stalking kindness, the important thing when stalking fearlessness is simply to pay attention throughout the whole process. Notice how the tension builds for a while, making you rather uncomfortable, at times on the verge of panic. Notice how you feel when the tension breaks, like stepping off a crazy roller coaster. You may feel a little shaken, but undoubtedly satisfied—somehow a little larger, a little more flexible than before your experiment.

A word of caution: Stalking fearlessness doesn't necessarily save you from the negative consequences of your actions. If you don't leave as much time to get to work in the morning, you may very well arrive late. If you quit working out, you will probably gain weight. Stalking fearlessness isn't some magical solution for doing away with feared outcomes. Rather, it is a way of recognizing you remain Who You Are, your personality totally intact, even when those things which you have most feared happen to you.

One more word of caution: A drunk stalking drunkenness, a lazy person stalking irresponsible behavior, or even a charitable person stalking good deeds isn't really stalking at all. Such a situation is nothing other than an excuse, a new concept used to defend an old behavior. The point isn't to act on already established ego boundaries, but to challenge them. A truly fearless action is always an action performed without the safety net of the ego story.

STALKING ABSURDITY

There is a famous Zen story from the *Mumonkan* in which a group of monks is quarreling over the ownership of a cat. Tired of all the bickering, the Zen master calls all the monks together and threatens to kill the cat if none of the monks can speak in its defense. The monks are speechless and, as threatened, the master kills the cat. Later, the master's star pupil shows up and the master presents him with the same dilemma. "What would you have said to save the cat?" The master asks. This pupil doesn't say a word. He simply takes off his sandals, puts them on top of his head, and walks out. The Zen master remarks that if that pupil had been there, the cat would have been saved.

When I first heard the above story, I was amazed. I thought, *How in tune to the Tao, the spontaneous flow of things, must such a person be in order to break the master's code, to perform just the right action to save the cat?* These days, however, I see things differently. There was no single right action, no complex code to be broken. Instead, *anything* would have sufficed, any seemingly arbitrary behavior, were it done with true confidence and complete indifference to the outcome. We stalk absurdity in order to gain such confidence. For our purposes, an absurd action is any action done without any rational purpose, for the sake of the doing, a kind of honoring of absurdity itself.

When I was in high school, my friends and I developed a game we called "Fall Guy." The rules of Fall Guy were pretty simple. You went into some heavily populated public place and, well, fell down. The more a fool you made of yourself in the process, the more truly ridiculous you looked to gawking bystanders, the better. To the degree that we were *consciously* performing an absurd action strictly for the sake of its absurdity, we were stalking absurdity. Slipping accidentally in the grocery store in front of the checkout counter is hardly stalking anything, other than possibly clumsiness. Try anything. Spend 15 minutes writing nonsense words on paper towels. Take all the dishes out of your cupboard and put them back in again. Take the most inefficient and circuitous route possible to work.

As you experiment with these absurd behaviors, you begin to notice something quite odd: They aren't so absurd after all. All such actions will have some decidedly positive, rational consequence in proportion to your level of attentiveness. Maybe on your circuitous route to work you discover what later turns out to be your favorite seafood restaurant. Maybe when you take all the dishes out of your cupboard you realize the shelf was cracked and was about to break at anytime. Probably you will notice something much more subjective, but positive nonetheless. The more confidence you gain in the positive outcome of *all* conscious behaviors, the freer your actions become. You no longer struggle so hard to make the right decision, as you have learned that any decision is the right decision. At the same time, however, until you have this degree of confidence, it doesn't really work to fake it. To act absurdly strictly as a kind of test isn't acting absurdly at all. Rather, it is nothing other than an attempt to manipulate the Tao—a project which is always doomed from the start.

STALKING THE SELF

Performed with focus and integrity, each of the stalking practices reminds you how arbitrary is the distinction between meditation and simply living. In stalking, you decide on an intended behavior in advance. This becomes your object of focus. As you go about your business, integrating stalking into whatever daily activities, you notice how your mind reacts to this object of focus. In observing whatever thought patterns tend to distract you from your intended object, you are essentially practicing concentration. Like all concentration practice, the goal is not so much to cling rigidly to your object of focus as it is to understand better the subtleties of your mind. For this reason, a mistake in stalking need not be a mistake. A distraction need not be a distraction. Once you have understood what the real object of your stalking is, there is no way to be distracted from it. What is the real object of all stalking and concentration practice? I am, you are—The One Self, which is our very own, everyday awareness is. You begin to notice, no matter what you do, no matter what bizarre and seemingly arbitrary decisions you make, you are always the Self quietly stalking the Self.

Ultimate Zhiné

As was the case with natural zhiné, ultimate zhiné is not so much a new technique as it is the experience of a new, much more spacious context from which to understand the practice of zhiné. Ultimate zhiné is a sort of way station between concentration and contemplation, or mindfulness, which I will discuss in chapter 7. As you continue to stabilize and deepen zhiné practice, you reach a point where your concentration comes quite easily and with very little conscious effort. Moreover, having penetrated deeply into your own mind, you may have started to question concentration practice itself on some very fundamental levels. Questions such as, "Who exactly is *doing* the concentrating here?" or, "Is there *really* a difference between concentration and distraction?" may have been turning over in your mind for some time. At deeper, subjective levels still, you have begun to realize that seemingly separate mental images, thoughts, feelings, physical sensations, and so forth are not actually distinct, nameable processes. Rather, each phenomenon that you formerly regarded as a single, simple occurrence is really composed of a vast array of infinitely smaller and smaller mental instants. As such a realization of the mind's incredible subtleties—a microscopic recognition of the parts within the parts, which somehow combine to form a seamless, organic experience—forms an essential base for the practice of true contemplation, we will look into this process in more detail.

As an illustration, consider the metaphor of a color picture in Sunday's paper. From a distance, this photo seems to be one continuous image. When you look at the photo very closely, however, you see that it is, in fact, composed of countless tiny pixels, which the mind automatically hooks together in order to produce the illusion of a single, coherent image. Look closer still and you will see that each pixel is really a little splotch of ink pressed onto several tiny fibers in the paper, and each tiny fiber is really. . . . You get the idea. So it goes with something like the feeling of happiness. As you begin to watch this feeling very closely as it unfolds from moment to moment, you begin to notice all these tiny pixels of color. You begin to realize that the experience we label as "happiness" is really an infinitely complex association of physical sensation, thought, and external stimuli. Does this mean happiness is somehow less real than before? Not at all. Rather, you begin to understand that you can never really grasp such a feeling as it necessarily contains *everything*—unhappiness as well as the would-be grasper.

At this stage in the practitioner's development—when concentration practice has begun to turn back on itself, and in so doing has begun to illuminate these infinitely tiny and intricate details of the mind—there is traditionally a pointing-out by the Dzogchen teacher of the natural mind. The recognition of the natural mind is essential for your cultivation of truly spontaneous presence. It is how you learn to relax and simply *be* in every moment. I will discuss this all-important concept of natural mind, along with specific methods of mindfulness meditation, in chapter 7. In the meantime, the chapter immediately following will help you to further cultivate your recognition of these intricacies of the mind, help you to identify them while still "in motion," continually giving rise—as is their nature—to complex subjective experiences you may tend to automatically, and rather simplistically, label as thoughts, feelings, and experiences.

AWARENESS IN MOTION

You cannot understand life and its mysteries as long as you try to grasp it. Indeed, you cannot grasp it, just as you cannot walk off with a river in a bucket. If you try to capture running water in a bucket, it is clear that you do not understand it and that you will always be disappointed, for in the bucket the water does not run. To "have" running water you must let go of it and let it run.

—ALAN WATTS[1]

ne of the first techniques the beginning swimming student learns is the survival float, which is a pretty simple affair. You take a big breath, hold it, lie face down in the water, and . . . float. If you happen to find yourself in an emergency, swimming instructors tell us, it is much better to conserve your energy with this simple maneuver than it is to thrash around frantically in the water. Even the non-swimmer, should he or she become stranded in the middle of the ocean, will find this technique quite effective. Provided he or she can keep calm and not be overwhelmed with panic, even the non-swimmer should be able to stay afloat indefinitely.

The survival float is not at all a difficult maneuver, so long as you stay calm and relaxed. Imagine dumping a non-swimmer in the middle of the ocean from a helicopter, however, and flying off. Even if this individual had practiced the survival float before, the person's natural tendency in such circumstances is probably going to lean toward a frenzied thrashing about in the water. For the non-swimmer who was never even acquainted with this maneuver, it would be pretty useless to yell instructions from the shore. "Just relax! Quit trying to save yourself! Just be calm and float!"

Spiritually speaking, if concentration practice is a life raft, mindfulness (or contemplation) is the survival float. As we have so far examined in various ways, there is necessarily a rather sticky dilemma involving all higher spiritual teachings. Until you reach a certain level of development—natural mind or no—you spend a good deal of time feeling like you are stuck in the middle of the ocean without knowing how to swim. Ramana Maharshi is yelling from the shore, "Be as you are! Just relax and float!" but it's not doing you much good. The fact of the matter is, even though you are never really stuck, it sure feels that way sometimes. In these circumstances when daily life seems to crowd in upon you, you become very much like a June bug who has somehow managed to flop itself onto its back. You're desperately kicking your legs in the air, trying to fix whatever went wrong, trying to get your feet back under you. You are not about to listen to any advice to the effect of, "There is nothing to fix here. You're just getting an opportunity to see the world from a new perspective right now. Relax and enjoy the spontaneous perfection of the natural mind!"

By definition, the obstacles that most commonly make us feel stuck are emotional obstacles. We feel stuck so we are stuck. Dzogchen describes different levels of spiritual practitioner. When the most evolved practitioner encounters negative emotions, the method prescribed is that of self-liberation. In one of the Dzogchen root texts, the *Zhang Zhung Nyan Gyud*, it is said, "The five poisons are energy. . . . Seeing the five poisons as negative is a mistake. . . . Leaving the poisons in their own nature is the method."[2] Here, the five poisons are the five passions, what practitioners of sutric (Theravada and Mahayana) Buddhism consider to be negative states, or obstacles to awareness. These five passions, or negative emotions are: anger, pride, desire, jealousy, and ignorance. As with the survival float, then, spontaneous self-liberation allows the highly developed practitioner to bobble calmly through the currents of these passions without kicking and flailing. Negative emotions continue to arise, but, as the skilled Dzogchen practitioner leaves them be, leaves them in their own nature, they spontaneously resolve themselves.

Most of us, however, encounter many situations in which this seems impractical. For this level of practitioner, the *Zhang Zhung Nyal Gyud* says, "When a vision is an obstacle, you need a friend."[3] Here, a vision as obstacle refers to the negative emotions. For those of us who find it difficult or impossible to simply float along (in certain emotionally-charged situations), we need a friend, a lifeguard who will reliably jump in the deep end and lead us to safety. We need, that is to say, some practical, systematic method of working with and resolving these conflicted feeling states.

The psychologist Michael Eigen writes about this same tendency to get stuck along the path.[4] He describes a therapy client named Owen, who was a respected meditation teacher. Despite his countless hours of meditation and years of experience in teaching meditation, Owen—by his own admission—still suffered much hatred and depression. Consequently, he had a pattern of engaging his students sexually and inappropriately. Owen described these events as simply part of his karma, simply more stuff of which to be mindful. To one degree, of course, Owen was absolutely right. The highest teachings do encourage us not to judge our own actions, not to engage them with the thinking mind, but simply to be aware of them, calmly recognize the unfolding karmic consequences. At another level, however— the more practical level in this situation—Owen was simply using spirituality as an easy excuse, a convenient whitewash to cover immature aspects of his personality. Unfortunately, this sort of cover-up is all too common in the so-called spiritual community where flagrantly self-centered individuals often masquerade as masters of this and that path or system. Until we reach a certain level of authentic understanding, however, no matter how we dress our mistakes in the flashy clothes of mindfulness and spiritual language, a mistake is still a mistake.

The Emotion Tree

Contemporary psychology contains much information that can help you learn to more easily recognize, and authentically connect to, your emotions as they arise. Using these insights, you can learn new ways to relate to and work through negative states so that your awareness is less likely to get stuck in various crowded corners of your unconscious. As you become increasingly comfortable from day to day working with your most authentic emotions—however pleasant or unpleasant some of these deep feeling states may be—you are preparing the way for a deep, intuitive and truly spontaneous experience of the natural mind. In order to help structure our examination of emotional states, I have constructed a conceptual device which I call the emotion tree.

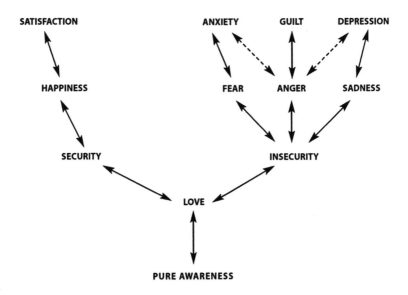

The bottom category in the tree, pure awareness, isn't exactly an emotion—not in the usual sense of the word, at least. Although pure awareness and love aren't really two distinct categories, I have chosen to delineate them as different shades, or layers, of illumination, since I believe most Westerners respond much more positively to the idea of love than they do the idea of pure awareness. If pure awareness is clear light, then love is a constantly shifting display of the rainbow spectrum. This sort of love is much more than romantic or sensual love, as such feelings tend to want to control and possess. "I'll love you forever . . . IF" is the motto of romantic and sensual love. The love that is much closer to pure awareness, however, is in no way conditional. It is an effortless, spontaneous manifestation of total acceptance and understanding. When you are moved by a beautiful piece of music, that's the sort of love I'm talking about. The music itself, for that matter, is a manifestation of love. You feel connected with the music because you are meeting and merging with it, *in* love. The same thing happens when you feel a sense of awe and wonder in the presence of nature. Unlike feeling impulses toward a romantic partner, you feel emotionally moved by the changing seasons without the desperate need to clutch at them and possess them. It is this sort of love, this sort of total compassion, that characterizes figures such as Christ and Buddha. It is the tendency of this love to flow freely, to constantly grow and emerge into new forms, rather than calcify into hard boundaries and stagnate. As the very source of all creation, this love is God, the Tao, itself.

In the emotion tree, two general categories of emotional states grow outward from this all-encompassing source. It is easy enough to see how those states on the left, which we typically associate with the positive, manifest as slightly different forms of love. If I am feeling happy, for example, I'm unlikely to protest if you assert that I am also feeling pretty secure. Likewise, we can move up on the tree and assume that, to the degree to which I'm feeling happy, I am also feeling relatively satisfied. It is this very tendency of the left side to flow freely up and down the tree, in fact, which makes us experience these states as positive in the first place. This is the state of non-grasping described by the Watts quote opening this chapter. To enjoy an open, spontaneously "running" emotional state, we must let go of our various feelings and let them run.

In a larger sense, what we are really experiencing when we say we are happy, secure, or satisfied, is a feeling of spaciousness and freedom. In such a state, our energy and awareness flows freely, often energizing those around us with a similar feeling. These positive states have an organic quality about them, which compels them to continuously merge with, and emerge from, one another, thereby producing an infinite variety of offspring. A good visual metaphor for the left side of our tree is one of a flame. This dynamic event of heat and light tends toward growth and expansion, spontaneously spreading outward into everything it touches. Significantly, fire transforms everything it touches. Practically speaking, nothing other than fire itself can maintain its original form in the wake of the powerful catalyst of flame. Love, like fire, if it is to spread, necessarily requires the surrender and transformation of all in its path. This is why the individual who has given him or herself entirely into love is described as "selfless." To be radically transformed by love, then, is to be willing to let go of our own self-importance and selfish desires.

The right side of the tree, however, is immediately more problematic, even at the conceptual level. Our first question tends to be, "How would insecurity possibly emerge from unconditional love?" Although this is probably the single most important question regarding the right side, let's save it for just a bit. It will be easier to address this difficult paradox after we look into the other branches further up the right side of the tree, to see how each of them likewise tends to resist dynamic transformation.

Although we can easily agree, in a purely intellectual sense, that anger, sadness, and anxiety all stem from our experience of insecurity, we tend to guard the distinction of these states in our daily lives rather ferociously. "No, I'm not *afraid* of anything," we say, "just angry. . . . It's not that I'm *depressed*," we tell ourselves, "I'm just a little blue right now." Contrary to the easy flow of left-side feeling states, right side states tend to contract into themselves and stagnate. A good metaphor for this category of negative feelings might be that of a monkey with his hand stuck in the gourd. As long as he is not willing to release what is in his clenched fist, he's stuck. Unlike the flame, the right side resists transformation in that it is more invested in the individual forms along the way than it is the larger process of growth. The traveler along the right-side feeling states tends to attach much more importance to the rather arbitrary boundaries between the varieties of emotional experience than does the left-side journeyer. He or she mistakes the bucket of water for the flowing stream. Some specific examples might make this pattern of resistance clearer.

THE GUILTY HUSBAND

Let's start with guilt. We will take this feeling and work it all the way back down the tree. Let's imagine a scenario in which I get a long-anticipated promotion at work and I rush home, beaming with pride, to tell my wife. My wife is not there, however. She has left a note saying that Aunt Nora has unexpectedly taken ill and she's had to rush off to take care of her. She will be back late that night, so don't wait up. I go out to dinner by myself to celebrate, feeling sorry for myself the whole time, of course, and get to bed before my wife gets home. The next morning, in discussing Aunt Nora's health over breakfast, my wife tells me she bought Aunt Nora a rather pricey birdhouse (Aunt Nora is a fanatic birdwatcher), hoping to cheer her up. I get absolutely furious. Why does Aunt Nora need yet another birdhouse? I want to know. How much money did this luxury bird palace cost? Doesn't my wife think she ought to discuss such gratuitous purchases with me beforehand? On and on I go round like this, right up until I set foot out the door on my way to work. Later that day, it sets in: guilt. I call my wife and apologize. I feel terrible about being so volatile this morning, especially considering poor Aunt Nora's failing health. Not to worry, my wife says. These things happen. In the future, she suggests, maybe we should discuss our individual purchases beforehand. Okay. So it's all been settled. I have apologized, been forgiven, a satisfying resolution reached. The only thing is, I *still* feel guilty. Now why is that?

As long as I continue to feel guilty, insisting that my wife must still be angry with me, I'm not going to get anywhere. My wife has sincerely forgiven me and I am not going to be able to convince her otherwise. Maybe, however, this feeling of guilt seems to linger because it's not *really* a feeling of guilt—not entirely, anyway. Maybe I can take my feeling state one more notch down the tree to anger. Am I still angry about the birdhouse purchase? No. That part has been settled to my satisfaction. What I'm *really* angry about, I come to realize—what I've been angry about the whole time—was the fact that my wife wasn't home to celebrate my promotion. I have no right to be angry, of course, as it certainly wasn't my wife's fault that Aunt Nora was feeling ill. Moreover, I would rather my wife tend to Aunt Nora than neglect her, so why all the irrational anger?

Well, it's true that my wife did nothing wrong here, nothing deserving of my anger. Still, when people don't get what they want, whatever the reason, they tend to get angry—not just angry in general, but angry with someone in *particular*. Rational or not, that is just the way anger seems to work. Okay, but why didn't I just recognize my anger at the time and tell my wife about it? Why didn't I just say, I realize I have no right to be angry, but I am nonetheless, so let's talk about it? Here is where we move down another notch in the tree: insecurity. I am afraid to express my anger to my wife because I don't want her to see how childishly I sometimes behave. I think that if I simply refuse to recognize my childish anger, maybe my wife won't see it either. I simply fail to accept certain immature parts of me and try to convince my wife that I'm strictly a sensible, mature adult. We will stop right here for the time being. The most important jump to make, and the most difficult, is always the last one—the one that returns negative feelings to their original source, which is always unconditional love. As I mentioned, we will visit this paradox a bit later. For the time being, let's look into another example of the right side's tendency to stagnate.

THE SAD MOTHER

Let's say I am a mother of two children. My children have recently grown up and moved away and I have been feeling a little blue. I've been eating more, getting out less, and having trouble getting out of bed some mornings. I go to see my primary care doctor. There is no medical cure for sadness, obviously, but there is medical help for depression. Helping me along to the next branch in our tree, my doctor shows me how my recent behavior fits depressive patterns. Recognizing my habitual tendency to get lost in feelings of sadness from time to time, I come to accept the fact that treatment for depression—despite my reservations about the stigma that may go along with a diagnosis of clinical depression—is in order. My doctor puts me on anti-depressant medication, which seems to help, particularly with the physiological symptoms.

Having loosened up a bit, having allowed myself to let go of my feeling of sadness long enough to recognize depressive aspects in my feeling state, I feel much better, but still a little stuck. Maybe I go see a therapist. The therapist wants to gently nudge me in the opposite direction on the emotion tree—into insecurity. The problem, however, is I'm *not* insecure. Okay, I'm sad, sure, a little depressed even, but that doesn't necessarily mean I am fundamentally insecure. After all, it would take a pretty *stable* person to raise two fine daughters like I have. This is where the therapist suggests that perhaps a big part of my personal identity has been anchored around the role of the caretaker. Now that my children no longer require caretaking, perhaps I feel unsure of myself, destabilized. Looking back, I begin to see this pattern playing out at other times in my life. There was the time I felt sad all summer when the girls were away at camp. I felt all out of sorts when the girls reached adolescence and started dating. This new level of insight helps and I feel much better, much less defensive, freer to explore my conflicted feeling states wherever they may wander along our tree. Still, it doesn't quite fix things. I *am* insecure, after all, so how do I get past this final emotional hurdle? Again, we will look into this question in just a bit.

THE ANXIOUS ADOLESCENT

One final example. Let's say I am a teenage boy and I have been feeling anxious lately. I've had excess energy, have been fidgeting in class, acting out, not able to sleep at night. I am not anxious about anything in particular, I'm just anxious in general. That seems to be the slippery nature of anxiety: *Something* seems wrong, but I'm not sure quite what. In meeting with the school counselor, I come to realize that I was extremely stressed and worried during the last several months, extremely fearful, as my grandmother was waiting on a kidney transplant. Loosening my grip somewhat on my vague anxiety, I come to realize that I was afraid, and reasonably so, that she might die. Increasing my mobility along the right side of our tree, I come to accept the necessary relationship between specific fears and a generalized anxiety. Just two weeks ago, however, my grandmother got the transplant and is doing very well. There is no longer any immediate threat of her dying, no concrete fear remaining, so why am I still so anxious?

In the weeks following my grandmother's surgery, we read *Hamlet* at school. I start to get very uneasy and fidgety in a class discussion in which we talk about Hamlet's struggle with mortality. The school counselor helps me to see that my beliefs about what happens after death are quite shaky. My grandmother's recent situation acting as a catalyst, I have started to realize that death is a real fact of life for everyone, myself included, which calls into question my whole life strategy at this time. Tracing my original anxiety deeper and deeper, I become aware of a deep, existential angst that has been just below the surface of my personality my whole life. Suddenly, I am no longer confident and secure in my present goals as none of them seems to be very useful in dealing with the inevitable fact of my death. Even so, I feel somewhat better with these new insights, more capable of consciously exploring broader aspects of my anxious feelings. Consequently, my jitteriness and sleeping problems have improved somewhat, making me feel more like my familiar self. Even so, I still can't seem to shake this constant lurking fear of impermanence, emptiness, death. *Of course* I'm insecure, but how can anyone be secure, I wonder, in the undeniable face of death?

GLAD, MAD & SAD

It has been said that there are only three core feeling states—glad, mad, and sad—and that all other emotions are essentially complications or derivations of these three. Although this statement is overly reductionistic, there is some truth to it. Assuming that happiness, anger, and sadness are at the core of emotionality, certain complications are implied. Society encourages and embraces feelings of happiness. A happy citizen is, after all, a safe and cooperative citizen. Similarly, sadness is allowed—if not enthusiastically cultivated—as it tends to be an inwardly-directed feeling state. Expressions of sadness are tolerated as long as they don't exceed socially-defined mores, manifesting in suicide and other self-destructive extremes. Anger, on the other hand, seems to stand in opposition to civilization itself. The angry citizen is, by definition, unhappy with other citizens and is therefore a social wild card.

Anger is, by far, the most consistently repressed of the three feeling states. Consequently, we would expect anger to manifest in cleverly disguised forms. We've already discussed how guilt is, in some ways, a wolf in sheep's clothing. Similarly, anxiety and depression (as represented by the secondary connecting lines in our tree) are likewise intricately tied to angry feeling states. When we don't feel able to express angry feelings outwardly, we express them inwardly, point them back at ourselves. Aggression is still there in full force—it has just become a mechanism of self-punishment. The anxious or depressed person is not necessarily "nicer" than the angry person. When working with anxious or depressed patients, one of the psychotherapist's primary goals is to circumvent the destructiveness of these emotions. From the psychological perspective, the most destructive feelings are often the most repressed feelings—regardless of their particular emotional flavor. It is especially important, then, to recognize our anger and express it honestly—albeit without indulging in childish explosions and so forth—if we are to feel whole and spontaneous. Once again, if anger is behind feelings of anxiety, guilt, and depression, and if insecurity is behind angry feelings, how do we finally resolve this restricted momentum of conflicting feeling states?

The Wisdom of Insecurity

To help us past this final emotional sticking place—the place where insecurity "gives up" and returns to the state of love—we can borrow a passage from the *Tao Te Ching*:

The Tao begot one.
One begot two.
Two begot three.
And three begot the ten thousand things.
The ten thousand things carry yin and embrace yang.
They achieve harmony by combining these forces.[5]

In the context of the emotion tree, we might translate this passage as follows:

Pure awareness begot love.
Love begot security and insecurity.
Security and insecurity begot all the other emotional states.
Each of these resulting emotional states contains both an active and a passive force,
    a positive and a negative aspect.

If we are to understand how insecurity could ever arise out of perfect love and understanding, we might begin by reevaluating our definition of insecurity. By way of contrast, let's look at security first. Imagine a kite flying high in the sky, a child running along underneath it, holding the string. We could call this kite secure to the degree that it has a fixed point of reference—a child with a string, in this case. The kite is carried here and there by the currents of the wind, as well as the child running along beneath it. Even so, the kite can operate only within the boundaries determined by other factors: the length of the string, the wind, the child's movements, etc. In another sense of the word secure, then, the kite is safe only to the degree that its movement remains limited.

To illustrate insecurity, however, imagine a helium-filled balloon released into the sky. The balloon is insecure in that, unlike the kite, it has no fixed point of reference. In one sense, this makes the fate of the balloon much less safe than that of the kite. It could easily fly too high and burst, get snagged in a telephone wire, etc. In another sense, however, the balloon has unlimited potential. There are stories of such balloons traveling across entire continents and remaining intact. For this increased potentiality of movement, we might say that the balloon necessarily risks its safety.

We can easily apply the kite and balloon metaphor to emotional states. A secure emotion, such as happiness, is, in one sense, necessarily limited in its potential creativity. We might say that all true creativity, all genuine artistry, seems to be born from a sort of longing, a loneliness, a desire for an external reflection of the artist's self. A state of perfect happiness and satisfaction, then, would necessarily lack the same urgency of expansion or change often caused by insecure feelings. This is only a provisional way of thinking about security and insecurity, of course. When taken to its extreme, such an idea would imply that the universe would have been created from the void only if the void—or God—itself was fundamentally insecure. Applied in a much more concrete sense, however, we can see the creative force of insecurity at work all around us. From a historical perspective, the overwhelmingly happy and satisfied artist seems to be a pretty rare artifact. Indeed, a disproportionate amount of the most influential artists from all periods and cultures have seemed to suffer from very volatile negative emotions, which is not to say their work itself was negative.

Although we might associate the positive emotions on the left side of our tree more with yang, an active force of heat and light, they seem to lack a certain kind of energy present in the right-side feeling states. Although fire represents an undeniable and irrepressible force, once a flame gets started, it is content to burn until it is out of fuel. It doesn't desperately require, that is to say, some change of circumstance. In the same way, happiness doesn't urgently long for the next thing, it just sort of sits there and smiles contentedly. To the degree that it moves at all, happiness, like fire, moves in a straight, well-mannered line.

Since every aspect of the universe is a manifestation of divine creativity, which makes each of our daily lives vast, ongoing works of art, the positive role of insecurity in regard to artistic expression is essential to our understanding of all negative feeling states. In this context, creative acts following strictly in the tracks of the left side, acts arising strictly out of security, would tend to be pretty straight and narrow. From our individual perspectives of relative cosmic ignorance, at least, such creations would tend to lack some of the interesting plot twists and tangents we so highly value. Instead, perfectly secure works of art—could such things ever exists— would sort of drift lazily along, easily flickering until the last bit of creative wick had been used up. This state of perfect calm and quietude is fine enough for the Zen master, perhaps, but not for those of us that are still working within the context of individual desire.

The best works of art, by contrast, seem to be much more complicated than this, much more ambivalent, delicately poised on the uncertain brink of something. Even the most famous of Shakespearean comedies, for example, however joyful and resolute their conclusions, incorporate a good deal of unhappiness and insecurity in their plots, particularly at the outset. A certain element of dissatisfaction, we could argue, is necessary fuel for any dramatic progression—our own, daily lives being the most immediately significant drama for each of us. Sadness, depression, anxiety, guilt—these emotions *demand* a resolution, build dramatic tension in that they require somewhere else to go. Such is the supposedly passive energy of yin at work, the stuff of desire, momentum, and progress. To the degree that each of us is going to participate in the bizarre Cosmic Journey, we accept and even cultivate insecurity in its many forms, however uncomfortable and frustrating those forms may be. After all, if things were perfect from the very beginning, there would be no journey whatsoever. We would have a perfectly lukewarm beginning of a tale, but no dynamically struggling middle, no satisfying, long-anticipated end.

HOLDING NOTHING BACK

Notice, however, that the passage from the *Tao Te Ching* doesn't actually divide the ten thousand things—a metaphor for every individual aspect of the material and immaterial universe—into distinct categories of yang and yin, positive and negative. Rather, it asserts that the ten thousand things harmonize through a *mingling* of these elements. The truest, most complete happiness, then, must necessarily *contain* unhappiness. Perfect security must integrate insecurity. Compare the satisfaction obtained from mowing the lawn to the satisfaction present at the moment of orgasm. Granted, mowing the lawn is a much safer experience, much less likely to stray into uncomfortable areas of anxiety and guilt, but it is rarely a really complete experience. The moment of orgasm, however, necessarily swirls all of these contrasting states into a single indescribable moment of desperation and fulfillment, yang merging with yin. Such is the very essence of genuine love and pure awareness. Many of us shy from this very experience, a truly unstructured and selfless moment of love, as we fear the negative emotions too much. We would prefer the pleasant and predictable safety of our lawns, or even the unpleasant safety of a carefully cultivated headache, to a dangerously unrestrained, insecure experience.

Without the darker emotions of the right side of our tree, life would theoretically be a very comfortable experience with very little pain and suffering. Even so, a Sunday nap, for example, is relatively free of pain and suffering, but is this what we want our lives to look like? For all save the truly enlightened individual, is this really an experience of perfect love and pure awareness? The right-side feeling states are what wake us from our Sunday nap, remind us who we are, show us that every individual being is a unique part of a dynamic, forever unpredictable, ongoing process. We are undoubtedly *alive*, these emotions remind us, and living sometimes involves a good deal of kicking and screaming.

Another passage in the *Tao Te Ching* states:

> The great Tao flows everywhere, both to the left and to the right.
> The ten thousand things depend on it; it holds nothing back.[6]

The Eastern traditions often refer to this experience of holding nothing back as that of "one taste." It's not that everything flattens out and becomes monotonous, but rather, even the most mundane experience comes to contain all of the varied flavors of existence. True loves accepts everything, even non-acceptance. As we begin to see the light in the dark, and the dark in the light, we begin to travel up and down the various branches of the emotion tree much more easily and freely. Over time, we come to appreciate, not so much the specific, and relatively limited, qualities of the distinct emotions along the way, as we do our fearless drifting from one into another. Change itself, transformation, becomes the essential emotion, the "one taste" which permeates, and provides a base for, all the other feeling states. It is then that we begin to authentically experience Dzogchen's self-liberation of emotions. We begin to live life like a passionate artist rather than a meticulous museum curator. A parade of emotions appears and disappears before us spontaneously—like "pictures drawn in water," as it is said in Dzogchen.

In one sense, then, the free life is a continual practice of insecurity, of letting go of one cherished thing and belief after another. We begin to give up our right to stake our claim to various emotional territories, as we learn that what we truly value is the constant flow from one state to another. Ram Dass tells a story about his guru, Neem Karoli Baba (Maharaj-ji). At the mention of Christ one day, Maharaj-ji falls to one elbow and is unexpectedly moved to tears. It is a very powerful moment of silence for all those involved. Then, just as suddenly, Maharaj-ji sits up and says, "The mind can travel a million miles in the blink of an eye—Buddha said that."[7]

Ironically, we can only find our security by way of our insecurity for, as the *Tao Te Ching* states, "Having and not having arise together."[8] To really "have" something, then, we must also accept that we won't have it for long. When a teacher of the law came to Jesus and said that he wanted to follow him, Jesus said, "Foxes have holes and birds of the air have nests, but the Son of Man has no place to lay his head" (Matt. 8:20). To be free is to be homeless. To be in love is to perform without a safety net. Untethered to any fixed point, we can bring all of ourselves into each passing moment, free to wander wherever both the safe and the dangerous currents of the Tao may take us.

An intellectual understanding of the emotional tree, I would like to emphasize, is by no means the most important factor here. Rather, if you are to be free, you must willingly and authentically *feel* every branch along the way, however rough or knobby. With this goal in mind, try the following two simple "feeling" exercises. You can think of these as simplified preparations for a much more involved Toltec practice, "the recapitulation," presented later in this chapter.

EXERCISE: FEELING THE PAST

■ Recall a situation in the past in which you strongly experienced some negative emotion. Don't just remember the various concrete facts or specific events that seem to have caused this feeling—actually try to feel it, try to re-experience this unpleasant emotion in all its original force and weight. Once you have reconnected with this feeling to the best of your ability, loosely categorize it somewhere within the right side of the emotion tree. Identify its primary character as sadness, anxiety, insecurity, etc. Next, try to trace this feeling along its suggested pathway, all the way up and all the way down the various branches. Rather than getting sidetracked with mere intellectualization, try to stay with the emotion, try to feel the different colors as it travels through different feeling states. At the same time, recognize the emotional similarities inherent to each of the "stops" along the right-side states. Notice, in particular, the various ways in which you are unable to smoothly flow from one feeling into the next. Be on the lookout for hidden aspects of anger coloring your emotions. Notice the ways in which you grasp at this or that form of your originally experienced feeling, while at the same time avoiding those forms that do not fit so easily with your own ego idea. Although I have indicated specific pathways in our tree structure, every feeling state is connected to every other feeling state, so experiment. Dive deep into the memory of your original negative feeling state, stretching and relaxing your habitual personality boundaries. Notice how, when the ego sufficiently lets go its white-knuckled grip, the various emotional states may travel into unexpected territory; anxiety may flow into happiness, security into guilt, etc.

EXERCISE: FEELING THE PRESENT

■ Throughout the day, notice when negative feelings arise in the present. This is considerably more difficult than the previous exercise, as we tend to push many negative feelings down below the surface of conscious awareness before they ever manage to see the light of day. They are still in there somewhere, however, so feel them as strongly as you can, but without getting stuck in them. Try not to categorize them as bad or inappropriate, but merely as distinct flavors of awareness. This is a perfectly safe exercise, for you are not trying to act out these conflicted emotions, but simply exploring them from within the familiar boundaries of your subjective space. Using the emotion tree, try to let each of your negative feelings freely flow into other feeling states. As in the previous exercise, notice your tendency to hold onto this particular emotion in favor of another one. Notice that as you relax and let go of certain habits of feeling and thinking, your emotions become very fluid. In the course of a few seconds, guilt may flow into anger, anger into insecurity, and back into guilt. While respecting the obvious differences between various feelings, try to recognize their interrelatedness, their "one taste." When your mind is sufficiently still and quiet, your personality not so fixated on itself, you begin to recognize this one taste as love itself, the indescribably pure and boundless space of the natural mind.

Defending the Fort

Most of us find it rather difficult to recognize our negative emotions as they arise. All too often, we may spend our entire sessions of meditation solely recognizing one positive feeling after another. Rather than genuinely quieting the mind through concentration, recognizing and accepting any feelings that may pass through our heightened awareness, we simply translate our everyday avoidance of negative states into our meditation. Every time a powerful negative feeling starts to emerge, we simply lose our awareness and get distracted until something more appealing comes up.

You can think of your ego—your individual story of "Who I Am"—as a kind of fort. Many of us mistakenly believe that we have managed to scavenge all the good stuff from "out there" and stack it up in a vault "in here," and that this vault of collected experiences, behaviors, and habits constitute our essential personality, our individual self. In reality, the individual self is barely a drop in the infinite ocean of the Self—each of our truest, spontaneously self-perfected identity. Nonetheless, because of our habitual misconceptions, we learn to defend this ego fort with all sorts of weaponry and military strategizing—psychological defenses that tend to work by simply misreporting or ignoring any uncomfortable "incoming" emotional material.

Deeper meditative practices, such as the contemplation practices described in chapter 7, try to work with emotion as it is. Before engaging in deep meditative practice, then, you need to recognize the psychological defense mechanisms continually at work in your daily life. Already, this recognition is, in and of itself, a form of mindfulness meditation. If you are to be cognizant of the ways in which your deeply entrenched mental patterns tend to obstruct your awareness in certain situations, you must apply a skillful, yet relaxed, focus. When you really begin to pay attention to your daily life, as opposed to perfecting your psychological defenses while engaging in repetitive daily dramas, feeling sorry for yourself, abusing yourself, or even sitting on the meditation cushion, it becomes much more difficult to substitute your mental fantasies for the actual, concrete reality of being. In the same way that perfect mindfulness necessarily leads to perfect psychological well-being, we could argue that perfect psychological well-being leads to perfect mindfulness. When pursued to their very end—fearlessly and with intense dedication and unrelenting focus—meditation and psychology arrive at the same place.

Even so, you need not venture far along any given path before you encounter numerous experienced psychologists and meditation teachers with some pretty huge gaps in their own development. Consequently, it is always the safest bet to integrate a variety of disciplines, thereby making use of a kind of system of checks and balances. Whatever you miss in your formal meditation sessions, perhaps you can catch in your therapy sessions. Whatever you miss when interacting with your therapist, perhaps you may catch in your solitary mindfulness sessions. Short of actually involving yourself in a therapeutic relationship, I advise you to utilize contemporary psychological thought in evaluating your meditative progress. If meditation techniques supply the actual needle and thread for sewing, psychology provides the guiding pattern, the underlying structure into which you stitch your awareness.

Psychological Defense Mechanisms and the Unconscious

Freud first "discovered" the unconscious, from which the defense mechanisms emerge, in his observation of hypnosis subjects. When given a post-hypnotic suggestion to perform some odd behavior, the subject would usually do so. When asked, however, why he was doing so, the subject tended to invent a reason. Freud deduced that the unconscious mind works to fit all behaviors into the individual's conscious idea of his or her self, his or her ego. Behaviors that don't seem to fit are simply translated into an acceptable form through unconscious defense mechanisms.

In her book, *Psychoanalytic Diagnosis*, Nancy McWilliams asserts that defense mechanisms serve two primary functions: "1) the avoidance or management of some powerful, threatening feeling, usually anxiety but sometimes overwhelming grief and other disorganizing emotional experiences; and 2) the maintenance of self-esteem."[9] Clearly, then, defense mechanisms, to the degree that they seek to avoid "disorganizing emotional experiences," are a way of "holding back," of clinging to the stagnant water in the bucket rather than entering the dynamic flow of the stream.

Defense mechanisms are generally put into two categories: primary and secondary. Primary defenses are mostly concerned with the boundary between the individual self and the outer world. They are considered primary because they develop first, in infancy, before the secondary skills of language and logic have developed. Consequently, the implementation of these defenses tends to be automatic and can be particularly difficult to detect. The general motto of primary defenses is: This is not happening.

In contrast, the motto of secondary defenses is more along the line of: This unpleasant thing happened, but I'll forget about it. Secondary defenses are more concerned with internal boundaries. The individual attempts to divide him or herself into doer and observer, and an ongoing struggle over territory then ensues. The doer can't deny the fact that an unpleasant thing was done, but the observer fights to look the other way. These defenses are developed later on, along with higher cognitive functions such as language and abstraction. They tend to be more sophisticated than primary defenses in the sense that they interact with the conscious mind in a more direct way and are thus more flexible and easier to work with.

To better understand the intricacies of the unconscious mind, I will provide some specific examples of each of these defense categories, starting with the primary. What follows is intended to give you a general feel for how these defenses work and is not meant to be a comprehensive list. My emphasis is on the ways in which the unconscious mind overworks to protect an essentially imaginary boundary.

As you read descriptions of the following psychological defenses, I suggest you keep in mind the words of Shakespeare's *Hamlet*: "The lady doth protest too much, methinks." Psychological defenses are not strictly for "crazies." In fact, most of us use most of the following defenses with some regularity. Instead of *defending* against them, then, try to recognize how each of these mechanisms might play out in your daily life. Ironically, the more we say, "Well, *that* particular defense certainly doesn't apply to me," we are likely just protesting too much.

Primary Defenses

Withdrawal is one of the most common primary defenses. When an infant is over-stimulated or disturbed, what does it do? Often enough, it simply goes to sleep, or withdraws from the situation. We carry this early pattern of avoidance with us into our adult lives. Imagine the husband who, every time his wife brings up an unpleasant subject, simply ignores her, absorbs himself in the evening paper, loses himself in drink, etc. Or imagine the insecure person who simply withdraws from all social contact by retreating into himself, spending most of his time alone, lost in his own ideas and fantasies. At the core, such seclusive strategies aim to avoid the unpleasant, yet truly unavoidable, facts of human reality.

Denial is a similar primary defense to that of withdrawal. When confronted with some unpleasant fact or situation, the individual simply denies that it is happening. Ironically, denial often brings about the very consequence that the individual was refusing to acknowledge or experience, usually in a much more forceful and unpleasant manner. Like all defenses, denial is never truly effective. It tends to merely postpone the inevitable. The individual who avoids going to the doctor—far from affecting a mysterious cure for the unwanted condition—will probably admit to this feared condition only after it is much too late for medical intervention. Or consider the elderly person who, fearing death, refuses to draw up his will. He may find himself in his final hours without the security of knowing even the most basic of personal and family arrangements have been tended to.

Projection is perhaps one of the most slippery of primary defenses. In this case, the individual takes those parts of him or herself he or she wishes to disown and projects them onto someone else. As with denial, projection can become a kind of self-fulfilling prophecy. Let's say I am angry at someone, but refuse to recognize my anger. Instead, I imagine *he* must be angry at *me*. If his actions don't fit with my idea of what an angry person's actions should look like, my defense can work much "better" if I provoke him until he is actually angry. I have managed, then, to externalize my anger and encounter it as a hostile foreign object rather than an internal conflict. The problem is that, in so doing, I tend to confuse myself with other people. To the degree that I don't make a clear distinction between my own emotional states and the feeling states of others, I am likely to feel confused and ungrounded about my basic identity.

Splitting is another common primary defense, involving the artificial division of experience into highly simplified camps. Imagine how a hungry infant might react to its caretaker. The caretaker who satisfies the infant's needs is, in that moment at least, "all good." The same caretaker, when he or she happens to neglect the infant's hunger, is perceived as "all bad." The infant simply doesn't have the cognitive functioning yet to sustain object constancy—in this case, the idea that different personal reactions to an external object don't necessarily indicate different caretakers. As adults, we also tend to group people into simplified categories. When I am in a fight with someone, they seem all bad to me. I indulge myself in a long litany of complaints against her since the day we first met. Likewise, the very same boss that I have found intolerable for all these years is suddenly all good the day I get that unexpected raise. The problem, of course, is that people are much more complicated than this. Even the worst villain is not without saintly qualities, nor is our most giving friend without flaws. As we become aware of this defense, we gain confidence in identifying the gray areas of personality that lie outside of our initial emotional reaction to a given person.

Secondary Defenses

Repression is the first defense that Freud identified. According to Nancy McWilliams, repression is "motivated forgetting or ignoring."[10] I was recently discussing psychology with a friend of mine who was rather skeptical of the subtle, yet pervasive role of the unconscious. I brought to his attention a handful of unpleasant experiences that had happened over the years, about which he had expressed much guilt. At first, he simply couldn't recall these events, although, by his own admission, they sounded probable. After I supplied a few details, he recalled these events in full, amazed that he had so easily and totally forgotten them.

It is best to remember that the unconscious, particularly when dealing with very sophisticated secondary defenses, is very subtle and crafty. Still, no matter how efficiently the unconscious seems to have erased things from our memory, they are still stuck in there somewhere, struggling to be found out. When we repress something, we necessarily feel a vague anxiety. Something is wrong, we are distantly aware, but what? This anxiety acts as a kind of clue or code, reminding us that there are still parts of ourselves lost out there.

Intellectualization is a very sophisticated secondary defense that is common amongst meditators. After practicing mindfulness meditation, or learning a certain psychological language, many individuals become experts at noticing and talking *about* their feelings, without ever really *connecting* to them. At a certain stage of awareness development, this is just what mindfulness meditation suggests—the cultivation of a detached, unaffected observer who merely watches the parade of various emotions go by. Although this kind of third-person-observer vantage point is useful in maintaining a certain calmness when entering the volatile spiritual path, if pursued to extremes it can easily disconnect a person from his or her emotions in a damaging way. To split ourselves into a central witness and periphery witnessed is merely a learning device as it is very dualistic. Ultimately, we learn to merge our witness with our actions and feelings themselves so that there is no boundary between the doer and the deed, or, the feeler and the felt. In the end, meditator or no, to merely observe or talk about our emotions—however accurately we have learned to observe and talk about them—is very different from fully integrating and experiencing them.

With the *displacement* defense mechanism, the individual removes feelings toward a potentially dangerous object onto a safer one. Imagine an abused child, for instance. Of course, he is angry with his parents for abusing him, but because of his dependence on them as caretakers, he perceives it wouldn't be a very wise strategy to express his anger toward his parents. Instead, he gets angry with his younger sibling, a much safer container for his feelings. As adults, we use displacement in a similar way. Studies have shown that when a spouse is unfaithful, for example, the injured party tends to get angry with the individual with whom the spouse cheated, rather than the spouse. Similarly, insecure individuals may displace anger onto minority groups. No matter how efficiently we displace our uncomfortable emotions, however, we can obviously never really work through them until we point them in the correct direction.

When an individual applies the secondary defense of *reversal*, he or she simply switches a desired role with its opposite, or complimentary role. For instance, let's say I want to regress to a childlike state and be taken care of by my spouse. I am embarrassed, however, to let my wife know that I still have such childish desires. Instead, I become the caretaker, encouraging my wife into the role of the cared for. I identify with my wife in this role and, therefore, get my cared-for fix vicariously without compromising my prideful idea of myself. Or let's say that I am very angry with my wife. I happen to believe that proper spouses should not be very angry at one another, however, so I do my best to convince myself that I'm not *really* that angry, after all. To "prove" to myself that I'm not really angry, I treat my wife with unusual kindness, pampering her to no end. My wife, as much as she is enjoying this special attention, is a little wary as she is waiting for the other shoe to drop. As with every other defense, reversal only postpones the inevitable. If I am angry with my wife, there is simply no way to truly sweep my anger under the rug. When it does finally get expressed, my anger will be even more explosive than it would have had I consciously recognized it in the first place. A good metaphor for most defenses is that of a garden hose. If you plug it up with your thumb and let the pressure build, when you remove your thumb the water comes gushing out with considerably more force than the usual, unobstructed stream. In the same way, all defenses plug up the processing of uncomfortable emotions and situations for only so long. When the defense finally gives way, the temporarily avoided emotion tends to come exploding forth in a pretty messy way.

Awareness of Defending Imaginary Boundaries

Let me clarify a few things about psychological defenses in general, both primary and secondary. First, the only thing that really makes defenses "defensive" is the fact that they are *unconsciously* employed. When we apply a self-protective strategy consciously, it tends to work much better. For instance, the problem with projection, as it is most typically employed, is that the individual never consciously recognizes him or herself as the owner of the projected feeling until it is too late. To use projection in an intentional manner, however, can be a very effective way of connecting with people, which is ultimately a self-protective investment. Take empathy, for instance. When a friend of ours is going through a tough time, we can never experience her feelings in exactly the way she is experiencing them. We can reference our own catalog of subjective experiences, however, and recall how we felt in a similar situation. We project our own feelings onto our friend and then relate to her as we would have wanted to be related to ourselves, in a similar situation. We are then using projection adaptively, a skillful means to do unto others as we would have them do unto us.

Consider the defense of withdrawal. Rather than unconsciously withdrawing from a disturbing stimulus, an artist might purposefully and temporarily withdraw from the external world, seeking refuge in his own artistic creation of fantasy. The artist is not trying altogether to avoid the harsh facts of reality in such a situation, but attempting to deal with the difficult external stimulus in a safer, internal environment in which he feels more secure. In so doing, he is choosing to consciously express his uncomfortable emotions in a relatively private way without directly entangling others. Freud called this mature drive to authentically transform disturbing emotions into something beautiful or useful "sublimation."

To be aware of our defenses, then, is much more important than trying to get rid of them. In fact, the more we struggle to override our defenses, the more violent they tend to become. When consciously recognized and accepted, psychological defenses are a perfectly natural, and often quite necessary, element of emotional experience. The problem is not with negative feelings such as anger and sadness in and of themselves. The tendency to get ourselves stuck and twisted inside our various little emotional buckets as the stream flows on around us is what causes us so many problems. All meditation practices, in fact, are themselves defenses to one degree or another. Even so, because we are, by definition, employing these practices intentionally, they tend to be much more effective means for working with uncomfortable emotional experience than are our habitual and often haphazard unconscious mechanisms of self-preservation.

Second, the boundaries we imagine we are defending are just that: imaginary boundaries. Although some psychologists might disagree and assert that the ego is a very real thing, the wisdom of the spiritual traditions claims that the ego is really nothing but our *idea* of the ego, an illusory bucket of illusory water. Trying to defend an imaginary boundary is very much like a child trying to defend an imaginary friend. It is never really clear whether the battle has been won or lost because there was never any real chance of whatever illusory treasure being taken from us in the first place.

In Buddhism, it is said that the "unborn" or the "not-become" is necessarily eternal. How can that which never existed in a concrete sense perish in a concrete sense? In the same way, our imaginary friends such as our egos can never be taken from us, as they never belonged to us in the first place. To say that the ego is empty or illusory, however, is not to say that it is not important or should be devalued. In fact, quite the opposite is true. The *Tao Te Ching* says:

> Thirty spokes are united around a hub to make a wheel
> But it is on its non-being that the utility of the carriage depends.[11]

In the same way, the "utility" of the individual rests on the emptiness of the individual's ego. As I mentioned earlier, the hole makes the donut. When you begin to watch the imaginary ego at work with increasing focus and intensity of awareness, you see that the ultimate absence of a true ego is not really an absence. Rather, it is a limitless, indefinable presence of the Self—a very real entity but one that is forever beyond conceptual grasp.

A third and final point regarding defenses—and this could be said about all other psychological matters as well—is that it is not enough to simply understand them in an intellectual way. Due to the unconscious nature of defenses, it tends to be much easier to observe the defenses of others rather than your own. The real point is to learn to observe, and fully experience, your own defenses in action, thereby bringing them into fluid, moment-to-moment consciousness. Many Westerners, in particular, find the path of psychotherapy very useful in this pursuit. Others choose to follow the paths of formal spiritual practice such as meditation. Whatever method you get started with—and, as I emphasized earlier, a multiple-disciplinary approach can be uniquely effective—the more you become aware of your psychological defenses, you see that they are present in virtually all of your daily activities. At this point, the specific methods you use to observe them is not so important. So long as you are able to authentically own up to your defenses as they arise time and again, your simple, day-to-day relationships become your most effective therapy, your most integrated meditations.

Even so, for many of us, the idea of being aware of our defenses can become one of the most crafty defenses in and of itself. Many astute psychologists are themselves unbelievably defensive, as are a good many skilled meditators. For this reason, regardless of your level of psychological or meditative expertise, it is often very useful to have certain stable guides along the way such as therapists or meditation teachers. As they are much less likely to fall for the same tricks you may play on yourself, other relatively mature individuals can often serve as reminders and road signs along the way when you unknowingly stray from the path. Even when such a person is imperfect in his or her own awareness—as he or she will inevitably be—this individual can be a valuable sounding board, someone who is less personally involved in your daily dramas, making that person a much more objective commentator.

EXERCISE: EXPERIENCING DEFENSES IN ACTION

■ Choose a quiet place free from distraction and sit in a comfortable posture. Using the concentration method of forceful zhiné (see page 95, chapter 5), apply intense focus to your breath or some other suitable meditative object for 5–10 minutes. Then release your focus, letting your mind wander freely, without attempting to restrain or organize your awareness in any way. Inevitably, your mind will eventually drift to some emotionally charged experience—some circumstance involving unfinished emotional business. Allow your awareness to explore this event freely, manifesting loose and nonlinear images, feelings, and associations. When you are done sitting, jot down any of the fragmented mental phenomena arising from this emotionally-charged event that you can recall. Review this list, assuming this event is "unfinished," due to various restrictive defense mechanisms at work. When you review the list of psychological defense mechanisms presented in this chapter, can you identify some of them at work in this scattered, unstructured moment of your awareness?

How We Store and Process Emotion

Most metaphysical traditions describe the individual self as being divided into various layers. Yoga and Kabbalah, for instance, divide the self into a handful of sheaths, each of which vibrates at a different frequency. Let's consider the individual as being divided into three primary layers: the conceptual mind, the physical body, and the subtle body. The self is actually an organic whole that flows seamlessly from layer to layer, but you can think of these various layers as differing methods of access, different pathways into the total, nondual Self. Although many systems extensively categorize these layers according to "lowest" and "highest," I don't find this way of thinking to be very useful. As disciplines such as Dzogchen and Zen emphasize, whatever means works for a given person is that person's highest method of access.

THE CONCEPTUAL MIND

Although "mind" has numerous definitions, the conceptual mind is the part that tends to deal with complex phenomena by representing them with a sort of shorthand, or concept. When we say we feel angry, for instance, we are using the *con-*

cept of anger to represent a highly complex process that takes place on all of the layers simultaneously. This method of shorthand reference is fine, so long as we remember that the concept of "angry" is, indeed, just a concept. As they say in Zen, it is important not to confuse the finger pointing at the moon with the moon itself. Emotions at the conceptual level tend to manifest in a variety of ways, typically in a verbal form. For this reason, "talking cures" such as psychotherapy tend to be a great way to access this layer. Oftentimes, we may discover that we sort of stumble onto our feelings while trying to discuss our state of mind. Unstructured talking and loose verbal associations, then, can be a very effective means to uncovering buried material.

Similarly, emotions tend to represent themselves as repetitive images and thoughts at the conceptual level. Let's say that I am in an argument with someone, only it is not my overall disposition to recognize or express anger at the verbal level. When I really pay attention to what is going on internally, however, maybe I notice that there is a persistent little film clip playing somewhere in the back of my head in which I throw the cup of water I am drinking into that person's face. Such a visual cue is a kind of conceptual code or reminder that, whether or not I put it in language, I am decidedly angry. Or maybe I find myself, seemingly for no reason, repeatedly "thinking" the lyrics to a certain song throughout this argument. "You ain't nothin but a hound dog. . ." keeps playing in my head, over and over. Well, if I stop and look into the content of these lyrics, assuming—and rightly so—that nothing in my head is there without some purpose, I might recognize that I am quite angry, after all. Although my anger may not manifest so easily at the verbal level, I am angrily battling with this person at the conceptual level nonetheless, privately conceiving of him or her as a whining dog who "ain't no friend of mine."

For many of us, although the conceptual level seems to be the most readily available layer of subjective experience, it seems to be the hardest to follow into the deepest levels of the self. It is tempting to intellectualize at this level. I observe my repetitive images and thoughts that seem to indicate anger. Therefore, I must be angry. Even if I express my anger verbally at this level, it is very likely to take the form of a concept—something more akin to algebra than it is an organic feeling state. Since a concept is always a mere representation of a complex process, it is important to find a way to access the deeper, more complex layers of the emotion as well.

Moreover, by the time an emotion has surfaced at the conceptual level, we have probably been struggling with it for quite some time on deeper, more unconscious levels. For this reason, we can use conceptual recognition of our emotions as a sort of marker from which we can then try to retrace the flow. As with each of the three layers, rather than clinging to the conceptual layer as the all-important layer of subjective experience, we can try to use the insights gained from this layer to access what is going on in the other layers.

THE PHYSICAL BODY

A deeper layer in which emotions are stored and processed is that of the physical body. Deeper doesn't mean more important; in this context, it simply means less conscious. Let's say, for example, that I am suffering from a headache and stomach cramps. Although I must be, by definition, conscious of this physical pain in order for it to be a recognized problem or distraction, I may not be aware that it is inextricably tied to a feeling of anxiety, for instance. In Gestalt psychotherapy, the mind and body are viewed as intricately connected parts of a whole. A disturbing feeling such as anxiety, in the view of Gestalt therapy, would simultaneously present itself at the level of body and mind. Oftentimes, when Getsalt's founder, Fritz Perls, suspected a client was not able to dive deeply enough into the unconscious to perceive authentic emotion on a conceptual level, he might redirect the client's awareness to his or her physical body, being a sort of reminder or placeholder for uncomfortable feeling states. In one such recorded instance, a man claimed that he felt relatively comfortable and was mostly free, at that time, from anxiety or emotional tension of any sort. Perls redirected the man to his knee, which had been bouncing anxiously throughout the session. In being guided to examine an unconscious physical manifestation of his anxiety, this man was able to recognize his true feeling state on a consciously mental level as well as the physical.

Many schools that work with the body such as Reiki, Hatha Yoga, and Rolfing believe that the physical body stores incompletely processed emotions as tensions in the physical body, a kind of "psychic armor" manifested at the material level. These schools work directly with the body, trying to alleviate physical tensions, a process that likewise tends to release psychological tensions. In my experience, physical sensations are often more reliable as indicators of emotions than are the products of the conceptual mind. As we live the vast majority of our daily lives from the level of the conceptual mind, it is simply too easy for most of us to trick ourselves at the strictly conceptual level. The body, however, seems much less prone to deceptions of this sort. Carefully observing our own bodily sensations, as well as the physical actions and reactions of others, can often provide much more immediate access to unfinished emotional material.

BODY SCAN EXERCISE

■ To experience how the body acts as a mirror of psychological states, you might try this brief exercise. Recall a particularly disturbing event or situation from the past. As you focus on the details of this event, trying to recall your emotional state at that time, perform a quick body scan from your head to your feet. To the degree that the recalled event was a traumatic one, you are likely to notice subtle muscular tensions in your head, neck, stomach, or anywhere else where you tend to store anxiety. As you encounter these various tensions, consciously relax them. Allow your entire body to relax into as comfortable a posture as possible. As these physical tensions decrease, you are likely to notice the emotional disturbances of the event likewise decreasing, if not disappearing altogether.

THE SUBTLE BODY

The deepest, least conscious, of our three layers of subjective experience is that of the subtle body. Most of us, in fact, are only vaguely conscious of its existence. The subtle body, also called the energy body, dreaming body, or astral body, is a luminous, egg-shaped tapestry of energy, emanating from and surrounding the physical body. Most spiritual traditions speak of certain areas where the subtle body intersects the physical body, usually called *chakras,* or energy centers. From each of these chakras, a complex system of luminous fibers extends outward, connecting us with the energy bodies of others, as well as energetic aspects of our environment. We can think of the subtle body as the first mechanism that encounters emotional material through its subtle energetic exchanges with other such bodies. Most of us tend to be almost entirely unconscious of such interactions until they become manifest at the physical level as various concrete sensations. Even then, we are often unlikely to recognize the original source of these physical sensations, which is typically unfinished emotional material gathered by the astral body. By the time our emotions are finally transmitted to the conceptual mind, then, they are often so diluted that they seem rather thin and empty.

All of us, however, have experienced moments in which we perceive material at the deep layer of the subtle body. For example, we might sometimes have a very strong impression of someone before we "know" anything about them. He or she simply gives off a certain kind of positive or negative "feel." Such a precognition is simply our energy body assessing his or her energy body. Or consider those moments of extremely high stress in which we seem to somehow shift gears and perform unusually smoothly and efficiently. The small mother who lifts an automobile to save her child is a perfect example. In such rare instances, the energy body simply takes over, bypassing the more cumbersome physical body and conceptual mind.

One of the most direct ways in which to access the subtle body is through dream material. Although each of us dreams on a nightly basis, our memories of such instances are often rather foggy and incomplete as our conceptual mind simply wasn't able to track what was going on at the time. Working with various meditative techniques and practices, we become increasingly aware of these subtler levels of feeling and intuition, and are thereby much less likely to get stuck in this or that negative emotion. Being of a much finer "vibration," the subtle body tends to be more malleable and fluid than are the levels of the conceptual mind and physical body, and thereby much less resistant to letting go of emotions and experiences. As we begin to free up the various knots in the astral body, we are likely to notice significant changes in our experiences of dream and sleep, as this is where our subtle body functions most obviously, while our physical bodies and conceptual minds are resting. (This phenomenon, along with specific techniques of dream yoga, will be considered in detail in chapters 10 and 11.)

The Recapitulation Method of Processing Emotion

The recapitulation is a Toltec exercise designed for direct access to emotional knots stored in the energy body. In releasing these knots, you release physical and psychological tensions, as each of these layers is intricately related. So far as I know, the first mention of this Native American practice appears in the work of Carlos Castañeda, in which he recounts don Juan's explanation of the recapitulation. More detailed explanations can be found in the works of Ken Eagle Feather, Taisha Abelar, and numerous other Toltec practitioners. I present this exercise here in a slightly modified form that I have found to be very effective.

STRUCTURING

Before beginning the recapitulation, it is first necessary to structure your past in such a way as to allow easier access to buried material. Your goal is to eventually include all layers in the process, the conceptual mind being one of them, remember, so it is best to choose a logically organized format that your mind and body can get hold of. To do this, make a list of a few categories of people from your past. Your categories might include sexual partners, high school friends, and present co-workers. I have found it is also useful to include other categories such as previous places of residence, particularly painful memories, people you strongly dislike, and so on. Whatever your categories, make a comprehensive list of every single person or item you can recall that falls under that heading.

To get started, rather than trying to fit your entire past into some complex structure, just decide on a handful of simple categories and make your comprehensive lists. Once you have thoroughly worked through, or recapitulated, these lists in the manner described below, you will be ready to choose some new categories. The ultimate goal of the recapitulation is to unblock the energy body of all repressed material. This process is very similar, though by no means identical, to psychoanalysis.

ACCESSING THE SUBTLE BODY

Having made your first series of lists, sit in a comfortable position. Try to feel your energy body emanating outward from your physical body, a foot or so in every direction. At first, it may be useful to actively imagine your subtle body as a warm, luminous sphere surrounding your physical body. Remember that the subtle body is as real as your physical body, albeit much less conspicuous to the average individual's senses. The active imagination of the astral body is a way to access this very subtle level of awareness. Staying focused on the subtle sensations of the energy body, breathe slowly and comfortably. Try to feel your awareness relaxing into the luminous space of the energy body with each exhalation. As you breathe in, feel and "see" the luminous body gathering the subtle energy from your environment and drawing it inward along luminous fibers that radiate from your naval. Feel the subtle heat at your naval as these energies are absorbed, merging with your physical body. As you exhale, feel and "see" the tensions of the physical body and conceptual mind flowing outward through these same luminous fibers. Know that with each breath, you are taking in fresh, luminous energy from your surroundings while simultaneously draining yourself of all tensions. With practice, you will begin to feel the subtle, warm glow of the energy body easily radiating somewhere halfway between your physical body and conceptual mind.

RECOVERING THE PAST

Once you feel calm and relaxed, in touch with the subtle energies of your astral body, you are ready to work with your list. Using the first item on your list as a focus, feel the luminous fibers somehow extending toward this item. Visualize this person, place, or thing as vividly as possible. See and feel it as a glowing, energetic object or experience. As you breathe, feel your energy body pulling this visualization into it, dissolving the essence of this energy into it. Allow your feelings and visualizations to wander somewhat loosely around this item of focus. Rather than intentionally choosing specific incidents to recall, focus loosely on the item from your list, allowing your energy body to take over and guide you wherever it wishes. If the images and sensations begin to come too quickly and you lose your focus, intentionally return your concentration to the list item at hand. Try not to internally verbalize your feelings too much at this stage. You can label your experiences with concepts later, after you have dealt with the material at this much deeper, pre-verbal level.

As you first begin this exercise, it may feel as if you are simply trying to remember past events. As your practice deepens, however, you will start to notice that your subtle body begins to access deeper and deeper levels of stored memories. You will begin to recall more intricate details of past events, recover more deeply buried emotional material. This exercise should be approached as a means to recover any energy that you have left behind in the past. As such, it is a way of filling in whatever "holes" may exist in your astral body, a method of untying the knots of various tensions so that your energy may flow freely and spontaneously.

INTEGRATING

As you gain familiarity with the recapitulation, you can begin to check in with your energy body from time to time throughout the day, becoming more aware of this deeper layer of your personality in various situations. If you find yourself in an emotionally draining experience, tune in to your subtle body and you are likely to notice a sort of external tug along the radiating fibers. Although negative emotions certainly won't disappear overnight, as you begin to encounter them closer and closer to this entry-level layer, you will find that they have much less of a hold on you, much less of a tendency to get you stuck in uncomfortable emotional patterns. Similarly, in situations in which you feel particularly happy and free, notice how luminously the energy body glows and radiates. Notice, in such situations, how easily you can connect to this subtle body as a very real aspect of your ordinary self.

WORKING WITH DREAMS

As the energy body is closely related to dreams and the astral plane, it provides a great way to work with dream material. Dream material tends to manifest directly from the deep unconscious layers of the self, which means it can provide direct access to emotional traces of unfinished business.

Each night before you go to bed, resolve to remember your dreams the next morning. Keep a notebook by your bed and, immediately on waking, jot down any dreams or dream fragments that you recall. You can then use the recapitulation exercise to work with this material. Visualize any fragment of the dream that stands out and try to use the astral body to reach out to this dream, drawing its energy along the luminous fibers. You will find that you are able to access much more of your dream content than you at first consciously remembered. Moreover, you will notice an almost immediate improvement in your ability to recall your dream material from night to night. This dream material has been there the whole time, collecting night after night, stored deeply within your energy body.

Due to our relative fixation at the physical and conceptual level of subjective experience, however, we typically fail to pay much attention to this subtle layer of ourselves. Recalling more dream material as you progress, you can then use this recovered content as a kind of pointer to particularly pressing unfinished emotional business. If you dream about a childhood friend of yours, for instance, try to recapitulate every incident related to this individual the next day. This process will, without a doubt, uncover some pretty surprising feelings. The recapitulation teaches you that even the most seemingly insignificant incident or situation can prove to be the storehouse of some deeply buried subjective material.

THINKING LESS

In general, the less thinking or conceptualizing you can do in any exercise involving the astral body, the better. It is the thinking mind that tends to distract you from this subtle subjective layer in the first place, demanding all of your attention so that you are unable to access these deeply buried memories and feelings. You can apply representative concepts to your experience later on as needed. The energy body, when left to work freely, will naturally seek out those places in which it is stuck. By disengaging and releasing the conceptual mind from its compulsive rambling, you shift your awareness to deeper and deeper aspects of the subtle body, thereby enabling a highly efficient cleansing and energetic recovery process.

Have Some Tea

When you feel trapped and bogged down in various concepts and methods, it might be best to relax and remember the words of the Zen master, Chih-men:

> If you understand in this way, it is still just a little bit of Zen perceptive understanding, not the whole experience of Zen.
> What is the whole experience? Go back and have some tea.[12]

It is important that you remember that all these various conceptual systems—psychology, the recapitulation, the emotion tree—are really just fingers pointing at the moon and not the moon itself. You don't need more sophisticated jargon with which to analyze emotional material, or more complex structures on which to hang your various feeling states. The point is to learn to truly connect with more of your total self, which necessarily includes the selves of others, as well as the entire Self of the whole universe.

WHEN MEDITATION ISN'T:
CULTIVATING PRESENCE

Yunton was a master of Dzogchen. He lived very simply, doing without formal religious clothing such as the traditional monk's robes, without formal meditation practices, yet surrounded by a large group of disciples. One day a Buddhist monk visited him, indignant that Yunton, a seemingly ordinary person, would pose as a master. The monk intended to test his knowledge against this supposed master, to prove him a fool in front of his many disciples. The monk showed up in his traditional robes, full of years of formal monastic learning and doctrine, and asked Yunton, "You practitioners of Dzogchen, are you always meditating?"

"What is there to meditate on?" Yunton replied.

"So," the monk said, "you don't meditate then?"

Yunton replied, "When am I ever distracted?"[1]

In paradoxical systems such as Dzogchen and Zen, it is often said that the best meditation is no meditation. Well, does this mean that a person who has never heard any spiritual teachings or never attempted any practices whatsoever is an advanced seeker? Obviously not. Meditation or no meditation, Yunton was nonetheless recognized as a Dzogchen master. Title aside, however, what differentiates an extraordinary individual such as Yunton from a person who is disinterested in all things spiritual?

Chuang Tzu said, "The one who doesn't know is right. . . . The one who forgot is pretty close. You and I aren't even close *because* we know."[2] This kind of paradoxical statement tends to make the seeker question his or her very efforts. If no meditation is the best meditation, and if the one who doesn't know is right, why bother ever trying to understand the strange and intricate workings of the Cosmic Dance? Ironically, to a certain degree, such an attitude is probably one of the most useful to adopt while following any particular spiritual path. At the same time, however, notice that Chuang Tzu didn't say, "The one who *never knew* is right." Rather, he said, "The one who *doesn't know* is right." The one who forgot is pretty close only because he did know something in the first place—he is simply not finished with his process of forgetting it.

Comparing the experience of a child to that of an adult might be useful. For a child to act like a child, carefree and unaware of the impending pressures and responsibilities of the adult world, is very different from an adult acting childishly. Here, I mean "childishly" in the most positive sense, as when Jesus said, "Except you become as little children you will not enter the Kingdom of Heaven" (Matt. 18:3). The responsible and unusually courageous adult, having been made aware of the potential burdens of adulthood, makes a conscious and informed choice when she chooses to cast them off, to "forget" them. It is not that this adult isn't perfectly mature and responsible, she is simply going about her adult affairs with the same carefree attitude a child goes about her "business." Such a choice, however, is only possible once the adult has passed through a certain process of growing up, becoming more integrated with aspects of awareness simply not available to the mind of a child. The carefree adult *consciously* chooses to be a carefree adult, whereas the carefree child is simply acting unconsciously, not yet able to fully appreciate his childish happiness.

Remembering How to Forget

In this chapter, we are going to examine the way in which mindfulness, or presence, naturally arises from the various practices we have so far described. What makes this discussion rather difficult is that presence, by definition, fully transcends any technique or effort. Alan Watts described the "method" of cultivating mindfulness as follows:

> Shortly after I had begun to study Indian and Chinese philosophy, I was sitting one night by the fire, trying to make out what was the right attitude of mind for meditation as practiced in Hindu and Buddhist disciplines. It seemed to me that several attitudes were possible, but as they appeared mutually exclusive and contradictory I was trying to fit them into one—all to no purpose. Finally, in sheer disgust, I decided to reject them all and to have no special attitude whatsoever. In the force of throwing them away it seemed that I threw myself away as well, for quite suddenly the weight of my own body disappeared. I felt that I owned nothing, not even a self, and that nothing owned me. The whole world became as transparent and unobstructed as my own mind; the "problem of life" simply ceased to exist, and for about eighteen hours I and everything around me felt like the wind blowing leaves across a field on an autumn day.[3]

According to Watts, then, two factors seem to be essential for an experience of presence: having no special attitude whatsoever, and owning nothing, not even a self. Once again, we are faced with a seemingly impossible method, a reiteration of Taoism's "work without doing."

In this context, you might think of meditation as a process of growing up rather than a specific technique, a spontaneously maturing awareness of the seeming burdens that life presents you. With this new, unflinching awareness, you gain the ability to make a truly informed and conscious choice that you will, quite simply, have none of it. As Watts suggests, you learn to solve the "problem of life" by deciding it is no longer a problem. It's not that you become an irresponsible, undisciplined individual, but that you are no longer interested in following the mindless patterns of the ordinary person—even meditation, as it turns out. Like Yunton, your ultimate goal is simply to be natural, thereby realizing the effortless state of "no distraction." You come to realize all spiritual practice is essentially a paradoxical un-learning, a process I like to describe as "remembering how to forget" what everyone else is trying to know.

The realization of true presence is intricately connected to the recognition of the natural mind. This being the case, let's begin our search for presence by trying to get a peripheral glimpse of this elusive base of awareness.

The Natural Mind

As you gain stability and focus through concentration meditation and other awareness-building practices, you begin to notice certain moments of total relaxation in which no effort of anxiety, conceptual thinking, etc. is expended. Such moments begin to arise entirely spontaneously, naturally—which means, paradoxically, there is no way of intentionally entering them. In Dzogchen, at this stage in the practitioner's development, there is traditionally a pointing out by the teacher of the natural mind. This pointing out is not the description of some new technique that leads to some new experience. The teacher simply provides a clearer context in which the student can better understand states he or she has already experienced. Describing the natural mind in a conceptual way can be very tricky, as any verbal explanation tends to place limits on the experience itself. Traditionally, the natural mind is pointed out through metaphor and symbols, encouraging the practitioner to rely on deeper, more intuitive layers of the mind rather than intellectualization.

Natural Mind Metaphors

There are three traditional metaphors for the natural mind: the butterlamp, the peacock feather, and the prism. To understand the natural mind metaphors in an intellectual sense alone is not the same thing as truly grasping the nature of mind, just like reading the word "joy" is not the same thing as feeling joy itself. Throughout your meditative practices and your daily life, you are constantly being drawn closer to a deep, intuitive realization of the natural mind. To try too hard to force it is very much like an amoeba trying to force itself to develop into a peacock feather. The irony of the situation is that there is nothing the amoeba needs to do—nothing the amoeba *can* do—other than *be an amoeba*. It ends up a peacock feather eventually, not through some effort of its own, but simply because such a transformation, such an evolution, is in the natural way of things.

Every so often, as you continue to progress in whatever formal or informal practices for deepening awareness, peace, and focus, come back to these metaphors and contemplate them. As you progress along your individual path, you will strengthen your connection to these images. The connection will be a deep, highly intuitive one—not one that you are likely to put into words. Trying to find the natural mind is like trying to find your own nose. The harder you look, the more confused you get. Even so, frequently revisiting the natural mind metaphors can bring you closer to spontaneous recognition of the natural state. Rest assured, if you persist in your practices with the sincere desire to know yourself, you *will* awaken to the natural state—if only for a few moments every now and then.

BUTTERLAMP

For the Westerner, a light bulb is a familiar object. When we turn a light on, light radiates from the bulb and illuminates the space around it. Of particular significance in our context, however, is the fact that the resulting light also illuminates the light bulb itself. This relationship between the space outside the light bulb, the space inside the light bulb, and the thin, yet very real, boundary of the bulb itself is very similar to the workings of the natural mind. You might think of your body as the light bulb in this scenario. Your body radiates a sort of light into the external world, which happens through your voice, your actions, anything you do or create in the external world. This is your natural energy radiating outward. You also radiate inwardly, however, illuminating your own thoughts, feelings, physical sensations, etc. The mind can recognize these components of itself because, like the light bulb, the mind also illuminates the mind. As you begin to understand the natural mind, you understand that both of these radiations, external and internal, come from the same source—which is your very self, the Divine Self. Even so, as with the light bulb, there does exist some subtle, albeit permeable, boundary between your energy and the energy of your external surroundings. The natural mind is the totality of your own self, at once separate from, and indistinguishable from, the play of energy between the internal and external.

PEACOCK FEATHER

Like many things in nature, the peacock feather is *spontaneously* perfected. The peacock has no more conscious control over creating its own feathers than each of us has over our natural hair color. Yet, even so, the feather *does* get created and it is beautiful. You might want to ask, "Who is the real artist here? Who is painting all these beautiful colors onto this peacock feather?" The answer: no one, everyone, everything. The peacock feather is part of a natural process that extends forever in all directions. Evolutionarily, the peacock feather—like everything else in the physical universe—is traceable all the way back to the Big Bang itself. And when the peacock dies, what happens to its feather? Even then, it continues to transform, manifest in yet other forms as it dissolves back into the earth.

To appreciate the beauty of a peacock feather is simply to focus on one relatively stable aspect of the entire dynamic universe. For that matter, what is the peacock feather's beauty without someone to appreciate it? Without your eyes to perceive the visual stimuli of the feather, and without your aesthetic sensibilities that understand the feather to be beautiful, do you really even have a feather at all? In this context, you might say that each of us is really a creation of the peacock feather itself, in order that it might consciously appreciate its own beauty. You are the eyes of the peacock feather perceiving its many colors, just as you are the conceptual mind of the feather appreciating its incredibly rich connection to all of history. You are both one with, and separate from, the spontaneous perfection of the peacock feather—which is a focal point of the entire universe. Such is the essence of perfect and effortless interrelatedness, which is the essence of the natural mind.

PRISM

Imagine the clear light of the sun shining through a prism. As the light emerges from the prism, it is broken into rainbow light. It is the same light that went into the prism, yet its form has changed. The end product of the rainbow light is part of a cooperative process involving sunlight, the prism, and certain natural laws—in this case, the law that clear light is really composed of many different energy wavelengths which, when combined, appear to us as clear sunlight. Imagine your own body as this prism. As a sentient being, some naturally manifesting energy or awareness—like sunlight—necessarily pours through you. Like the prism, your body, your individual self, breaks this energy down into beautiful patterns and projects it outward through your eyes. The external world, then, becomes the manifestation of this original sunlight filtered through your own inner experiences and then projected back out into the external world. To interact with the external world, then, is really to interact with certain aspects of your own self reflected back to you.

In this metaphor, the entire universe is a kind of cooperation between this original sunlight, our own bodies, and the external world. There are three distinct things, yet there is only one thing. The question might arise, "Now where does this metaphorical sunlight come from in the first place?" Well, like the peacock feather, this sunlight is just there, it just happens. The best way to understand where the sunlight comes from is to simply step outside on a sunny day. The feel of the sun across your face, the look of the sunlight playing across the grass, *that* is where the sunlight comes from. You are the original source of that, and that is the original source of you. Yet, you are nonetheless distinct from the sunlight. If you were not somehow distinct from it, you couldn't fully appreciate its beauty, which is the indescribable beauty of otherness.

&.

A few of you, upon reading the preceding descriptions, whether you have spent a lifetime in meditation or never performed any practices whatsoever, will grasp the natural mind immediately. A little bell will go off in the back of your head somewhere and you will realize this is something you have been trying to understand for a long time, most likely all the way back to your earliest memories of childhood. If you have really "gotten it," you will probably chuckle at how ridiculously simple "it" is. There is really nothing to be comprehended, you understand, nothing new to be grasped, because it has been there the whole time. You have been waiting for just this moment of pointing out, the moment when you were finally ready to consciously experience the natural mind.

However, due to fear, self-importance, anger, and other obstacles to accurate perception, many individuals find it takes considerable effort to grasp the natural mind. Even so, know that these very obstacles to direct perception are part and parcel of the natural mind itself. When it is time for each of us to directly experience the natural mind, we will directly experience it. Just like the peacock feather is spontaneously created, albeit within an infinite span of time, so will your own, perfect understanding one day manifest in beautiful patterns of energy and acceptance.

MANIFESTATION OF THE NATURAL MIND IN MEDITATION

Let's suppose you have decided to work with the mantra RAM. You start off with a lot of effort, the stage of forceful zhiné, forcefully gluing your mind to that one vibration of energy. As your concentration deepens, you begin to notice that you can loosen your concentrative grip a little without losing your anchor to your mantra. At this stage, the stage of natural zhiné, there is this constant RAM turning over and over at your center while everything else, all other distracting thoughts, pass through your awareness without ever pulling you away from your center. As your practice continues to deepen, you notice a very odd thing: *Everything* is RAM, every external sound, every distracting thought, is simply variations on this single mantra. You begin to hear all sounds as RAM, you begin to see all colors as subtle vibrations of that same mantra, feel all sensations as the play of RAM. This is the state of ultimate zhiné. At this point, you realize you can leave off concentrating altogether, because wherever you look, there is RAM, over and over again. You realize the energy of RAM has somehow taken over and begun to concentrate for you. This is the point at which you are ready for true contemplation.

WHEN A MOUNTAIN IS JUST A MOUNTAIN

As your confidence grows from this paradoxical realization, you begin to get rid of RAM altogether. As they say in Zen, whereas the world was temporarily turned upside down as you dove headfirst into the seemingly bizarre spiritual stream of awareness, you now begin to appreciate that a mountain is just a mountain, a river is just a river. The same simple truths that you held before starting down your path in earnest—each of which you relentlessly questioned and deconstructed along the way—are apparent once again, albeit from a much richer, broader perspective. Moreover, you now realize, RAM is just RAM.

Anything you focus on at this point automatically connects you to everything else. Formal meditative practices begin to seem redundant. Like Yunton, once you have reached a certain state of awareness, you no longer feel the need to meditate because you have realized it is impossible to ever be distracted. It's not that you have attained some superhuman level of constant concentration, it's that you have realized there really is *no such thing* as concentration. You have realized that everyone is in a state of constant concentration—only the vast majority of individuals fail to recognize that state for what it is. At this point, there is really nothing to do but live your life, however simple or messy, and wait. You are like the amoeba who is slowly transforming into a peacock feather by the perfectly natural process of amoeba-ness—a perfectly natural process you can call "grace." However strange this essential truth may sound to some of you just now, every breath you take, every beer you drink, every foul word or kind word you utter ultimately becomes part of this automatic, profoundly beautiful process of self-realization.

Contemplation

To a certain degree, contemplation is a technique you employ to cultivate mindfulness, which is direct experience of the natural mind. At the same time, however, true contemplation *is* mindfulness, is presence itself. Ultimately, the means merges with the end.

I have been teaching music for years now, and I'm learning more and more that there is no right way to go about cultivating music skills. Music, like meditation, is such an intensely personal thing that it can never be captured in this or that method or concept. It can certainly be *learned*, mind you, it just can't be *taught*—not directly. With this in mind, remember that all these various categories of meditation progress are, at the very best, loose approximations. Don't feel that it is necessary to approach meditation "by the book." In my experience, such an attitude is often one of the most cumbersome obstacles to further understanding. Feel free to experiment. Piece these various methods and stages together in any way that makes sense to you and remember: There is only one true direction on the spiritual path, which is always forward. No matter how orthodox or unorthodox your methods at present, be confident that they are continuously pulling you along toward an increasingly deeper knowledge of yourself.

As for contemplation proper, however we approach it, it isn't a practice in the same way that concentration is. In fact, it's not really a practice at all, in the same way that you don't consider taking a breath from moment to moment a practice, or allowing your heart to pump blood throughout your body a practice. Understood properly, contemplation is an effortless, natural process that is always going on. The more awareness you cultivate through various intentional practices, the more you become conscious of this process. Contemplation practice, then, is simply learning—almost accidentally—to recognize the pervasive energy of contemplation that is going on all the time, everywhere and in everyone and everything.

The Three Essential Points of Contemplation

Perhaps the most succinct description of contemplation is found in a Dzogchen text, Garab Dorje's *Three Statements That Strike the Essential Points*.[4] Rather than paraphrase or explain them directly, I'll relate how these three simple points have played out in my experience.

1. *One is introduced directly to one's own nature*.
Throughout various meditative experiences, I somehow found myself "wandering into" the natural mind. This would be the first essential point, my direct introduction to my own nature. What does this state feel like? Put simply, it is a state many of us enter when we are truly absorbed in some task. It is nothing new, that is to say, but something each of experiences on a daily basis. Once you learn to consciously recognize this state of no distraction—and this is what is meant by an "introduction to one's own nature"—you begin to notice when you fall back out of it into your normal awareness full of self-conscious distractions. Although my understanding of the natural mind would often be quite rich and profound in these meditative states, I noticed myself losing it again and again. As I became more aware of my daily activities, I began to notice that sometimes I seemed to be merged—albeit without conscious intention—with this state, and sometimes I didn't. There wasn't much I could do other than notice when I was natural and notice when I wasn't.

2. *One definitively decides upon this unique state*.
After much experimentation, I definitively decided this natural state was by far the simplest and most satisfying way to go about my daily life. All effort, I gradually realized, was a kind of distraction, a splitting of the One Self into two parts: one a disciplining military officer, one an anxious recruit. This effortless state of natural mind, I finally decided, is entirely unique and simply can't be improved upon

or manipulated in any way whatsoever. Such is the realization of the second essential point: The state of natural mind is present to the degree that each of us is truly natural.

3. *One continues directly with confidence in liberation.*
I now continue in this state or, rather, I continue to become more aware that I never leave this state in the first place! I can't emphasize this point enough. This is the crazy thing each of us is already beginning to realize in our own way: Even when I don't get it, I still get it! Such seeming nonsense and confusion is very much a natural part of the gradually unfolding maturation of contemplation. The natural mind is, above all, natural. This means that it is *always* there . . . naturally. When you try to enter into it, that is one particular manifestation of the natural mind. When you don't try to enter into it, there it is again, in a different manifestation. As you see this effortless presence playing out again and again, both in your own experience and the experience of others, you begin to gain the "confidence in liberation" of the third essential point. In addition to becoming confident of your own liberation, you also begin to perceive the spontaneous perfection in every individual, regardless of whether he or she may be able to perceive it just yet. Such is the point at which you begin to experience true, Christ-like compassion.

As you gain more confidence in the continuous, unbroken presence of the natural mind, your actions become increasingly free. Once you understand that the natural mind is always present, it doesn't really matter what you do or what circumstances befall you—not in the same highly pressurized way that most of us live our lives on a daily basis. You still suffer, just as every imperfectly enlightened being suffers, but your suffering no longer has the same sort of anxious hold on you. Regardless of your individual actions, regardless of the various karmic consequences and situations in which you find yourself from day to day, you experience a deep, unshakeable confidence at your spiritual core. Whatever may come to pass, you have finally come to realize, all things work toward one, and only one goal: the spontaneous self-perfection of each and every individual being within the entire cosmos. As such, there are no good actions, no bad actions—there are only actions. As the Zen master I-Hsüan said, "In Buddhism no effort is necessary. All one has to do is to do nothing except to move his bowels, urinate, put on his clothing, eat his meals, and lie down if he is tired. The stupid will laugh at him, but the wise will understand."[5]

Until you are perfectly confident, however, it is easiest if you stick to actions and situations within a reasonable context of "Who I Think I Am." This is the ego story, one of the most deeply imbedded habitual structures imposed onto every aspect of your daily life. Although this structure necessarily limits your actions, thoughts, and feelings, it is essential nonetheless. Without it, until you reach a state of authentically heightened awareness and confidence, you run the risk of thoroughly confusing yourself, deeply entangling yourself in this or that messy circumstance or subjective experience. From inside this relatively safe cocoon of the ego story, you can begin to comfortably observe how the natural mind is always present.

As your confidence continues to grow, you begin to understand that you are never in danger of choosing the "wrong" action, somehow outside the realm of the natural mind, because *you're* not really choosing in the first place. Each of your actions is simply the natural mind flowing *through* you, illuminating both internal and external as in the example of the light bulb. How could you ever possibly do something outside of your own nature? How could you ever be, in every bone and muscle, every neuron and cell, anything other than yourself, which is *the* Self? At this point, the ego story begins to stretch and expand, become more malleable. At such a state—the state in which true and unconstrained integration comes more fluidly—you begin to understand the following Dzogchen scripture in a very deep way:

> In the mind of Samantabhadra [the Self, the Tao, the natural mind]
> Experience called "present" or "absent" is erroneous.
> That one excludes not the other is the ultimate excellence,
> Clarified without effort, neither ascertained nor conceived.[6]

Integration in Contemplation

The Dzogchen teachings speak of three different states that we must learn to blend, or integrate, with the state of presence or contemplation. It is very important to remember that this integration is already happening in all of these states, apart from your own efforts. Through the practice of integration, you are simply learning to become more aware of this automatic process. The three states with which to integrate are positive, neutral, and negative.

Positive Integration

Positive states include all those actions that we tend to label as "good." Spiritual practice, donating time to charity, helping a friend in need—all of these actions fall under the category of positive states. Positive actions are, without a doubt, the easiest to integrate with a state of mindfulness. To one degree or another, whenever you engage in positive actions, you are already looking into your state of mind. If you sit down to meditate, for example, your energy is focused on maintaining an unbroken awareness of all your thoughts and sensations, however subtle. Likewise, if you are trying to sincerely resolve a longstanding interpersonal conflict, for instance, your awareness must be focused and nonattached. You watch your mind move in such situations, veering toward its entrenched habits of impulsive anger and superiority, but you remain focused on the task at hand. In short, when you perform positive actions, negative impulses rarely cease to exist, but—to the degree that you skillfully recognize them as they arise—you refrain from indulging in them.

As you begin to integrate contemplation more completely with positive behaviors, you begin to understand that the ease of such integration is the very thing that makes such actions positive in the first place. This simple, self-evident fact is often overlooked, so people tend to cling to concepts like morality, benevolence, or duty to explain positive states. As your awareness deepens, however, you see that the actual content of your behaviors has little to do with their being positive. Rather, any behavior is automatically positive if performed with true confidence and awareness—within the state of contemplation, that is to say.

THE SECRET HELPER

What if, while trying to perform positive actions, you lose your awareness from time to time, and briefly lapse into negativity? The truest, steadiest state of contemplation, although it does recognize such lapses, does not judge them as ultimately negative. The authentic state of mindfulness, in fact, doesn't even consider such seeming lapses of awareness as "lapses." The self-sustaining energy of contemplation recognizes these seeming mistakes as manifestations of a different quality of awareness—a state of awareness which is called *dran shes* in Dzogchen, meaning "secret helper." After all, if my awareness was truly absent in such a moment, how would I ever know it was absent? Ironically, the very thought, "I just lost my awareness," is a secret helper to the fact that our awareness always remains unbroken, albeit sometimes disguised in the mask of absence. Think about that elusive paradox for a minute. When you wake from sleep each morning, you are most definitely aware that you were just asleep, right? You *think* you lost consciousness in that state, but if that were true, how would you ever know you were just asleep in the first place?

Contemplation teaches you that this secret helper follows you everywhere, even into states of deep, dreamless sleep, and states of agitated distraction and forgetfulness. The secret helper is the essential, unbroken thread of awareness that spontaneously connects one moment of your experience to the next, the very means by which *you* can recognize yourself as *you*. As you learn to recognize the secret helper, and to place your confidence therein, you learn to merge with it and follow it into whatever states may arise, allowing you to remain conscious in all states of awareness. Recognizing the secret helper is very, very important if you are to rediscover your natural state, so let's continue to explore the role of the secret helper as it applies to states of neutral and negative integration.

Neutral Integration

Neutral states include activities such as eating, sleeping, and driving to work. We tend to view such states as neither good nor bad; they are simply necessary. Let's look into the act of eating, for example. As you begin to increase your awareness of contemplation, you may notice it manifests in many different forms while you eat. The easiest way to recognize it is in a state of effortful mindfulness, a state similar to that produced by the practice of forceful zhiné. The Buddhists, for example, perform a practice in which they keep a running account of their eating process. As they eat, they mentally say to themselves "chewing, chewing . . . tasting, tasting . . . swallowing, swallowing . . . " If such a process were to happen entirely naturally, without the slightest effort, *then* I would call it integrated contemplation. If it is happening from a kind of forced-witness observation point, however, although it might be a very useful practice, it is decidedly not contemplation.

By contrast, let's say you are eating a meal and your mind starts to wander. You begin to fantasize about an upcoming fishing trip. When you finally snap out of your fantasy, you realize you have eaten your entire meal almost accidentally. Well, in that exact moment—the moment of direct perception—it is important to recognize you never truly lost your presence in the first place. Your mind wandered, sure, but what's wrong with that? Minds wander—that is part of what makes them interesting. Notice, however, your meal did get eaten nonetheless. That's the secret helper again, the quiet maintainer of a subtle, almost invisible awareness in all states. For that matter, even though you completely lost yourself in your fishing fantasy, your body kept breathing, your heart kept pumping. No one was manning the ship, but the ship stayed afloat and perfectly on course.

If you don't yet understand the importance of these automatic functions, it simply means you don't yet have full confidence in the state of contemplation. Consequently, you will probably continue to apply one sort of effort or another until you do. When you finally perceive this process directly, finally experience the perfect ease and simplicity with which contemplation sustains itself, all the strenuous effort you previously applied seems rather comical. Paradoxically, these very efforts are what make the eventual discovery of the natural state possible.

CONFIDENCE AND INTEGRATION

The best advice I can give you on integrating contemplation with positive and neutral actions is this: Assume your awareness is a very fine, unbroken thread connecting every single moment. If you think you must have lost awareness in a situation, look closer. Review your actions closely, as well as your most fleeting thoughts and momentary feelings. All things considered, did you really lose awareness? Properly examine the actions you performed in that state, as well as the emotions and mental images that engaged your attention and you will realize them to be just as useful, just as positive, as actions, thoughts, or feelings arising from a more conscious state. Such is the way of the self-perfected universe. It is the way of the natural mind, aided along by its secret helper. A seeming absence in awareness isn't really an absence—it is simply a different manifestation, a subtler quality of awareness.

Think of an expert athlete. If he were to run down the field thinking "running, running . . . jumping, jumping . . ." he would very likely short circuit. Only by entering a state of automatic absence is he able to turn on his innate athletic ability. Consciously or unconsciously, he creates a kind of mental and bodily vacuum, which is spontaneously filled by the natural mind. Focused on the task at hand, he ceases to be concerned about states of so-called presence or absence. In so doing, he allows his body and mind to move naturally, effortlessly—to man the ship without his habitual, ego-driven self getting in the way.

Confidence, then, is essential to the practice of true integration. Returning to Garab Dorje's Three Essential Points, you must first recognize and confidently decide upon the state of natural mind. Although this state is ultimately beyond description, you can conceptualize it in various ways as you progress along the path. You need only decide on one thing in which you authentically and totally believe. Love, beauty, truth, the sat guru—whatever you take at present to be the most genuine, all-pervasive form of the sacred—this becomes the root of your confidence, the original mold of the natural mind. This becomes the all-important task at hand. Through surrender and devotion to this one governing principle, you recognize that your life is not your own, your actions are not your own. You give up, as best you are able, your individual self in service of the Self. Having done so, you watch your life go by, watch the universe go by, calmly and resolutely, certain of your ultimate liberation, as well as the liberation of your fellow beings. You fully participate in the human drama, sincerely and without reservation, but you are not ruled by it. Your individual desires, you come to recognize, are not really individual. Rather, they are the elusive stuff of the Tao itself, the fundamental fuel of spontaneous self-perfection. Consequently, your deepest, most comprehensive practice of integration becomes the simple recognition that things—just as they already are—are perfectly integrated from the very start.

Negative Integration

When the great Tao is forgotten,
Kindness and morality arise.
When wisdom and intelligence are born,
The great pretense begins.[7]

In the above passage from the *Tao Te Ching*, the "great Tao" is really just another name for presence or mindfulness. Lao Tzu is suggesting that true mindfulness transcends the need for such pretense as kindness and morality. As I discussed in chapter 4, it's not that Taoism is encouraging cruelty or wrongdoing. Rather, Taoism—along with traditions such as Zen, Dzogchen, and even Christianity at the esoteric level—recognizes that establishing concrete rules of any sort necessarily implies a lack of confidence in the spontaneous way of things. If we are to have true confidence that the natural mind is *always* present, spontaneously perfected within every person and every situation, we need to feel comfortable recognizing the subtle good within the bad, the hidden light within the dark. This is where the practice of negative integration is uniquely useful.

In *Dzogchen: The Heart Essence of the Great Perfection*, His Holiness the Dalai Lama talks about negative integration as it appears in certain Dzogchen texts. "The purpose of this is to help the practitioner transcend the polarities of normal ethical conventions. . . . to engage in actions that usually would carry negative associations and be an affront to normal ethical conventions."[8] I was rather disturbed by the idea of negative integration when I first encountered it in Tenzin Wangyal Rinpoche's *Wonders of the Natural Mind: The Essence of Dzogchen in the Native Bon Tradition of Tibet*. The idea of deliberately allowing negative actions into my daily life didn't seem quite right to me, certainly not very spiritual. No doubt, many of you may share a similar discomfort with this practice. To ease your discomfort, let me emphasize a crucial lesson I learned through my own practice of negative integration: *A negative action performed with full awareness in the state of contemplation, contains just as much, if not more, genuine love and compassion than a kind action performed in a state of distraction or ignorance.* Such was Lao Tzu's point in the above excerpt. To the degree that you remember the Tao, to the degree that you place your confidence in the automatic perfection of the natural mind, there can be no such thing as a truly harmful action.

Like it or not, we all perform numerous negative actions every day. Whether or not we consciously practice negative integration, every one of us still "on the path" indulges in anger, fear, envy, etc. with some regularity. To the degree that you consider yourself imperfect, in fact, is the degree to which you are aware, however vaguely, of your tendencies toward these negative feeling states. The real problem with negative actions isn't that they are mean or immoral, but simply that the states in which they are carried out can foster the habit of disconnecting from conscious awareness. Properly understood, this—and only this—is what makes such actions negative.

Each of us has a story running in the back of his or her mind at all times—the ever crafty ego story, which says that, *whatever* I mean by negative actions, *I* am not attracted to them. Negative actions are something the other guy does, my ego assures me, the bad guy. Far from preventing all negative thoughts, feelings and actions in myself, however, all this ego story really does is compel me to disown those parts of myself that I have conceptualized as negative. I still behave just as "badly" as the next person, by simply looking the other way while it is happening. Likely, as I discussed in the previous chapter, I even go so far as to project those unwanted aspects of myself onto others around me, reassuring myself again and again that I am a relative saint in a sea of sinners.

Then again, sometimes our egos use yet craftier means to defend the personality fort. Maybe my ego recognizes my negative actions as they arise, but quickly goes on to construct a story of irredeemable guilt, self-loathing, and self-pity. My ego fixates on these negative tendencies, that is to say, as a way of creating a kind of distance between myself and my undesirable actions. I am incorrigibly bad, my ego tells me, so what can I do possibly do to save myself? At the core of such a strategy is a deeply entrenched fort of self-importance. When we look deeper and deeper into our seemingly self-deprecating thoughts, feelings, and behaviors, we recognize an underlying foundation of resentment and blame of others. We are so lost in feeling sorry for ourselves, disgusted with ourselves, etc., that we fail to truly recognize and take responsibility for the consequences of our actions.

Tenzin Wangyal says that, "The principal nonvirtuous mental actions are those called the five poisons. These are: attachment to people and to things; anger, which can manifest when simply seeing someone gives rise to an unpleasant sensation; pride, which can manifest not only by thinking oneself to be very important but also by thinking one is the worst kind of person; jealousy, which means all kinds of comparison and competition; and ignorance, which means not understanding the real condition."[9] In learning to integrate with such states, "one makes all [mental] activities expressions of contemplative awareness; they become aids to spiritual development and so virtuous in the truest sense."[10] Rather than burdening yourself with abstract concepts, you might do best to jump in headfirst and try a brief experiment in negative integration. Your ego will do its best to talk you out of such an experiment, because honest, open-minded evaluation is the arch enemy of the ego story. But for those of you who are brave enough to take an unflinching look at your individual personality, you can use the following exercise as a means of harnessing the seemingly negative energy of certain mental states to further your experience of the natural mind.

EXERCISE: WORKING WITH NEGATIVE THOUGHTS AND FEELINGS

■ Think of someone you strongly dislike. Rather than questioning your reasons for anger and so forth, actively cultivate them. Recall situations from the past in which you were wronged, and allow your anger to flare. Fantasize about various means of revenge—angry words, vicious gossip, a punch in the nose, even. This is a perfectly safe experiment, remember, in that you are simply exploring your own subjective space. Feel the power of your anger. Enjoy its fleeting taste.

Or think of an attractive coworker, friend, acquaintance—anyone who you find physically or romantically desirable despite his or her being "off limits." Indulge in sexual or romantic fantasies. Nothing is too obscene, in this context, nothing too intimate. This is your own mind, after all, and you have the right—the obligation even—to explore it.

Better yet, imagine that you have been elected as Supreme Ruler of the World. You make the laws, you distribute the world's wealth and resources however you see fit. Finally recognizing your superior importance and wisdom, the governments and citizens of the world have agreed to humbly and joyfully honor your every wish and whim. I am not being ironic, facetious or even metaphorical. I am suggesting a very real and specific exercise, so challenge yourself—take a few minutes and try it out.

When you engage in this exercise with sufficient honesty and focus, you notice something rather peculiar: This is all somehow extremely *familiar*. Each of us, consciously and unconsciously, indulges in these sorts of negative thoughts and feelings on a daily basis. We usually do our best to ignore these unpleasantries of our mind, but they inhabit our subjective space nonetheless. For most of us, if we can really pay attention, really bring an intense energy of awareness to our daily lives, we will likely notice we absentmindedly dabble in each of the above fantasies on our way to work every morning!

Ultimately, remember, the point of negative integration is neither to condone nor encourage such negative fantasies. So long as you have such fantasies—however typically quiet and hidden they may be—you are much better off to have them out in your open mind than you are to cultivate them in private, where they become more exotic and compelling in their negativity. Ironically, fully recognizing your negative tendencies, and totally accepting your undesirable habits of thinking and feeling, is the most direct way to free yourself of their unnecessary burden. Once you allow your negative habits into the full light of day, you are able to recognize the incredibly subtle influence of the secret helper which has been at work the whole time, converting seeming negativity into ultimate positivity.

NEGATIVE ACTIONS

"[Physically] expressing the passion of anger . . . telling lies . . . insulting and quarreling with people,"[11] are, in Tenzin Wangyal's words, examples of negative actions appropriate for the practice of negative integration. For the sake of simplicity, we will say there are two primary types of negative actions: actions that affect only oneself negatively, and actions that also have negative effects on others. A personal example may help to illustrate the first of these categories.

I have always been extremely health conscious. For years, I have exercised religiously, monitored my diet strictly, and drank alcohol only in moderation. At some point, I began to sense that these so-called good habits weren't so much the result of a mature, focused attention as they were compulsive acts. I was very fearful, I began to realize, of becoming one of those people who indulged themselves in mindless pleasures. I decided to try an experiment. For one month, I decided to quit working out, eat anything I wanted whenever I wanted, and drink alcohol whenever I had the slightest urge to do so. Ironically, this practice required much more honest discipline and restraint than did my previous habits. Daily, I would find myself trying to rationalize going to the gym, eating healthy, etc. I began to realize that I was just as addicted, or attached, to the healthy lifestyle as an alcoholic is to alcohol.

Strange as it may sound, during this month, my moment–to-moment awareness increased tenfold. I began to experience more deeply mystical states, more stable and joyful presence than I had ever known previously. When this practice ended, I returned to my old lifestyle, albeit more moderate and considerably less fearful. Enjoying newfound confidence and a sense of expansive personal freedom, I had learned that I could act like one of "those people" without truly *becoming* one of "those people."

EXERCISE: WORKING WITH NEGATIVE ACTIONS

■ Examples of negative behavior that affect only oneself are numerous. Experiment with whatever negative actions seem reasonable for you, but be careful to sit back calmly and observe the ensuing consequences. If you fear physical fatigue, for instance, deprive yourself of sleep for a night or two, just to see what happens. Hypochondriac? Take a walk in the rain, minus your shoes. Penny pincher? Stuff a hundred dollar bill or two down the garbage disposal. You do such behaviors, not to indulge in childishness or stupidity, but to authentically stretch your ego-boundaries, see what is left of the ego story after it has taken an unexpected beating.

More difficult still are those negative actions that involve others. Undertip an excellent waiter. Leave your trash in a parking lot. Tell your friends you went out last night to a great restaurant when you actually stayed home. Be intentionally unproductive on the job. Once again, as was the case with negative integration with thoughts and feelings, consciously indulging in negative actions reminds you just how often you already lose yourself in such habits—albeit mindlessly and defensively. Honest and genuine awareness is the key here. Tenzin Wangyal writes, "The point of integrating with negative states is not to justify wrong action. It is, rather, the best way to minimize harm and, ultimately, to overcome negativity. If we all mastered the practice of [negative] integration, there would be no harm or injury since we would all be in the non-dual state [of the natural mind] and when we are in the non-dual state we cannot cause harm."[12]

To one degree or another—until you are fully and completely absorbed in the natural mind—negative behaviors still bring about negative consequences. Until you are entirely liberated from old habits, the practice of negative integration does not promise total alleviation of guilt, suffering, or any other negative consequences you will likely incur. The ultimate point to realize is that—negative consequences no matter—*you* are still *you*. Whatever rigid ideas you may maintain regarding your personality, you will not melt into a puddle of egoless goo when you skillfully question these habitual limits. Throughout all states, however negative, impassioned, or seemingly distracted, the natural mind's secret helper is at work holding the Self together.

RESPECTING YOUR LIMITS

When working with negative integration, it is of utmost importance to pick actions within a reasonable range of your ego boundary. Most of us simply aren't ready to start a fistfight with our neighbor, for instance, or curse our boss to his face. Negative integration need not be—and for the vast majority of us, *should* not be— anything nearly so scary. Whatever your personal rules of behavior are at present, the point of negative integration is to realize you don't have to be bound by any rules whatsoever. As Nietzsche emphasized, it is one thing to be honest, charitable, etc., because you enjoy it. It is quite another to do so out of simple fear of retribution, or a supposedly moral obligation. Paradoxically, the staunch environmentalist, by the deliberate act of littering, may very well come to appreciate his or her original environmentalist viewpoint in a much deeper, and less fearful, way.

Overestimating your ego flexibility and choosing behaviors beyond your means does more harm than good. If I have never so much as received a speeding ticket and decide to go out and rob a bank, I am simply creating an unnecessary mess for myself. Dzogchen or no, I am creating an overly stressful identity crisis, to say the least, and will most certainly begin to anxiously rationalize my behavior, convince myself that I am nothing other than elated and liberated, drown myself in fear and guilt, etc. If your negative actions simply cause you to look the other way, you are no longer performing skillful negative integration practice. You are simply indulging in mindless and habitual negative actions—a so-called practice at which most of us are already quite expert.

CULTIVATING EMPATHY

The practice of negative integration is not meant to encourage you to act without feeling, or that you should withhold empathy for others. Rather, the more you can honestly pay attention throughout your negative actions—which, as your daily life proves time and again, are going to happen whether or not you "allow" them—the more you can be fully present in the situation. The more presence you bring to any situation, the better able you are to see things as they truly exist. Opening up to the energy of the natural mind, you necessarily become more aware of the consequences of your actions, the way they affect those around you as well as your environment. Rather than defensively pretending so-and-so simply "got what he deserved" in an angry exchange, for instance, you can learn to stay with the situation, more fully appreciate the humanity of your seeming enemies even in the midst of heated battle.

How can you be confident you are recognizing the difference between legitimate negative integration and mere self-righteous defensiveness? Well, the real point is not so much to answer this question as it is to keep asking it relentlessly. You are bound to make mistakes. If not, then you are probably living your life strictly within the cozy walls of your time-honored ego boundaries.

As your practice of authentic negative integration deepens, your life will become more full of love and understanding for yourself and others. You will experience new levels and layers of legitimate empathy. You will feel more free, less constrained by objective rules and regulations. At the same time, you will paradoxically develop more confidence in those guidelines you had previously chosen to keep for yourself. These "rules" will have become celebrations of your truest self rather than fearful superstitions. The five poisons of attachment, anger, pride, jealousy, and ignorance will have been spontaneously liberated into the five wisdoms. Such is the state of total empathy and compassion, the state free of nervous limits and compulsive categorizations. Even so, anger still *feels* very different from happiness, pride still *feels* very different from security, and so on. Such distinctions remain, but are no longer a sign of limitation, some obstacle to be overcome. Rather, they have become relaxed and unselfish reminders of the infinite beauty of variety within oneness.

Thogal Practice

With the possible exception of negative integration, the Dzogchen teachings consider the contemplation practices we have examined so far to be *Trekchod* practices. These practices are, by definition, effortless. As I have emphasized, such so-called practices involve not so much specific methods or techniques as they simply provide a stable conceptual context in which to view the various manifestations of contemplation. Trekchod practice, then, is consciously recognizing your already perfected ability of "remaining in the state of contemplation, abiding in the natural essence of the pure state of mind."[13] Negative integration, not so easily or automatically recognized within the state of the natural mind, is a little different in that it seems to be helped along, in the beginning at least, with more deliberate actions. By my definition, then, we might place negative integration in the Dzogchen category of *Thogal*. Referring to practices that involve consciously "exerting oneself for direct realization,"[14] Thogal practice encompasses deliberate techniques for working with the movement of energy present in the natural-mind state.

More specifically, however, Thogal tends to work with vision. Traditionally, the Dzogchen practitioner gains stability in Trekchod, or contemplation, before proceeding to the practice of Thogal. In my experience, Thogal practice develops on its own as a result of stability in Trekchod. Even so, and even if you have yet to have total success in mindfulness practice, a brief introduction to Thogal may be in order at this time, as a direct experience of the dynamic energy explored in this esoteric practice can immediately deepen your understanding of contemplation. We will deal with Thogal in much more detail in chapter 11, which examines dream practice. I will introduce a very simple Thogal practice here, however, which will allow you an immediate glance into the innate movement of the natural state.

EXERCISE: SEEING THE MOVEMENT

■ Find a patterned surface such as a carpet, grainy wood or stone, tile, etc. Sitting comfortably, gaze at this surface. Relax deeply into this surface allowing your vision to slightly blur. This is sometimes called a soft focus, which tends to result in a slight crossing of the eyes. As you continue to gaze in this way, not looking at the patterned surface directly so much as just in front of it, you will begin to notice a very slight movement. You may observe a subtle shimmer or heat wave-like effect. Continue to gaze and you may see the patterned surface begin to wobble, almost as if it is breathing, or rolling over itself like the waves in an ocean. There are many different ways in which this visual phenomenon may manifest. The important point is that you notice movement of some sort. The more you relax your body and mind, and the calmer your breathing becomes, the more you are likely to observe this movement.

Well, what is this movement? Is it a hallucination? Is it your imagination? Properly understood—which is to say, *directly* experienced—this play of energy is an external projection of your own internal state. This movement is the movement of your own mind, but not in quite the same way that a hallucination or fantasy is. It does little good to observe this movement if you don't somehow recognize it as yourself, something that arises from deep within you—a kind of mirror that is reflecting the energetic play of your own mind back to you.

As you gaze, you may notice subtle shapes within the textured surface arising and disappearing. Such a recognition is very much like children finding shapes in clouds. As you observe such shapes, notice that your thoughts move with them. At the same time you notice the face of your grandmother, for instance, you may recognize you were just internally humming her favorite song. Or, perhaps you notice your thoughts first. Maybe you are thinking of grocery shopping later that day when you notice produce begin to appear, very subtly at first, in the field of your gaze.

In much the same way that you can never stand directly beneath a rainbow, these various shapes and moving patterns will likely disappear if you try to look at them directly. This is due to the fact that your process of observation is organically and intricately intertwined with the manifestation of these subtle visual stimuli. It is not that your thoughts *cause* these shapes to appear, neither that the shapes *cause* your thoughts to arise. Rather, these mental objects and external objects arise *together*, at exactly the same time. Whichever you notice first—the inner or the outer—depends on where your present focus lies: internal or external.

With continued experience in Thogal, you begin to understand that all external objects and situations are simply manifestations of your own mind. Whereas the three natural mind metaphors at this chapter's outset help you conceptualize the natural mind, Thogal helps you to directly experience the reality behind these metaphors. As you gain experience in Thogal, Taoism's message of interrelatedness no longer seems so abstract. You begin to see literally more and more of yourself reflected back to you in the world around you.

EXERCISE: INCREASING THE MOVEMENT

■ If you don't get any results with Thogal at first, I suggest you find a way to increase your internal movement of energy. Practice after having a few cups of coffee. Practice after you have performed vigorous exercise. The more the energy in your body and mind is stimulated, the easier it will be to notice this same energy projected onto your external environment. States of fatigue can also be very useful in this way as they tend to suppress the rational mind—a relatively narrow, goal-oriented mechanism that normally filters out this external play of your own energy. Try Thogal practice when you are dizzy with hunger or exhausted from lack of sleep. Try it just as you drift off to sleep or upon first waking in the morning. Try it after you have had a couple of glasses of wine or are running a fever. The more strangely your internal state is behaving in regard to your daily, ordinary awareness, the more likely you are to recognize this same atypical behavior reflected in your environment.

One final word regarding Thogal practice and any other practice that might lead to mystical experience: The goal of these practices is not, necessarily, mystical experience in and of itself. For that matter, mystical experience is genuinely useful only to the degree that it increases your enjoyment and understanding of the most simple and mundane of daily tasks.

The Indescribably Ordinary Beauty of Kansas

SOME TIME AGO I HAD A DREAM in which I was climbing the steps of an ancient Mayan pyramid. Halfway up, I recognized the fact that I was dreaming. Moreover, I recognized that this was no ordinary lucid dream, but a dream of particularly heightened awareness—what Dzogchen would call a dream of clarity. At this point, I became quite excited, practically sprinting up the pyramid steps, eager to see what sort of dizzying mystical encounter might await me at the top of the pyramid.

When I reached the top, I felt it was appropriate that I launch into flight. I tried to do so several times, but kept falling to the ground. Finally, after much struggle, I stabilized in flight and swept over fabulously beautiful fields of golden corn and luscious valleys of green grass.

At some point, I felt that I was meant to fly higher and higher. As I ascended into the vast expanse of an incredibly blue sky, I was periodically overtaken with waves of fear and panic, anxious of whatever might await me at some ultimate height. A violent tornado funnel appeared just above me and I flew toward it, despite my increasing anxiety. I was fearful, but I was also very excited to see where this tornado might carry me. I thought of Dorothy being whisked away to Oz just as I entered the funnel. There were several moments of dazzling commotion, a fireworks display of sound and color, and I could feel I was being flung higher and higher.

Just at the moment I could feel I was about to be catapulted into some bizarre and exotic realm of consciousness, I closed my eyes tightly, bracing myself for some inevitable impact. When I finally settled, I opened my eyes, somewhat hesitantly, and found myself simply lying on my bed, looking up at my very ordinary ceiling.

The moral of this story is an obvious one: The highest spiritual experience is nothing other than the most ordinary moments of our daily lives. Even Dorothy returned from Oz, remember, ending up back where she started. Despite her bizarre adventures, Kansas was *still* Kansas—her familiar and ordinary home—which is not to say that her trip to Oz didn't change her forever in some profound ways. After all, every time Dorothy looked at Aunty Em from then on, she couldn't help but see traces of Glenda, the Good Witch. . .

JAILBREAK OR REDECORATE?
THE RIDDLE OF SELF

You do not realize your own situation. You are in prison.
All you can wish for, if you are . . . sensible . . . is to escape. But how to escape?
—G. I. GURDJIEFF[1]

Whether you practice formal concentration or contemplation as described previously, or simply try to be more present in your daily life from moment to moment, you begin to gain an increasing awareness of certain personality patterns that tend to play out over and over throughout your everyday routine. These patterns may take the form of certain repetitive behaviors or habits, such as eating when you are anxious, sleeping when you are unhappy, driving recklessly when you are angry and so on. These patterns may also manifest as habitual thoughts and feelings such as, "I am bored today, I need to lose weight, no one appreciates me," etc. Moreover, you begin to appreciate that even certain objective facts about yourself, such as "I am tall, I am a dentist," and so forth, tend to be much more complex than you previously recognized. As you learn to attend to subtler and subtler workings of your mind, you increasingly appreciate just how complex, compelling, and pervasive this phenomenon we call "personality" or "self-identity" really is. In short, you begin to notice that every moment of your life is woven together from a virtually infinite array of interconnecting patterns of thinking, feeling, and behaving.

The Sense of "I-ness": East vs. West

The collection of those patterns each of us favors as an individual makes up what we typically call the self, the ego, or simply "me." Both Western psychology and

Eastern spiritual disciplines recognize the essential necessity of working skillfully with this pervasive, deeply entrenched sense of self or "I-ness." The specific strategies each system employs in working with this experience of self, however, seem to contradict one another. At first glance, in fact, Freudian psychology and traditional Buddhism, for example, seem to stand in exact opposition to one another regarding the methods for "curing" the maladies of the self. Masao Abe writes, "The most conspicuous difference between Buddhism and Western psychology is perhaps found in their respective treatments of the concept of "self." In Western psychology, the existence of a "self" is generally affirmed; Buddhism denies the existence of an enduring "self" and substitutes instead the concept of *anatman*, 'no-self.'"[2]

For the psychologist, then, our experience of self is a kind of cozy apartment, or securely boundaried living area. To improve our experience of self, we need to improve this apartment, redecorate it, strengthen its walls and foundation. Jack Engler states, from the perspective of psychotherapy, that "The deepest psychopathological problem . . . is the lack of a sense of self. The most severe clinical syndromes . . . are precisely failures, arrests or regressions in establishing a cohesive, integrated self or self concept. In varying degrees of severity, all represent disorders of the self, the inability to feel real or cohesive 'in being' at all."[3] Consequently, the psychologist works to repair these "failures" of identity, using various therapeutic techniques and strategies to help the patient cultivate a more cohesive, integrated feeling of individual being.

By contrast, the Buddhists believe the most fundamental problem of being is "The presence of a self and the feeling of selfhood. According to Buddhist diagnosis, the deepest source of suffering is the attempt to preserve a self, an attempt which is viewed as both futile and self-defeating. The severest form of psychopathology is precisely *attavadupadana*, the clinging to personal existence."[4]

From the Budhhist perspective, the self is an illusion, a trick of smoke and mirrors. To cling to it, thinking it to be real and enduring—especially seeking to further solidify it—is like the thirsty man in the desert, desperately crawling toward a mirage of water. Jeffrey B. Rubin summarizes this viewpoint in *Psychotherapy and Buddhism*: "We imagine there is a unified, independent self because without special perceptual training, such as meditation, we view subjectivity grossly. Like nonphysicists attempting to examine the particles of a table without the benefit of an electron microscope, we do not see the fluidity, discontinuity and insubstantiality of subjectivity underneath the apparent solidity, continuity, and substantiality."[5] As far as the Buddhist is concerned, then, the self is less a cozy apartment than it is a confining jail cell. Rather than redecorate, the Buddhists say, we need to break out.

Throughout the remainder of this chapter, we will be examining these seemingly opposing perspectives in relation to one another, placing particular emphasis on the character organization schemas of analytic psychology. Although the differences between the psychological and meditative systems are significant, to say the least, these disciplines are by no means mutually exclusive. Properly understood, both Western psychology and Eastern wisdom traditions are means to the same end: a direct experience of "AM-ness," a feeling of individual freedom and natural spontaneity. Rather than dogmatically pursuing the methods of one particular strategy, I suggest an integrated approach. When approached from the right context, the imaginary boundary between meditation and psychotherapy is just that: imaginary. If we are to pursue either of these disciplines to their ultimate conclusion, in fact, we must necessarily be willing to step across to the so-called other side.

Psychology and Self-History

Gurdjieff suggests that the first step in breaking out of prison is realizing you are in prison. From both the psychological and Buddhist perspectives—whether or not you decide the ego is a jail cell—you must begin the search for your core identity through a better understanding of the current strengths, structures, and confines of your personality.

One of the primary ways in which analytic psychology approaches the phenomenon of self is to ask "Where did it come from? How, or why, did *I* start feeling like *me*?" To better understand how the self was originally formed, asserts psychoanalytic thought, is to better understand its habitual actions within, and reactions to, its various present-day environments. In general, three different approaches have been cultivated toward answering this question: classical drive theory, ego psychology, and object relations.

CLASSICAL DRIVE THEORY

Freud originally believed that the individual's sense of self was developed in relation to the management of early instinctual drives, which Freud defined as *libido*. In the first six or so years of the child's life, said Freud, these instinctual drives passed through three stages: oral, anal, and genital. Consequently, the caregiver's response to these various stages would have highly significant formative effects on the individual's adult personality. For example, let's suppose an infant doesn't receive sufficient food when passing through the oral stage of libidinal development. Later, as an adult, this person is likely to still be stuck at this stage. If he feels that he is not receiving enough affection, career fulfillment, or sexual satisfaction, he may substitute the comfort of food, thereby unconsciously translating his adult desire into this unresolved infantile need. Similarly, if the individual encounters significant obstacles during potty training, for instance, she may suffer from poor digestion as an adult, or manifest other "anal-retentive" characteristics such as compulsive housecleaning, etc. The individual who feels particularly rejected or overstimulated during the genital phase, likely encountering much guilt and shame at the onset of puberty, may later find it extremely difficult to engage in a normal, adult sexual relationship.

In many psychological circles, classical drive theory is considered rather archaic. Nonetheless, the idea that the difficulties the individual encounters early on play a very important role in the development of the self still pervades psychological thought. Moreover, examining the differing effect of emotional conflict at various early stages of personality development is still considered an essential means to understanding and addressing adult personality traits. For that matter, Freud's oral, anal, and genital stages aren't nearly so arbitrary and odd as they may initially sound. Correlations between personality organization and these developmental phases have been well documented by both early and contemporary psychologists. The anal-retentive individual, for example, commonly has dreams with various problematic bathroom scenarios—situations in which he or she is unable to control his or her bladder, can't find a suitable restroom, etc. Likewise, an individual partially arrested at the oral stage of development commonly dreams of enormous feasts, experiences frequent dream scenarios in which adult sexual hunger is somehow mingled with childish food hunger and so on. Intuitively—however bizarre we may find Freud's early ideas at first glance—most of us seem to find some significant merit in classical drive theory as, to this day, phrases such as "oral fixation," "anal-retentive," "penis envy" and so on, are quite common in popular culture.

EGO PSYCHOLOGY

Freud introduced this approach to personality later in his career. Although it doesn't exactly counteract his earlier drive theory, it does suggest a different emphasis in understanding the individual's experience of self. Although ego psychology continues to be expanded upon and refined even now, the basic structure Freud originally suggested is still more or less intact.

Loosely corresponding to the oral, anal, and genital stages of drive theory, ego psychology is concerned with the three structures that make up the personality: id, ego, and superego. The id is present at birth and consists of strong, undisciplined urges for self-preservation, love, and sexual satisfaction, as well as unrestrained aggressive desires and destructive impulses. Operating on the pleasure principle, the id wants *all* of these desires gratified, and *fast*—the fact that many of these urges are mutually exclusive being beyond its understanding. At about six months of age, the ego develops. Introducing the reality principle, the ego mediates the conflicting demands of the id, essentially teaching it that not all desires can be fulfilled all the time, but must sometimes be postponed until the appropriate circumstances arise. When the child is about five years old, the superego emerges. Whereas the ego seeks, rationally and realistically, to merely postpone the gratification of the id's conflicting desires, the superego wants to permanently cancel them. For all practical purposes, this aspect of the self is the moral or ethical conscience of the individual, representing learned social rules and standards.

The ego psychologist works with the patient to integrate these three layers, or aspects of self—the primary emphasis being on strengthening the ego. The ego is the location of the "coherent organization of mental processes,"[6] Freud said, or, in Jung's words, the "center of the field of consciousness."[7] As this center acts as a kind of referee between the id and the superego, working to strike the most comfortable balance between childish desires and restrictive moral conscience, the therapist attempts to cultivate a more flexible, resilient ego within the patient's personality. Weak or inflexible egos are easily overpowered by the id's childish urges, manifesting in habitually impulsive and irrational behavior in the adult. Similarly, when the ego is dominated by the superego, the individual is frequently overwhelmed by feelings of guilt and shame, unhealthily restraining his or her instinctual desires. The psychotherapist works with the patient to bring more awareness to the imperfect workings of his or her ego, allowing him or her to better recognize, and rationally manage, the various battles that persistently wage between the id and superego.

OBJECT RELATIONS

For the purposes of our discussion, this is the most current development of psychoanalytic thought in regard to the development of the self. Psychologists such as Melanie Klein, Ronald Fairbairn, Margaret Mahler, and Otto Kernberg have been pioneers in the cultivation of this influential contemporary theory. (There are, in actuality, numerous other significant schools of psychological thought such as Heinz Kohut's self-psychology and Gerhard Adler's individual psychology, which—due to the limited scope of my present discussion—I will not address.)

As its name suggest, object relations is concerned with the ways in which the self relates to external "objects" at various developmental stages. Here, an object is most typically a person, such as a family member, but may also be a more traditional object such as the father's belt or a favorite toy. In the first few months of life, the infant is essentially unaware of external objects—a state which Mahler describes as normal autism. Around the fourth month, the infant enters the separation-individuation phase, in which he or she begins to develop various strategies for relating to different objects. Various conflicts between dependence and independence emerge, bringing about feelings of separation anxiety. At about three years of age, the child has resolved these conflicts to the degree that he or she now recognizes object constancy, which is a permanent sense of both self and external object. At this stage, the child realizes that he or she is both related to, and separate from, objects within the environment.

One of the primary interests of object relations is the understanding of introjected, or internalized, objects. Let's imagine, for example, a woman raised by a distant, yet hypercritical mother. Early on, fearing separation from her mother, this individual learned to introject this critical quality of the mother, to sort of borrow it as part of her own personality. This becomes her way of staying close to the mother, internally relating to her in times of separation. In so doing, perhaps she also becomes distant with, and hypercritical of, others as an adult. Moreover, perhaps this individual becomes hypercritical of *herself*, devaluing her career endeavors, physical appearance, etc. She does this as a way of maintaining emotional contact with her mother, a way of holding on to whatever familiar feelings she had toward her, and toward herself, growing up—even when these feelings are mostly negative or unpleasant in character. From the object-relations perspective, the patient is encouraged to seek more adaptive ways of connecting to this sense of early emotional security. In learning to distinguish more clearly between her own self and external objects, she better appreciates the fact that she is an organic whole, an individual related to, but not dependent upon, her environment. In so doing, she learns to accept her ambivalent feelings toward others, accepting both love and aggression—feelings of closeness and separateness—as natural human responses to mature interpersonal relationships.

THE COMPLEXITY OF "I"

There is an enormous, and ever-growing, body of psychological literature devoted to the many intricacies, inconsistencies, and seemingly infinite expressions of personality and self. My aim here is really not so much to provide an authoritative account of psychological views concerning the development of self, as it is to suggest that the history of the self is an amazingly complicated, and often quite murky, affair. If nothing else, these summaries of psychological thought remind us that the phenomenon we typically describe as "I" is much more complex than it appears on the surface. Who I am, from the psychological perspective, is a complex being formed from past and present circumstances, relationships, and events, many of which are well outside of my conscious awareness. Consequently, it would be safe enough to assume that most of us simply don't really know ourselves nearly as well as we would like to think. With this in mind, I would like to present a very simple guide to a do-it-yourself psychological character diagnosis in the following section.

Character Organization

From the psychological perspective, before we can effectively work with the individual self, we must know what color it is, understand its flavor. In what follows, we will explore various types of character organizations, our immediate goal being the recognition of our own self's primary color and flavor. As discussed in chapter 6, each of us regularly employs a whole arsenal of psychological defenses. To a large degree, those defenses each of us habitually favors determine the primary organization of our personality. In addition, as each of the aforementioned psychological schools emphasizes, our developmental history goes a long way toward forming our character type. With this in mind, we will explore the various defenses and developmental sticking points that tend to dominate various character organizations, as well as describe those organizations from the inside, describe how a depressively organized individual, for example, might typically experience him or herself and his or her environment.

Although organization *type* describes the general flavor or qualities of a given character, within any given type, we find various *levels* of organization. Here, "level" refers to the individual's general strength of self-identity, be it hysterical, masochistic, or schizoid in flavor. No one character type is obviously "crazier" than any other. One can easily have an obsessive-compulsive personality organization, for example, without repeatedly locking the doors, counting footsteps, etc. Within any given type, we will find individuals at the neurotic or well-adjusted level, capable of maintaining healthy relationships, careers, etc. These, for the most part, are the individuals most of us would recognize as "normal." On the other end of the self-identity continuum, we will find the psychotic individual, who often does not feel like the same person from one moment to the next. Such individuals, says Nancy McWilliams, "have grave difficulties with identity—so much so that they are not fully sure *that* they exist, much less whether their existence is satisfying."[8] Those individuals who fall in the rather murky, gray area between neurotic and psychotic are known as "borderline." I will explain the character organizations as they tend to manifest at the neurotic level, assuming that the majority of you most easily identify with this developmental stage of self-identity.

While each of us tends to have one primary character type, we are by no means exclusive specialists. In fact, each of us manifests thoughts and behaviors from all of the following types—even if only occasionally. For this reason, take notice of any particularly strong negative reactions you have when reading the following. If you find yourself thinking, "This obsessive-compulsive type is so obnoxious!" remember that you must also manifest this character type to some degree. Moreover, you are probably irritated by it to the degree that it reminds you of some deeply hidden aspect of your own personality.

It is all too easy to read the following within a strictly intellectual context, treating this material merely as academic musings or theoretical curiosities. To receive the most benefit from what follows, however, it is important that you read with a focus of practical application rather than intellectual scrutiny. If the following is to do you much hands-on good, you should read with an eye for diagnosing yourself as well as others. Because this is no easy task, I suggest the following preparatory exercise.

EXERCISE: PREPARING TO RECOGNIZE YOURSELF

■ Take a few minutes to consider certain problems that have persisted throughout much of your life. Maybe you have been unable to feel sexually satisfied in committed relationships, unable to hold down a job, have a tendency toward addictions of various sorts, etc. Whatever your most habitual problems—*you* know what they are. As you consider these, ask yourself:

- What is going wrong?

- Why do I tend to keep discovering myself in these same sorts of situations over and over? Is it me? Is it someone else?

- Do I habitually make poor choices, or am I just an "unlucky" person?

- What kinds of situations make me particularly uncomfortable?

- Which types of people do I find especially irritating?

Explore these questions as long as you would like, jotting down your thoughts, but try not to come to any ultimate conclusions. In fact, try to keep these questions open as you read along. Our character types most clearly manifest themselves, as it turns out, in difficult situations, recurrent problems, persistent areas of conflict and so forth. For this reason, as you consider the following material, be on the lookout for additional insights that may help you to glimpse a piece of the situation in question that you habitually miss.

THE DEPRESSIVE CHARACTER

Two major feeling states accompany the depressive character. First, the depressive person feels a persistent and relatively pervasive sadness. In acute cases, this sadness may manifest as a certifiable depressive episode, or clinical depression. In such an instance, this feeling may very well be incapacitating, making it very difficult for the individual to maintain a job and other responsibilities. The individual's motor skills will be noticeably slower, appetite will likely fluctuate, and he or she may experience sleep pattern disruption. Frequent bouts of crying and an inability to enjoy things that normally give pleasure also tend to accompany such an episode. Although it's common for a depressive person to experience one or several such concentrated episodes throughout his or her life, it is not a requirement for the depressive character. Just as often, this feeling of sadness is not so acute. It is experienced, rather, as a kind of constant, low-grade melancholy. Although this person may not be depressed in the strictly clinical sense, relatively small upsets may affect him or her considerably. The depressive individual tends to get rather shaken by seemingly minor failures and incidents of loss. If not properly attended to, such upsets may develop into the depressive episode.

Second, the depressive character tends to weigh heavily with a pervasive feeling of guilt. A good example of this is William Goldman's statement, "When I'm accused of a crime I didn't commit, I wonder why I have forgotten it."[9] The depressive person, then, tends to blame him or herself for any conflicts or difficulties that may arise in his or her relationships. This tendency is due largely to the depressive person's difficulty in expressing anger. Rather than getting angry with someone "out there," the person turns his or her anger inward, pointing it back at him or herself. For this reason, the depressive individual often benefits considerably from learning to redirect anger externally, realizing he or she is not solely responsible for all of life's crimes.

These feelings of sadness and guilt seem to stem from some early experience of loss. Perhaps one of the child's parents was physically absent throughout childhood. This loss may also be much more subtle—having a depressive mother, for instance. It is known that depression tends to run in families. One of the primary reasons for this may be the fact that depressive parents tend to lack the necessary energy to sufficiently attend to the needs and wants of a child. In the context of object relations, the depressive character deals with this sense of loss by forming a kind of mental representation of the lost person or object, and carries it throughout life, interacting with it internally in an attempt to heal earlier wounds. As this process is described in *Psychoanalytic Terms and Concepts*, the depressive individual maintains "an intense but ambivalent internal relationship with the mental representation of what is lost. Love for the object represented leads to the mechanism of identification in order to keep it within the self, while feelings of hate demand its destruction. Since the individual identifies with the representation of the lost object, he or she experiences these destructive forces as if directed toward the self."[10]

A child who is raised by a depressive mother, for example, would form a mental image of the mother and relate to it internally as a way of protecting herself from an imperfect caretaker. The feelings of anger that the child would necessarily develop toward the imperfect caretaker get redirected back at this internalized object, resulting in feelings of guilt. In essence, that individual goes on to act the part of both herself *and* the lost mother, punishing herself as a kind of stand-in for the mother.

In terms of drive theory, this early loss is thought of as a fixation at the oral stage of development. Perhaps the depressive mother didn't have enough energy to feed the child properly or attend to its other needs during the oral stage of libidinal development. Consequently, the depressive individual goes through life feeling somehow "hungry"—as if his or her life wasn't properly nourishing. Not surprisingly, then, many depressive people eat, smoke or drink to lessen this pervasive oral longing. It is not uncommon, then, for depressive individuals to become overweight, develop eating disorders, or to develop substance abuse problems.

All things considered, depressive people tend to be quite warm and amiable. McWilliams writes, "Unless they are so disturbed that they cannot function normally, most depressive people are easy to like and admire. Because they aim hatred and criticism inward rather than outward, they are usually generous, sensitive, and compassionate to a fault."[11]

THE HYSTERICAL CHARACTER

This character organization is also known as "histrionic," and is most common in women—although not uncommon in men. According to *Psychoanalytic Terms and Concepts*, the hysterical individual is "exhibitionistic, seductive, labile in mood, and prone to act out oedipal fantasies, yet fearful of sexuality and inhibited in action."[12] One of the main characteristics of the hysterical individual, then, is a tendency to dramatize her emotional states in an effort to captivate the attention of others. These dramatic moods tend to change often and abruptly in an attempt to keep the "show" interesting. In a process known as conversion, the hysteric converts these emotional exaggerations into physical symptoms. In Freud's time, this was the mechanism behind the infamous swoon of the romantically affected woman. These days, conversion tends to be much more subtle. Sudden onset of sleepiness, hiccups, headaches, back pain, stomach cramps, and many other relatively minor physical discomforts are common in hysterical individuals.

Another major characteristic of the hysteric is sexual repression. For developmental reasons discussed further on, the histrionic individual feels particularly ashamed of her sexual desires. Consequently, she tends to not find much legitimate satisfaction or enjoyment in the sexual act. Ironically, however, due to the intense compression of her sexual urges, these urges tend to "leak out" unconsciously, manifesting in non-sexual areas of her life. For example, the hysteric tends to be highly seductive, knowingly and unknowingly sexualizing relationships through flirtation, seductive dress and mannerisms, etc. This advertising of sex without the expected follow-through is the primary characteristic associated with the stereotypical sexual "tease." This repression also tends to show up in pervasive feelings of generalized anxiety, stress, and explosive fits of anger and emotionality.

This sexual repression can likewise manifest in physical symptoms. For instance, Freud describes women suffering from glove paralysis, a condition in which loss of feeling and mobility is experienced in one hand. As Freud discovered in working with these women, this condition resulted from the woman's anxiety about her sexual desire—specifically her practice of masturbation. If she masturbated with her right hand, that hand would become chronically limp, preventing her from satisfying her sexual desire in this particularly guilt-inducing manner. Although such a direct form of conversion is not as common these days, hysterical women often suffer from some persistent physical symptom or symptoms with an unclear medical diagnosis. Once these women learn to reconnect with their sexual desire, these symptoms—as was the case with Freud's glove paralysis patients—are significantly alleviated, or go away altogether.

Developmentally, the hysteric tends to come from a family in which the female role was somehow denigrated in relation to that of the male. Perhaps the mother was viewed as weak and passive in relation to the dominant father. Similarly, the female hysteric may have an older brother whom she believed to be favored for his masculine qualities. "Girly" qualities may have been criticized in such a household as being inferior to "manly" traits. Consequently, the hysteric comes to perceive men as more powerful than women. Wanting to balance this power differential, she seeks to "borrow" the power of a dominant male. Feeling that the primary quality she has to offer is that of feminine sexuality, she attempts to seduce this man through her "feminine wiles." Even if this attempt is successful, however, the sexual aspect of this relationship quickly becomes a hostile battleground. Due to her false notion that men are somehow innately more powerful than women, the hysteric resents this and tries to gain power by withholding sex, disengaging, or acting indifferently to the sexual act.

In terms of drive theory, hysteria can be understood as being "stuck" at two different phases: oral and oedipal. Typically, much like the depressive, the hysteric would have experienced the mother as being inattentive at the oral stage. Whereas the depressive attempts to solve this problem by internalizing the mother, the hysteric strategically devalues women in general, defensively deciding that she will never depend on the unreliable feminine object for fulfillment. When she reaches the oedipal phase and begins to have sexual feelings for the father, she displaces all of her earlier dissatisfaction with the mother onto this stage, unconsciously intensifying her sexual feelings. As the father is not an obtainable sexual object for her, however, the hysteric develops a strategy of seduction without fulfillment. As Freud discovered in his work with hysterics, she tends to represent unobtainable male power through the symbol of the penis—hence the infamous term "penis envy."

Although the hysterical character is often perceived as shallow and false in many respects, the hysteric is also commonly experienced as warm and engaging. Her attempts to capture the attention of others often result in a highly energetic and entertaining personality, the "life of the party." Despite the ambivalence and various contradictions that go along with hysteria, the histrionic individual is typically emotionally expressive and genuinely open in certain ways, and can be a charismatic and sincere person.

THE OBSESSIVE-COMPULSIVE CHARACTER

This character organization relies heavily on repetitive patterns of thought and behavior. Obsessions involve repetitious, circular patterns of thinking, whereas compulsions involve repetitive doing. Although these defenses tend to go together, the obsessive-compulsive person may rely more heavily on one than the other.

According to *Psychoanalytic Terms and Concepts*, obsessions are thoughts that "occur against one's will" and can include "rumination . . . brooding . . . reflection, musing or pondering . . . All these mental phenomena involve an effort made to solve an emotional conflict by thinking, but the conclusion or solution is avoided, and the person starts the process over again repeatedly."[13] When such a person encounters a difficult emotion, then, he or she will likely engage in some unsolvable thought riddle. The person may wonder what he or she will be doing 20 years in the future, or consider infinite subtle meanings of a coworker's curious smile earlier that day. Rather than experiencing an emotional conflict directly, the obsessive person tends to get lost in the impossible labyrinth of the "meaning of life," or some other mental abstraction.

"Compulsions and rituals are persistent and irresistible urges to engage in apparently meaningless acts; they are the motor equivalent of obsessive thoughts and often accompany them. . . . The person so afflicted usually knows that his or her acts are unreasonable but is unable to control them."[14] Rather than face certain emotional difficulties, the compulsive individual may become a workaholic or an overachiever. They may engage themselves in housecleaning, meticulous straightening and arranging, and other minutely detailed tasks. Acts such as exercise, eating, intoxicant use, gambling and sex can also be used as outlets for compulsive tendencies.

Classically, the obsessive-compulsive character has been conceived in terms of fixation at the anal stage. According to Freud, certain characteristics—"cleanliness, stubbornness, concerns with punctuality, tendencies toward withholding"[15]—which form the basis for childhood potty-training scenarios, are also prevalent in the "anal" adult, or obsessive-compulsive individual. Though this emphasis of the importance of potty-training may at first seem rather bizarre, Freud's conception was highly logical. When we consider that "toilet training usually constitutes the first situation in which the child must renounce what is natural for what is socially acceptable," this early stage seems a likely breeding ground for the obsessive-compulsive character. Similar to the potty-training child, "the basic . . . conflict in obsessive and compulsive people is rage (at being controlled) versus fear (of being condemned or punished)."[16] Parents who are particularly harsh or critical at this stage, then, would be more likely to contribute to the formation of an obsessive-compulsive character.

The object relations school describes this same conflict, albeit with less emphasis on the potty-training particulars. From this perspective, unusually critical or demanding parents are likely to behave as such throughout all phases of the child's development. Although parents who are strict and consistent in punishing bad behavior and rewarding good behavior often contribute to a sense of a sturdy self-esteem, emotional stability, and responsibility in the developing individual, this is not always the case. Parents who punish and reward without much emotional warmth or affection are likely to exacerbate obsessive and compulsive tendencies. Moreover, parents who emphasize moralistic aspects of behavior are likely to complicate the situation. For example, parents who say, "A *good* person doesn't do such and such," or, "I'm doing this *for your own good*," tend to encourage obsessive and compulsive defense mechanisms.

These defenses are essentially intended to distance the obsessive-compulsive person from uncomfortable emotional material. Fearing a loss of control in certain situations, the individual occupies him or herself with detailed thoughts and behaviors, attempting to be safely isolated from the emotional situation at hand. Fantasies of omnipotent control are at the core of the obsessive-compulsive character, often resulting in magical rituals such as the athlete's elaborate incantations before the big game. There is often a sense of atonement about the thoughts and behaviors of this character type. If such an individual takes a day off work, for example, he or she may seek to "atone" for this act through compulsive housecleaning, or obsessively considering some problem at work.

Although the obsessive-compulsive individual can be highly frustrating and stubborn, at the higher-functioning levels he or she tends to be highly responsible and dependable. This person's attention to detail often makes him or her a great employee and caretaker. Moreover, many important innovators of philosophy, science, and other exacting mental disciplines, have shown obvious signs of the obsessive-compulsive character.

THE MASOCHISTIC CHARACTER

Originally, masochism referred to the tendency of certain individuals to seek out physical and mental pain as a means of sexual gratification. In the context of the masochistic character organization, however, this sexual component is de-emphasized. Very likely, the masochistically oriented person—also known as self-defeating—will relate to suffering in two primary non-sexual ways. First, the masochist thinks of him or herself as a kind of martyr. Although, like the depressive, the masochist experiences a pervasive feeling of sadness, he or she directs the blame outward rather than inward, having a "tendency to complain about being a victim of fate and of malevolent people."[17] Typically, the masochistic individual would describe him or herself as being underpaid, underappreciated, or mistreated by employers, suffering these work conditions out of a sense of obligation or responsibility. Similarly, the masochistic character tends to perceive relationships as being imbalanced, the other person being a bit of a tyrant who habitually takes advantage of him or her. The masochistic suffers these various conditions with a hidden sort of arrogance, perceiving him or herself to be morally superior to his or her unjust detractors.

Second, the masochist tends to manifest pervasive self-defeating behaviors through an "unconscious need for punishment, based on a sense of guilt, which leads to neurotic symptoms of unconsciously self-inflicted suffering via accidents, financial loss, unhappy relationships, failure, or disgrace."[18] This mechanism of self-punishment—unconsciously choosing a poor employer, bad relationships, etc.— closely correlates to the above-mentioned mechanism of martyrdom. The masochist unconsciously becomes involved in unpleasant circumstances and blames these circumstances on morally inferior individuals whom he or she patiently "tolerates," thereby maintaining his or her self-image as a graciously long-suffering, morally or ethically superior person.

It should be emphasized, however, that the masochistic individual does not become involved in all this suffering because he or she truly *enjoys* it. Rather, masochism, like all other character organizations, is a kind of strategy. The masochist suffers, believing this to be a necessary means toward some greater individual good. This strategy tends to play out in three primary ways. First, due to some early loss—a depressive or absent mother, divorce, physical abuse, etc.—the masochist, much like the depressive, tends to feel guilty, imagining his or her own "badness" as having caused these painful situations. As I mentioned earlier, the masochist differs from the depressive in that he or she attempts to deflect this guilt onto some external object. For example, imagine a child who undergoes the trauma of his parent's divorce, blames himself, and then later interacts with a stepfather. As a strategy for dealing with his deep, unconscious guilt, the child decides that the *stepfather* is bad, that *he* was somehow the cause of his parent's divorce. As a way of proving this notion, the child then goes on to act out in an attempt to provoke volatile or violent behavior from this "immoral" person.

Second, closely related to the above mechanism, the masochist defeats him or herself as a subversive means to obtain power. Due to early experiences, he or she believes that it's just a matter of time before authority figures are going to punish him or her. Rather than deal with the constant anxiety of waiting for the other shoe to drop, the masochist takes matters in hand. Fearing punishment from her employer, for instance, she may unconsciously provoke that very behavior. Not only does this reduce the tension of anticipatory anxiety, it also reassures the masochist of her personal power. Internally, she has managed to transform a situation in which she was vulnerable, seemingly dependent on the whims of some authoritative party, into a case of "I'll get you before you get me."

Third, the masochist employs the strategy of "I'd rather be hit than not touched at all."[19] As a child, the masochistically-oriented individual may have noticed that his or her negligent caretakers were most attentive when he or she was in a state of suffering. As an adult, then, the masochist seeks the attention and affection of others by repeatedly displaying, and often exaggerating, his or her own difficult conditions. Should these conditions fail to impress, the masochist tends to seek out worse and worse circumstances until he or she achieves the feeling of being properly appreciated and attended to.

THE NARCISSISTIC CHARACTER

In the context of clinical psychology, narcissism refers to "people whose personalities are organized around maintaining their self-esteem by getting affirmation from outside themselves."[20] This reliance on others for their self-esteem results in a "curious apparent contradiction between a very inflated concept of themselves, and an inordinate need for tribute from others."[21] On the surface, the narcissistic person tends to appear very grandiose, self-satisfied, and judgmental of others. These appearances are merely red herrings, however, attempts to cover up the narcissistic individual's core reliance upon the opinions of others. This seeming contradiction may be best appreciated when viewed from a developmental perspective.

Typically, the narcissistic adult was a highly sensitive child, attuned to subtle emotional and behavioral cues from his or her parents. It has been suggested that many narcissistic people were uncommonly gifted in this way as children. Certain caretakers, unconsciously aware of this gift, make use of it to inflate their own self-esteem. They may view the child as a narcissistic extension of themselves. If such a parent wanted to be a musician or an athlete but was never able to do so, he or she may decide that the child must fulfill this lacking aspect of him or herself. Similarly, if parents are unhappy with some aspect of themselves—being over-weight, for example—they may project this criticism onto the sensitive child, becoming hyper-vigilant of the child's eating patterns. The child grows up, then, experiencing two very different images of him or herself. First, he or she feels somehow empty of self-identity, having been habitually treated as an aspect of someone else. Second, he or she feels the urgent desire to fill this emptiness by staking a claim in the world, achieving perfection, proving him or herself to be unique and superior to others.

Two emotions are at the core of the narcissistic self: shame and envy. Shame, it should be emphasized, is quite different from guilt. Whereas guilt is a kind of inter-nal judgment, a feeling of "I am bad," shame is a feeling that one *appears* bad to others. It is decidedly an externally-focused feeling. For this reason, the narcissistic person is more concerned with proving his or her goodness to others than experi-encing it within. Consequently, he or she is very interested in objective rankings, consistently seeking ways to rank as best. Attending the best school, wooing the most attractive or successful partner, winning the highest award—these are priorities for the narcissistic individual. Most narcissistic individuals don't *appear* very shameful, of course. Rather, an external audience would likely view them as highly confident, accomplished, and full of pride. The narcissistic person goes to great lengths to encourage this false view of him or herself, typically to his or her own detriment.

Closely related to the narcissistic character's shame is an equally pervasive envy. Once again, the narcissistic individual does not envy those he or she personally believes to be successful or satisfied, but rather, those whom a *general audience* con-siders as such. Consequently, celebrities are favorite targets of narcissistic envy. The narcissistic individual defends against his or her envy by criticizing such "audience favorites," affecting the illusion of superiority and disinterested self-sufficiency. Narcissistic envy is also defended against by becoming a narcissistic projection of the envied individual. If I envy the fame of Beethoven, for example, I may decide that he and I belong in the same camp of exceptional individuals. It is then safe to openly admire Beethoven as I am really admiring myself *through* Beethoven. Such narcissis-tically organized individuals tend to be "characterized by a sense of entitlement and fantasies of omniscience, omnipotence, and perfection of the self"[22]—often to such a degree where they more or less mistake themselves for a kind of celebrity, thereby defending against the inescapable failures of human competition.

Aware at some level of feelings of emptiness and fragile self-esteem, the narcissistic individual often avoids intimate relationships. Sincere apologies and expressions of gratitude or affection are rare among narcissistic people, as they essentially resist this basic recognition of "otherness." When his or her inflated sense of self is called into question, the narcissistic individual commonly flies into a narcissistic rage, morally indignant that his or her habitual sense of entitlement and superiority is not being properly gratified.

Although the narcissistic character is obviously full of difficulties, especially in interpersonal relationships, it should be mentioned that such individuals are frequently admired for their unique giftedness—which is to suggest that their feeling of specialness may not be altogether without justification. Their core drive toward artistic, physical, or moral perfection, albeit pathological and unrealistic, often motivates such a person to excel in numerous, objectively recognizable ways.

THE SCHIZOID CHARACTER

The schizoid personality organization is characterized by a "defensive tendency to retreat from the complexity of interpersonal reality to the familiarity of a simplified world of inner objects."[23] It should be emphasized, however, that although all levels of schizoid organization involve a withdrawal into a kind of inner fantasy realm, this is not to suggest that all schizoid individuals are schizophrenic. As with all the character types considered so far, the schizoid personality is found on a continuum from highly adaptive to psychotic. With higher functioning schizoids, this tendency to withdraw often leads to creative, sophisticated works of art, philosophy, and spirituality.

In terms of classical drive theory, there is much debate as to which stage the schizoid is stuck. As many schizoids report a pervasive fear of being engulfed, or "swallowed up," by intimate relationships, many psychologists have supposed that the schizoid fixation is an oral one. Others, however, have suggested some genetic hypersensitivity that causes schizoid infants to avoid motion, bright lights, and affectionate embraces. Whatever the case may be, a certain style of rearing does seem common to most schizoid individuals. Over-involved, intrusive parents sometimes foster a sense of emotional claustrophobia that can lead to schizoid characteristics. This situation seems to be exacerbated by parents who are both invasive and emotionally dishonest, sending confusing messages throughout development. The schizoid character develops as a means of withdrawing from both unwanted external intrusions, as well as ambivalent inner states.

Typically, the schizoid individual is conceived as a kind of detached onlooker or observer, watching his or her own feelings as well as the external world with a kind of cool objectivity. "Affectively, one of the most striking aspects of many high-functioning individuals with schizoid dynamics is their lack of common defenses. They tend to be in touch with many emotional reactions at a level of genuineness that awes and even intimidates their acquaintances."[24] This objective sort of openness comes with a price, however. The schizoid is able to accurately observe and comment on his or her own feelings as well as those of others so easily only because he or she fails to connect to them in a genuinely "feeling" way. He or she often feels much more like a scientist participating in an experiment, or an actor crafting a scene, than a person participating in normal human emotions.

As the word *schizoid* implies, the essence of the schizoid character involves a kind of "splitting." This splitting takes two forms. First, fearing engulfment from his or her environment, the schizoid splits the self from the outside world. As stated previously, one of the ways he or she does this is by entering into emotional states only indirectly—*recognizing* them more than *feeling* them. When interacting with a schizoid individual, one is likely to feel both very engaged on a personal level, as well as curiously disengaged. Oftentimes, the schizoid feels more comfortable experiencing emotional states through his interactions with internal objects. The musician may have more "romantic" interest in his or her instrument than his or her partner. The writer may react more emotionally through his or her created characters than daily situations. "One of the most striking aspects of people with schizoid personalities is their disregard for social conventions."[25] Through personality eccentricities and often bizarre behaviors, the schizoid attempts to maintain a safe distance between himself and the agreed-upon world "out there."

Second, seeking to avoid the deep emotional conflicts that he or she encountered early on, the schizoid individual splits his or her experienced self from his or her own desires. The schizoid may project these desires for food, sex, or aggression onto his or her environment, which he or she then perceives as devouring or overwhelming. One of the most common ways schizoids create distance from their environment is through intellectualization. They recognize their desires, may even be willing to discuss them and examine them quite openly, but somehow never connect to them in a fully organic way. Consequently, the schizoid individual's rich inner world, as expressed through art, music, literature, etc., is likely to be rampant with bizarre and childish manifestations of violence and sexual desire, alongside striking oral and anal fixations.

Although the schizoid person often appears quite odd and non-sociable, he or she can be a very insightful and original thinker or innovative artist. His or her interpersonal relations may seem rather cold and mechanical at times, but when one catches a glimpse of this person's inner reality, much human warmth and emotional complexity tends to be revealed.

THE MANIC CHARACTER

Mania, according to Nancy McWilliams, is the "flip side of depression."[26] Whereas the depressive tends toward sadness, slowed motor response, and feelings of guilt, the manic individual is often elated, constantly "on the go," and grandiose. The manic person is highly energetic, sociable, and seems to be in a near-constant, quite exhausting state of excitement.

Like the depressive character, the manic character seems to develop in response to some early loss, the main difference being that the manic individual typically suffers some significantly more traumatic or painful circumstance. Whereas the depressive individual may be inadequately attended to by a depressive mother, the manic person may have literally lost his or her mother in an accident, or been severely abused. Likewise fixated at the oral level, the manic tends to talk non-stop, eat or drink excessively, chew gum, bite his or her nails, etc.

It should be emphasized that, although the manic may appear at first glance to be highly entertaining and "full of life," this is not the whole story. Like all other personality organizations, mania is an unconscious strategy to deal with disowned pain and emotional ambivalence. The two main defense mechanisms of the manic individual are denial and acting out. Whereas the depressive attempts to heal old wounds through introjection, directing his or her childish anger toward the lost object inward, the manic simply tries to ignore any reminders of childhood traumas. When feelings of anxiety or loss start to arise, the manic person urgently engages in one distraction after another. Wanting to avoid deeply painful feelings at any cost, the manically organized individual is overwhelmed with a "hunger for stimulus and new experience," frequently manifested as "pressure of speech" and "flight of ideas."[27] This acting out may take the form of compulsive humor, flirtation, grandiose schemes and plans, or virtually any other means of frantic doing. At the core of this intense avoidance is a deep fear of emotional attachment. To prevent him or herself from re-experiencing some traumatic early loss, the manic attaches to others on a rather superficial level, never "settling" long enough to risk rejection or abandonment.

Since mania is really just a more energetically charged version of the depressive character, most manic individuals frequently lapse into states of depression. In more extreme cases, this alternation between mania and depression is known as bi-polar disorder—what was once referred to as manic-depression. Many charismatic celebrities have suffered from this, and less extreme versions of mania. Although exhausting, the perpetual flight of the manic individual can be very exciting and engaging, and fuel episodes of intense creativity and expression.

I have chosen to forego summaries of three character types—antisocial, paranoid, and dissociative—as they are not within the scope of this work. Although each of these three is not unheard of at the neurotic level, they are far more common at lower-functioning borderline and psychotic levels. For those readers who are interested, detailed descriptions of each of these, as well as elaborations on the above, can be found in Nancy McWilliams' work (see Bibliography).

EXERCISE: DISCOVERING YOURSELF ON THE WAY TO NO-SELF

■ Take a few minutes to focus, rather loosely, on any simple object as described in the chapter on concentration practice (see page 95). As you concentrate on this object, notice any distractions that may arise—gently returning your focus to your object each time. Try this for 15 minutes or so, noting how the longer you sit, the more compelling the distractions. Afterward, mentally review your list of distractions. Did you mentally review the details of your finances or think about house-cleaning? Did you lose yourself in an elaborate fantasy or recall your favorite TV show? Were you surprised by feelings of sadness, emptiness, or anger? Were you distracted by physical aches and pains or sexual desire?

When you examine it carefully, you can probably recognize how your list of distractions fits into one or many of the character organization types. Whatever your distractions, when described psychologically, they could be classified as compulsions, obsessions, anxiety, guilt, etc. In contrast, for the Buddhist, distractions are distractions, personalities are personalities.

No-Self

Buddhism's description of the self stands in striking contrast with psychology's detailed categories of character type, defense mechanisms, and developmental theories. To engage ourselves in naming and categorizing our individual character type is simply to indulge in our own egocentric perspective, to become morbidly fascinated and captivated by our own sickness, asserts traditional Buddhism. Although this is a gross reduction of Buddhist conception of the self, we could say that many Buddhists tend to view psychology as a "cure" worse than the original sickness.

Regarding the individual self, *The Dhammapada* says that "All states are without self; those who realize this are freed from suffering. This is the path that leads to pure wisdom. . . . Him I call a *brahmin* [individual free of selfish desire] who has turned his back upon himself. Homeless, he is ever at home; egoless, he is ever full."[28] This is known as the doctrine of *anatman*, or "no-self," which forms the very core of Buddhist teaching. Walpola Rahula clearly summarizes this doctrine:

> Buddhism stands unique in the history of human thought in denying the existence of such a Soul, Self, or *Atman*. According to the teaching of the Buddha, the idea of self is an imaginary, false belief which has no corresponding reality, and it produces harmful thoughts of "me" and "mine," selfish desire, craving, attachment, hatred, ill-will, conceit, pride, egoism, and other defilements, impurities and problems. It is the source of all the troubles in the world from personal conflicts to wars between nations. In short, to this false view can be traced all the evil in the world.[29]

From this perspective, then, psychology's elaborate representations of this and that type of self are as useless as a madman's complex categorizations and manipulations of his various hallucinations. The point, according to Buddhism, isn't so much to recognize, strengthen, or repair the self, so much as it is to let it go, recognize it as mere imagination.

Even so, Buddhism is not without its own description of self or character type. When discussing this ego-mirage, the Buddhists refer to the five *skandhas*, or "aggregates." These five are: form, feeling, physical perception, mental constituents or mechanisms, and consciousness. In any given moment, say the Buddhists, the experiential, individual self is a dynamic swirl of these five aggregates. When I watch my mind in meditation, I will notice these five components constantly arising and dissolving, each one of them competing for the energy of mental attachment. Notice that the *specific* feelings, physical perceptions, etc., are de-emphasized. In this context, all feelings, all forms, are distracting in that they are impermanent. Feelings change from moment to moment, as do the various mechanism of the mind, so to get caught up in labeling them is useless. In the Buddhist doctrine of "no-self," there is only one character type— that of delusion or self-centeredness. Whether our delusion takes the impermanent, ever-shifting form of depression, mania, or narcissism is of secondary importance.

The ultimate goal in meditation, then, is to essentially deconstruct the self, dissolve these five aggregates back into their most elemental form. In *Transformations of Consciousness*, Jack Engler describes the meditative experience of this deconstruction: "The normal sense that I am a fixed, continuous point of observation from which I regard this object, now that, is dispelled. . . . When my attention is sufficiently refined . . . all that is actually apparent to me from moment to moment is a mental or physical event and an awareness of that event. . . . No enduring or substantial entity or observer or experiencer or agent—no self—can be found behind or apart from these moment-to-moment events to which they could be attributed."[30]

Put simply, our typical experience of an individual "I" or ego merges into one continuous stream of "things happening" during meditation. To say that I am a depressive or manic person in such a moment no longer has much significance, for my so-called personality is merely another object that is floating by in a liquid chain of moments. Engler goes on to say, "the stream of consciousness literally break[s] up into a series of discrete events which are discontinuous in space and time. . . . When this total moment-to-moment 'coming and passing away' . . . is experienced, there is a profound understanding of the radical impermanence . . . of all events."[31]

To examine this concept of "no-self" less abstractly, imagine a scientist peering into a microscope studying some bacterial organism. While studying the bacterial cell structure, the scientist's intense focus may unfold to an awareness that the scientist's *own* being—the observer—is also a collection of similarly structured cells and so forth. If the scientist's focus continues to deepen, all notions of "scientist" and "bacterial organism" dissolve into one seamless process of cellular *happening*. It's suddenly cell meeting cell meeting cell—the individual "flavor" of each specific cell becoming much less significant than the indescribable, ownerless, and dynamic awareness of oneness itself.

Integrating Self and No-Self

It may appear that psychology and Buddhism simply don't mix all that well. Traditionally, the two disciplines have been rather hostile toward one another. These days, however, there is decidedly a movement underway—among both Buddhists and psychologists—to integrate the two. Differences in method aside, these two disciplines obviously share a common goal: alleviation of suffering. With this in mind, it seems likely that Buddhism and psychology would essentially compliment rather than threaten one another.

As I have been emphasizing throughout this book, Buddhism, psychology, art, and philosophy are all simply different paths, different angles of approach toward the same ultimate goal: self-knowledge and realization. Consequently, to judge one discipline or path as superior to another is to miss the whole point of *all* paths and systems. It is important to recognize that whatever path you are drawn to, *that's* the highest path for you. There is only one path—the "spiritual" path—although it may appear to us in many different forms along different legs of the journey. It is ultimately ridiculous to bicker about the superiority of psychology or Buddhism, because properly understood, no clear line can be legitimately drawn between the two. Jack Kornfield writes in *A Path with Heart*:

> We have acknowledged that these [psychological] issues cannot be separated from spiritual life. It is not as if we get our psychological house in order and then strike out to attain nirvana. As our body, heart, mind and spirit open, each new layer we encounter reveals both greater freedom and compassion and deeper and more subtle layers of underlying delusion. Our deep personal work and our meditative work must necessarily proceed together. What American practice has come to acknowledge is that many of the deep issues we uncover in spiritual life cannot be healed by meditation alone. Problems such as early abuse, addiction, and difficulties of love and sexuality require the close, conscious and ongoing support of a skillful teacher [or therapist] to resolve.[32]

The opposite side of this point should also be emphasized. Just as psychological strategies are often necessary if meditation is to work most effectively, psychology alone often fails to go deep enough to uproot the most fundamental, core issues underneath our emotional difficulties. In what follows, I am going to describe a cooperative journey of development that can be conceptualized in three distinct phases. Although, as Kornfield suggests, psychology and spirituality are necessarily equally present and important at each successive stage, I am choosing, for the sake of clarity, to consider each discipline as a kind of "specialty." In this context, psychology and Buddhism differ primarily in their overall emphasis of particular stages of the journey and, consequently, the specific methods in which they "specialize."

PHASE 1—IGNORANCE

At this stage, the seeker has very little psychological or spiritual awareness. This would describe all children and a good many adults. The seeker is not quite a seeker just yet, but rather a frantic chaser of pleasure. He or she wanders from one experience to the next, sometimes elated, sometimes miserable, but lacking any real sense of meaning to hold the overall context of experience together. Happiness and unhappiness appear to be random situations in which the individual haphazardly "finds" him or herself. His or her feelings and behaviors—the true cause of his or her happiness and unhappiness—are mostly automatic and unconscious at this point, emotions, actions and circumstances appearing as one vague blur of happening. If "ignorance is bliss," the ignorant seeker is not yet aware of it.

PHASE 2—THE THERAPEUTIC SPLIT

Once the seeker has experienced sufficient pain and disillusion in his or her journey—and this happens to each of us sooner or later—he or she begins to look for some larger meaning, some more stable context from which to understand and experience him or herself. This stage is the specialty of psychology. For example, whether or not I, as the seeker, actually enter therapy, I begin to develop what psychologists call the therapeutic split. Whereas the self was previously one big blur of acting and reacting, it now begins to divide itself into two parts: observing ego and experiencing ego. This split is crucial if I am to understand my own psychology. If I am so totally involved in being compulsive, for example, how am I supposed to *recognize* I am being compulsive? I begin to cultivate a calm, detached part of myself, which learns to sit back and watch the other part of myself—at best, non-judgmentally. From this "outside" perspective, I learn to relax my self-centered grip enough so that I can honestly recognize my defensive patterns, organizing character type, and other aspects of myself. Doing so, I begin to make decisions about which aspects of myself I would like to leave as is, and which I would like to improve. At this point, I'm no longer so "full of myself" that I fail to recognize that my own thoughts and actions are the cause of my most persistent pain and struggles.

Spiritual systems approach this same phase from a similar angle—albeit relatively de-emphasized. Here is when the cultivation of "the witness" comes into play (see page 103). Through concentration practice, as in therapy, the individual learns to split his or her experience into watcher and doer. He or she begins to notice when he or she loses this focus and gets caught up in old habits of thinking and behaving. The individual's focus gradually strengthens to the degree that he or she can watch the intricacies of his or her mind and personality unfolding from moment to moment without chasing after them. Even so, the path of intensive meditation can be very confusing and destabilizing at this stage. Kornfield cautions us:

> All too often the mistaken belief that enough sincere practice of prayer or meditation is all that is needed to transform their lives has prevented teachers and students from making use of the helpful teachings of Western psychology. In an unfortunate way, many students of Eastern and Western spirituality have been led to believe that if they experience difficulties, it is simply because they haven't practiced long enough or somehow have not been practicing according to the teachings. . . . In truth, the need to deal with our personal emotional problems is the rule in spiritual practice rather than the exception. At least half of the students at our annual three-month retreat find themselves unable to do traditional Insight Meditation because they encounter so much unresolved grief, fear, and wounding and unfinished developmental business from the past that this becomes their meditation.[33]

A good way to think of the particular method of self-realization at this point of the journey, then, is as a strategy of making the recognition and understanding of your own psychology your primary meditation. Traditional meditation can be practiced, of course, but it seems to work better as a supplement to psychological work at this point rather than an intensive, exclusive path of inquiry. Like it or not, most of us will need to participate in formal psychotherapy if we are to proceed beyond this stage. The vast majority of us are so firmly entrenched, so impossibly stuck in our emotional past, that we require the help of a skilled professional if we are to truly uncover and process this highly-charged personal material.

PHASE 3—PRESENCE

Whether by way of therapy, meditation, or both, when the individual becomes sufficiently calm and self-aware, he or she naturally begins to progress into this next phase. In many ways, this leg of the journey is much less "personal" than the previous two, as the individual has now begun to authentically remember and yearn for The One. This is the specialty of spirituality. As Freud noted late in his career, the therapy patient often reaches a place where he or she has considerable insight into the nature of his or her problems, but the problems still persist—albeit with much less urgency and disruption of the patient's daily life. Although contemporary psychologists continue to grapple with this dilemma and refine their methods and theories, the most general, often unspoken conclusion seems to be this: Being a person *necessarily* involves frustration, dissatisfaction, and suffering. Although we can never fully transcend these human limits, traditional psychology asserts, we can ease the burdens they place upon us.

At the same time, however, a psychological focus and intensive psychotherapy can still be highly effective at this point. In the words of Kornfield, "The best of modern therapy is much like a process of shared meditation, where therapist and client sit together, learning to pay close attention to those aspects and dimensions of the self that the client may be unable to touch on his or her own."[34] Our psychological strategies begin to take on a slightly different flavor at this stage, then. Our individual personality is still of great significance, but we are most interested in the ways it reacts with other personalities. It is this overall process of psyche reacting with psyche, we are beginning to understand, that is our truest self, our truest "personality."

Although Buddhism doesn't exactly disagree with psychology's attitude regarding the necessity of human suffering, it does turn it on its head at this stage. If being a person is necessarily dissatisfying, Buddhism asks, why not be something *more than* a person? Why not let go of egocentric individuality once and for all so you can become it *all*—a context in which words like "suffering" and "frustration" no longer carry negative meaning? At this stage in the journey, these ideas are no longer simply mystical theories or highfalutin abstractions. Rather, the seeker has begun to experientially appreciate oneness as a practical and necessary means of self-realization. Issues such as personality and individual desire are becoming increasingly less important—or at least conceptually less meaningful—and he or she is simply going about his or her business from moment to moment. The seeker is coming full circle at this point, healing even the hard-earned therapeutic split between observing ego and experiencing ego. His or her actions and feeling are once again automatic and spontaneous, but now the seeker truly understands the meaning of the phrase, "ignorance is bliss." Legitimately accepting unhappiness as a necessary condition for happiness, the seeker begins to accept all experiences willingly, without resistance, being more fully present in every aspect of life. In a manner of speaking, the seeker has become so focused on the path itself that he or she begins to be blissfully ignorant of selfish desires and preferences. At this point, even habitual scarecrows such as death no longer have a hold on the seeker, as he or she has begun to identify with the infinite whole more than with the finite, individual "me."

Ironically, from the perspective of this last phase, there was never a journey to go on in the first place, never anyone *in particular* to go on a journey. It's all been part of the One Dance, the Divine begins to remember through each of us, which has necessarily been perfect at every stage of so-called development. And the greatest mystery of all is this: Even though words such as "personality" and "desire" no longer have any real, objective meaning at this stage, nor do words such as "enlightenment," and "progress," there *you* are, nonetheless—your familiar old personality perfectly intact, your old desires perfectly satisfied, and you are content to simply be who you are from moment to ordinary moment, effortlessly shining with the spontaneously perfected clear light of awareness.

THINGS CHANGING:
DESCRIBING THE DREAM DANCE

Always know, sometimes think it's me,
But you know I know when it's a dream.
I think a "No" will be a "Yes," but it's all wrong.
That is, I think I disagree.
— "Strawberry Fields Forever"[1]

s your awareness continues to deepen, you may come to relate more to the above Beatles' lyric. As all your old boundaries continue to blur and dissolve, you may likewise—from time to time—perceive life as a confused jumble of opposites: always versus sometimes, knowing versus thinking, no versus yes. The only certainty amid all this uncertainty, according to John Lennon, seems to be the fact that he knows when it's a dream. No matter how much of a mess things get to be, the lyric seems to be saying, at least there is still a knowable distinction between dream and reality. In the context of the highly demanding path of self-realization, however, you might wonder if even this fundamental boundary must also be reconsidered.

This knowledge of dreaming versus waking, the real versus the unreal, is probably the single most important determining factor in the Western view of sanity. An individual is considered to be sane to the degree that he or she can establish and maintain a clear boundary between reality and unreality. Individuals who suffer from borderline and psychotic episodes are considered problematic to the degree that they are unable to distinguish between internal and external states, private thoughts and objectively measurable facts, subjective feelings and real-world events. One of the questions an interviewing psychologist asks a potentially psychotic patient is, "Do you hear voices that no one else can hear?" The idea is that the psychotic individual can't distinguish between voices "inside" and "outside" his or her head very well. According to Western psychology, a mentally healthy individual regularly performs reality tests, periodically checking what is inside against what is outside, looking out for discrepancies. In Freud's words, reality testing involves "a question of external and internal. What is unreal, merely a presentation and subjective, is only internal; what is real is also there outside."[2] An individual is considered psychologically mature to the degree that he or she is able to work with these discrepancies skillfully, consistently seeking the most comfortable balance between internal events and what is there, outside.

Since the Western evaluation of sanity is based on an individual's ability to distinguish the real from the unreal, we might want to take a closer look into the West's traditional definition of this all-important reality idea. Well, to say the least, this definition turns out to be a pretty slippery fish. When I looked up "real" in a handful of dictionaries, I found what boils down to about four definitions: (1) not imaginary; (2) something that is actual or factual; (3) something that is relatively fixed, stable or permanent; (4) something of, or related to, objective fact—which means, more or less, something concretely observable and measurable by *more than one* person. Now the first two definitions say little more than, "A real thing is a thing which is real." The third and fourth definitions, however, are much more interesting. To associate the real with the fixed or secure—as in definition three—is a reminder that we are most likely to call "real" those things that we believe to be somehow *safe*. The fourth definition is this very same idea, albeit in a slightly different disguise. If several people agree on a certain observation, for instance, then that observation is real, objective. By implication, then, the more people who agree on some observation, the more real that observation becomes.

A few people believe in astral travel, for example. That being the case, you are not going to be immediately dismissed as crazy if you say, at a block party, that you believe in astral travel, but you will probably be whispered about when you leave the room. The Statue of Liberty, however, is real beyond the need for whispers. How do we know? Well, almost *everyone*—all sane and educated people—agree to its location, its physical measurements, etc. I'm not taking much of a chance, that is to say, when I assert among a group of reasonably sane folk that the Statue of Liberty is real. Moreover, the Statue of Liberty is a decidedly secure object in many other senses of the word: It is probably going to be in the same place year after year; its physical measurements are relatively stable, which means predictable over time; it is not very likely to do anything of its own accord anytime soon to surprise us.

This last point, the avoidance of the surprise element, is a significant one. For the Westerner, real things tend to be those that seem to fit within a set of preexisting rules, fixed knowns, or laws governing the natural world. Observations that threaten to significantly modify these laws are initially treated with much skepticism. Science at large finally accepted the world was really round, for instance, only after this property had been observed several times by numerous authoritative individuals throughout history. Notice that such a fact becomes reasonably safe to admit into our communal repertoire of knowledge only after we have had time to visit the huddle and rework our game plan. Rather than own up to the fact that some of our society's most cherished knowns were entirely misguided, we simply readjust our existing views to the point where they are not going to be turned on their head by this new addition. Okay, say the supposed authorities, so the world is round. As it turns out, our longstanding belief in God, religion, morality, etc., didn't *really* require that the world be a flat slab, after all.

Leaping Before We Look

The real, then, is basically the safe, the secure, the dependable. The individual who can accurately distinguish the real, consequently, is likely to be a much safer individual than the psychotic or borderline individual. Freud says, regarding the individual who performs proper reality tests, that by "interposing the process of thinking, [that individual] secures a postponement of motor discharges and controls the access to motility."[3] A sane person *looks* before she *leaps* and is therefore a relatively safe person.

It is interesting the way Western culture seems to enjoy blurring the distinction between reality and unreality. Consider our collective fascination with intoxicating substances, for instance. These substances are valued, not despite their tendency to dislodge us from the steady foothold of the real, but because of it. We certainly tend to act pretty freely while intoxicated, not so likely to "postpone our motor discharges" until we have thought things out. Still, we pursue these substances because they seem to make the world a bit larger somehow, seem to increase the scope of our experience. You're drunk at a party, for instance. You realize you are likely to embarrass yourself in front of all these people and you are *sure* you'll wake up with a miserable hangover tomorrow. Still, you're very high and full of life somehow as you sort of float from room to room, full of the dangerous potential of revealing something of yourself that you wouldn't normally reveal. Such is the alluring essence of high danger.

Or consider contemporary art and music. Don't these forms try to blend dreamy elements with more familiar ones, confuse our senses a bit, encourage us to question our basic assumptions about the world? Rather than interposing the thinking process, doesn't contemporary art try to loosen us up a bit, encourage us to feel and act without being so sure of what is really there outside? There is a standard movie trick, for example, we have all seen a hundred times: Abruptly cut to an unexpected scene that will startle the viewer. The main character, who has been in a wheelchair all his life, for instance, jumps up and starts waltzing around the park with his elusive love interest. Now, just when the whole fabric of the movie's plot threatens to dissolve, just when the viewer is about to stand up and shout, "Hey! This isn't *making sense* anymore!" the main character wakes up. Ah ha. You just *thought* what you were seeing was genuine, but it was really just a dream sequence. Much like our use of intoxicants, such methods are ways of temporarily sneaking in some extras, covertly stirring in some more hazardous materials without really damaging our cozy security, without fundamentally attacking our basic, existential expectations.

Well, why is this? Why all the dabbling in confusion? If we like to be safe and safety is all about maintaining clear boundaries between the real and the unreal, why are we so drawn to this sort of blurring? For that matter, what happens when our sense of security *is* fundamentally attacked? Do we just melt like the Wicked Witch of the West, or is there something else, something even more essential at our core?

The Lobster Limbo—Are You Dreaming, Or ...?

Starting in early childhood, I began having dreams in which I apparently "woke up." I would climb out of bed in such dreams and stumble into the bathroom, brush my teeth, comb my hair, and then it would hit me: Something was wrong. Something was very wrong. I was still asleep, I would realize, and just dreaming I was awake, going about my daily business. So I would pinch myself, slap myself in the face, whatever I thought it might take to jar my sleeping body back into the real world. I would finally manage to wake myself up and then I would go about my business for real. There I go, stumbling into the bathroom, brushing my teeth, combing my hair . . . but wait. There's that something wrong again. I was still asleep. So I would go round and round like this, falling for the same trick every time. Well, my feet can really feel the floor, I would reason, I can really feel my toothbrush in my mouth, so this time I *must be* awake. This must be *the real thing*. And there I would go again a few minutes later, screaming, slapping myself, pinching like a rabid lobster.

To this day, this phenomenon still happens to me—much more so in fact, as a result of the dream practices I discuss in chapter 11—only I have given up trying so hard to wake myself up. I still experience moments of pure panic and desperation in such dreams, but I have learned that these pass. For that matter, I have begun to ask myself, "What would be so terrible about living out the rest of my days in a dream world? My dream sink doesn't look all that different from my real sink after all." Ironically, every time I start to accept my crazy predicament, there I am suddenly, lying in my real bed, staring at my real ceiling. As far as I can tell, anyway. How am I to be sure, after all, that such an experience isn't taking place within a particularly long dream? For that matter, how can I know the entirety of my current life isn't just the result of one of those times I accepted the possibility of perpetually living in dreamland, only I accepted it so well I have forgotten accepting?

This is what I call the dream dance. We all do it on a daily basis, it just not may involve all the literal pinching. *I feel this person likes me, but does she really? I'll check and see by asking her to work my shift for me.* There we go, reality testing, pinching away. Or it can be much more complicated: *I feel like there is a God, but how can I know? Maybe I'll try out a little prayer, do a little rain dance, give God a little hoop to jump through. I know it's short notice, God, but could you maybe work this Friday for me?* The more we test, the more ridiculous the whole dance gets. There is simply no logical end to it, in fact. Okay, we reason, God did make it sleet on Friday so no one had to go into work, but sleet doesn't really *prove* anything. After all, sleet could happen without a little old man in the sky . . . Pinch, pinch, pinch.

We might rename the dream dance the "Lobster Limbo." What we really want to know, while dancing our crazy dance, is if this dance can ever be enough. Can we ever really pinch ourselves sufficiently hard, we wonder, to make sure we are awake? For that matter, *am* I awake right now? *Are* you awake right now? Am I simply someone you are dreaming, a figment of your imagination? And if so, how would you ever know? How would you ever wake up?

Chou, a Butterfly, Some Blind Guys, an Elephant

> Long ago, Chuang Chou dreamed he was a butterfly fluttering among trees, doing as he pleased, completely unaware of a Chuang Chou. A sudden awakening, and there, looking a little out of sorts, was Chuang Chou. Now, I don't know whether it is Chou who dreamed he was a butterfly, or whether a butterfly dreams he's Chuang Chou. But between Chuang Chou and the butterfly, we ought to be able to find some sort of distinction. This is what's known as Things Changing.[4]

Notice, in this passage from the writings of Chuang Tzu, the questions of "Which is real? Which is dream?" go unanswered. Chuang Tzu recognizes a distinction between the two, but he doesn't seem to ultimately favor one over the other. Instead, security seems to be found in the idea of "Things Changing." But what is this idea exactly? For that matter, if the Western idea of real and secure requires fixation and stability, what sort of safety is there to be had in Things Changing?

Here's another famous metaphor: Three blind guys are asked to describe an elephant, only they can't exactly take a look, so they have to feel their way. The first guy gets hold of an ear and says, "No problem. The elephant is like a palm leaf." The second guy gets hold of the trunk and says, "Simple. The elephant is like a man's arm." The third guy gets hold of a leg and says, "You guys must be *crazy.* We're obviously dealing with something very much like a tree trunk here." Each of them is, of course, right in a way. The moral of the story is that you can't really get a feel for the elephant until you have had, well, a feel of the *entire* elephant.

In our context, the elephant is Chuang Tzu's Things Changing. The three blind guys are philosophy, science, and psychology. Each of these disciplines has been feeling-up various parts of the elephant for quite a while now, and have come up with some pretty interesting descriptions.

As it turns out, looking into Things Changing through the specialized lens of whatever discipline is—in one way or another—to dance the Lobster Limbo, to ask the old question of What is real? Am I awake? This is not an intellectual question, however. Despite what philosophy, science, and psychology may have to say on the matter, it is, first and foremost, a dance, an artistic endeavor—even, or especially, when the dancers don't *know* it's a dance. As with any artistic endeavor, thinking or reality testing is only going to get us so far. It's like the difference between studying a piece of music and actually listening to a piece of music. I encourage you to contemplate each of the following pursuits of Things Changing as you would enjoy a piece of music. Use the sheet music for reference, that is to say, but make sure you put a quarter in the jukebox as soon as you get a chance. Even if the languages of philosophy, science, and psychology are a little dry and academic at times, keep in mind there is *something* very mysterious and strangely artistic going on underneath.

Philosophy's Take on Things Changing

The safest general characterization of the whole of the Western philosophical tradition is that it consists of a series of footnotes to Plato.[5]

Around 400 B.C., Plato, perhaps the first full-fledged philosopher in the Western tradition, set out to tackle our metaphorical elephant. In one of his most famous dialogues, *Meno*, Plato describes his theory of Forms. Plato begins by considering groups of things that share at least one particular quality. Consider, for example, the following three items: an apple, a rose, a fire truck. The most obvious quality each of these things has in common is color. They each share the quality of "redness." Plato goes on to ask a seemingly simple question: How do we *know* all of these things are red? What is some quality that all red things—and only red things—possess that allows us to identify them as red? (You're dancing a crazy little dance, remember, feeling your way in the dark.) Obviously, not all red things have to grow on trees like an apple, and obviously not all red things have to include wheels like a fire truck.

In Plato's outlook, in order to recognize redness in an apple, a rose, a fire truck, or anything else that is red, we have to be able to compare it to something, some pure form that has no qualities other than perfect redness. Clearly, we couldn't use an apple for such an example because we might get confused and think that redness must necessarily include the quality of being edible, for instance. Neither could we use a fire truck for our redness mold, as we might mistakenly deduce that redness must involve rubber and clanging bells. In fact, no actual, *concrete* red thing would work as such a perfect example. Why? Simply because all actual red objects have—by definition—some other qualities, some other forms, mixed in alongside their redness.

To solve this dilemma, Plato postulates a world of pure Forms, some realm separate from the world of concrete things that possesses nothing other than perfect, abstract molds of qualities such as redness, tallness, smallness, etc. Items in our everyday, concrete world are what Plato calls "sensibles," which are degraded versions of these original, pure Forms. The main function of sensibles, says Plato, is simply to remind us of, to reconnect us with, these perfect original Forms.

IN PLATO'S CAVE

To illustrate the relationship between the world of Forms and the world of sensibles, Plato offers his famous analogy of the cave in a later dialogue, *The Republic*. Imagine, Plato suggests, individuals that have been imprisoned in a cave-like dwelling since birth. As it so happens, this cave is open on top, whereby figures pass back and forth, casting shadows below along a certain wall of the cave. Our prisoners, who are unable to turn their heads away from this wall, spend their entire lives watching and interacting with these shadowy forms that move back and forth aimlessly. Consequently, these cave dwellers—who are entirely unaware of the world outside the cave—believe this to be the whole world, the real world. Should one of them escape, however, he or she would realize that the hazy figures the prisoners had been watching for so long were really shadows, mere projections of the authentically real figures wandering above.

The philosophically ignorant, Plato says, are like the prisoners inside the cave. They are trapped watching mere shadows, mistaking the play of degraded sensibles for reality itself. The enlightened individual, however, has escaped from the cave and become aware of the world of Forms, the genuine world. Such an individual, according to Plato, is then able to appreciate the sensibles for what they are: cardboard reminders of the molds of true reality. For Plato, then, our everyday waking world is essentially a dream world. The real world lies just beyond and above somewhere. We get there—if we ever get there at all—by climbing the ladder of the sensibles.

ARGUMENT FROM ILLUSION—ARE WE OUT OF THE CAVE, YET?

There is at least one infamously major problem with Plato's analogy. How does the escapee know that he or she hasn't simply escaped into a much larger cave? How does he or she know that what he or she now perceives as perfect Forms aren't simply complex artifacts of some yet *more* authentic entities? The escapee has already been fooled once, after all, so he or she must not be an entirely dependable observer. This objection is called "the argument from illusion." It states simply that the perfect hallucination, for instance, never *looks like* a hallucination. Each of the blind men really believes *he's* got the inside track on this elephant situation, the uniquely authoritative understanding, right? For that matter, says our argument from illusion objection, even if he could get a feel of the whole elephant, how does any one blind man know this elephant is not just a hood ornament on some much larger elephant?

We have all experienced this argument from illusion phenomenon. How many times, for example, have you been absolutely sure you have something figured out, some basic truth of life uncovered, only to later realize that you were way off target? You just thought you had escaped from the cave when, in fact, you simply stepped from the cave's closet into its dining room. In this context, there is the cave of childhood, then the cave of adolescence, then the 20s cave, then the mid-life crisis cave, and so on. We pass through developmental stage after stage, handling more and more extensive belief systems all the while, but when can we be sure we are really standing on solid ground? How do we know that the minute we plant our next philosophical tent, it won't get rained on? For that matter, do we ever reach a stage of development where we quit putting up tents at all, preferring to sleep under the stars? "I'm going to be moving on any day," you might say at such a fabled point, "so I might as well travel light."

When I was trying to determine if I was awake or asleep, I performed several reality tests, all of which came back positive. My environment felt, tasted, and smelled as real as my environment does at this very moment. How can I be certain, then, that I haven't simply escaped into a larger cave, woken into an even more convincing dream from which I've yet to awaken? Don't just think about it. Don't just work with these ideas as if they were silverware. Instead, try to really feel yourself as a dream of someone else, an idea in the mind of God. This deeply intuitive sense of something abstract was what Plato seems to be after and, ultimately, such is the only way to squeeze the real juice from the philosophical lemon. You're wandering around in the dark, something deep within tells you, clumsily feeling your way—and all the while your very next breath is a thought in the mind of an infinitely large being.

All philosophical schools of thought are ultimately based on non-verifiable assumptions. No matter how solid and self-evident certain ideas may appear within any conceptual framework, we always have reason to doubt the conceptual framework itself. Like all cognitive systems, philosophy necessarily reflects its own limited set of supposed rules and arguments. Ultimately, no matter how elaborate these arguments, no matter how seemingly logical and convincing, we are inevitably brought back to slapping and pinching ourselves, asking, "Now, is this the real thing? Am I really awake this time?"

At the same time, although philosophy can never answer the fundamental question it often pretends to answer—the riddle of Things Changing—it does go on asking the question. More and more blind guys keep joining the dance, pawing in more and more intimate elephant regions. Like science and psychology, philosophy does keep turning the problem over, continually changing its perspective—now Chuang Chou, now the butterfly. Ironically, this relentless questioning may turn out to be the very key to Things Changing, may be the very elephant within the elephant.

Science's Take on the Dream Dance

Whereas philosophy seems to be engaged in an endless debate as to which cave is the real cave, science appears to be more concerned with simply describing the inside of the most readily observable cave—in our context, the process of sleeping and dreaming. I know there's a whole elephant out there somewhere, science says, but I'm busy mapping out the wrinkles on this particular eyelid just now.

Not until relatively recently did scientists discover that all of us dream on a nightly basis. In 1953, Dr. Nathaniel Kleitman, while conducting sleep research at the University of Chicago, noticed that rapid eye movements occurred regularly during sleep.[6] Wondering if the sleeper might be looking at something, such as a dream, the research team began to wake individuals during these episodes of rapid eye movement and discovered that, in fact, these individuals had been dreaming. Following this breakthrough discovery in sleep research, what has science learned about sleep? Not all that much.

REM (rapid eye movement) sleep happens in four phases each night, spaced at about 90 minute intervals. This means that if you sleep the typical six to eight hours, you will probably have at least four dreams or dreaming sessions each night. Interestingly, the dreaming sessions gradually lengthen from the first to the fourth phase. Whereas the first session tends to last about five minutes, the final dreaming episode of the night tends to last about 30 minutes. Toward the morning, then, most of us are having our longest, possibly most intensive dreams. Research has shown that, despite all this nightly REM activity, the average individual is unable to recall the vast majority of his or her dreams unless he or she happens to awaken in the middle of a dreaming session. We might then raise the logical question, "Why all this dreaming business if we can't even remember it? What's it for?"

SPECULATIONS ON THE PURPOSE OF DREAMS

Although science is still uncertain as to the exact function of dreaming, research has shown it is an essential process in maintaining mental health. In REM-deprivation experiments, individuals who are deprived of dream time for a few days get very anxious and agitated. They are much less able to inhibit some of their primary drives such as eating. Studies done with male cats, for example, show that, when REM-deprived, the male cats will attempt to mate with almost anything—including wooden blocks. In extreme cases of dream deprivation, individuals have undergone psychotic breaks, hallucinating and so forth, seemingly dreaming while awake in an attempt to recover lost dream sleep.

Interestingly, most individuals show physiological signs of sexual arousal while dreaming, regardless of the content of the dream. It seems relatively safe to assume that wherever you have sexual arousal, *something* important is going on, although science has so far been unable to satisfactorily explain the specific function of sexual arousal while dreaming. When it comes to the scientific study of sleeping and dreaming, this lack of definitive explanation is pretty much par for the course. Scientists have managed to gather scattered information concerning our states of sleep and dream, but without making much overall sense of it.

Considering the fact that we spend about one third of our lives asleep—which we mostly can't remember—along with the unexplained fact of sexual arousal while dreaming, the apparent correlation between dreaming and mental health, etc., scientists seem to agree on one basic point: Sleeping and dreaming seem to serve some important function. Exactly what that function is remains highly speculative. Science or no, it seems rather odd, common sense would suggest, that individuals would forget so much of their dream content—apparently highly charged, sexually arousing material that has to be processed in REM sleep if mental health is to be maintained. Although there is no conclusive body of scientific evidence as to the exact function of dreaming, there are a number of theories.

Mental Waste Discharge

One common view of dreaming function is that dreams, although apparently essential for mental and psychological health, are simply a meaningless discharge of a kind of mental waste material. J. Allen Hobson of Harvard Medical School, for example, believes dreams are the result of a dream state generator located in the brain stem.[7] This generator, says Hobson, fires neurons randomly and the dream state results from the brain's attempt to make sense of all these garbled signals by fitting them into a kind of semi-logical story. Similarly, other scientists have suggested that dreams occur so that we can unlearn useless information. Unimportant and arbitrary cognitive connections that have been temporarily stored, theorize these individuals, are allowed to dissolve and discharge in the dream state. For these scientists, dreaming is a process much like clearing out a computer's random access memory by rebooting.

In the context of our elusive elephant exploration, such waste discharge theories may be best represented by the blind guy that has an intimate encounter with the elephant's hindquarters. There is nothing mythical or even all that curious about dreaming and sleeping, says this school of thinking, however romantically we humans like to imagine the mostly invisible processes of our subconscious. Our brains, if they are to remain efficient thinking machines, simply need to wash out the garbled cognitive and sensory gunk that inevitably collects throughout our day on a regular, nightly basis.

Increased Intuition and Creativity

Other scientists, such as Carl Sagan, question this waste-disposal theory.[8] Due to a number of famous creative acts that have occurred while dreaming, these scientists believe dreams may allow an extraordinary kind of intuitive building that is not readily available while waking. Albert Einstein is reported to have discovered his theory of relativity in a dream. Similarly, Friedrich August Kekule discovered the structure of the benzene molecule while in REM sleep. Many artists have also reported all sorts of creative phenomenon resulting from the dream state. Paul McCartney, for instance, describes dreaming the entire melody of "Yesterday," one of the most popular pop songs ever recorded. Upon waking, McCartney says, he simply wrote it down, as if taking dictation.

According to scientists such as Sagan, these curious acts of creativity result from an uninhibited working of the right brain during sleep. Whereas the more analytic left brain tends to dominate waking activity, the right brain is more active during sleep. Less restrained by the linear workings of the left brain, individuals are able to make much larger cognitive leaps while dreaming, often resulting in highly original and intuitive ideas, as well as works of art. Contrary to their more mechanistically minded contemporaries, this scientific school of thought seems to ascribe a kind of cognitive magic to the processes of dream and sleep—heightened, creative mental states that somehow transcend base functionality.

Whatever goes on while we sleep and dream, I think most of us would agree it seems to be more significant than waste disposal. It certainly doesn't *feel* that way, at least. Most of us still remember, quite vividly, certain dreams from the past, as far back as early childhood even. It seems unlikely that our mental "computers" are so emotionally affected by their most memorable hard drive scans. For that matter, artists haven't traditionally been particularly inspired to write famous pop songs after an unusually poignant bowel movement. What is it, then, about the automatic, yet necessarily elusive, dreaming process that seems to affect people on such a profound level? Could it be that dreaming is a mostly untapped, though fundamental, aspect of each of our personalities?

LUCID DREAMING

Lucid dreams are those in which the dreamer is able to integrate his or her normal waking awareness with the dream, thereby remaining conscious of the fact that he or she is dreaming throughout the process. In fact, lucid dreamers are often aware of the curious situation of their consciousness to the point of being able to actually control the dream events, bringing about certain dream content at will.

Despite the fact that this wakeful dreaming experience was recognized as significant by Aristotle and numerous other thinkers throughout history—not to mention its widespread prevalence in cultural myths, folktales, and spiritual systems the world over—Western science didn't generally accept this phenomenon until the research of Steven Laberge was made known. In the 1970s, Laberge was able to prove, throughout various controlled studies, that certain individuals were able to repeatedly signal—by means of a prearranged eye movement—that they were dreaming while in the dream state. Moreover, Laberge's studies indicate that dream lucidity is, for many individuals, a learnable skill.[9]

If some of us can learn to somehow integrate our waking conscious during the dreaming process, the whole functional, waste disposal idea of dream and sleep seems to be overlooking some pretty major facet of human awareness and cognition. Might both the process and content of the dream state allow much greater access to some relatively hidden part of our personalities and daily activities—some deeply significant facet of our natural human awareness—that we have yet to learn how to operate? We will look into this curious phenomenon of lucid dreaming, which is of utmost importance in many spiritual systems, in greater detail in chapter 10.

Psychology's Analysis of Dreaming

Compared to the disciplines of philosophy and science, Western psychology's approach to understanding the dreaming process is, in many ways, the most practical. Psychology doesn't get too directly worked up about the metaphysical dilemma of what is real and what is illusion. Neither does it bother too much with the technicalities of the various REM phases and so forth. Instead, psychology simply asks, "What use is this dream material to daily life? How can it shed new light on psychological obstacles?" In other words, we don't care what the damn elephant looks like, just tell us how much stuff it can carry.

In an indirect way, the whole discipline of psychology grew out of this desire to harness dream material. As discussed earlier, Sigmund Freud noticed, in working with hypnosis patients, that something seemed to be going on just below the rational surface of the mind, some compelling, hidden force that led the patients to mis-remember certain facts. "We're dancing around a pretty big elephant of some kind or another," Freud might have said. What he actually ended up saying: "The interpretation of dreams is the royal road to a knowledge of the unconscious activities of the mind."[10]

FREUD AND THE PERSONAL UNCONSCIOUS

Freud hypothesized that the mind is composed of two basic parts: the conscious and the unconscious. The unconscious is simply that part of the mind that we can't access in an intentional way—not directly, at least. After all, that's what *makes* it the unconscious. For Freud, the unconscious consisted mostly of two sorts of data: latent, or temporarily unconscious, and repressed.

We each know we have forgotten certain significant life experiences, but *how* do we know? Such experiences, according to Freud, are simply latent. They *were* conscious once, but now—for whatever reason—they have faded from our readily accessed, daily consciousness. Even so, such experiences leave a sort of footprint in our head somewhere—a kind of secret elf, half-suspected but never quite caught, making shoes in the shadowy corners of our mind. We could say that latent unconscious material is recognized, however vaguely, through the "secret helper" of the natural mind discussed in chapter 7.

Some psychological data, says Freud, has never exactly been conscious. Freud considers this to be repressed data—"processes . . . which if they were to become conscious would be bound to stand out in the crudest contrast to the rest of the conscious process."[11] Due to these habitual repressions, many emotional difficulties tend to recur. Some time in the past, each of us has unintentionally held back certain thoughts or wishes that we thought didn't fit in very well with our idea of "Who I Am." As a kind of automatic strategy, we have stored these unacceptable thoughts and wishes for later processing in the deeper layers of the psyche, and learned to protect them from conscious manifestation through a complex array of psychological defenses. These packages are too heavy and unwieldy right now, we decide, so we'll let the elusive elephant of the unconscious carry them awhile. . .

Unconscious material remains hidden from our everyday awareness. We may vaguely suspect that elf of lost internal and external experiences is in there somewhere, but as soon as we poke our head around the corner, trying to catch him, he disappears into impossible nooks and crannies. Over time, we can imagine this elf calling over other elves to join the party until we have a confused, tangled knot of drunken elves heaped up in a stuffy little psychological corner somewhere. Freud called this tangled, pressurized little knot of unconscious material, be it latent or repressed, a *cathexis*. The main goal of psychoanalysis, then, is to achieve a catharsis, or discharge, of the mental energy tangled up in these little knots. Using the processes of dream analysis and free association, Freud believed we can somehow sneak up on our secret elf colonies and break the party up. Approaching from the mental periphery, we can gradually unpack unconscious material into our ordinary conscious, where we can then neatly tuck it away into the cozy drawers and cupboards of our daily awareness.

Not surprisingly, given his view of the unconscious, Freud believed dream material was primarily motivated by traumatic memories, repressed wishes, and forbidden impulses hidden just out of our conscious reach. Consequently, dreaming somehow releases this charged energy by acting out our wishes in a disguised or symbolic way.

Let's examine a theoretical dream to see how a typical Freudian dream analysis might be applied. Suppose I have a dream in which my much-beloved childhood dog, Fido, is angrily trampling through a garden of yellow roses. Now given just this much, there is no secret psychoanalytic decoder ring, no prearranged interpretation for the elements "childhood dog" and "yellow roses." Instead, I would be encouraged to talk freely about any associations I might personally have to these elements—a process known as free association. Well, as it turns out, I always thought of Fido as an unfailingly loyal companion, in much the same way I imagine myself to be a steadfast and faithful friend to others. I *identify* with Fido, that is to say. As for the yellow roses, I find myself suddenly remembering a family reunion from my childhood in which my mother was wearing a dress with a yellow flower print. This was the same day, it so happens, that my mother wouldn't let me eat my chocolate cake because I hadn't finished my barbecue sandwich. A possible interpretation of this dream, then, might be that Fido—who represents me—trampling the yellow roses—which represent my mother—is symbolic of my repressed anger toward my mother. Why not just dream about yelling at my mother, then? Once again, like Freud said, maybe I consciously adore my mother and couldn't integrate such feelings of intense and childish anger very easily into my normal, waking awareness. Consequently, I let the elephant handle the dirty work, let the unconscious absorb the burden of my undesirable feelings. Here enters Fido and the roses as camouflaged pointers of a sort, trying to sneak these unacceptable impulses past the gate of my conscious awareness.

For Freud, then, the unconscious is very much a personal matter. Each person has developed an autonomous set of symbols that can only be decoded by allowing the conscious mind to relax and wander onto a sort of translation. It is on this last point that Carl Jung, another psychologist famous for dream work, departs somewhat from Freud.

JUNG AND THE COLLECTIVE UNCONSCIOUS

Jung agreed with Freud, for the most part, that dreams seemed to represent hidden or unacceptable aspects of an individual's personality. Dreaming, both men more or less agreed, was a secret balancing act that kept a coded record of the entire individual. Jung, however, distinguished between a personal unconscious, which was more or less the Freudian unconscious, and a kind of shared, or collective unconscious. In Jung's words, the contents of the collective conscious "have never been individually acquired, but owe their existence exclusively to hereditary."[12] This collective unconscious, according to Jung, was most clearly present in dreams of a particularly powerful, and relatively impersonal nature. Such dreams contained archetypes, deeply implanted symbols repeatedly referenced throughout the history of spiritual belief, myth, art, and folk tales. According to Jung, these archetypes are "pre-existent . . . definite forms in the psyche which seem to be present always and everywhere."[13] Instead of these personally pesky elves inhabiting the hidden regions of our mind, we now encounter something much more abstract. Rather than actual elves, we might say we encounter the pure, pre-existing idea of, or original mold for, Elf.

To illustrate these Jungian ideas more clearly, let's reexamine my Fido dream, but this time adding the Jungian element of the archetype. Fido isn't just trampling any old garden of yellow roses. This time, the flowers are planted in rows of repeating circles. These circles, for Jung, call to mind the mandala. For Jung, the mandala and other archetypal symbols, "beyond question . . . originated in dreams and visions, and were not invented by some . . . church father."[14] Such a symbol, then, doesn't exactly arise out of my personal experience—it's just sort of "in there" from birth. Now, I'm not just angry with Mommy. Now, as indicated by the appearance of an archetypal symbol, I am also interacting with something much more ancient than any one person or group of people. We might say that I seem to be questioning the very order of the universe itself, the mind of the divine Self. My attempt to break the perfect circles of the roses, then, is no longer strictly a personal matter. My dream is now part of a sort of pervasive heritage of symbols in which a person struggles to individuate amid the impersonal ocean of awareness, the collective conscious. This idea of a communal, shared unconscious is of great significance in the practice of dream yoga.

FRITZ PERLS AND THE GESTALT METHOD

Another important innovator in psychology's understanding of dream material is Fritz Perls. Although his essential theories regarding dream material are not all that different from Freud's idea of the "repressed wish"—Perls thinks of it as the "disowned part of the self"—his specific method of dream work is highly interesting. Perls' intention was to enable individuals to realize that each dream represents the whole, or *gestalt*, of their being. His specific method of dream work requires that individuals break their dreams down into distinct parts and then dramatically "play" those parts against one another. In doing so, that individual would theoretically reconnect to those hidden, rejected parts of his or her personality by, once again, sneaking up on them. Using his or her dream material as a means of access to the unconscious, the patient would recognize the fragmented nature of his or her mind and learn to reintegrate, or harmonize, these seemingly contrary parts.

For example, in a gestalt dream work seminar, one man relates a dream in which a train moves over a barren desert. This man thinks of himself like this scene: stagnant and lifeless. Perls has this man alternately play the parts of the train and the desert, has him act out a spontaneous dialogue between these two seemingly opposing elements of his dream. Through the train's dialogue with the desert, this man discovers a very dynamic process hidden at the heart of his dream. The straight and unbending progress of the train through these perpetually shifting desert sands only appears stagnant on the surface. Once the man dives deeper into this content, bringing some real emotion into his dialogue between the train and the desert, the dream becomes a rich dramatization of the life process itself, the individual's courageous journey through the vast and impersonal ocean of Jung's collective unconscious. Using Perl's unique method of dream work, then, this individual has managed to sneak up on the elf of his unconscious, act out a drama with him, and end up appreciating those secret shoes he's been making the whole while.

THE ELEPHANT UNBURDENED?

Each of these psychologists, then, sees dreams as a means to recover lost parts of our individual identities. Although highly useful tools along the road to wholeness, notice that each of these psychological paths stops short. If the dream dance represents, and is chiefly motivated by, an interaction with the unconscious, what happens as the individual integrates more of this hidden aspect of awareness into his or her ordinary conscious? What happens to the elephant, that is to say, once we have completely released it of its load? Such a liberation obviously doesn't happen very often, but is it possible? Can we eventually uncover so much of our hidden self that we remain awake at *all* times, sleeping and dreaming included? Can we somehow become both the elephant *and* the blind men, the whole crazy dance at once?

Spirituality's Dream Dance Lessons

It would seem, then, that dreaming and waking, the illusory and the real, are not exactly two distinct states or phenomenon. Instead, they seem to be opposite ends of a continuum on which we continually wobble back and forth. I call this continual wobbling "the dream dance." Spirituality's approach to the dance is, at its core, radically different from that of philosophy, science, and psychology, which, along with the informal school of common sense, primarily attempt to understand and *explain* the dream dance, to step outside of it long enough to take the choreographer's chair. Spirituality is much more interested in providing dance lessons—refining the dance itself, making it more beautiful. The wisest spiritual seekers have simply given up trying to distinguish between the real and the unreal, knowing this apparent boundary itself to be part of the dream. Chuang Tzu says:

> How am I to know that this life is not merely a delusion? . . . Your Master Kung and you are both dreaming. And my saying you're both dreaming is also a dream. . . . Ten thousand years from now, you may meet with a great sage who will know how to unravel this mystery for you. Or maybe you will this morning. Or this evening. . . . The alternating noises of dispute await their turns, but you need not attend them. . . . Forget judgments! Flap your wings and fly to the palace without boundaries and live there![15]

In this way, we might say spirituality has much more in common with art than it does philosophy, science, or psychology. We could say that our ultimate goal as spiritual seekers is to *become* the elephant rather than *know* the elephant—to simply flap our wings rather than stand around wondering if we can really fly or not. Paradoxically, we could also say our goal is to dance so freely and intensely that we forget all about the elephant—not to mention the dancer and the dance.

In one way or another, most spiritual systems center around the idea of our metaphorical elephant of Things Changing as God, the Divine. Interestingly, the Hindus represent one of their most beloved gods, Lord Ganesa, as an elephant who is often depicted dancing. He is known as the "Lord of Obstacles" in that he is primarily concerned with the overcoming of individual difficulties each soul has to encounter in its spiritual development. In our context, we might say that Lord Ganesa is acutely aware of, and dedicated to help resolve, each dancer's particular blindness.

CLAIRVOYANT DREAMS

Not all spiritual systems portray the divine literally as an elephant, of course. Even so, most spiritual teachings convey example after example of dream as a means to connect with the infinitely mysterious divine. One common manifestation of this direct connection is the foretelling of important future events. The Bible records a warning Joseph, husband of Mary, receives in a dream, telling him to beware of King Herod. Similarly, a different Joseph has prophetic dreams that symbolically predict his eventual ascent to high offices in the Pharaoh's court. Yahweh also speaks to Jacob in a dream, making a sacred promise to him. "Your descendants will be like the dust on the earth," God tells Jacob. "All peoples on earth will be blessed through you and your offspring. I am with you and will watch over you wherever you go" (Gen. 28:14–15). The biblical examples of such clairvoyant dreams are numerous. Suffice it to say that—historically speaking, at least—some of God's most important messages have been conveyed through the dreaming process.

Dreams are equally important, if not more so, in the traditional Buddhist teachings. In numerous scriptures, accounts are given of Queen Maya's famous conception dream in which the birth of her son, the historical Buddha, is predicted. In Tibetan Buddhism in particular, dreams often foretell the seeker's future meeting of an important spiritual teacher, as well as sometimes revealing the physical location of *terma*, "dream treasures," or hidden tantric teachings and sacred objects. A contemporary Tibetan Buddhism master, Namkhai Norbu, relates a personal experience of terma discovery. While on a visit to a site of ancient Tibetan ruins, he dreamed of a certain mound of earth at that location. In the dream, he dug down into this mound and extracted a *garuda* (a mythological bird-man) statue. On waking, he located this same mound of earth. Digging down into this mound as far as his shoulder, Namkhai Norbu discovered a statue identical to the one in his dream.[16]

Dreams also play a significant predictive role in Native American cultures. In these cultures, vision quests often lead a young person to dreams that predict his or her future roles in that society, sometimes resulting in the renaming of that young person. In the writings of Carlos Castañeda, it's clear that his apprenticeship with don Juan was highly influenced by Castañeda's dream experiences. Often, before proceeding with a new teaching, don Juan will analyze Castañeda's recent dreams for omens indicating Castañeda's future success, or lack thereof, with that teaching.

In my own experience, predictive, or so-called clairvoyant dreams have been fairly common. Sometimes the information they contain is mundane. For instance, I may dream of an encounter with a stranger, only to meet that same person the next day as a new music student. Other times, however, such dream predictions seem much more significant. I had a series of such dreams that helped with the diagnosis of a certain chronic medical problem, for example. In indicating a different direction my treatment was to take in order to be successful, these dreams allowed me to ask the right questions of my physicians, eventually leading to alternative treatments that were much more effective.

Such examples pervade spiritual teachings of all sorts. Examine any culture you want, any esoteric spiritual system, and you are likely to happen on some very important prophetic dreams surrounding the core teachings. And in each of these examples, remember, the prophecies are believed to come from the divine itself. The individuals who dream these dreams are typically considered to be mostly passive vessels, blind dancers who happen to encounter—however momentarily—some hidden aspect of God. The elephant is holding out its trunk to a certain blind man and saying, "Do something useful with this information."

AUTHORITATIVE DREAMS

Dreams that have this flavor of divinity often confer spiritual authority onto the dreamer. God says to Moses, for example, "If there be a prophet among you, I will make myself known unto him in a vision and will speak to him in a dream."[17] Not just any old blind man will do, it seems. The correct interpretation of dreams is also viewed as a sign of spiritual authority. After Joseph correctly interprets the dreams of the Pharaoh and his servants, claiming that he does so only through the power of God, the Pharaoh says to him, "Since God has made all this known to you, there is no one so discerning and wise as you. You shall be in charge of my palace and all my people are to submit to your orders" (Gen. 41:39–40).

Likewise, in Buddhism, certain dreams are a sign of significant spiritual maturation. Buddhist scripture describes certain sequences of dreams that all buddhas necessarily have as their individual awareness develops, many of which can occur only after the developing buddha is sufficiently "ripe," thereby activating new layers of spiritual accomplishment. In Tibetan Buddhism, disciples are typically advised to take note of their dreams as they undergo formal initiations into new practices and teachings. Certain sorts of dreams, echoing symbols and events within the Tibetan heritage—what Jung might identify as archetypal symbols—are believed to signify a strong karmic connection to various teachings and deities, thereby encouraging the seeker forward along specific spiritual pathways. Moreover, due to the harsh climate and terrain of Tibet, it is common for the disciple to meet the teacher face to face only a handful of times. Rather than requiring the disciple to attempt a difficult physical journey time and again, the vast majority of the teacher's spiritual guidance and instruction is simply transmitted to the disciple in dreams. Bypassing the need for more typical teaching methods, this or that part of the elephant is simply—and relatively directly—passed along for a feel.

In other traditional cultures, the shaman or medicine man is often the individual who dreams "big" dreams, the content of which is applicable to the entire tribe or individuals other than the dreamer himself. In Colin Wilson's *From Atlantis to the Sphinx*, for example, he relates a well-documented story of "porpoise calling." A British colonial minister was working in the Gilbert Islands when a certain shaman said he was going to call the porpoises. The shaman retreated to a hut, where he said he was going to connect with the porpoises in a dream, inviting them to join a feast. Sometime later, the man came out of the hut and said the porpoises were on the way. The British administrator, along with the villagers, went to the shore where the porpoises soon appeared, flopping placidly onto land and lying still while the tribesmen prepared them for the feast—a meal of porpoise meat, of course. Jungians might assert that such a shaman is simply the individual most consciously connected to the collective unconscious—a communal pool of awareness shared, in this case apparently, even with the porpoises.

In shamanistic cultures, certain individuals gifted in this way enter into the dreams of afflicted community members in order to diagnose their sickness or promote direct healing. Carlos Castañeda's mentor, don Juan, is considered a *nagual*, or accomplished teacher, partly due to his own success in dreaming. In the Toltec tradition, it is the nagual's principle role to guide and protect the apprentice throughout the various dreaming states, "meeting" him in dreams whenever difficulties or questions arise.

A DREAM OF CLARITY

In each of the above examples, we are reminded, yet again, that dreams are often perceived to connect the dreamer to events and information well outside of what is conventionally knowable through ordinary means. Whether Christian, Buddhist, or Native American, such dreams are commonly considered a kind of gift, a rich blessing from some mystical guiding force or being. To illustrate how such phenomenon might play out for the individual seeker, I offer a personal example of what the Tibetans call a dream of clarity.

A few years ago, I had a dream in which I was attending, along with a handful of others, a lecture given by His Holiness the Dalai Lama. The Dalai Lama was using a sort of overhead projector to display a compass. At the center of the compass was a white sphere, which we students were told represented Tibet. In each of the four directions, there was a sphere of a different color. Each of these spheres, the Dalai Lama said, represented a certain lineage of the dharma (teaching), along with a symbolic depiction of specific geographic regions in which the teaching had been spreading over a very long time. Upon waking, I made a mental note of this dream, committing as much detail as I was able to memory. Although I didn't fully understand the teaching conveyed in this dream, I did feel it was highly significant. As is often the case with such dreams, I decided to put it away in safe keeping until the proper circumstances arose that would allow me further insight.

About a year later, I was researching the role of dream practice in Buddhism when I came across a very familiar sounding dream in Serinity Young's *Dreaming in the Lotus*. In this work, Young describes the "four pillar" dream of Milarepa, one of the most important historical figures in Tibetan Buddhism. In this dream, Milarepa is shown a snow-covered mountain. Surrounding this mountain in the cardinal directions, are four pillars, each one with a different animal on top. Milarepa's teacher, Marpa, interprets this dream for him. He says that the snow-covered mountain at the center represents Tibet. Each of the four pillars with its corresponding animal represents a certain lineage of the teaching. This dream, said Marpa, predicted the enduring success for each of these lineages.

The similarities between Milarepa's dream and my own compass-like dream were obvious. To the best of my knowledge, I had never encountered a description of Milarepa's dream prior to my own. Although I am still far from fully comprehending the significance of this dream, I do recognize it as having come from some central source outside of myself—a kind of astral library that the Hindus call the Akashic record. I also understand that I am only able to access such esoteric information at this time through the guidance of much more mature individuals and highly evolved spiritual teachers, represented in my dream by the Dalai Lama.

WHEN YOUR WINGS START FLAPPING

In my experience, these types of dreams—dreams of clairvoyance, esoteric spiritual teachings—come when you are ready for them. They are spontaneous, naturally arising, self-perfected gifts that tend to mark new milestones in your spiritual development. You need not go to Tibet or India to search for this or that guru, this or that esoteric teaching, that is to say. The elephant will rub up against you when you are ready. In the meantime, you need only work on opening yourself to an unfolding process, trace the powerful currents of love and awareness deeper and deeper into your center, and whatever teachings or teachers you need will appear at just the right time as a manifestation of your own innate clarity.

For those of you who have yet to have these kinds of dream experiences—and this describes the vast majority of individuals—a lot of what I have been describing probably sounds like a lot of hogwash, which brings me back to one of my favorite refrains: See for yourself. Don't guess—find out. Learn to work with the dream state directly, learn to bring more and more awareness into sleep and see what happens. As you have seen, most of us have been conditioned by philosophy, science, psychology—and just about every other Western intellectual institution—to *think about* the dreaming process rather than make an art form of it. Just like any other art form, effective dreaming requires certain learnable skills. For this purpose, I will share with you a simple, yet highly sophisticated methodology called dream yoga in the next two chapters. The Tibetans have developed these dream yoga practices into a beautifully precise system, which is described in *Tsongkhapa's Six Yogas of Naropa*.[18] These practices describe, in detail, various means for bringing full, waking awareness into the dream state, as well as actively guiding those dream states. Similarly, the Native American tradition of the Toltecs has developed a strikingly similar dream technology over thousands of years of experimentation. From time to time, I supplement the Tibetan practice with Toltec ideas, hopefully providing a broader context in which to understand dream practice in general.

In bringing immediate awareness into the dreaming and sleeping process, both of these systems look much deeper into the question of "What is real?" than do the various theories and elaborate guesses of philosophy, science, and psychology. As you examine these dreaming practices in some detail, you see the significant way the spiritual path works to shift the focus of the "What is real?" question. When you begin to experience yourself as a continuous, unbroken thread of awareness that runs throughout both waking and sleeping states, you begin to experience the equal reality of all states of consciousness, to truly remember the totality of the Self. As this ancient memory deepens, the fundamental question becomes not "*What* is real?" but "*Who* is real? Who exactly is it," you begin to ask, "that is doing all this dancing?" It is at this crucial and irreversible moment that, to paraphrase Chuang Tzu, your spiritual wings really start flapping.

THE THREE CLASSES
OF DREAMS

Don Juan contended that our world, which we believe to be unique and absolute, is only one in a cluster of consecutive worlds, arranged like the layers of an onion. He asserted that even though we have been energetically conditioned to perceive solely our world, we still have the capability of entering into those other realms, which are as real, unique, absolute and engulfing as our own world is. . . . Believing that our energetic conditioning is correctable, don Juan stated that sorcerers of ancient times developed a set of practices designed to recondition our energetic capabilities to perceive. They called this set of practices the art of dreaming.

—CARLOS CASTAÑEDA[1]

Spiritual systems tend to classify dreams according to the nature of their connection with the divine, the layer of the cosmic onion from which they arise. According to the Tibetans, there are three basic classes, or types, of dreams: ordinary, clarity, and clear light. In the context of our continuing metaphor, you can think of these classes as three different dances the blind man does with the elephant of Things Changing. Before you begin to work with each of these dances directly, however, let's map out the dance floor to better understand the size and shape of the ballroom.

When you first begin dream practice, you can assume that the vast majority of your dreams belong to the first class, that of the ordinary dream. As you learn to bring more awareness into dream and sleep, you will begin to experience more of the other classes—clarity and clear light. These three types of dreams fall along a gradual continuum of awareness. Many dreams of clarity involve certain elements of less stable, ordinary dreams. Inversely, ordinary dreams may sometimes involve very subtle hints of a clear light experience. The point here is not to precisely identify each and every element of your dreams, placing them in the appropriate class. Rather, the goal is to simply identify the overall "feel" of the dream.

Different kinds of dreams require different methods of practice in order to maximize their potential use. In order to fully understand your dreaming and sleeping experiences, as well as better appreciate your developing skills as a dream practitioner, it is important that you learn to apply the appropriate practices to whatever class of dreams you are working with. In what follows, I will describe each of the three classes of dreams in some detail. In chapter 11, we will look into the various practices most effective for each of these classes.

Ordinary Dreams

This is a dance step I call "Blind Man Touches Elephant." By far, these are the most common variety of dreams. You have such dreams when you are wanting *something*, but you're not exactly sure what. This somewhat confused state probably describes most of us most of the time. Vaguely aware that there is an elephant out there somewhere, you are groping around in the dark, trying to catch hold of an elusive tail or an ear. If you are not already a serious dream yoga practitioner, it is highly unlikely—although not impossible—that you experience the other two classes of dream with any regularity. Even if you *are* already a serious practitioner, it is important to understand that it takes most of us a good while to encounter the other classes of dreams. Patience is particularly essential in dream practice. As with any other spiritual practice, the more you try to hurry yourself on to higher states of awareness in dream and sleep, the more your practice tends to suffer. Consequently, if you are having ordinary dreams at present, then you should be content to work with ordinary dreams. The other classes will come along when you have learned to work skillfully with this most common type of dream.

Tibetans call common dreams "karmic trace dreams." As all dreams of any class involve karmic traces to one degree or another, however, I think this phrase is a bit misleading. Rather, I would suggest the phrase "personal karmic traces." You can think of karmic traces as unfinished business. Somewhere in the past, seeds have been planted, which have yet to mature. Namkhai Norbu says in *Dream Yoga and the Practice of Natural Light* that all personal karmic trace dreams are "related to an event that touched the person deeply and left traces of the tension, fear or other strong emotion."[2] This is the type of dream Western psychology has so far been most interested in. When Freud suggests that dreams express hidden wishes or desires, he is referring to the unfinished business of personal karmic traces. A hidden desire is a desire nonetheless, which means that it is going to have to be dealt with in one way or another. The seed of whatever repressed or otherwise neglected feeling or situation is going to grow one way or another, so you might as well provide a comfortable growing environment.

In working with ordinary dreams, the first step in resolving these hidden desires, then, is simply to consciously recognize them. Once you can bring these desires into your everyday, waking awareness, you can better release the tension created by your anxiously buried, unacceptable wants and wishes. The longer a desire goes unrecognized, the more urgency it accumulates, the more tension it creates and the more likely it's going to be acted upon.

A crude metaphor might be that of an ingrown hair. If a hair follicle gets plugged somehow, the hair is forced to grow unnaturally, which causes pain. So it goes with unrecognized or disowned desires. Like unwanted hairs, they will not go away simply because you stubbornly ignore or avoid them. Rather, they will bury themselves deeper and deeper in your psyche, steadily increasing your emotional and psychological discomfort. This is why many people seem to "explode" unexpectedly, suddenly leaving their spouse after decades of a successful marriage, for example. The psychological tension having finally become unmanageable, the repressed desire seems to pop out of nowhere one day, destabilizing such an individual's nervously maintained ego boundaries to the very core of his or her personality.

You might think of recognizing hidden desires as going on a diet. Before you attempt to diet, you probably don't pay all that much attention to your desire to eat. When you are hungry, you eat. It is, for the most part, an automatic process. When you go on a diet, however, these food desires begin to stand out in increasingly vivid, neon detail. Such a recognition, however, doesn't mean that you act on each of these desires—not if you are going to diet successfully. Rather, you learn more skillful ways to satisfy these desires. If, for example, I desire ice cream, maybe I can eat low-fat yogurt. If I want a hamburger, maybe I'll eat a chicken sandwich. Unlike my eating process prior to my diet, these days I notice my desire as it arises, then make a *conscious* choice as to the best way to satisfy it. In the same way, simply recognizing a hidden desire such as wanting to cheat on your spouse can present you with alternative ways to fulfill this want. Maybe you'll get into couples counseling. Maybe you'll try to bring more excitement and romance back into your relationship. By contrast, if you continue to simply suppress this desire, this stored tension will necessarily erupt sooner or later, very likely creating a needlessly messy situation.

MARKS ON PAPER

In *The Tibetan Yogas of Dream and Sleep*, Tenzin Wangyal Rinpoche says that ordinary dreams lack an innate meaning. He compares the interpretation of dreams to the process of reading a book. "A book is just marks on paper," he says, "but because we bring our sense of meaning to it we can take meaning from it."[3] No book has one, concrete meaning, of course. In fact, books are interesting to the degree that we *are* able to find multiple meanings in them, emphasizing those that are most communicative to us personally. This is not to say ordinary dreams are "meaningless" in a negative sense. "Infinitely flexible" might be a better way to describe them. What

Wangyal Rinpoche is saying mirrors Freud's own idea about dreams. Rather than fitting the elements of your ordinary, or karmic trace, dreams into some systematic decoding chart, you have to work to find the most personal meaning, the meaning that seems to best reflect your own daily life. You can do so only by looking into both your waking and sleeping experiences openly and honestly.

As you begin to work with your ordinary dreams, learning to better correlate their hidden messages with your waking wishes, conflicts, and desires, you will notice an almost immediate increase in your capacity to recall dream material. You may still be wandering around in the dark of the unconscious mind, but now you have got a specific dance to do. At least now you know there is an elephant of some variety involved. Your unconscious processes may remain mostly a mystery to you, that is to say, but at least now you are on the lookout, conscious of the fact that you are missing something. With this new, albeit imperfect, awareness of your total personality, you may begin to experience nights in which you are able to recall every dream in vivid detail. At this time, you may even begin to experience varying degrees of lucidity in your dreams. At first, lucidity will probably be very unstable. Even after much practice, you may only be able to remain lucid for a few seconds here and there. Still, this is a very encouraging sign of progress. At this point, you are likely to experience an occasional dream of clarity.

Dreams of Clarity

I call this dance step "Elephant Touches Blind Man." If ordinary dreams reflect personal karmic traces, then dreams of clarity express *transpersonal* karmic traces. Although such dreams still deal with unfinished business of some sort, this business tends to be much less urgent than does your own, individual hidden wishes and desires. According to Namkhai Norbu, "When a practitioner has matured or developed, there is a diminution of the obstacles that usually function to obscure the natural clarity of the mind."[4] He compares the dream state to the sky. In ordinary dreams, there are many dark clouds—the obscuration of repressed wishes and desires. Although the sun is shining, you catch only a ray here or there. In dreams of clarity, the sky has begun to clear up, and you begin to perceive the sun's rays more directly. The sunlight has been there the whole time, of course—being nothing other than the innate illumination of the natural mind—only you were previously too absorbed in the weighty, unfinished business of your own desires to recognize it. At this point, we tend to settle down a bit so that the elephant can come to you, present you with whatever part of the elephant that is the most useful to you.

Transpersonal karmic traces are very similar to Jung's idea of the collective unconscious. Once you begin to access this storehouse of phenomenon, you begin to process not only your own unfinished business, but also the unfinished business of other individuals and groups of individuals. You are beginning, that is to say, to encounter larger areas of the elephant. For this reason, before you begin to experience transpersonal karmic traces, you need to attend to your own urgent desires. If you are running around like crazy in a dark room, you're going to keep falling down. If you are involved in a very tumultuous romantic relationship, for example, you're probably going to be too distracted by the ongoing drama of the situation to be aware of much subtler karma. You have got to be able to stand in one place long enough before the elephant can find you. As Tenzin Wangyal describes it, "In the dream of clarity it is as if something is given to or found by the dreamer, as opposed to the *samsaric* [personal karmic trace] dream in which meaning is projected from the dreamer onto the purity of fundamental experience."[5] Only when you begin to experience a kind of calm steadiness from day to day do you begin to open up to dreams of clarity.

Much of the material in dreams of clarity can look like ordinary dream content. How do you distinguish between them? Although there are some objective criteria, the only truly reliable way to distinguish is by feel. A good rule of thumb is: If you are not sure whether you're having dreams of clarity, you're probably not. Moreover, you can take a look at your waking life. Is your waking life very calm? Do you remain stable and centered even in stressful situations, or do you tend to get lost in dramatic emotional experiences? Many people are too much in a hurry to dive into dreams of supposed clarity before they take care of some of their most pressing personal issues. It's too easy in such a situation to put our own problems off on others. "This dream doesn't represent *my* unfinished business," we tell ourselves, "but my co-worker Gina's unfinished business."

A dream of clarity really is a kind of reminder. You are being reminded that other people's unfinished business *is* your unfinished business. There is just one elephant out there, which belongs to all of us collectively. There is a Zen saying that asserts that spiritual practice doesn't cure merely the practitioner, it also cures the birds and the grass. This means the more you attend to your own internal sticking points, the more your external life begins to make more sense. All those people "out there" that you previously thought were so obnoxious—now you're beginning to see more and more light in them. Consequently, the more you desire to truly love and accept other people, the more you begin to experience dreams of clarity. If your primary desire is simply to be entertained by mystical experiences, or to impress others with your clairvoyant knowledge, you are just getting yourself stuck more deeply inside your own personal drama.

Dreams of clarity come in an almost infinite array of forms. Let's look at a few of the most common varieties, as well as explore some key dream-practice concepts.

CLAIRVOYANT DREAMS

These dreams contain information about individuals not normally available to us. The clearest dreams of this nature tend to contain objectively verifiable facts. For instance, I recently had a dream in which a relative of mine became pregnant. There was some medical concern about the pregnancy. In this dream, however, I could see that the baby was going to be fine and told this relative so. (This is a distant relative, with whom I speak only once a year or so. As we are not all that close, we wouldn't normally discuss intensely personal issues such as planning a pregnancy.) About a week after this dream, I learned that my relative was, in fact, pregnant in waking life as well. Moreover, as in the dream, there were indeed some significant concerns about the baby's safety. I shared my dream with my family in the hopes of providing them with some comfort and reassurance. In the end, the baby was perfectly healthy.

Dreams such as this are common in the literature. Many practitioners have such dreams containing objectively verifiable facts with some regularity. I should emphasize, however, that the occurrence of such dreams does not confer some sort of spiritual mastery. In fact, these sorts of experiences are very natural manifestations of progress along the path. Rather than congratulating yourself for your amazing powers of awareness when you experience dreams of clairvoyance, you might do better to ask yourself, "What use can I make of this information? How might this knowledge be used to help myself and others?" If you seek after such experiences simply to inflate your ego, you will only make things more difficult for yourself.

As you begin to see larger patterns of karma unfolding, getting your hands on more of the elusive elephant, it becomes increasingly clearer that pursuing greater love and awareness is the highest human endeavor. If nothing else, dreams of clairvoyance remind us that as we delve more and more deeply into our own layers, we discover the presence of others. It's what all the spiritual books and teachers have been yelling at us: *We are all one.* I am you, you are me. Literally. Go deeply enough into your own awareness and you will discover Buddha and Jesus sitting there calmly, patiently waiting for you to reintegrate this highest aspect of your own self.

TEACHING DREAMS

As your awareness stabilizes, you begin to meet your teachers on the inner, or astral, planes. These are simply the alternate realities—deeper layers of the cosmic onion—you encounter while skillfully dreaming and in heightened states of awareness. Very deep teachings are revealed in such states. In fact, it may take you quite a while to "catch up" with these teachings in your waking awareness.

The Toltecs believe that we are guided on two levels as we pursue the spiritual journey: the *tonal* and the *nagual*. At the tonal level, we receive relatively concrete, verbal instruction that we can recall and make sense of from day to day. Most spiritual books, for instance, address the reader primarily at this level. With nagual teachings, however, we are also being instructed at a much deeper level, the level of the dreaming body. This is the level that, although sometimes present in the written word, has a kind of mysterious, non-conceptual "shimmer" to it—teachings that can only be grasped indirectly, from the corner of our spiritual eyes. As you, the seeker, progress in your practices, you become more aware of this esoteric level of teachings that have been going on the whole time in other states of awareness, particularly those of dream and sleep. In the context of Namkhai Norbu's analogy, the sun—the nagual level teachings, in this case—has been shining the whole time, you just couldn't see it because of the habitual clouds that inhabitant the tonal level teachings. In my own dreaming experiences, for example, I frequently meet some teacher who seems very familiar to me at the time. Upon waking, however, the teacher and the teaching are somehow foggy to me—almost like a very early childhood memory. This imperfect recollection, or assimilation into waking consciousness, is evidence that I have simply yet to stabilize my normal, everyday awareness to the point where I am able to fully integrate this deeper level of teachings.

At the same time, many teaching dreams convey relatively simple messages from teachers familiar to us in our waking consciousness. If you purchase a book by a very mature teacher, for instance, that teacher is already sending out teachings to you on every level. As you begin to connect more deeply with his or her verbal teachings, you may very likely begin to meet such an individual on the inner planes, where you receive even more powerful and personalized teachings. I should emphasize, however, that not all dreams that seem to contain one of your beloved spiritual teachers are "authentic." Very often, you may be encountering your own projection or *idea* of that teacher. Tenzin Wangyal says that making "the mistake of believing that *samsaric* [personal karmic trace] dreams are offering us true guidance . . . is also a way to become stuck in personal drama, believing that all our dreams are messages from a higher, more spiritual source."[6] How can you tell the difference? There is no hard-and-fast rule. Generally, one of the best ways to distinguish so-called teachings arising from ordinary dreams and authentic teachings present in dreams of clarity is simply examining the teaching itself. Whether it came from your own mind or a seemingly external teacher, is it a useful teaching? Ironically, as you progress along the path, you begin to understand that these supposed external teachers are—at the most esoteric level—really aspects of your own highest self reflected back to you. You encounter such individuals externally at present—through books, lectures, and dreams—only because you are not yet able to fully recognize your own, self-perfected, innate wisdom.

As you begin to pay attention to increasingly subtle aspects of your own awareness, you start to see that these teachings were present the whole time. Maybe you notice a quiet little voice in the back your head, maybe a fleeting, yet recurring, mental image. When you begin to recognize these subtle inner teachings, you no longer feel so dependent on others to show you the way. You begin to understand that you *are* the way. Your very own, everyday self, is already the perfected Buddha or Christ nature.

ABSTRACT TEACHING DREAMS

Teaching dreams need not contain a teacher in physical form. Rather, as recorded in

BUILD A BETTER BUDDHA

the literature of dreaming practice, it is often as if you are visiting a kind of cosmic library (the Akashic record). In my experience, it is as if some impersonal librarian is showing me various writings and oddly familiar drawings, teachings that often seem just outside of my waking understanding. For example, I was once shown a beautiful mandala with the letters ATI inscribed all over it. The next day, I looked up this term and discovered that Dzogchen, which is now my principle practice, is often referred to as Ati Yoga. Similarly, I've often encountered a disembodied voice while dreaming, typically instructing me in some new dreaming technique. Don Juan calls this voice the dream narrator. He tells Castañeda that this voice isn't really telling him anything other than what he already knows. As I stated previously, this seemingly mysterious, astral authority is simply some heightened aspect of your own, ordinary self contacting you in a way you can more easily understand.

DREAMS OF INCREASING LUCIDITY

By the time authentic dreams of clarity begin to arise, you have probably begun to experience more lucidity in your dreams. You may have experienced fully lucid dreams. In these dreams, you are completely aware that you are dreaming, in much the same way that you are now aware that you are awake and reading this book. As your lucid experiences increase, you will find you have more conscious control over what goes on in your dreams. In a perfectly lucid dream, you are in complete control over the dream material. Stabilized in your awareness, you create whatever dream you desire, rather than letting the dream automatically carry you this way and that. If you believe you may be having dreams of clarity, but experience lucidity in dreams very rarely, I suggest you approach the content of such dreams with a grain of salt. Whatever legitimate teachings these dreams may contain, they will be of little use to you until you can approach them with the steadiness and confidence that naturally give rise to lucid dreaming experiences.

DREAMS OF DAKINIS

Dakinis are benevolent astral beings with feminine energies. The Tibetans frequently mention dakinis when discussing dream practice. As Tenzin Wangyal defines these beings, a dakini is a "female sky traveler [literally] . . . [She] can be a human woman who has realized her true nature, or a non-human female or goddess, or a direct manifestation of enlightened mind."[7] I would like to emphasize that these beings, bizarre as they may sound, are very real. When I first began dream practice, I thought dakinis were simply metaphors, cartoon icons for the superstitious—rather like the angel on top of the Christmas tree. My experiences since, however, have led me to believe very differently. If you embark on the path of dream practice, you will encounter one of these beings sooner or later. They are beautiful, angelic creatures that gently guide you in many ways. They are not necessarily enlightened beings, nor are they typically spiritual teachers in the common sense of the phrase. Peculiar as it may sound, they are very much like the benevolent fairies of popular myth. They assist you, the dreamer, in your travels, freely offering kindness and love. They seem to be guardians of dream practice, ensuring that you do not get lost as you journey through alternate realities. As you embark on your nightly dream journeys, then, be confident that there are benevolent, nurturing creatures "out there" helping you along.

PARALLEL LIFE DREAMS

The Buddhists call this sort of dream of clarity a past life dream. "Depending on the dreamer's capacity," Namkhai Norbu says, "it might be possible to remember a past life in its entirety. One hundred or even a hundred thousand lives can be remembered in a dream."[8] I think this term "past life" is a little misleading as, the more awareness we bring to the dreaming process, the more our idea of time changes. In my experience, our journey as a spiritual being is not so much a sequential passing from one body and personality to the next as it is one large, simultaneous movement. We are all of our many lives at this very moment, that is to say, trying to reconnect with our total self. For whatever reason, we are simply most identified with—the Buddhists would say most "attached" to—this one particular layer of the onion at this point in our evolution of consciousness. For this reason, I prefer the phrase "parallel lives" to "past lives."

THE TOLTEC WISDOM ON PARALLEL LIFE DREAMS

Because they bring into question some of our most basic assumptions about reality versus appearance, parallel life dreams have particular significance for our understanding of who we are. As this sort of dream is really about realigning your perception in very important ways, the Toltec view of personal perception can help you understand how to work with the parallel life dream. Certain experiences I will describe, as well as the systems that make sense of these experiences, are well outside the average individual's daily awareness.

Interestingly, it is not even necessary that the seeker along whatever path believe in such things in order to start encountering them. Believe it or not, such seemingly bizarre stuff is a very natural part of spiritual development. For now, I encourage you to maintain a healthy skepticism. After all, taking someone else's word on such important matters isn't really going to get you very far. For those of you who have yet to encounter parallel life phenomenon, it might be best to simply think of it as a useful metaphor for the time being, a useful way to illustrate the way human perception works. As your experience of such phenomenon deepens, you will decide for yourself as to the reality of these experiences.

The Dreaming Body

In the Toltec system of perception, the dreaming body—also known as the subtle, energy, or astral body—is absolutely essential for our perception of all phenomenon, ordinary as well as non-ordinary. As I explained earlier, the Toltec seers perceive this body to be a luminous sphere that surrounds the physical body.

Most of us, whether we recognize it or not, are tuned in to the dreaming body to one degree or another. Some individuals refine their awareness of this subtle body to the degree that they can actually see or feel it. Many such individuals describe the awareness of the dreaming body as involving something halfway between seeing and feeling, something that combines the physical senses with a very subtle sort of intuition.

Toltec seer or no, we all experience awareness of the subtle body from time to time. For instance, consider the well-known experience of feeling as if you are being watched. Maybe you turn suddenly and find that, in fact, your vague sensation or intuition was accurate. Such is the work of the dreaming body. From this body, the Toltecs tell us, there radiates a number of luminous fibers or tentacles. We interact with the external world by sending and receiving information through these fibers.

At a certain point along the surface of your luminous astral body, there lies a kind of condensed bundle of these fibers, which the Toltecs call "the assemblage point." The assemblage point is the central processor of the dreaming body in that it directs and organizes the flow of energy along the radiating fibers. An important aspect of this point is that it can be moved, intentionally or accidentally. A good visual metaphor for the dreaming body and its assemblage point is that of a round, touch-sensitive novelty lamp that pulses with static electric fibers. As you touch the surface of the lamp at various points, the fibers change their shape in reaction to your own electricity. The point at which your finger touches the lamp is similar—both visually and functionally—to the assemblage point of the subtle body.

Moving the Assemblage Point

When the assemblage point moves, the energy body's luminous fibers react, causing you to perceive your world in a different way. For example, when you are intoxicated, running a high fever, or under enormous emotional stress, the assemblage point moves automatically. As a result, you perceive the world in a slightly different way, confusing the supposed real world with your own "hallucinations." Notice, however, we don't question the fact that the drunk person, for instance, really experiences the room as spinning—we simply say that his or her perception is somehow "off." Although we probably don't think of it as a shifting of the assemblage point, we recognize the fact that some internal change within the drunken person is causing him or her to assemble, or organize, his or her perceptions of the world in a slightly different way.

The most important shifts of the assemblage point happen while sleeping. Everyone undergoes numerous shifts of the assemblage point every night. These shifts are usually very erratic and without conscious purpose. This is why our dreams, if recalled at all, are remembered as a kind of foggy blur of fragments. Let's say, for example, you are having a dream in which you are back in ninth grade, sitting in your favorite teacher's classroom. You notice your teacher looks like your uncle and suddenly, there you are in your uncle's garage, already having forgotten all about your ninth grade classroom. Your assemblage point has *erratically* shifted.

In one way, all of spiritual practice might be considered an elaborate means to stabilize the assemblage point, and gain conscious control over it. When you first begin spiritual practice, your assemblage point is very undisciplined. This is why you do concentration practice. As you sit there bringing your focus back to your object time and again, you are essentially training your assemblage point to heel. You are learning to consciously point it somewhere and make it stick.

Stabilizing the Assemblage Point

When you have trained your assemblage point to a fairly high degree of stability, your dreams become much less erratic. The Toltecs refer to this process as "cultivating intent." You may even stabilize your assemblage point to the degree where you begin to "wake up" in your dreams, which simply means you are firmly planting your assemblage point in some parallel reality. It's not that reality is changing, it's that you are realigning your perception to notice aspects not usually available to you. As you begin to stabilize your assemblage point with increasing skill, you begin to understand that what you previously called reality was nothing other than a certain setting of the assemblage point. Everyone you encounter in your ordinary, waking perception, is simply another individual who prefers this very same setting. There is nothing at all wrong, in and of itself, with this particular setting of the assemblage point. There is nothing innately lacking in the world you have learned to identify as the *real* word. What you call reality, however, is just one tiny dial marking on the cosmic receiver. Once you begin to learn how to turn this dial, you discover something amazing: You are much, much more than you thought you were. This life, your so-called real life, is simply one of an infinite number of dramas you are playing out all the time in parallel dial settings.

The more you learn to stabilize your assemblage point, and consequently, the more you begin to wake up on increasingly bizarre planes of reality, the more you begin to remember deeply buried aspects of yourself and appreciate the uniqueness of individual lives. This is why the goal of spiritual practice isn't to simply find your favorite dial setting and plant yourself there. In fact, this sort of stagnation is much like death itself. Rather, you want to learn the art of infinite flexibility, what Chuang Tzu calls "Things Changing." John Lennon sings about "Strawberry Fields where nothing is real/and nothing to get hung about."[9] Well, that's just it: There is *no* thing to get hung about, no one truly "real" awareness setting where you need to stick your assemblage point. Herein lies the eternal beauty and mystery of Things Changing.

Reincarnation Reconsidered

Let's reconsider the Buddhist's idea of reincarnation in our new context. In their view, the assemblage point has been born again and again into new settings so that our current setting is really the latest in a long line of shifts. Like I said earlier, while I think there is certainly some truth to this view, rather than viewing our "past lives" as linear, or sequential affairs, I think it is much more useful to view these alternate awareness settings as simultaneous happenings.

Interestingly, when you wake up into a parallel reality, you will find that all your same old problems have followed you there in one way or another. Maybe in the real world you had a problem with high blood pressure. Well, in some parallel life you may experience this stress as a strange and pesky creature that hangs out by your front door, harassing you on your way to work every morning. The point is not to "escape" into some other reality. Rather, you learn to work out your familiar, very ordinary problems in numerous planes of reality, thereby offering you numerous angles of attack.

The good news is, not only do your problems follow you, so do your loved ones. In my experience, the very definition of closeness is the sharing of assemblage points. The closer you are to someone, the more assemblage point settings you share with him or her. Someone very close to you, then, shares a virtually infinite number of assemblage settings with you. Consequently, wherever you go, there he or she is, albeit in a slightly different form.

The most spiritually evolved people are the ones that maintain the most stable identity throughout *all* planes. No matter what bizarre astral circumstances in which I meet him, my guru, Maharaj-ji, is always clearly Maharaj-ji. He once told a devotee that he could never be angry with him—not even in a dream. This consistency arises from the fact that Maharaj-ji has simply woken up, is "all there" on every plane, whereas most of us are still sleepwalking through the vast majority of the cosmic onion layers.

For this reason, individuals of heightened awareness are still "out there" even when they die, or simply abandon ship, on this particular plane. In dreams of clarity, it is not uncommon to encounter highly evolved individuals who have been considered long-gone in this world. When Buddha was enlightened, he was said to have experienced a sudden knowledge of each and every one of his past lives. In that single moment, we might say Buddha suddenly woke up to all of his concurrent lives, suddenly tuned in to the infinite array of dramas playing out all around the awareness dial. Consequently, the fact that Buddha left his body a long time ago, is not all that significant. This simply means he has shifted his primary focal point to some other plane—a plane that is nonetheless accessible to those who would go on the journey. If you truly desire to encounter him—or any other historical spiritual teacher—in the recognizable form of an individual being, you can certainly do so. The key, once again, is simply cultivating both flexibility and stability throughout your waking and non-waking states.

Why This Reality?

You might wonder, given that there are all these various parallel lives apparently going on the whole time, why we seem to be so stuck on this one. As it turns out, the very same obstacles that bring about suffering on this plane—fear, anger, envy, self-importance, etc.—are the same hurdles of awareness that compel our narrow-minded attachment to this, and only this, reality.

In many of these parallel astral planes, the basic rules of engagement are very different from those of our everyday plane. For example, on some planes, everyone close to you may manifest as a single entity, a kind of conglomeration of each of their individual traits. Your spouse, parents, and best friends may be melted into a single blob of consciousness. For that matter, you may be melted in with them. Such a fundamental transformation of your ego identity—and this is only one example of infinitely strange possibilities—could be pretty traumatic until you are ready to experience it. This is why you experience such oddities only once you have learned to discipline your assemblage point, which becomes an essential grounding device. Throughout the various planes, you discover that people can fly, animals can talk, the dead live, inanimate objects can become animate, etc. The possibilities are literally endless—a prospect that can be pretty terrifying to most of us.

There is no reason to worry about wandering onto other planes until you are ready, however, as fear—along with its many other forms of self-centered craving and negativity—is the single most powerful obstacle to increasing awareness in other planes. Rest assured that until you have gained confidence that your true identity, your core essence, will follow you wherever you may find yourself, you are unlikely to be discussing Plato with your family pet.

Art as Reminder

As don Juan tells Castañeda, everything that can be written, any story that has been or can be told, is happening somewhere within the vast cosmos. In this context, your favorite book is probably your favorite book because it somehow reminds you of some astral plane for which you have a kind of homesickness. We tend to say, after all, that such books "connect us" to other aspects of ourselves, open up dormant avenues of our personalities. Moreover, there are planes of pure music, winged angelic choirs, indescribable symphonies of light and sound. There are planes in which Van Gogh's paintings are swirling, physical realities, planes in which everyone looks like a Picasso portrait. In short, anything you encounter here, in this plane, in whatever form—book, movie, joke, song—rest assured that, on some astral plane or another, it is just as real as your own face.

Think of art and music, movies and books, etc., as placeholders similar to Plato's sensibles. Such ordinary phenomenon act as extraordinary pointers, that is to say, to hidden or disowned aspects of your own self, doors to the most distant rooms of your transpersonal awareness. You may feel a kind of bittersweet nostalgia when you watch your favorite movie, for instance, because you are reminded there is still some significant part of yourself, some aspect of the One Self, "out there" somewhere. In this way, all creative acts and artistic works stem from the artist's not-quite-conscious contact with other realities, other lives and worlds, reminding all of us that our journey of remembering will ultimately take us well beyond our current boundaries of ego, intellect, sensory perception, and even physical laws.

Larger Than We Think

I will further discuss parallel realities in chapter 11. For now, the most important point to consider is that the universe—being composed of both internal and external space—may be much larger than you think. *You* are much larger than you think—infinitely large, in fact. Stay with your everyday awareness long enough, follow it deeply enough back and back throughout the intricate corridors of the natural mind, and you will reach the space of experiencing It All, the space of pure *being*. As you explore new frontiers of your awareness, following your conscious *and* unconscious mind even into states of deep sleep and dream, you discover that you have been both Chou and the butterfly the whole time, both the blind men and the elephant dancing the crazy dance of Things Changing.

Clear Light States

I call this class of dream "Elephant Touches Elephant." It's not exactly a dance in the same way the other two classes of dreams are. Rather, the dancer and the dance are one thing here, one dynamic whole. For this reason, of the three classes of dreams, clear light dreams—more properly called "states," as you shall see—are, by far, the most difficult to describe. This difficulty arises mainly because, unlike ordinary dreams and dreams of clarity, clear light dreams are not dualistic.

What exactly does "not dualistic" mean? According to Tenzin Wangyal, "The clear light dream is not defined by the content of the dream, but is a clear light dream because there is no subjective dreamer or dream ego, nor any self in a dualistic relationship with the dream or dream content. Although a dream arises, it is an activity of the mind that does not disturb the practitioner's stability in the clear light."[10]

In an ordinary dream or dream of clarity, regardless of the degree of lucidity you bring to it, you are still mostly an actor participating in a drama. You identify strongly with your own individual awareness, the center of your subjective lens. You film all these objects around you, all these events and characters interacting with you, and you operate under some automatic, albeit very quiet, assumption that your drama is composed of two main elements: I and other. In clear light states, however, this duality dissolves. Everything is part of this central "I." Things don't happen to you. Rather, you are *things happening*. Like Chuang Tzu said, you are Things Changing. A good analogy might be you scratching your own arm. You probably don't think to yourself, "Scratching is happening to my arm." Instead, you probably think, "I *am* scratching my arm." It's all one happening—experience and experiencer are not two.

To facilitate your understanding of the clear light state, we are going to explore three manifestations of this elusive experience. Owing to the confines of language and concepts, I will present each of these manifestations as distinct forms of the one clear light. Know, however, that such distinctions are, at best, loose approximations. More accurately, each of these manifestations necessarily contains the other two. For that matter, to say that the clear light can be somehow experienced separately, somehow isolated from the ordinary context that includes every mundane aspect of your daily life, is to be fundamentally misleading. In the end, the best we can legitimately assert is that the clear light is what it is—an elegant existential truth that can only be tasted through direct experience.

NON-REM CLEAR LIGHT

Another thing that makes clear light experiences difficult to talk about is the fact that they need not happen during REM sleep. They need not be dreams at all. Whereas ordinary dreams and dreams of clarity, regardless of their content, necessarily arise during one of the nightly four dream phases, the clear light can be experienced between these phases as well. In my experience, this occurrence of the clear light state is a little different from the clear light in the REM phases.

Typically, as you fall asleep, you lose all sense of yourself for a bit, and sort of slip into darkness. This is the state of deep, dreamless sleep—the non-REM state. The first time you regain any slight recognition of "I" is when you emerge into REM sleep and have your first dream of the evening. In a clear light experience, however, as you fall off into this non-REM darkness, your awareness shifts to some much deeper aspect of yourself, what Dzogchen calls the "base." In my experience of this state, I am aware of myself gradually drifting off, then suddenly I'm awake inside a warm white light. It's not exactly that I am looking out into this white light—which would still be dualistic. Rather, I *am* the white light, the white light *is* me—yet I am still somehow aware of the white light. You might say I am the white light being aware of itself, but be careful with such statements. There aren't really two things, remember. The best I can say about this state is that it's perfectly peaceful and calm—to the degree that I'm perfectly peaceful and calm, at least. There is no desire in this state, no fear or typical emotion of any sort. In many ways, it is much easier to recognize this state—in a verbal or conceptual way, at least—as I am emerging out of it into dream sleep. At that time, a separate, observing "I" could refer to the clear light as a distinct object, and note that it has been very restorative, somehow replenishing and realigning my basic elements.

We all enter into the clear light every night. It is not something that starts happening only after we have reached a certain stage of awareness. Even so, most of us aren't able to follow our individual awareness into this state. In deep sleep, most of us couldn't even say we experienced darkness. We experience absolutely nothing. We are temporarily dead, we might say, void of conscious experience of any sort. By contrast, to experience the clear light is to begin to recognize that your individual awareness always remains unbroken. Stability within the clear light state teaches you that awareness can never be truly lost, not even for an instant—it can only be over-looked by your habitual-thinking mind.

THE DUMB MAN'S DREAM

This significant variation of the clear light experience also occurs in non-REM sleep. Whereas in the aforementioned experience, there is a distinct element of clear, or white, light, in this experience, there isn't even this phenomenon to report, which is not to say there is darkness, because there's not. In such a state there is absolutely nothing other than awareness itself. "What exactly is it aware *of*?" you might ask. Itself and nothing else. It is pure awareness staring silently into pure awareness. In Dzogchen, they describe such an experience as "like a dumb man's dream."

You might wonder how—if you are aware of absolutely nothing in such a state—this dumb man's dream is different from the state of ordinary, dreamless sleep. There is a definitive, qualitative difference, but one that is nearly impossible to describe. The best I can say is it feels as if I somehow shrink into a tiny pinpoint of light in such a state, and then that light . . . swallows itself. The clear light is so full of love, you might say, it can't help but gobble up even the last little speck of its own body. Here is the really amazing part, however: Even in this state of formless-ness, *sunyata*, the state of so-called emptiness, I'm still there in my entirety. And I don't mean just the mystical "I" as in "We are all this I," either. I also mean the James Robbins "I." Moreover, my cats are still there, each with their individual personality perfectly intact, John, Paul, George, and Ringo are there, as are chocolate ice cream, light beer, spaghetti Westerns, and the kitchen sink. These things remain because love remains. Love remains because this is who you are: spontaneously perfected pure awareness, which is love, itself.

To have this experience, even once, is incredibly liberating. You begin to real-ize that there is nothing to fear, death included, because whoever you are, wherever you find yourself along the path, you are not going anywhere. If you look deeply inside of yourself right now, you can feel the truth of this, feel the incredible joy of this ridiculously beautiful dance going on. It's there at the very center of your spiri-tual heart, this quiet little explosion of light and music. At the same time, all these various experiences I am describing, all these various practices you are about to look into in the next chapter—understand that these are nothing other than training wheels. Love is the thing. Your daily life, just as it already is, is the thing. Truth, Beauty, God—whatever you want to call it, is ever-present. But you know this already. You couldn't possibly be reading these words—which are simply aspects of *you* being reflected back to *you*—right now if you didn't. Dzogchen, Zen, Buddhism—these are ultimately nothing more than insignificant, comedically complex footnotes to the infinite beauty of Who You Are.

THE CLEAR LIGHT "DREAM"

In comparison to the above experiences, the clear light dream proper, which necessarily happens in REM sleep, is somewhat easier to describe. It is still non-dualistic, understand, but at least now you've got a little more scenery to work with. Imagine looking into a mirror. This is no ordinary mirror, however. It doesn't merely reflect your physical appearance, it also reflects your every thought and feeling, every fleeting memory that passes through your mind. How exactly does this mirror do that? What does all this stuff look like as it is reflected back to you? Imagine looking into a kaleidoscope. Not only are there beautifully intricate patterns of color, there is an unspeakably graceful motion, all these strange shapes melting into and out of one another. Well, *that's* you. This very dance within the kaleidoscope mirror is you, all of your internal and external thoughts, sensations and feelings being reflected back to you in dynamic Technicolor. This is you translated into your most basic, essential form, what the Tibetans call "the elements."

Imagine if you took a Shakespearian play and represented it with all the minute chemical interactions that were going on in Will's brain as he composed it. The clear light dream is similar to this, except that chemical interactions are very small, artistically speaking, in comparison to a Shakespearian play, right? The clear light, despite its elemental form, somehow manages to represent the artistic *totality* of individual awareness. We can further complicate things by giving our magic mirror some speakers. As it turns out, every color in our kaleidoscope also has an accompanying sound. Colors are just vibrations, after all, differing wavelengths of energy, as is sound. Put all these things together—the vividly colorful, shifting kaleidoscope patterns, the seed syllable sounds that are a part of this same energetic vibration—and you have an infinite mandala, extending forever in all directions. This is your true body—what the Tibetans call the Body of Light.

When a fully-realized Dzogchen master dies, his physical body is transformed into this much subtler form of energy and awareness. Namkhai Norbu explains, "usually one who practices this realization, when he or she decides to die, asks to be left closed up inside a room or a tent for seven days. Then on the eighth day, only their hair and nails, considered to be the impurities of the body, are found." He goes on to describe such an event witnessed by his uncle—himself a Dzogchen master—in 1952. An old Tibetan left all his belongings to a local monastery and announced that he would die within a week. He gave instructions that he be shut up in a tent for seven days. "On the eighth day many people rushed to take part . . . including some Chinese officials who were convinced that they would be able to show . . . how foolishly superstitious the Tibetan people were. . . . When the tent was opened, all that was found inside was the practitioner's hair and nails."[11]

We learn to integrate our awareness with the state of deep sleep so that we can ultimately integrate our awareness with the moment of death. Those of us who do so perfectly achieve the clear light body. Although the vast majority of us will not realize this ultimate human endeavor in this current lifetime, we can, with practice, learn to experience this pure mandala form of our own bodies. It is an incredible symphony of color and sound, this body—composed of what the Tibetans call the sounds, rays, and lights—dancing in such a way as to remind us of our highest selves in every moment. Temporarily liberated in such a state, we are entirely free to look where we want to look, listen where we want to listen. Wherever our focus wanders within this vast body of sound and light, *there we are*, looking back at ourselves. In such a moment, you are that whole dance of Things Changing. You are that dance, dreaming of the dance, dreaming of the dance . . .

THE ELUSIVE ART OF
DREAM YOGA

You are dreaming now. Try to recognize the dream as the dream.
—HIS HOLINESS THE DALAI LAMA[1]

ream yoga is not a method, technique, or science. Not exactly. Like all spiritual practices, when properly actualized, dream yoga is an art. Anyone who has ever created something with an artistic goal in mind has, to some degree or another, practiced dream yoga. Consider, for instance, the art of Vincent Van Gogh. In Van Gogh's work, you see a fascinating blend of the subjective and objective. Although Van Gogh's landscapes are presumably based on some actual, external scene, rather than simply trying to create an "accurate" depiction, he superimposes his own, dramatically swirling, mental and emotional experience onto the "apparent" surface of things. A Van Gogh painting, then, always tells us as much about him as it does the model. Dream yoga is essentially concerned with this very same artistic blending of the inner and outer, the conscious and unconscious, the real and imagined.

As far as art forms go, dream yoga is particularly slippery, particularly elusive. Why is this? Well, the medium you are working with here is the mind itself. Whereas the artist has paints *and* canvas, the dream yoga practitioner has only his or her own inner experiences to work with. The mind is both the paints and the canvas. To complicate things further, dream yoga, by definition, mostly happens while you sleep. To a certain degree, then, you don't do dream yoga—it does you. As a practitioner of dream yoga, all you can really do is learn to increasingly open your heart and mind to make room for this spontaneous artistic creation.

Careful Carelessness

The art of calligraphy is an important Zen practice. If the calligrapher is too careful, uses too much technique, the work is dull and contrived. In the dream yoga context, if you rely too heavily on technique, you will probably simply wake yourself up. If the Zen calligrapher is too careless, however, the work will be a sloppy mess. Similarly, the unfocused practitioner of dream yoga will simply go to sleep, fall into the same deeply unconscious state that pervades most individuals' sleeping states. The ultimate goal in Zen calligraphy is an artistic blending of careful technique and careless relaxation, of becoming involved in a cooperative process of integrating conscious intention with the so-called random flow of the ink, and the seemingly accidental grain of the surface. In the same way, the dream yogi learns to blend effort and spontaneity, intense focus and "dreamy" relaxation. Once achieved, this blend produces something transcendental and beautiful. Although the dream yoga practitioner, like the Zen calligrapher, may very well learn something along the way, the real goal here is joyful and dynamic creation, not static knowledge and self-improvement.

Even so, it's often easiest to discuss dream yoga in terms of technique and method. After all, we have to discuss what is discussable. Keep in mind, however, as you read the following descriptions of this and that practice, the real practice of dream yoga is always somewhere between the lines. We talk about Van Gogh's brush stroke, post-impressionistic philosophy, etc., because we don't know what else to talk about. In the end, the best we can really do is point at one of Van Gogh's paintings and say, "See!" So it goes with dream yoga. All of the following techniques and methods are simply fingers pointing at the indescribable artwork of our own minds.

I have adapted the majority of the following dream and sleep practices from the most widely-known and highly-respected treatise on dream practice, *Tsongkhapa's Six Yogas of Naropa*. In applying these techniques, both carefully and carelessly, you stand to gain incredible insight into Chuang Tzu's forever slippery slope of Things Changing.

Working with Recall in Ordinary Dreams

The first goal of dream yoga is to bring more of your ordinary, waking awareness into the dream and sleep states. Once you begin to recall more of your dream material, as well as participate more consciously in this process, you learn to work with the dream content itself in various ways. Philosophy, science, psychology, and spiritual practice all recognize that the processes of sleeping and dreaming seem to hold some very important keys to our most fundamental identities, our most core selves. Most of us spend about one third of our lives sleeping. Each night, we have four REM states, which means we have at least four dreams. If you are to recover your whole, organic person, then, it is extremely important that you learn to be more present in this relatively shadowy third of your daily life.

To achieve this goal, Tsongkhapa makes a very simple suggestion: One of the best ways to recall your dreams, he asserts, is to firmly resolve to do so.

> There is a point that should be made on the practice of retaining conscious awareness in the dream state by means of cultivating resolution. In general, even people who are not trained [in meditation] sometimes can experience a clear dream and retain awareness in it. Therefore it is not only through the path of meditation . . . that the ability occurs. . . . Consequently if we make some effort during the daytime to cultivate a strong resolution to recognize and remember our dreams, and we make the resolution strong and continuous throughout the day, then at night dreams will certainly arise and one will probably be able to retain them. This level of practice is not difficult to accomplish.[2]

Throughout the day, think of sleeping that night and be confident that you will recall your dreams. Before you go to bed, you might spend a few minutes relaxing with a concentration exercise. Once you feel calm and centered, you can make an extra firm resolution to bring more awareness into your dreams that night. As you wake throughout the night, you can give yourself a gentle reminder to stay more present in your dreams. On waking the next morning, allow 15 minutes or so to recall any dream material. I strongly recommend that you enter these recollections in a dream journal.

DREAM JOURNAL

As part of cultivating your intention to remember your dreams, many dream yoga systems suggest that you keep a dream journal. Purchase a special blank book for just this purpose. Having a concrete artifact can be a great way to remind you of your practice. You can keep this journal by your bed so that you see it each night as you drift off to sleep, as well as the next morning, consistently reminding you of your goal on both conscious and unconscious levels.

It is quite common to remember a dream very clearly in the morning on waking, but quickly forget it as the day progresses. For this reason, I suggest you make a thorough entry each morning for any dream fragments you might recall, however insignificant. Moreover, it can be a great aid to dream recollection to carry your journal around with you during the day. You can periodically review your earlier entries, which are very likely to trigger additional fragments. Sometimes, due to any number of internal and external triggers, you may find yourself suddenly remembering a piece of a dream from several days ago. In such cases, the dream journal can be a very effective yet simple way to motivate and structure your dream practice.

When you begin to remember even one dream clearly each night, consider this a significant sign of progress. In time, you will find that you recall more material each night, more details from every dream. You may discover over time that you can remember all or most of every single dream on a nightly basis. At this point, you may feel that you have discovered a whole section of your life that has remained hidden for a long time. The question then arises, "What do I *do* with this newly uncovered chunk of my daily experience?"

UNDERSTANDING DREAM CONTENT

This is where Western psychology has some great ideas. If, like most psychologists believe, dreams contain coded aspects of ourselves, secret desires, or personality traits that we don't feel comfortable processing during our waking hours, the more we learn to break this code, the better we may understand our seemingly inconsistent actions and stubborn sticking places.

There is simply no magical decoder ring when it comes to understanding dream content. As a very general guideline, however, it's best if you look into your dreams assuming they must point to some aspect of yourself that you are reluctant, or altogether unwilling, to accept. This can be tricky, of course, because—by definition—there is probably some firmly entrenched reason you *don't* want to accept these unwanted aspects. After all, part of what makes the unconscious mind *unconscious* is its amazingly sophisticated strategies of resistance. For this reason, you can expect much subtle and persistent resistance when trying to decode your dream content.

EXERCISE: BREAKING THE DREAM CODE

■ A very simple exercise can help you see through some of your habitual defenses. Take note of any difficulties you have been experiencing lately. This could include trouble at work, relationship problems, or even physical pain. You could also take note of any major decisions or situations that you have been considering, such as a new promotion at work or a vacation that is coming up. In short, consider anything that is likely capturing a good deal of your emotional energy at present. It might be useful to jot these things down, make a brief list in your dream journal.

Next, review your recent dreams, assuming that they may help to uncover repressed feelings and wishes related to the items in your list. Rather than isolating specific dreams, you may want to look over a whole week's worth at this time. You may perceive certain undeniable patterns when you examine several dreams at once. Don't get too literal. Look for broader themes at first, such as aggression, guilt, etc. The vast majority of dreams represent repressed wishes, unsatisfied desires, and persistent anxieties. Be on the lookout for these elements as you review your dream material.

Remember: Think symbolically, metaphorically. If you have a dream in which you punch Aunt Jenny in the nose, there is probably much more to it than being angry at Aunt Jenny. For that matter, Aunt Jenny may be more of a dream stunt double than she is Aunt Jenny in this situation. The unconscious mind is trying to sneak coded messages past your conscious mind, remember, so if it seems too obvious, it probably is.

To a certain degree, if you don't uncover some persistent tension in your dream content, if you don't stumble on certain elements that make you rather uncomfortable, you are probably just not ready to integrate certain aspects of your unconscious just now. You may need to further calm your mind through meditation practice, guru yoga, and so forth. As you consider your dream content in relation to your waking experience, note that part of you—the unconscious part of you—keeps working through difficult or significant emotional, psychological, and even physical material even while your conscious mind rests every night.

DO-IT-YOURSELF GESTALT THERAPY

Tsongkhapa says that if you are really clear about a dream, you "should be able to describe it in detail to others upon waking."[3] Inversely, as Western psychology has found out, talking about dreams can also be a useful tool for gathering more clarity about the material. Obviously, if you're in therapy, discussing dream material with your therapist is a great way to learn to break your own dream code more skillfully. If you're not in therapy, consider the further understanding of your dream material as a good motive for trying it out. This is a good therapist's specialty, after all: bringing the unconscious into the conscious. Either way, whether or not you are in therapy at present, I would like to suggest an additional do-it-yourself method for working with your dream content.

For starters, you are going to need to find someone else who is interested in talking about his or her dreams. To mentally go over your own dreams with a fine-toothed comb is one thing—to enlist someone else to assist you in this process is another. Your codes are codes for a reason, remember—mostly to keep certain unpleasantries hidden from your conscious mind, disguised within your ego story. Left entirely to your own devices, then, you are very likely to miss some of the most obvious stuff. I suggest using a modified Gestalt technique.

Gestalt's idea of dream work is that every element in your dream represents some aspect of you. For example, let's say you present a dream to your partner in which you are washing your new car with your nephew, Max. Now if your partner simply asks you, "What aspect of yourself does Max represent?" and so forth, you probably aren't going to get very far. The unconscious is sneaky, so you will also have to be sneaky. Instead, your partner might utilize Fritz Perl's favorite technique and have the elements of your dream interact with one another. Your partner might ask, "What might Max be thinking of your new car?" or even, "What might your new car say to Max if it could talk?" These various dream elements are all different aspects of you, remember, so what better way to see how you work as an organic whole—

at both the surface level of daily awareness and further "behind the scenes"—than getting these aspects talking to one another?

How Gestalt Works

TO ILLUSTRATE THIS TECHNIQUE MORE FULLY, the following is an abbreviated excerpt from a Gestalt seminar conducted by Perls:

> Liz: I dream of tarantulas and spiders crawling on me. And it's pretty consistent.
>
> Perls: Put the spider in that chair and talk to the spider. . . .
>
> Liz: (sighs) I don't know what to say except to get it off of me.
>
> Perls: Now be the spider. . . .
>
> Liz: I wanna get somewhere and you're in my way and so I'll crawl over you. . . . I feel as though you're inanimate and it doesn't matter if I crawl all over you.
>
> Perls: You feel this toward Liz? . . . Toward whom do you feel this?
>
> Liz: I don't feel that way. I think the spider feels that way.
>
> Perls: Oh, you're not the spider.
>
> Liz: No.
>
> Perls: Which means you're not what?
>
> Liz: Aggressive.
>
> Perls: Give us all the negations, all of what you're not. "I'm not a spider, I'm not aggressive. . . ."
>
> Liz: I'm not ugly, I'm not black and shiny, I don't have any more than two legs. . . .
>
> Perls: Now let the spider say the same—"I am ugly and I want to be beautiful."
>
> Liz: I am ugly and I want to be beautiful. To a spider-lover I probably am. . . .
>
> Perls: Talk to the spider in terms of you. "You are important because you. . ."
>
> Liz: You are important because you keep the insect population down, and you are important because you build beautiful webs. . . . and you're important because you're alive.
>
> Perls: I would like you to try and let the spider return the appreciation.
>
> Liz: You're important because you're a human being.[4]

In getting Liz to integrate her spider self with her Liz self, Perls helps Liz to appreciate herself as an organic whole, an appreciated human being. In order for this to happen, however, Perls guided Liz into some uncomfortable territory, encouraging her to bring some honest emotionality into the situation.

❧

Of course, despite the infamous fireworks of Fritz Perls' seminars, it's not very likely you will fully reconnect to rejected aspects of yourself simply by understanding your symbolic content. This is where your daily, waking life comes in. If you discover, for example, a recurring theme of aggression in your dreams, you can be on the lookout for this feeling, albeit cleverly disguised, from day to day. "Well, I don't exactly *feel* angry right now," you might notice yourself thinking throughout the day, "but I have been replaying this violent scene from a movie last night in my head. For that matter, I can see that I was pretty irritable with my co-worker, Chuck, this morning—which is odd, because I really love Chuck." You will probably discover that you tend to repress feelings that don't fit in nicely with your idea of yourself. Feelings of anger, envy, superiority—such are the natural emotional reactions that we habitually try to overlook, but which necessarily arise time and again.

Consequently, when discussing your dream content, notice any interpretations your partner or therapist suggests that you find *particularly* offensive, ridiculous, etc. Chances are, such interpretations may be much truer, and much more obvious to everyone else, than you would like to think. Think of dreams as a kind of secret referee, a way of keeping you honest. No matter how much you may be disturbed by certain repressed feelings and desires, they are, first and foremost, *your* desires, and they are simply not going to let you be until you have consciously recognized them and genuinely worked them through.

Developing Lucidity in Ordinary Dreams

The more you are able to recall your dream material and, most importantly, the more you are able to recognize these same hidden patterns at work from day to day, you are going to start experiencing occasional moments of wakefulness in your dreams. Just as you are beginning to wake up to your repressed feelings of anger, for instance, you are going to begin to wake up more inside those most hidden aspects of yourself: the experiences of dream and sleep.

Lucid dreaming may begin with a single flicker of doubt inside a dream. "Now wait a minute," you may ask yourself, "does my next door neighbor really have a pond in her front yard? Do I really still take care of my childhood pet, interact with friends from my adolescence?" Over time, these little flickers of recognition—these fleeting moments of dream lucidity—will grow more substantial, eventually to the point where you can stay entirely "awake" throughout whole dreams and sequences of dreams.

This lucidity is important to cultivate directly as, inversely, the more you wake up inside your dreams, the more you will wake up inside your daily life. Right now, you may think you are perfectly awake from day to day, perfectly alert and aware. Maybe. But how about those recurring feelings of anxiety and sadness—that feeling there is a hole somewhere, an unsatisfied gap in your life? Well, there probably is a very real hole or two in your life. Like Buddha said, that elusive satisfaction we all have been chasing by getting more and more stuff—more money, sex, power, etc.—isn't really working, right? Our compulsive strategies of accumulation are much like someone who is missing a limb trying to fix things by wearing a new hat. Overlooking our most essential metaphysical and existential problems, that is to say, is just that: overlooking. Increasing your lucidity in your dreams is an authentic, direct way of filling in these spiritual and emotional holes. Unlike various material accumulations, or even impressive individual accomplishments, the kind of satisfaction you gain from rediscovering more of your deepest, most elemental self doesn't go away—not ever, not even at the moment of death. Such is the ultimate reason for practicing dream yoga. Once you have really remembered Who You Are, really reconnected to every aspect of yourself—the totality of which is nothing other than the One Self—nothing can change this stability of presence, not pain or tragedy, not the unavoidable fact of the impermanence of the individual self.

DREAM INCUBATION

Tsongkhapa suggests a few simple techniques to help dream lucidity along in the beginning. One of these is "consciously initiating a particular dream pattern,"[5] which is commonly known as dream incubation. Pick someone or something to which you feel very connected. Create a detailed, visual imagine of that someone or something. As you lie down to sleep each night, concentrate on this image, firmly resolving to dream about it. As a slight variation on this incubation technique, don Juan suggests that Castañeda "set up dreaming" by resolving to find his hands in his dreams. When, after considerable effort and frustration, Castañeda is finally able to find his hands while dreaming, it momentarily triggers full lucidity.[6]

It is important to pick something very simple at first and to stick with it. Patience is an absolute necessity in dream practice. Give yourself two weeks at the very least for any particular incubation. Even if you don't get it exactly right, feel satisfied with anything in the general ballpark. If you are trying to have a dream about a childhood friend, for example, feel encouraged if you begin to have more dreams about childhood. If you are looking for your hands, dreams in which you notice someone's rings or wristwatch are significant signs of progress. If you persist but still have no luck at all, try a new "target," something even simpler and more immediately meaningful to you. If you still have little or no success, move on to an entirely new method of developing lucidity. This isn't a paint-by-numbers process, remember, so approach dream yoga creatively, flexibly, and with an attitude of determined patience.

RECOGNIZING THE DREAMINESS OF WAKING LIFE

Another simple technique Tsongkhapa suggests is the daily "practice of repeating to oneself that whatever appears is like a dream occurrence and should be recognized as a dream."[7] Throughout the day, simply try to connect with the beautiful "dreaminess" of waking life. Notice the surreal play of light and shadow at twilight. Observe the waves of heat shimmering on the hot pavement, the sleepy breeze rustling the trees, the surreal ice cream truck music off in the distance. . . . In *Exploring the World of Lucid Dreaming*, LaBerge suggests we schedule five to ten of these "checks" daily.[8] Don't just merely say to yourself, "This is like a dream." Really connect to that deep place in which you know these phenomena are somehow messengers from the "other" world, the dream world, subtle reminders of the totality of Who You Are. Use recurring dream elements to structure your practice. If you frequently dream about attractive women, for instance, connect to the surreal qualities of waking life when you see an attractive woman. If you frequently dream about classroom settings, allow elements within waking life that remind you of school to trigger this same technique. With continued effort in this manner, you will begin to have dreams in which you find yourself looking at a certain cloud in the sky, thinking, "This cloud reminds me of the dream world," and all of a sudden it will click: Hey! This *is* the dream world! These moments of waking will probably be very brief and unstable at first, but rest assured, they will gradually stabilize with continuing effort.

INTEGRATING CONCENTRATION PRACTICE

One of the most direct ways to increase lucid dreaming is by working with concentration meditation. This integration is only effective, however, when you have progressed to a fairly loose kind of concentration, referred to as natural zhiné in chapter 5. Let's say you have been working with your breath every day for a while, and you have arrived at the point where it takes little effort to follow your breath even as you go about your daily business. At such a point, you can try this very same technique as you lie down to sleep. Relax into a very easy and loose focus on your object. Try to follow it, loosely, as you drift to sleep. Even when you have gained considerable skill with this method, you are probably going to lose your focus more often than not throughout the night. When you wake in the middle of the night, gently reinstate your object of focus. You will probably begin to notice dreams in which you're doing concentration practice. You may find yourself having a dream in which you are riding on a subway, for instance, and following your breath, repeating a mantra and so on. Stay with your concentrative object long enough, your focus sufficiently loose and flexible, and that little bell deep within your awareness will go off, telling you this is a dream.

This technique also has the advantage of integrating your daily practice with your nightly practice. As you work with your object of focus during the day, you might notice how everything around you is somehow illusory and dreamlike—not so concrete as the conceptual, ego-dominated mind would like you to think. While practicing natural zhiné in this way, you might begin to look into the question, very gently at first, of "I know I am awake right now, but *how* do I know?" This question may soon develop into: "I know *someone* is awake right now, but who is this someone?"

THE ROLE OF THE THROAT CHAKRA IN DREAM YOGA

Tsongkhapa suggests a certain object of focus as being particularly beneficial in dream practice. Because the "throat chakra is the site from which dreams are generated," Tsongkhapa recommends visualizing a "small red four-petalled lotus"[9] at this site. The throat chakra (also known in Sanskrit as the *visuddha*) is located near the center of the throat. It is associated with the energy of speech. Make a low, long hum and you will feel your throat vibrate near the center. This is where the throat chakra is. As I discussed earlier, chakras are those places where our subtle, or dreaming, bodies intersect our physical bodies. They are concentrated places of subtle, whirling energy or awareness, which can be accessed through focused visualization techniques such as described by Tsongkhapa.

EXERCISE: WORKING WITH THE THROAT CHAKRA

■ At your throat chakra, feel the red lotus (any red flower will do), about the size of a golf ball. Understand that rather than merely visualizing it, you are trying to tune into it. Feel the color as a radiant red, vibrating with an inner glow. Feel the luminous red petals at your throat chakra and you will notice a subtle sensation of relaxation, or sleepiness associated with this chakra and the red lotus; this is partly what makes this object of focus and its color so ideally suited to dream practice.

To bring a bit more energy of awareness to this visualization, feel a small white sphere at the center of the lotus. Don't let this sphere shine too brightly or it will keep you awake. Rather than agitating yourself with all the visual detail of the red lotus and the white sphere, simply tune into them by feel and notice your sensation of relaxed drowsiness associated with the luminous red petals, mixed with the calm alertness of the white sphere. As you lie down to sleep, try to merge gently with this feeling of drowsy, loosely focused awareness at your throat chakra. As you wake throughout the night, take a moment to reconnect with the red lotus and white sphere at its center.

If this visualization is keeping you up all night, relax your focus. Try letting go of the white sphere and simply dissolving your awareness—all of your passing thoughts and physical sensations—deep into the luminous red petals. The point of dream practice is not to interfere with your habitual sleeping patterns, but to bring more awareness to these states.

On the other hand, if you find yourself simply falling into the dulled awareness of normal dream and sleep each night, despite continued practice, you might want to intensify your focus a bit—emphasizing, in particular, the white sphere at the center of the flower. As you drift off to sleep, know that this white sphere is the center of your mental alertness. Bring more luminosity, more glow to the sphere, recognizing that this same radiance is the radiance of your natural state.

Much more detailed description of this, and other dream yoga techniques, can be found in Namkhai Norbu's *Dream Yoga and the Practice of Natural Light*, as well as Tenzin Wangyal's *The Tibetan Yogas of Dream and Sleep*. As in all other dream practices, however, it is important that you keep your methods simple. Distracting yourself with complex visualizations and overly intricate meditative techniques will probably do little more than interfere with your much-needed sleep.

WORKING WITH THE FOREHEAD AND ROOT CHAKRA

For those of you who experience difficulties with the throat chakra practice of the red lotus, Tsongkhapa offers two alternative objects of focus. If, despite continued efforts, dream retention and lucidity doesn't seem to be improving, Tsongkhapa suggests that you "meditate on the drop in the chakra at the forehead."[10] This chakra is called the *ajna* in Sanskrit, and is located between and above the eyebrows, more or less at the center of the forehead. Once again, don't worry so much about locating this chakra "correctly." Simply try to feel it where it already is. The drop at this chakra is a luminous white sphere about the size of a dime. As this chakra is strongly associated with wakefulness, Tsongkhapa emphasizes that the drop should not be visualized too brightly. If you experience difficulties sleeping, you should visualize, or feel, this white sphere rather dimly.

If, on the other hand, these visualizations still "cause one to be unable to sleep, or to sleep fitfully," Tsongkhapa says, "then concentrate instead on the drop at the secret place,"[11] or the root chakra (also known as the *muladhara* in Sanskrit). This drop is a small, purplish-black sphere located behind the genitals. This chakra is associated with a dim, very relaxed state of awareness, as is its purplish-black sphere. Consequently, a sufficiently loose focus on this object—while still advantageous in bringing more awareness to your states of dream and sleep—isn't likely to keep you awake.

EXERCISE: PROGRESSIVE RELAXATION

■ If, after continued experimentation with dream practice, you still have problems sleeping, it's probably best to do without any objects of focus altogether. Some personalities already tend toward mental restlessness and agitation. If you are one of these individuals, it might be best to work with a simple progressive relaxation exercise. At this point, simply relaxing into the natural space of your thoughts is the best sleep practice.

• Place yourself in a comfortable position for sleeping.

• Imagine a warm sphere of light entering through the crown of your head, spreading warmth and relaxation throughout your face, head, and neck.

• Gradually follow this light down your body, step by step, until it passes out the bottoms of your feet. Allow five to ten minutes for this process.

- As it progresses, allow the warm light to calm your body and mind, relaxing deep into your skin, muscles, and bones.

- Perform this exercise multiple times, if necessary, until you feel you are sufficiently calm and relaxed.

- Watch, very loosely, your awareness drifting in and out of your thoughts and sensations, gently slipping back and forth over the brink of sleep like the ocean's waves gliding back and forth on the beach.

WHAT IF INSOMNIA PERSISTS?

Occasional difficulty in sleeping is one thing, as are initial disturbances in sleep patterns arising from dream yoga practice. Chronic insomnia, however, is a frustrating problem unto itself. Although various meditative techniques presented throughout this work may help to alleviate persistent sleeping difficulties, such matters often require a multi-disciplinary approach. Cognitive-behavioral modification techniques, for instance, as detailed in various popular books are often quite effective in addressing chronic insomnia.

At the core of this problem, however, is very likely an unrecognized state of psychological unrest. Unconscious tendencies toward depression and anxiety often go unnoticed and commonly result in all sorts of sleeping disturbances. For this reason, if you experience persistent difficulty in falling asleep, early awakening, or disturbances throughout the night, it might be advisable to consult with a qualified psychotherapist, psychologist, or sleep disorders specialist.

GURU GUIDANCE IN DREAM YOGA

In working with all dream yoga practices, invoking the presence of the guru can be very supportive. Whatever practices you have chosen to work with, visualize the guru hovering over your head as you lie down. Connect to the immediate presence of the guru, confident that he or she will watch over your practice, and bring more awareness throughout the night. If you don't favor a physical form of the guru, simply connect to the infinite goodness of the universe. Bring that pervasive feeling of comfort and connection with you down into sleep. However you choose to invoke the guru in your practice, try to gently reconnect to this loving, nurturing presence as you wake up throughout the night. Know that the guru never leaves you during the night, but is there in every moment, watching over you, protecting you.

Working with Dreams of Clarity

As you bring more awareness into the dream process, dreams of clarity will begin to arise. The best advice I can give you on working with dreams of clarity is simply this: Don't make too much of them. Don't get distracted by trying to determine if this or that prophecy is true, this or that astral meeting with a teacher *really* happened. You will encounter many bizarre experiences, no doubt, but keep your foremost goal in mind: rediscovering disowned aspects of yourself, letting your own mind be shaped into a beautiful and pliable piece of art. No matter how sacred or profound, such experiences are useful only to the degree that they cultivate more love and awareness in your daily life.

A dream of clarity has a certain unmistakable "feel" to it, a certain depth and stability of presence that an ordinary dream does not have. As you begin to experience such states, be confident that your practice is going well. Compare your nightly experiences to your daily experiences. If you are truly having dreams of clarity, then your mundane, daily experiences should be much richer and calmer as well. You may find yourself noticing very subtle things in your daily life, significant little details of both your internal and external experiences that were previously lost on you as you were so hurriedly getting things done. The more you are able to be present and aware from moment to moment, you start to notice a kind of relaxed, mystical glow about mundane tasks such as doing the laundry and buying groceries. Your dreams of clarity, however odd they may initially appear, are ultimately nothing less than creative, self-perfected reflections of your ordinary daily happenings.

DREAM ONE, DREAM TWO

When Ramana Maharshi was asked if he still dreamed after full realization, he said that all experience was now dreamlike for him. The waking from a night of sleep and reentering the daily world, he said, was like passing from dream one into dream two. As you begin to bring more presence into your dreams, you will begin to understand that Ramana Maharshi wasn't being cryptic or theoretical. Your daily life is simply one of an infinite number of dreams that, for some reason or other, is particularly fascinating to you. When you wake up in another realm, as evidenced by your continuing progress in dream practice, you can test physical reality and see that it is entirely intact. If you encounter beings in these realms, you may find that you have access to a long and detailed history of relationships with them. There is a definite continuity in the dream world, that is to say, in just the same way you think of your waking life as a continuous and unfolding process.

As you begin to experience more of the detailed intricacies and continuities of the dream world, you may begin to ask yourself, "What exactly *is* real? Which is my real life?" When you really look into these questions, and when you really begin to fully and consistently wake up in other realms, you will understand that there is simply no logical way of answering such existential riddles. This is why the Buddhists refer to all reality as *maya*, or illusion. I personally prefer to think of all phenomenon as real, dream and waking experiences alike. Ultimately, there is no real difference in the meaning of these two statements, each of which simply discourages attachment to this reality—or unreality—over that one. Whether you think of all experience as real or illusory, you begin to understand that your attachment to this one little strand of your being—your so-called ordinary life—is just restrictive attachment. As you become more comfortable being yourself in other realms, however, much of this fearful attachment starts to dissolve. You begin to identify much more with the kinetic, infinitely potential beauty of Things Changing than you do your clinging to Chou or the butterfly.

Even so, there does remain a distinct difference between Chou and the butterfly, between this realm and other realms. This seemingly obvious statement is of the greatest importance. This simple recognition of distinction without preference, in fact, becomes the very stuff of love itself. This is Things Changing. This indescribable process—the dynamic dance in which the One repeatedly becomes the many, the many repeatedly become the One—is the fuel of the entire material and immaterial universe.

Furthering Lucidity—Heart Chakra Practice

As your practice continues to develop, you may want to try other means of increasing and working with lucidity. In addition to the previously described practice using the red lotus at the throat chakra, Tsongkhapa describes another similar practice using the heart chakra, also known as the *anahata* in Sanskrit. This visualization is sometimes more associated with sleep yoga, or clear light yoga, whereas the throat chakra is more strongly associated with dream retention and lucidity. Once you have gained some stability in the throat chakra practice, however, it's best to work with the heart chakra. Tsongkhapa states that, "the vital energies naturally withdraw into this drop (at the heart chakra) as one goes to sleep."[12] Since the vital energies are stored here, working with the heart chakra is the most direct method to control them. Although the throat chakra is usually a bit easier to work with when you are just getting started with dream yoga, the heart chakra has a much broader application, and can be used to work with ordinary dreams, dreams of clarity, lucidity, and clear light.

The heart chakra is typically described as located somewhere between the center of the chest and the tip of the sternum. The important thing is to locate your own heart chakra by "feel." Wherever you locate this chakra, you should be able to feel the central channel flowing through it (see page 58). Once you have located the heart chakra, you should feel immediately connected to this primary subtle channel.

Exercise: The Blue Lotus

■ At the heart chakra, Tsongkhapa directs us to visualize a blue, four-petalled lotus. Bring more energy into this visualization by emphasizing the natural radiance, the inner luminosity of the blue flower. Compared to the red lotus at the throat, the blue lotus is calmer and closer to your core of awareness. As you tune into it, you feel an intelligent warmth located there, peacefully radiating throughout the rest your body in subtle currents.

As you did in the throat chakra practice, visualize a small white sphere at the center of this lotus. Feel that this white sphere brings a bit more energy, a bit more awareness to this chakra. Remember, it is important not to visualize this drop too brightly, as this will likely keep you awake. As you lie down to sleep, loosely focus your awareness in the central channel and the heart chakra. Feel your awareness being drawn deeply into the luminous blue lotus and white drop; you are *sensing* it rather than concretely *seeing* it.

As your awareness stabilizes, it may feel almost as if you have relocated from your head into your heart chakra, as if you have left your physical body behind and are sitting on this blue lotus, radiating energy and love outward. To withdraw into this center is to recognize the divine within you. As you merge with this site, drifting off to sleep, you are essentially engaging in an act of worship, making an offering of your very sleeping and dreaming experience. More than accurate visualization, this practice relies on this feeling of authentic devotion and surrender. You may want to picture the guru seated on this blue lotus. As you drift off to sleep, you become the guru, merge your individual awareness with that of the divine.

TOWARD THE CLEAR LIGHT

When you first begin working with the blue lotus at the heart chakra, it is unlikely you will directly experience the clear light. In fact, I suggest you don't worry too much about the clear light at this point. Simply connect with this practice as a very deep act of worship, a means of connecting directly with the source of all love and understanding. You will probably find that this practice allows you to sleep a bit more deeply than the throat practice, while gaining even more lucidity in your dreams. You may begin to experience very abstract dreams that have no real plot or story, but are mostly formless intuitions, vague plays of color and sound. This means you are well on your way to the clear light experience. Even so, it is important not to mistake the final goal of dream yoga as the clear light experience. No matter what your specific practice of dream and sleep, the better able you are to train your focus on your innate yearning for pure love and awareness, the more success you will enjoy.

Advanced Lucid Dream Practices

Over time, the above practices will certainly increase your experiences of dream lucidity. As your lucidity stabilizes, you are able to work more deliberately with various practices while you dream. It is often said that any practice performed while dreaming is seven times more powerful than its waking counterpart. I have personally found this to be true. Often, I've gained more understanding of a certain practice through a single experience of it while dreaming than I have with hours and hours of waking meditation. Tsongkhapa suggests several specific ways in which to practice while dreaming lucidly.

CONTROLLING DREAM CONTENT

If you have been practicing dream incubation, you have already begun to explore the idea of consciously controlling dream content. Maybe you have been able to find your hands in a dream by resolving to do so as you went to sleep. Maybe you have been able to increase dreams of certain events, locations, or people by intentionally "targeting" them throughout the waking and sleeping periods. The control of dream content is simply an extension of this same process. Rather than deciding in advance what your dream goal is, however, you work more directly within the dream experience itself to bring about certain content.

WORLDLY DREAMS

In the context of controlling dream content, Tsongkhapa differentiates between two types of lucid dreams: "worldly" and "beyond-the-world."[13] Worldly dreams are those dreams that involve the ordinary objects of your daily life. It is relatively common for me, for instance, to wake up into a lucid dream while observing a certain room in my house. This is an example of a worldly dream. Such dreams tend to vary widely as far as accuracy. I might have a lucid dream in which I am floating in my music studio, for instance, and notice that I accidentally left some piece of equipment on. On waking, I sometimes find such an observation to be accurate, sometimes not. Some individuals have become so skilled in accurate worldly dreaming that they have been used by the military to act as spies. David Morehouse, ex-special forces operant and "remote viewer" describes his own experiences within this covert branch of the military. In *Psychic Warrior*, Morehouse describes how he and other remote viewers learned to project their subtle body to the desired location and bring back pertinent, objectively verifiable information. Robert Monroe details this same sort of accurate worldly dreaming in *Ultimate Journeys*, as well as describing his bizarre experiences in otherworldly dreaming. Your own experience of worldly dreams need not be so exotic. A lucid dream that involves your family, friends, or any other element of your ordinary waking life is also a worldly dream.

OTHERWORLDY DREAMS

Otherworldly dreams involve parallel reality content. This content might stay fairly close to your ordinary, daily life. You might dream of familiar individuals and environments, for example, only all of these individuals are casually flying around within these environments, appearing in their astral bodies. As this sort of flying is not exactly "allowed" within your daily physical realm, you would have to consider such a dream as occurring elsewhere—within some other world or astral plane, that is to say, however closely such an environment may resemble your waking reality in most respects. From here, otherworldly dream content quickly becomes bizarre beyond description. There is really no limit to the sort of content you might encounter in other realms. For detailed descriptions of otherworldly landscapes and encounters with beings not typically met in this plane, you might want to take a look at the works of Robert Monroe, Carlos Castañeda, Florinda Donner, Ken Eagle Feather and numerous other writers concerned with astral travel (see Reading List on page 315).

As I mentioned in the context of parallel life dreams in the previous chapter, the rules of reality are often quite different in other worlds. It is common to communicate telepathically, for instance, or to be able to transfer consciousness from one individual to another. In your otherworldly dreaming, you may come to recognize certain worlds in which you "wake up" very frequently. Over the years, for instance, I have found myself often revisiting a beautiful watery world populated with intelligent sea creatures. For whatever reason, I feel very at home in this place, swimming with otherworldly dolphins, communicating with these astral beings in a telepathic manner. Consequently, whenever I wake up in this realm, it feels very much as if I am visiting a relative's familiar old house. There is some part of me apparently, that still considers this realm home.

Accurate Projecting

Tsongkhapa suggests that working with both worldly and otherworldly dreams "involves consciously projecting oneself in the dream state to various"[14] locations. In a worldly dream, you might want to visit some geographically distant friend of yours. You might want to see the Empire State Building. Again, there is no limit to the places you can visit.

Keep in mind, however, that until your dream presence is very, very stable, much of the material you observe in your visits is likely to be inaccurate to varying degrees. In the same way that all of us often "project" our feelings onto others in waking life, it is all too easy to project your thoughts and wishes onto your dreaming experiences. Your sincere wish that your fourth grade teacher is doing well might cause you to project a scene of good physical health in the dreaming state. In reality, you may come to learn that this person, despite your best wishes, is currently suffering a rather severe illness. For this reason, it's important to keep examining the reality of all situations, dreaming and otherwise. If you notice that you repeatedly distort certain information—be it in waking or dreaming experiences—this knowledge can be a great tool to learn more about your various psychological defense mechanisms, repressed desires, etc.

Buddhafields

For otherworldly dreaming, Tsongkhapa specifically recommends that we visit various "Buddhafields" so that we might receive teachings.[15] A Buddhafield is a heavenly realm in which accomplished spiritual teachers reside. Strange as they may sound, these realms are very real. The landscape of such a realm might consist of swirling colorful patterns and a single mantra, or you might encounter a choir of angelic beings. You might meet some teacher in a recognizable form, or the realm itself might be the teaching. It's easiest to visit those teachers or teachings with which you feel most connected. If you have a particular teacher to which you feel strongly tied, such as Ramana Maharshi, for instance, you might try to project yourself into his realm.

Whatever teaching you might receive in such a circumstance, it is likely to be so densely compressed that you won't have much luck "unpacking" it in your ordinary awareness. Think of such teachings as seeds of knowledge planted very deeply within you that will reveal more and more of themselves as they grow over time. Like the lotus flower, our spiritual understanding tends to grow of its own accord, even within the muddy terrain of our ignorance.

THE PRACTICE OF INCREASING

Increasing in dreams simply refers to the practice of multiplying the number of objects encountered. If you have a dream involving an elephant, for instance, you might try to manifest a thousand elephants. The idea here is to work closely with the dream content you have already been provided with. It doesn't have to be increasing, of course. You might want to alter the size or the color of an object. You might want to rotate objects or turn them upside down, etc.

Sustaining Presence

In getting started, I suggest you try relatively small alterations. If you encounter a blue vase in a lucid dream, for instance, simply try to transform it into a dark blue vase. If you try for more dramatic alterations before you are ready, such as manifesting ten thousand giant tarantulas from one tiny one, you are likely to lose your presence and either wake up or slip into an ordinary dream. The dreaming body tends to get lost in minute detail. In such a situation, it is all too easy to get absorbed in this or that detail of some object or sensation, thereby causing the dream to fade. For this reason, it's useful to keep your eyes moving during a lucid dream, giving quick glances at objects rather than intently gazing at them. Very often, employing this quick glancing technique will sustain your lucidity in a dream or bring a fading dream back into focus. Similarly, if your lucidity starts to fade, try spinning. This movement tends to dislodge the rational mind's fixation on detail.

Another great way to ground dreaming awareness is to attend to the sensation of touch. Sights and sounds tend to be very captivating in lucid dreaming, so it is particularly tempting to get lost in them. When this starts to happen, you might shift your focus to the feel of the ground beneath your feet or take some object in your hand. Taste is another good one. Keep shifting your focus around to different sensations within the dream, particularly those relatively subtle ones of touch and smell, and you are much less likely to lose your presence.

Remembering Your Goal

AS YOU BEGIN TO HAVE INCREASING success manipulating the items in your dreams, it's important to stop and reconsider what the practical goal in all this exotic craziness might be. Dream practitioners often mistake the practice for the goal itself, the means for the ends. The real reason you are engaging in all these odd practices is very simple: to increase the flexibility of your everyday behavior and perception, to bring more artistry into your daily life. The more creativity you can manifest in dream, the more you can manifest waking. Obviously, most of us are not going to be able to levitate objects in the real world just because we can in the dream world. Some extraordinarily gifted individuals, however, such as Sai Baba, are able to manifest this same flexibility in waking as in dreaming. To learn more about this fascinating miracle worker, I recommend *Sai Baba—Man of Miracles* by Howard Murphet.

Your goals are probably much more modest, however. Let's suppose you suffer from chronic stage fright. Every time you are called upon to give a presentation in a company meeting, you are absolutely terrified. Well, once you have developed some presence in dreaming, you have a great opportunity to practice. Illusory or no, lucid dreams feel quite real—often more real than waking experiences. Even so, there is considerable more flexibility in your individual ego story on the astral plane, which would allow you to give your presentation more easily within a dream meeting—however real it might seem. Inversely, you might try a relatively subtle transformation practice while waking. While in a real world meeting, remind yourself that this, too, is only a dream of sorts, all reality being ultimately pliable. Opening up your habitual awareness in this way, you can mentally transform the faces of your presentation audience into the familiar faces of supportive friends and family members.

It is all too easy to get lost in the weirdness of spiritual practice. As your practice evolves, you can get so involved in various mystical states and so forth that you lose sight of your deeper goal. If all of your extraordinary experiences aren't enriching even the most mundane of your daily errands, what good are they? Your ultimate goal, remember, is to find total satisfaction in *every* experience, be it visiting a buddha realm or folding laundry.

❧

Divine Creativity

I HAD A DREAM IN WHICH I WAS practicing altering various dream content. In this case, I was practicing changing the color of the walls in my house. At one point, after having successfully done so, I heard myself say, "And it was good." I was immediately reminded of the opening of Genesis, in which the divine creative act is described. "And God saw that it was good," is a refrain that runs throughout this creative act, a kind of divine stamp of approval on God's own work. When I used this same phrase within a lucid dream to describe my own work, I was essentially participating in the divine consciousness, remembering my own divine heritage. When you create or alter content in dream yoga, you are directly reconnecting to your own Godlike nature. In this context, you might think of Yahweh as the ultimate dream yogi. When you practice creating in dream yoga, you are, quite literally, re-learning the very tools by which the entire universe was originally manifested. The ultimate success in dream yoga, then, is nothing less than you remembering yourself as God, the Tao, the Original Creator.

ва

OVERCOMING FEAR

The key to this method, Tsongkhapa says, is simply to "Recognize dream objects as dream objects."[16] Interestingly, even if you are experiencing a very stable lucid dream—meaning you are aware and confident of the illusory nature of your environment—your old cognitive habits are likely to interfere. I have a real problem with snakes, for example, and I can't even look at one without feeling a little uncomfortable. When I first began dream yoga, I would encounter snakes time and again. I would be fairly sure I was dreaming, but not entirely. Often, when these snakes began to crawl around on me I would panic, waking myself up. In time, however, I learned to stay relaxed and focused. As hundreds of snakes would crawl around on my body, I would remind myself that dream snakes couldn't harm me. Soon enough, these snakes would dissolve into my body and I would be transported into higher and higher realms. Once again, this practice of fearlessness should translate into your daily life. If you have a fear of elevators, for instance, you might recognize that all elevators, waking and non-waking, are essentially dream elevators and can't harm you.

Practicing Waking Fearlessness

Overcoming fear in your daily life will greatly increase your success in dream yoga. Obviously, it's important to be reasonable. If you lie down on the highway, you are just going to get run over by a very real vehicle. Say you have always wanted to get up and sing at a Karaoke bar, however, but have just been too intimidated. This is a pretty safe, although likely terrifying, exercise. Once again, remind yourself that all Karaoke bars are dream Karaoke bars in the sense that no true harm can come to you from getting up and singing. This doesn't mean, I should say, that you won't be terribly embarrassed, nor does it guarantee that people won't laugh at you. In fact, if such guarantees were possible, it wouldn't even be a worthwhile practice, right? Instead, no matter what might happen, no matter how humiliating the experience, *you* will still endure. Your awareness will continue. Moreover, to the degree that such an experience is truly difficult and terrifying, it will only bring deeper confidence into your experience of yourself as a continuous unfolding of awareness, thereby allowing for the loosening of the various limits and rules you place on yourself from day to day.

Beyond Limits

As in so many of the other practices we have so far explored, the ultimate goal of overcoming fear in dream yoga is to become a being without limits, a being without compelling preferences and strong dislikes. Once you realize that, in a very real way, you are the author of your own experience from moment to moment, what need is there for fear? If you find yourself in some unpleasant situation, you can simply alter its contents to better suit you. On the other hand, as a practical example, if I'm stuck in a traffic jam in the real world, I can't exactly levitate my vehicle and fly to my destination. Still, I can change my mental focus, alter the way *I* perceive the event. It's not that something obnoxious, or even unfortunate, is happening to me, it's simply that the other drivers and I are doing a kind of karmic dance together. I am being given an opportunity to grow, to learn more about my awareness. Detaching from my habitual ego story in such a stressful situation, the external circumstances remain real, but I am able to perceive as illusory the various reasons I used to fear such situations.

Ironically, the more you lessen your fear, the more you realize every moment is already just the way it needs to be. A traffic jam may very likely make you late for work, but such unpleasant circumstances can become uniquely effective tools for increasing flexibility. The more your practice of fearlessness develops in dream yoga, you begin to realize that all of your individual preferences are manifestations of one sort of fear or another. As you recognize this innate problem with attachment, it is not that you melt into some sort of homogenous blob of awareness. Rather, you simply learn to enjoy more satisfaction regardless what happens to you. Your attachments remain, but—all things being illusory and impermanent—you no longer cling to them so urgently. As your flexibility in the dream state continually expands, your seemingly individual wants, wishes, and desires are gradually, bit by bit, becoming the way of the Tao itself.

SUCHNESS

Meditating upon "suchness" in dreams is one of the most powerful dream yoga practices. Unfortunately, it is also by far the most difficult to describe. When you find yourself in a lucid dream, you are aware that the objects within your environment somehow lack concrete, objective reality. In this context, Tsongkhapa suggests one connects to suchness in the dream world by meditating "on how all these appearances are empty of a true self-nature, yet manifest as illusions."[17]

Let's say I encounter a penguin playing a banjo in a lucid dream. This penguin and his banjo are real in the sense that I can see them, hear them, touch them, etc.

I can successfully perform all the same reality checks on these dream objects as I can on objects in my waking world. How do I know, then, that this penguin is an illusory penguin—a penguin "empty of true self-nature"—whereas the penguins of my waking life are real penguins? I can't. Such is the whole point of dream yoga. Such is the simple, self-evident truth of Chuang Tzu's Things Changing—the recognition that all aspects of our experience, waking or otherwise, lack some fixed, conceptually graspable "self-nature." We could say that all penguins are *dream* penguins, or we could say that all penguins are *real* penguins. Either way, the point is that reality—or unreality—doesn't quite work the way we have been taught it does. When viewed from the perspective of a sufficiently open and contemplative mind, reality is infinitely more flexible and fluid than our restrictive ego stories would have us believe.

Just Because

If it's all just a big illusion, then—all waking and non-waking experience, all our passionate feelings, hard-won principles and cherished ideals being "empty of a true self-nature"—what is the point to life? Moreover, if I am just another illusion, an object for God to practice with in his dream yoga experiments, why bother trying to improve myself or "realize" myself at all?

Here is where suchness comes in. As an artist, I am often asked how I came up with an idea for a certain story, or a chord progression for a particular song. When it boils right down to the essence of the matter, the most honest answer I can give in such a situation is: I have no idea. Although the creative process can be structured and conceptualized up to certain point, there is always an overwhelming aspect of "just because" in any artistic or creative endeavor. Such things come from wherever they come from. They are such as *they* are. The ideal artist has finally given up on trying to control or consciously manipulate the process in any way. Rather, he or she stays open and alert to the spontaneous process of creativity, recognizes his or her role almost as one of detached reporter more than inspired innovator. These things arise from nothingness, the creative individual realizes, and parade before our minds on their own mysterious initiative. The artist is simply the individual who pays the closest attention to their passing and goes on to describe this strange parade as best as he or she is able.

In the context of my banjo-playing penguin dream, I might begin by asking myself, "What's this banjo-playing penguin doing in *my* dream in the first place?" Let's suppose I have no particular interest in penguins or banjos, no deep psychological associations or feelings regarding either of these objects, haven't recently encountered any television programs about penguins, haven't recently visited Nashville, etc. How, then, did this penguin get into my dream? Once again, the best answer I can give is simply "just because." The penguin, like every other impermanent thought, sensation, and feeling that tumbles around in my head, is there *such as it is*. This incredibly simple fact, this ridiculously obvious truth, is the most fundamental essence of the self-perfected natural mind. Herein lies the eternal mystery that makes life truly and deeply beautiful and profound.

We might say that this penguin is there in my head simply because *he* wants to be. Maybe he wakes up from *his* dream and wonders what the hell this bizarre looking penguin—that would be me—was doing in *his* head. Such is the very essence of Things Changing, the very stuff of love and art. It's a very quiet realization—one that is so obvious and all-pervasive, nonetheless, it is impossible to point at directly. You are here *just because*. I am here *just because*. And here goes this infinitely amazing dream of our relationship, this bizarre dance we do because it's the only dance in town, such as it is. It's Chou and the butterfly all over again, perpetually encountering and reencountering Chou and the butterfly. . .

Already as They Are

This lack of concrete purpose or objective reality, this so-called emptiness that pervades all internal and external experience, doesn't make life meaningless. Just the opposite is true. In fact, the authentic recognition of suchness—the realization that all things are "empty of a true self-nature," yet undeniably and mysteriously present, nonetheless—reminds us that an infinite variety of meanings can be projected onto our own experience, each of them as legitimate as the next. This divine gift of ultimate subjectivity, ultimate pliability, allows us the freedom to quit trying so hard to discover The Truth, struggling to recognize things As They Are. Things are, after all, already as they are. The Truth is already The Truth. It's no one's personal responsibility to keep the cosmic Ferris wheel spinning. Instead, each of us is free—within this very moment—to sit back, relax, and watch this crazy movie of life going by with whatever attitude we want. Whatever you find the most enjoyable, whatever you feel to be the most deeply passionate, artistic expressions of your total, undivided self, simply rest within these aspects—already abundant within the present moment—as experience streams and trickles around you, within you, without you. Once you begin to experience the deeply liquid nature of reality, the satisfying core of existence that is illuminated from within by the indescribable beauty of suchness, you realize—as Dozgchen says—there is truly nowhere to go and nothing to do when you get there.

Experiencing Clear Light States

In the context of dream yoga, clear light states are the most difficult to work with, as ideas of method and technique don't exactly apply to the actual clear light dream. Remember, clear light dreams aren't dualistic, which means there isn't exactly an observer to "work with" some separate dream content. Once clear light dreams start arising as a spontaneous sign of progress along the path, they become their own instruction manual. The more you have clear light dreams, the more likely you are to have clear light dreams. For this reason, I will focus primarily on techniques for establishing a stable foundation for understanding the clear light state. In doing so, I hope to help you prepare to recognize the clear light when it arises—and it happens every night, by the way—as well as allow yourself to recognize more of the clear light in every waking moment. Before you begin to practice the integration of your awareness with the clear light, you should understand the basic process through which it manifests.

RECOGNIZING THE ELEMENTS

The core building blocks of each of our experiences, as well as our own personalities, attachments, etc., are manifest in what the Tibetans call the elements. There are five basic personality elements, each of which is associated with a certain color, emotion, body location, and so forth. I won't go into all of the specifics here, as such particulars are not important to a basic understanding of the clear light. Think of the elements simply as your personal tendencies or preferences stripped down to their most fundamental "seed" or core. Throughout the day, these five elements gather in our heart center—the chakra at which we visualize the blue lotus in sleep practice—and are projected out through our eyes. The seemingly external objects with which we interact throughout the day, then, are really aspects of our own, most essential selves projected outward. You might think of your body and mind as a movie projector that is able to project its images onto an external screen while at the same time watching its own show, even experiencing internal reactions to these projected images—only you may have forgotten where these projections are coming from. Much like Plato's deluded cave dwellers, most of us watch this projected show in ignorance, fundamentally misunderstanding the nature of its many sights and sounds. Throughout the day, you essentially interact with your self, typically misunderstanding your experiences as interactions with external objects, the world "out there."

In much the same way, when you go to sleep each night, these elements gather at your heart center and are essentially projected against your closed eyelids. It is this sort of movie, in fact, that we call "dreaming." In a clear light dream, however, you recognize your elements in their most basic form *before* they have been molded into specific, concrete images. You have turned your attention from the shadows on the cave walls to the figures above that cast these shadows. You are essentially merging with the elements at the heart center itself—watching the reel as it spins in the projector rather than being captivated by its projected images. As such, in a clear light dream you experience the elements as abstract motions of color and sound as opposed to the familiar objects that populate your daily experience.

Overcoming Attachment

What is the advantage to observing your elements in this more basic form? Put simply, you are much less likely to form the same sort of emotional attachments or intellectual confusions regarding these core, elemental abstractions than you do the objects they eventually become. The clear light dream is like being able to slow the movie down and study it frame by frame. Once you experience your basic elements in this form, you begin to truly appreciate that everything in your daily life—every aspect of the entire universe, in fact—is simply some aspect of your own, ordinary self.

I should emphasize that once you begin to appreciate this fact of ultimate interrelatedness, these more "degraded" forms of the elements—the ordinary objects of your daily experience—don't go away. Instead, you are able to recognize more of your own fundamental self within every object of your daily experience. Perfect love and compassion means refining this ability to recognize the inner within the outer, the subjective within the objective, to its highest state. As Jesus said, we are all a part of The One—the totality of which is none other than God. Once you begin to appreciate this core, existential fact, hating your neighbor becomes as unnecessary, and as impossible, as hating your left hand. Anyone that manifests some annoying or rude behavior toward you is really an extremely valuable marker, a highlighter of some aspect of your own personality that you have been overlooking. For this reason, the ultimate goal in practicing with the clear light should be to cultivate a perfect love and understanding of everyone and everything around you, which are all aspects of your very own self.

CLEAR LIGHT PRACTICES

The following are exercises that can help you get acquainted with your own clear light elements. To better understand these exercises, imagine your awareness as a hand. A hand can touch foreign objects as well as parts of your own body. Moreover, a hand can touch itself—finger interacting with finger and so forth. Your awareness functions in much the same way, only it tends to forget it can "touch" itself. To experience the clear light directly, you must turn your awareness back on itself, draw it inward, rather than project it outward. To do so with intense focus and stability is to realize the perfect Oneness of all reality.

■ *Pressing on the Eyelids:* One of the easiest ways to observe your own elements directly is simply by gently but steadily pressing on your closed eyelids. Maintain pressure for several seconds, and blobs of colored light will begin to emerge. These are the elements manifesting in a rather crude form. Notice how these patterns tend to change, swirling in and out of one another. This is your very own perception changing as you watch these elements, the spontaneous movement of the natural mind. Release the pressure on your eyelids and what happens? The patterns fade rather quickly, withdrawing back into your heart center.

This exercise may initially seem like a simple visual trick. After all, most of us have experimented with this sort of thing as kids. Even so, perhaps the reason most of us *did* experiment with this traditional Dzogchen practice as kids, albeit unknow-ingly, is because we recognized something very familiar in it. The true clear light dream or experience is similar to this practice. In sleeping states or in meditation, however, the experience is much more vivid and profound. These dynamic blobs of color will be crystal clear, forming incredibly intricate geometric patterns and sounds, and—most importantly—they will do so without any effort on your part. You won't need to press on your eyelids in such states because you will be looking directly into your heart center. More accurately, as the clear light teaches us, your *heart center* will be looking directly into your heart center.

■ *Connecting the Thigles and the Sounds:* Now that you have a very basic under-standing of the clear light experience, let's look into some more sophisticated exer-cises. As stated in chapter 7, the Tibetans refer to such practices as Thogal, practices that deliberately work with the clear light energies.

• Begin by sitting in a comfortable posture and entering into a very relaxed medi-tative state. Spend a few minutes in concentration, contemplation—whatever it takes for you to calm your mind and body.

• Close your eyes and observe the tiny pixels of color that flutter in the blackness. If you are missing them, you are probably looking for something a little too spec-tacular. They are simply tiny little dots of color that are always in your field of vision, subtly vibrating and shifting. The Tibetans call these little pixels *thigles* (pronounced "tí-glaze").

• Once you have noticed these thigles, focus your attention on your inner ear. You are listening for something internal rather than external. The sound of your inner ear is a kind of high buzz or "eeee," similar to the quiet hum of a computer.

• Try to blend this inner sound with the inner sight of the thigles. Think of these two elemental forms of energy as manifesting from a single, subtle electric cur-rent that continually energizes your individual awareness—a current that is known as *prana, kundalini,* or *chi* in various spiritual disciplines.

Notice that these two forms are somehow one experience, parts of a whole. What is this whole? Your own perception, the kinetic base of all internal and external expe-riences. Your are turning your perception back on itself, pointing the camera lens back at the camera lens. Think of the inner sounds and thigles as a kind of dance. Notice how the sounds somehow vibrate along with the thigles. Notice how there are continual, subtle movements among the thigles, accompanied by very subtle changes in the inner sounds. Try to merge into this process, relaxing deeply into your own perception until you become this movement itself, this fluid base of cre-ative, elemental energy.

■ *Integrating Music:* Once you are feeling calm and tuned in to these subtle inner experiences, try listening to some relaxing instrumental music. With your eyes still closed, notice how the movement of the music somehow fuels the movement of the thigles. As you relax more and more, you may notice the thigles merging into broader, more obvious swirls of color. At the same time, notice that the buzz of the inner ear is still there. Think of it as the internal, energetic foundation from which the external music emerges. As you listen to the music, recognize that it, too, is ultimately internal rather than external—a kind of projection within your mind's vast movie theater.

Contrary to our habitual, everyday way of perceiving the world, all seemingly external experiences, objects, individuals, etc., are inside rather than outside, just as the thigles and the inner sounds are inside your own mind. Allow yourself to merge more and more deeply into these inner experiences—the thigles, inner sounds, and external music gradually dissolving into one another. Don't try too hard. Don't think about what you are doing. Simply relax into the inner music, becoming the inner music. Your body has expanded to fill the entire room and you are effortlessly floating around inside of it, exploring more and more expansive aspects of your boundless self. Your body gradually expands to fill the sky, the planet, the entire universe, and all the while you are calmly floating inside of it, exploring it, just as the inner sights and sounds effortlessly swirl and float inside the infinite space of your mind.

■ *Integrating Sleep:* As you relax more deeply into the space of the natural mind, you may drift in and out of a very light sleep. This is fine. This is an essential part of the practice, in fact. Simply try to notice what happens as you drift in and out of the dream and sleep states. With practice, you can begin to observe the abstract swirls of thigles forming more concrete dream images as you drift off. The abstract colors may spontaneously form into the face of a family member or close friend. As your relaxation deepens, you may find yourself somehow watching the room you are in with your eyes closed. You may find yourself staring back into your own face or observing some other part of your body. This is simply your own awareness exploring itself. Your physical senses, although one aspect of your sensory awareness, are by no means the only one, or even the most efficient one. As you drift in and out of waking consciousness, more subtle, habitually dormant aspects of sensory awareness activate. Your own experiences with states of heightened awareness will verify that the constricted rules of everyday sensory perception simply do not apply to your elemental, or clear light, awareness.

Who Is Practicing What?

WHILE BRINGING MORE CONSCIOUSNESS INTO the process of your elemental awareness, notice that you are not exactly directing or controlling this perception, nor is it directing you. You *are* this process of awareness. This strange little movie you are watching—this is you in your most basic, most elemental form. This is where you come from, where you return to. As soon as you step outside of the clear light state and try to get a hold of it with your normal awareness, you will lose it. If you are able to relax deeply enough into this experience of the Self, you may discover yourself merged into a warm white or golden light. This is one of the purest manifestations of the clear light. It is that part of the Divine Self that is shared by all of us. To experience this state, then, is to experience oneness, to experience perfect love and compassion. Each night as you drift off to sleep, whether or not you are consciously aware of it, you rejoin, or re-member, this timeless, core aspect of Christ consciousness or Buddha nature. It is this automatic, self-perfected remembering, in fact, that makes sleep so refreshing and essential to your physical, mental, and spiritual self.

ⓢ

■ *Gazing*: This is a slight variation on the preceding exercises.

• Sitting about a foot or so from a white wall so that you see nothing but the wall itself, gaze at the wall, and let your eyes soft focus, blurring or crossing just a bit.

• It is important that you find a gaze that you can hold with complete relaxation.

• As you gaze into the wall, notice that the white surface begins to break down into its fundamental elements, which manifest as countless small, colorful thigles. This process will be very, very subtle at first.

• The more you relax, the more you may begin to notice circular rainbows or mandalas appearing. You may notice Buddhist or Christian icons fluidly emerging and disappearing into the surface of the wall. Know that the surface of the wall is no more than a projection screen for your own mind. These subtle objects that continually come and go, fluid images that spontaneously arise and dissolve, are the movement of your own awareness.

• You can also listen for the "music" of the wall. If you can listen deeply enough, openly enough, every visual movement is accompanied by a subtle movement of sound.

• Allow yourself to relax and merge into these movements, dissolving into the space where sound and image are one, parts of a dynamic whole. As you do so, you may notice the wall changing colors—red, blue, almost black.

• When you are at your most relaxed, the wall may merge into a single blob of white light. At this point, there is no you and there is no wall. There is only the clear light of perception.

In Dzogchen, this same practice of gazing is often done using the sky.

- Find a place outdoors where you can comfortably lie on your back and stare up at the sky. If possible, your vision should be unobstructed by trees, buildings, or anything else that might distract your mind from the vast expanse of sky.

- As with the practice of wall gazing, subtle images, movements of sound and light will arise in sky gazing.

- Realizing that your awareness is infinite like the sky, beyond all limits and concepts, allow your awareness to expand higher and higher, until you recognize the movement of clouds across the sky as the movement of thoughts within your own mind.

■ *Working with Sunlight*: A final variation on Thogal practice involves sunlight, a very pure energy that allows for a uniquely direct manifestation of the clear light.

- Try working with this practice in the morning, just as the sun is coming up, or at twilight, just as the sun is setting.

- Watch how the sunlight appears through slightly open window shades. There is a very faint rainbow glow just at the edges of the shades, a kind of elemental energy.

- Try holding your hand up between your eyes and the window shades. Notice how this same rainbow glow outlines your hand. It is very subtle at first, so try to soft focus on the exact point where your skin meets the sunlight.

This rainbow light is your very own awareness being reflected back to you. The rainbow border drawn around your hand is a direct manifestation of the way your discriminating mind works. Due to conceptual habits, your mind draws a border around your hand and the window shades as a way of separating the clear light into distinct objects. *Visual* borders, that is to say, however subtle, are simply reflections of *mental* borders. As you observe the sunlight falling across the carpet or the trees outside, know that you are this essential energy. You are, literally, this very sunlight, as well as the observer of this sunlight. Your daily life is an ongoing process, a constant dynamic exchange of energy between the personal, everyday you and this more abstract, mystical you.

THE CLEAR LIGHT OF DREAM AND SLEEP

As you begin to recognize the clear light more easily in the previous practices, you may begin to recognize it spontaneously in the dreaming and sleeping states. Visual perception tends to be much more fluid in dreams, so you will likely experience a more dramatic manifestation of the clear light in such a state. You may be watching a sunset in a dream, for instance, when the whole sky suddenly merges into blazing rainbow light, allowing you to recognize your core self in the movement of the dream. Or, you may begin to wake up out of some ordinary dream into a clear light dream. While still asleep, you may find yourself suddenly staring at a shifting mosaic of vivid mandalas accompanied by a buzz, mantra, or beautiful, ethereal music. However strangely compelling and exotic such experiences may be, try to simply recognize yourself, try to realize the presence of your natural mind. Know that it is your own innate creativity, your self-perfected, elemental energy, that gives rise to these beautiful visions within sleep and dream.

Unlike an artist who creates a painting, however, this creative process is entirely without effort. These visions arise without conscious purpose or strategy, outside of desire and personal attachments. Similarly, each day when you wake up, you spontaneously create an entire universe without even realizing it. In the same way the clear light energy gives rise to dreams and visions while you sleep, it spontaneously forms every aspect of your waking experience, seamlessly reflecting the essence of Who You Are from moment to moment. As you begin to recognize the clear light of awareness, the fundamental base of all experience, you begin to directly reconnect with God, the sat guru, Truth—whatever you prefer to call the impersonal, creative aspect of the Divine Self. This aspect is eternal, infinite, without flaw—it is, in fact, you.

THE CLEAR LIGHT OF EVERYDAY EXPERIENCE

In Dzogchen, it is often said that the clear light is so close we tend to overlook it. The more you learn to recognize the clear light, the better you realize it has been there the whole time—right in front of you, in fact, in full Technicolor. Notice that the phrase is "clear" light rather than "white" or "golden" light. This is because the clear light, perfectly integrated, is entirely *transparent*. In many ways, to "see" the clear light is to become distracted. Why is this? Well, the ironic thing you learn from clear light practice—and this is what makes such a practice so elusive and difficult to describe—is that there is no such thing as a separate, clear light. Rather, the clear light is the ordinary, daily illumination that allows you to see the objects of your daily life. Turn on an ordinary light bulb and there is the clear light. Step outside into the sunshine and there it is again. Paradoxically, you don't need to go looking for the clear light because it is always there, always reflecting you back to you, us back to us.

THE CLEAR LIGHT OF COMPASSION

Among spiritual systems, Dzogchen is arguably unique in its relatively direct approach to clear light awareness. All spiritual paths work with the clear light, however—to perfectly integrate the clear light is to be "enlightened," after all—albeit in different ways. Rather than emphasizing direct, meditative experience such as the exercises described above, many systems—Christianity, for example—emphasize love and kindness toward others. Without a doubt, without love and kindness we can never truly recognize the clear light.

In addition to working with the previous exercises, then, it is absolutely essential to remember that every individual and situation you encounter in your daily life is a very real, concrete part of this perfect and spontaneous artistic creation. If I dislike someone, or am unkind, I should ask myself, "What disowned aspect of my own personality is this person reminding me of?" Likewise, if I find myself in a very uncomfortable or stressful situation, I should ask myself, "How is this drama of my daily life reconnecting me to the whole, helping me to remember the One?" As I have emphasized time and again, perfect compassion *is* perfect understanding. For this reason, kind behaviors, in and of themselves, are not the ultimate goal. If you perform an act of kindness toward someone, yet all the while you are thinking, "How lucky this poor sod is to have someone like *me* around," you are not really recognizing this person as an aspect of your own self, a self-perfected manifestation of God's own mind.

Oftentimes, it may be more useful to simply observe your daily experience rather than actively intervene. If someone insults you, try working directly with that immediate experience, try to observe it with complete clarity in the moment of its arising, rather than donating your time or money to charity, for example. Strange as it may sound, as much "worldly good" can be accomplished through accurate, individual perception as can any personal or collective behavior. Simply sitting in meditation and trying to legitimately reconnect with those disturbing aspects of yourself is, quite literally, to heal the external world, to influence your environment through love and understanding. The purer you become, the purer the world becomes. Such was the entire message of Buddha and Jesus. Since everything you see "out there" is really some aspect of the self "in here," once you can sufficiently let go of your competitive, fearful, and judgmental tendencies, you begin to see the clear light in even the Adolph Hitler's and Charles Manson's of the universe. At such a state, you begin to emanate a kind of automatic love and compassion by your very presence. With direct, non-deluded perception—viewing the world from a place of total selflessness and acceptance, every moment you simply *are*, the entire world benefits from your ongoing desire to realize The One Self.

PICKPOCKETS, PERVERTS
AND SAINTS:
A SUMMARY OF SEXUAL POSITIONS

Is sex dirty? Only if it's done right.
—Woody Allen, *Everything You Always Wanted to Know about Sex*

how a pickpocket a saint, the Hindus say, and all he will see are pockets. This state of affairs doesn't apply only to pickpockets, of course, but to all of us. Our individual desires obviously affect the ways in which we perceive the world—which is why it's not a good idea to go grocery shopping when you haven't eaten all day.

"If you have a toothache, you do what you do, but the mind remains on the tooth."[1] This quote from my guru, Maharaj-ji, reminds us of this same quirk of desire or attachment: Whatever we imagine we want, whatever we imagine we lack—such desires fundamentally affect our relation to the world around us. We go about our business from day to day, but all the while there is a persistent throbbing, a distracting "toothache" in our awareness.

Throughout this work, we have been looking at this bizarre dilemma of desire—which is the very same bizarre dilemma of *being*—from all sorts of angles. Meditation, devotion, psychology, dream work—follow any of these various paths of inquiry far enough, deep enough, sincerely enough, and you end up face to face with the same old riddle: Who Am I? Properly understood, Who I Am is simply a collection of ever-changing wants, needs, and satisfactions, thoughts, feelings, and behaviors. At the core, there is *nothing* there, there is *everything* there. However you choose to describe it—the Self, yourself—you are beginning to catch these little glimpses every now and then of its spontaneous perfection. You are beginning to have those moments here and there of: Wow! This Is It! Even so, you will probably keep losing sight of this spontaneous perfection, this indescribable love and grace, time and time again—but why is this? Once again, you're back to where you started, back at the core teachings of Buddha and Jesus: Understand desire, truly see how it plays out in your daily life, and you—just as you already are—become pure love and truth and understanding. "The Lord God is one," (Mark 12:29) said Jesus—and you are that one.

Sex on the Brain

As a means of furthering our exploration of this Who Am I? riddle, this chapter will focus on the infamous toothache of sexual desire. In general, sexual desire works like any other desire. Recall Buddha's analogy, "Suffering because life cannot satisfy selfish desire is like suffering because a banana tree will not bear mangoes." In this respect, your desire for sex—as with any other desire—is only a problem to the degree that you think life can ever truly satisfy it. Although sexual desire, in this context, isn't qualitatively different from any other desire, it seems to be quantitatively different. Sexual desire—more so than any other, it would seem—is literally everywhere. In this way, sexual desire is at once one of the clearest paths toward, and most frustrating obstacles blocking the way to, self-realization.

Returning to the pickpocket metaphor, you could assume that each of us so clearly has "sex on the brain" simply because we are not very satisfied with our sex lives. Give a pickpocket a million dollars, and you can be pretty sure he or she is not going to be so fascinated by the saint's pockets anymore, right? Like the typical pickpocket, most of us are, sexually speaking, starving and impoverished. Many of us claim to be sexually satisfied, but, given the compulsive fascination most of us seem to drag around when it comes to sex, such claims are highly suspect. You could follow just about any one of us throughout his or her day and easily observe how this sexual pickpocket mentality tends to play out. Consider any situation you would like—a trip to the grocery store, evening television, billboard advertisements, the workplace, the gym, Sunday church service, PTA meetings—and you are likely to discover one seductively stuffed "pocket" after another.

Some of us will confess easily enough—"Guilty as charged." Others, no doubt, will indignantly exclaim, "Not me! I've got better things to do with my time than get all googly-eyed at the convenience store magazine rack!" Quite likely, such individuals are making use of the same strategy the dramatist, Alan Ayckbourn, writes about: "My mother used to say . . . if S-E-X ever rears its ugly head, close your eyes before you see the rest of it."[2] Such individuals are like the guilty pickpocket who convinces himself he is just clumsy. Eyes closed tightly, he keeps "accidentally" bumping into people, their wallets unexpectedly tumbling into his hands. In the same way that the accidental pickpocket is just as likely—probably more so, in fact—to get caught as the intentional pickpocket, the person that refuses to recognize the way in which sexuality pervades his or her daily life is also going to be "found out." Ironically, in trying to avoid the various difficulties that go along with sexual desire, such a person simply creates new problems for him or herself, typically inventing a cure that is worse than the original sickness. As Freud describes it:

> Psycho-analytic work has shown us that it is precisely these frustrations of sexual life which people known as neurotics cannot tolerate. The neurotic creates substitutive satisfactions for himself in his symptoms, and these either cause him suffering in themselves or become sources of suffering for him by raising difficulties in his relations with his environment and the society he belongs to.[3]

If we claim to be sexually satisfied, or if we claim to be disinterested in sex altogether, Freud is suggesting, we should be on the lookout for "substitutive" behaviors. Eating, drinking, and smoking are favorites, as are compulsive exercising, housecleaning, and working. In such circumstances, we are simply taking the frustrations of sexual desire and displacing them onto a frustratingly "filthy" house, for instance, or a "filthy"—yet highly compulsive—habit such as smoking. Then there are the stand-in "satisfactions" of guilt, depression, anxiety, explosive anger, etc.—not to mention various sexual stresses and tensions stored all over the body in the form of seemingly unrelated physical pains and discomforts, which psychologists call "somaticizations." Show me a person who is free of all of the above, *then* I will consider the possibility that he or she may be one of those rare humans who has found the Holy Grail of sexual satisfaction.

THE NECESSITY OF DIRTY SEX

My point, then, is a simple one: Whether you feel comfortable recognizing it or not, sexual desire does pervade just about every facet of daily life. In and of itself, this doesn't have to be a problem. An artist sees life in terms of art, a philosopher in terms of philosophy—so why should seeing life in terms of sexuality be such a problem? In Buddhist terminology, we would say that sexual desire tends to confuse us more than does artistic or philosophical desire because, quite simply, we are more *attached* to it. We somehow expect sex, unlike art and philosophy, to magically solve all our problems. Or, inversely, we can be negatively attached to sex: If I have sex in such and such a way, or with such and such a person, I'm simply *no longer the person I used to be.*

As we all know, there is something about sexual desire that is highly confusing and frustrating—so much so that many of us, whom Freud calls "neurotics," try to avoid the whole disorienting business altogether. There seem to be two main solutions to this pervasive sexual problem: (1) have more and more, wilder and wilder sex; (2) avoid sex like the plague, or at least repress it to a bare minimum. Ironically, both of these seemingly different attitudes come from the same assumption: that sexual frustration is unnecessary, something that can be avoided or fixed. As Woody Allen pointed out, however, there seems to be some necessary connection between "dirty" sex and sex "done right." In our current context, we could interpret "dirty" loosely to include sex that involves feelings of guilt, anxiety, frustration, depression, etc. If Woody is right, good sex necessarily involves these complications, or "filthy" elements, which both camps—the more sex camp as well as the less sex camp—are so trying to avoid.

My main thesis for this chapter could be put like this: To want to have sex without pervasive difficulties and core dissatisfactions, is like wanting to go on a diet of beer and fast food without gaining weight. To return to a Taoist writing we examined earlier:

> Under heaven all can see beauty as beauty only because there is ugliness.
> All can know good as good only because there is evil.
> Therefore having and not having arise together.
> Difficult and easy complement each other.[4]

Wanting to have sex is a problem, then—sort of. As "having and not having arise together," we can only have sex to the degree that, well, we *don't have* sex. The bigger the hole, the bigger the donut, right? I am not suggesting, of course, that the greatest sexual satisfaction comes from literally not having sex. Rather, I am simply suggesting that sex, by definition, can never truly be *had*. Such is the way of life itself, the way of love, awareness, truth, whatever. We can only have these things to the degree that we are willing to not have them. Elsewhere in the *Tao Te Ching*, we find this equally paradoxical passage:

> Observers of the Tao do not seek fulfillment.
> Not seeking fulfillment, they are not swayed by desire for change.[5]

Therefore, the most uncomfortable feelings we have about sex come from our mistaken belief that it *should be* fulfilling. We don't feel guilty and anxious about brushing our teeth each morning, for instance, because we never think this experience is really going to fix our lives in the first place. We don't exactly "seek fulfillment" when we brush our teeth—we are just looking to get our teeth clean.

Interestingly, everything I have so far said about sexual desire can also be said about spiritual desire—that is, the desire for total self-realization or enlightenment. Truth be told, the distinctions we draw between the two are entirely arbitrary. When it comes to enlightenment, as with sex, the more we chase it, thinking it will fix us, or the more we avoid it, thinking it will ruin us, the more we suffer from "Zen on the brain." Paradoxically, the highest realization of spirituality is nothing other than our daily lives, just as they already are—however "dirty" they may be. With this in mind, we are currently considering sexual desire rather than spiritual desire simply because it is easier to talk about, seemingly more concrete and immediately present.

The same strategy of ultimate fulfillment applies to both paths, or obstacles, however: Give up our rigid views and behaviors concerning our all-important goal and there we have it—wholeness, oneness, the Self—the experience of total and satisfactory merger, The Great Orgasm in the Sky.

Rather than getting ourselves hopelessly tangled in this paradox of "having" and "not having" just now, we can simply recognize that sexual desire is a lot more complicated and elusive than we tend to realize. At the same time, of course, sex—like spirituality—is much simpler and attainable than we tend to realize. What keeps us from seeing things As They Are? Why do we habitually fail to see life, and sex, As It Is? Well, there's those sticky attachments and personal hang-ups, again, spoiling our view of the Big Picture. With this in mind, in what follows, we are going to assume various sexual positions—to look at some of the innumerable ways in which desire plays against satisfaction, examine a few of the infinitely varied dances of The One— many of them quite "filthy." As you survey the following schools of thought regarding sexual desire, remember that what you are ultimately after is not necessarily satisfying sex or even spiritual progress. Rather, you are seeking the seeking itself, dancing the crazy, perfectly transparent dance of being until you are, at long last, one with the dance.

Sex and Evolutionary Psychology

Strategies are essential for survival on the mating battlefield."[6] So says psychology professor Dr. David Buss, in his groundbreaking book, *The Evolution of Desire: Strategies of Human Mating*. This idea of "mating" as comprising strategies in an ever-evolving war between the sexes, is the infamous battle cry of evolutionary psychology. Actress Carrie Fisher sums up the war this way:

> Here's how men think. Sex, work—and those are reversible, depending on age—sex, work, food, sports and lastly, begrudgingly, relationships. And here's how women think. Relationships, relationships, relationships, relationships, work, sex, shopping, weight, food.[7]

Although evolutionary psychology doesn't necessarily agree with all of Ms. Fisher's specifics, this basic idea of tension created from fundamentally differing wants is believed to be at the core of the sex war. From this perspective, we are so compulsively fascinated by sex because we don't have much choice—not if we want to succeed in passing our genes along. Men and women learn to see sex everywhere— although that seeing may take very different forms—in much the same way a soldier learns to constantly scan the terrain, looking out for ambushes, mine fields, booby—no pun intended—traps, etc. We can't help but check out that sexually attractive person in line at the 7-11 because, hey, this is war, this is love—and you know what they say about love and war.

Over a hundred years ago, Charles Darwin took an interest in peacocks. Darwin noticed that the brilliant plumage of the male peacock, at first glance, doesn't seem to be very advantageous, evolution-wise. Not only is it a kind of bright red bull's eye for possible predators, its extravagant plumage is also very costly, calorically speaking, to maintain. After observing numerous such examples of seeming inefficiency throughout various species, Darwin came up with the idea of sexual selection. Sexual selection is simply the natural process of the evolution of certain traits—not for survival benefits, however, but for reproductive benefits. Both of these natural processes, natural selection as well as sexual selection, are necessary arsenals in what Darwin called the "war of nature," whose end result is "the production of the higher animals."[8] Right alongside each organism's desire for immediate physical protection—this is the primary role of natural selection—Darwin was asserting, is a desire for a kind of genetic, or long-term protection, which motivates strategic sexual selection. To the degree that an organism passes on its genetic material, that organism somehow lives on beyond its own individual life, partially transcends the limits of physical death, thereby winning the "war of nature." Granted, you probably don't go around from day to day thinking, "I must guarantee the future success of my genetic material!" Still, you have to admit, to the degree that we are here right now at all— each of us "higher animals" necessarily the product of sperm meeting egg—we must have come from a very long line of successfully reproducing ancestors. After all, not a single one of us could claim a biological ancestor who never managed to attract, or select, an evolutionarily viable sexual partner.

WHAT IS SEXY?

Until about 20 years ago, this idea of sexual selection wasn't widely accepted by scientists—not when it came to humans, at least. With the huge amount of data recently collected by evolutionary psychologists, however, mainstream science is doing an abrupt about-face. In his research involving over 10,000 people from 37 cultures worldwide, David Buss has shown that certain traits are universally preferred in the selection of a sexual partner. His conclusion: Women want—in their mates—money, status, dependability, health, intelligence, and commitment. Men want youth, physical attractiveness, health, good caretaking skills, and sexual fidelity. Sound unfair? Well, let's be honest: Unfair or not, we see a beautiful woman with an unattractive man, what do we say? "I'll bet he must be loaded." Or we hear about a brilliant, rich man dating a rather obnoxious, uneducated woman, what's the chorus line? "She's a bimbo." In this context, "bimbo" means, among other things, sexually attractive. If Buss is correct in asserting the universality of certain sexually attractive traits, we might wonder how particular traits came to be favored over others.

Interestingly, Buss asserts, we can trace the whole mess back to a simple difference in sex cells, or gametes. Put simply: Women have—practically speaking—a limited supply of big ones, men have pretty much an infinite supply of little ones. In actuality, a woman has many more sex cells than she could ever need. The primary limiting factor here is one of access. That is to say, women typically release only one egg per month, whereas men can release a virtually unlimited amount of sperm. Women, then, can't afford to give away their monthly egg to just anyone—not if they want to insure the success of their offspring. Moreover, any sexual encounter could possibly require a nine-month investment for the woman, not to mention an additional three or so years of lactating. Although it is true that modern birth control significantly reduces the risk of unwanted pregnancy, we are dealing with ancient hardwiring here. To complicate things further, it does little good, evolutionarily, if a woman simply cares for her child until the age of three and then leaves him or her to fend for him or herself. Rather, she has to spend a good many years nurturing that child if that child is to survive, eventually doing his or her own part to further the genetic line.

Due to the relatively limited availability of female sex cells, combined with the considerable investment of energy and time women must make to rear genetically successful offspring, women seek men who will be able to dependably provide for their financial needs and material comforts for a good while. Once again, the cultural situation of vocational roles is radically different these days, of course. Modern women commonly work and support themselves as well as multiple children without male assistance, but this new development is beside the point when it comes to prehistoric biological know-how. What, after all, is one of the first things a woman wants to know about a potential suitor? She wants to know what his career is. "Will he still be able to provide resources 20 years from now?" her primal brain wants to know. Indicators of physical reliability are important in this same context. If the man is sick, clumsy, physically weak, or small in stature, he is more likely to die early, get eaten by a wild beasty and so forth. He also needs to be intelligent, because if the child is to survive, flourish, and eventually find a mate, that child—who shares her father's genes—needs to be intelligent. I could go on and on, but you get the idea. Despite the recent, so-called sexual revolution, sex is still no small matter for women. Any time a woman engages in sexual activity, her primal brain believes a good portion of her future life, as well as long-term genetic success, is likely at stake. Consequently, those qualities that would seem to guarantee a good father—which means a stable, committed, physically reliable, providing father—are of utmost importance in the selection of her sexual partner.

Which isn't to imply that, all things considered, sex is a lesser matter for men. Although men can afford a much bigger "gamble" when it comes to sex cells and potential time investment, this is only part of the story. After all, it does a man little good, sexual selection wise, if he attempts to impregnate a hundred infertile women. We would predict, then, that men are more attracted—both in the context of so-called casual sex and lifelong mates—to women who exhibit signs of fertility. What are these signs? One of the most obvious, of course, is youth. Women are only fertile for about the first third of their life, so it stands to reason that men would typically seek out youngish women. In fact, many of the feminine features considered attractive across cultures are direct indicators of youth. Supple skin, shiny hair, energetic mannerisms, clear eyes, etc.—all universal features of feminine beauty, according to Buss—are evidence that a woman is more likely to be within the fertile age range.

The psychologist Devendra Singh has made a particularly interesting discovery in this context.[9] He has shown, in numerous cross-culture studies, that men prefer a certain waist-to-hip ratio in women. Not surprisingly, this same ratio—which describes mathematically the stereotypical hourglass figure—is, even with today's modern technology, still predictive of increased fertility, as well as better overall health. And the man doesn't just need his long-term partner to be fertile, of course, he also needs her to be a good mother. Good mother means, in this context, a kind and nurturing caretaker, a healthy and reliable woman who can be counted on to see to the child's long-term health and genetic success. Every time a man has sex, that is to say, he has also got quite a lot going on. Despite our popular misconceptions, although he would likely be much more open to the idea of "casual" sex, the man is not ultimately shopping for an "easy" sex partner so much as he is a nurturing, physically robust mother to raise his offspring.

THE WAR RAGES ON

In case it's not already obvious, viewing sex from this evolutionary perspective points to some pretty big problems. Let's consider the man first. Not all men are rich, of course, nor are they six feet tall or even dependable. Sexual selection, that is, is decidedly not a democratic process. And even if a man does seem to possess these ideal traits, who is to say his partner won't "trade up" at some point for a richer, taller, more dependable man? After all, Buss asserts that one of women's strategies of sexual selection is, while being committed to one man, maintaining several male friendships on the side. From the woman's primal brain perspective, such men more or less function as back-up providers in case her mate is, for whatever reason, no longer able to provide sufficient resources sometime in the future.

Aware of this, at least at the unconscious level, the man is always somewhat insecure. He has learned to be jealous, carefully monitoring his partner's activities, particularly whom she spends time with. Then there is the added pressure of the woman's relatively limited supply of eggs. If she does happen to have sex with another man and become impregnated, she is giving away a treasured resource—a full year of her childrearing time and energy, at the very least. In addition, if a man's mate is impregnated by a genetic rival, he may unknowingly commit his own resources to the upbringing of that child, suffering a kind of evolutionary "double whammy."

For this reason, the man watches his partner closely during the sexual act, wants to make sure that she is truly enjoying it, looks out for the slightest sign of sexual straying. For example, did you know that men have at least two different types of sperm, "defenders" and "impregnators?" When all is well and his mate shows consistent signs of sexual devotion and satisfaction, the man primarily produces sperm of the impregnator variety. When he becomes suspicious that his partner may be straying, however, his body automatically produces a much larger ratio of defender sperm, whose sole function is to kill off any strange sperm that may be hanging around trying to crack that egg.

My primary point, once again, is that sex is a very, very charged act—much more so than most of us are consciously aware of. The man has learned to surround the sex act with competition, jealousy, and constant watchfulness as a way of guaranteeing his genetic survival. For that matter, men have consistently sought, throughout history, to repress and outright forbid the female sexual drive. Is this because men are simply domineering tyrants? Not according to evolutionary psychology. Men have tried to limit feminine sexual desire, Buss would suggest, as a means to encourage their partners to carefully guard access to their eggs, to maximize—in the man's opinion—their limited fertile years. The negative emotions and behaviors men direct at women are actually, from the evolutionary standpoint, highly effective and necessary strategies. In the context of evolutionary psychology, the saying, "Nice guys finish last," becomes "Nice guys finish first." Men who don't employ strategic negativity in their sexual strategies are much like an army that goes to war without weapons—they are, genetically speaking, very quickly "finished." So far as the man's primal brain is concerned, sex is quite literally a struggle to outmaneuver, vigilantly guard against, and ultimately outlive the next guy—a matter of genetic life and death.

By no means are things easier for the woman, of course. Assuming she is, physically speaking, among the sexually "elite" at present—meaning she happens to be young and attractive with just the right waist-to-hip ratio, etc.—how long will these physical features last? Her body shape is going to change as she ages, not to mention after having children, so how can she ever be perfectly secure? She sees her partner admiring some younger actress or model, some colleague with an even more ideal waist-to-hip ratio, more energetic and engaging mannerisms, and she gets angry. Fearing her mate may himself try to "trade up" for a more fertile partner, a more nurturing mother and so forth, she strategically tests the relationship bond, measures her mate's commitment to her by going on more shopping trips (think "dependable financial resources"), demanding more of his emotional attention at home, etc. Maybe she even learns to withhold sex as a strategy. The more she withholds, the more her partner is likely to suspect infidelity, right? And the more he suspects infidelity, the more he is going to defend his valuable "resource," the fiercer he is going to compete with this imagined cuckold, becoming more and more attentive. It's what Buss calls an "evolutionary arms race." The more dangerous the arsenal one partner brings to the sexual act and surrounding emotional territory, the uglier the weapons the other partner feels compelled to amass.

So sex becomes a war. The act of lovemaking becomes entangled with an often brutal territory dispute. Aggression and affection become military strategies, fuel for a violent, albeit very quiet, power struggle. Every trip to the movies risks happening on a landmine. Every office party hides Indiana Jones-style booby traps behind each cocktail. He constantly measures himself against other men, she constantly measures herself against other women. Sexual intercourse becomes a strange gauge of success, a competitive event: Am I good enough? Is my partner good enough? Is sex—can it *ever* be—good enough?

Freudian Relationships

As a way of introducing Freud's take on sexual partnering, I would like to borrow an exercise, slightly modified, from Dr. Harville Hendrix's *Getting the Love You Want: A Guide for Couples*. Get out a sheet of paper and make a list of all of your parents' qualities that come to mind. Try to list both positive and negative character and/or physical traits, significant as well as seemingly insignificant personality characteristics, mannerisms, etc. You don't need to separate these out into mother and father, good and bad, just jot them down as they come to mind. To get the most out of this exercise, I suggest you spend a few minutes on your list before reading on.

Now you are going to make the same list for your spouse or current romantic/sexual partner. If you are not involved in an intimate, opposite sex relationship at present, you can use a significant someone from the past. If you have never really had what you consider to be an intimate romantic relationship, you can use a close, opposite-sex friend, past or present. Whoever you choose, take some time making your list of both positive and negative physical traits, mannerisms, personality characteristics, etc., as honestly as possible before continuing.

A quick comparison of the two lists will probably prove interesting. If you are like the vast majority of us, there will be some striking similarities between them. Most likely, whomever you chose for the second list probably exhibits many of the traits from the first list, both positive and negative characteristics belonging to your mother and father. The fact that we have chosen someone who exhibits our parents' positive qualities is hardly surprising. If my mother had a great sense of humor, for example, it stands to reason that I would look for that same quality in a potential mate. How about those negative qualities, though? If you've been sufficiently open and honest in your list making, no doubt some of those particularly annoying parental qualities have also reared their ugly head in the second list. In examining why this might be the case, we can start by taking a look at the Oedipus myth.

THE OEDIPUS MYTH

Roughly told, the story goes like this: Oedipus was born to King Laius and Queen Jocasta. Before he was born, however, an oracle had told his royal parents that

Oedipus would grow up to kill his father and marry his mother. Trying to avoid this unpleasant prophecy, the king and queen abandoned their infant Oedipus in the mountains. Happened upon by kind strangers, Oedipus was adopted and raised with love and care, never knowing his adoptive parents weren't his real parents. When Oedipus reached adulthood, however, he visited an oracle at Delphi who told him of his true origins, as well as the terrible prophecy surrounding it. In horror, Oedipus fled across the mountains toward Thebes, hoping to save himself from this supposed fate. In his flight, he encountered his father, King Laius, and killed him in a violent struggle. Oedipus went on to Thebes, but his way was blocked by a kind of guardian monster, the Theban Sphinx. He successfully solved the beast's riddle—we'll get to that later—and arrived in Thebes. There, just as the oracle had originally foretold, he ended up marrying Queen Jocasta—both mother and son ignorant of the fact of their intimate biological relationship. To make a long story short, Oedipus eventually found out that he had, in fact, blindly fulfilled the terrible prophecy. Oedipus then literally put out his own eyes as punishment for his "unseeing" actions.

Freud's infamous Oedipus complex derives its name, of course, from the above myth. Freud's Oedipus story goes like this: As an infant develops, it seeks out various objects for its libido. Freud defines libido as: "a quantitatively variable force which could serve as a measure of processes and transformations occurring in the field of sexual excitation. . . . The analysis of the perversions and psychoneuroses has shown us that this sexual excitation is derived not from the so-called sexual parts alone, but from all the bodily organs."[10]

By the strictly Freudian definition, then, libido refers specifically to the energy of sexual desire, present from the infantile stage on, in one form or another. Moreover, for Freud, the entire body is essentially one large sexual organ, meaning all of our bodily and mental processes—eating, thinking, hurting, etc.—are actually sexual experiences to one degree or another. Many contemporary psychologists, however, have modified this idea of libido to include friendly affection, warmth, and love. In this context, libido refers to any feelings of human companionship, ranging from highly charged eroticism to simple, everyday feelings of friendliness and kinship. For these psychologists, it is no more fair to call the body one large sexual organ than it is to call it one large brain, emotional vessel, oral cavity, etc. We don't need to go into all the details of theory here—we just need to understand that there is an ongoing psychological debate as to how much of our desire, or libido, is necessarily sexual.

However we choose to define libido, the first object the infant finds for these libidinal feelings, whatever their quality, is simply himself. This is what Freud called the auto-erotic phase of development. At this stage, the infant doesn't really distinguish between himself and his environment. All of experience is one big sloppy goo of needs and means to meet those needs at this point. Soon thereafter, however, the infant does begin to discriminate. At this time, the mother, who has been breastfeeding the infant, caretaking, nurturing, etc., becomes the infant's libidinal object. In contrast to the earliest stage of self-absorbed development, the infant now learns to associate the meeting—or not meeting—of its needs with Mother. Around the age of four or five, says Freud, the infant's libido becomes more directly sexual. The infant begins to experience more mature, genitally motivated sexual desire, and who does he expect to satisfy those sexual desires? Mother, of course, his historical need-meeting object. The infant quickly learns, however, that this isn't going to work. Unlike his desire for food, affection, and so forth, Mother is not going to satisfy this particular desire. As for Father, he has become a rival of sorts, the winner in the competition for Mother's sexual attention. Even if Mother were to meet his sexual needs, the infant realizes, he would be in big trouble with Father.

So what does the infant do with his sexual want at this stage? Not much. Due to the incredible tension created by this problematic and "inappropriate" desire, these entirely natural—according to Freud—libidinal needs get set aside for a while, a stage which Freud calls latency, only to be re-encountered in puberty. At this time, as the individual begins to understand sexual desire from a more conscious, adult perspective, this new information "has in fact awakened the memory-traces of the impressions and wishes of his early infancy, and these have led to a reactivation of certain mental impulses. He begins to desire his mother herself in the sense with which he has recently become acquainted (adult sexual desire, my parentheses), and to hate his father anew as a rival who stands in the way of his wish; he comes, as we say, under the dominance of the Oedipus complex."[11]

All hell breaks loose at this point, of course, as the adolescent suddenly has to deal with all the guilt and anxiety arising from these deeply repressed oedipal wishes. In his unconscious drives, the adolescent male, like Oedipus, is set on a blind course to kill his father and marry his mother.

That said, how about the female child? There is a lot more confusion surrounding her libidinal development, particularly in the writings of Freud. Originally, Freud said the oedipal dynamics played out pretty much the same for the female. Like the male, she attached to her mother as the first need-meeting object and later, at age four or five, began to desire her sexually—albeit in a very confusing manner. Later on in his career, however, Freud began to revise his view. He decided that, although the mother was necessarily—through breastfeeding, etc.—the first libidinal object for both male and female children, the female child somehow "switched over" to the father as object at age four or five. This sexual desire for the father by the female child has come to be known, in contemporary psychology, as the Electra complex. There is still much disagreement among Freudians about the specifics of this stage in female development. In my grossly simplified account of libidinal development, I would just like to emphasize that although the female infant's development closely parallels that of the male, it is necessarily a significantly different dynamic. No doubt, this early developmental discrepancy may go on to cause all sorts of misunderstandings between adult men and women. It is not in the scope of this work, obviously, to look into all these variously complex issues. Once again, I would like to simply emphasize that whereas all children attach to their mothers as the first libidinal object, only the female seems to "make the switch" later on.

THE OEDIPAL STUNT DOUBLE

So here is where things get confusing for us as sexually mature adults: To the degree that our opposite sex parent never met our sexual fantasies, said Freud, we carry around a repressed wish to somehow fix things as an adult. This doesn't mean, usually, that we go around with the literal desire to have sex with our mother and kill our father, of course. We have learned, very early on, through our pervasive process of socialization, that such things are strictly not allowed among civilized people. Instead, we try to substitute someone else—someone who somehow reminds us of the taboo parent—to try to satisfy our old, infantile wishes through this new, sexually appropriate relationship.

Sound like a lot of bunk? Well, take a look at your list. You have obviously chosen someone who is sort of a stunt double for your parents, right? This universal phenomenon, assert the Freudians, arises due to this unfinished libidinal business, these unsatisfied early wishes. It would be much more *rational* to choose a partner that doesn't exhibit all these frustrating characteristics—your parents negative characteristics—that caused you so much grief throughout childhood, of course, but this simply isn't a rational matter. In fact, because we are trying to heal old wounds, we unconsciously assume it is necessary that our parental stand-in be as accurate as possible, flaws and all. The more our stand-in looks like a composite of our parents, say the emotional and cognitive remnants of our conflicted infantile experiences, the better we will be able to adjust the lighting for the real stars of our unconscious Oedipus movie.

It's a pretty good psychological strategy overall, except for one major sticking point: Like Oedipus, we tend to go around blind to our own psychological "fates." Failing to realize that we are trying to heal childhood wounds through our adult sexual relationships, we cultivate highly unreasonable, childish, wants and expectations from our partner. Inevitably, to the degree that we are unaware of our unconscious motivations, typical, real-world adult sex simply can't be satisfying enough. Why? Well, we have still yet to learn to distinguish between our parental relationships and our sexual relationships. We are still, in one way or another, doing our utmost to marry our parents.

Once again, if your immediate reaction to all of this is to dismiss it as ridiculous "psycho-babble"—and this is probably the most common initial reaction—take a minute to think about how you behave in, and around, sexual matters. Are your wants not typically rather childish? Do you not carry around deep feelings of guilt, shame, and resentment about your sexual wants and fantasies, as well as those of your partner? Do you not cultivate the childish notion that just the right partner could

magically fix all of these problems? Like Oedipus, whether or not we consciously recognize it, we have gone looking for trouble, and trouble is never hard to find. How
often, when in a heated argument with our partners, do we think to ourselves, I can't
believe we're fighting *just like my parents*? These oedipal patterns tend to be so deeply
entrenched that they play out over and over again in our most intimate relationships,
despite the fact that we, as mature, rational adults, clearly "know better."

To make matters worse, not only do we seek out romantic partners that exhibit
our parents' most difficult traits, we try to directly illicit such qualities in the most
charged circumstances—sex being foremost among charged circumstances. Let's say
you are a woman and your father was emotionally volatile while growing up, prone
to explosive fits of anger. Well, what "better" way to heal this old libidinal wound
than to choose an emotionally volatile romantic partner and incite him into a similar fit—a kind of dramatic re-enactment strategy? Do you find yourself repeatedly
getting into volatile fights just before, or just after, the act of sex? If so, you are probably trying to make your stunt double act the part more convincingly so that his sexual acceptance of you, despite—or rather, *because* of—his emotional volatility, will
be all the more satisfying.

Or let's say you are a man and your mother was always after you about your
physical appearance. Tuck your shirt in, was your mother's favorite motto, comb you
hair, wash your face, etc. Well, wouldn't it be satisfying if your wife—unlike Mom—
accepted you despite your unruly appearance? So you set up unconscious test after
test, presenting yourself in more and more physically or emotionally unkempt states
to your wife, furious and defeated when she sometimes—and not at all
surprisingly—rejects you sexually. As a strategy to heal old wounds by way of a sub-
stituted object, whatever your parents' most upsetting qualities were, you are likely
to try to provoke them in your partner in and around the issue of sex.

Then there is the problem of triangulation. Your sexual partner probably does-
n't make a perfect stand-in for both of your parents. Common sense would tell us
that she is probably more like Mom than Dad, he is probably more like Dad than
Mom. Nonetheless, we likely experience some pretty big unresolved problems with
both parents, remember. To varying degrees, we still carry around the old wish—
albeit deeply unconscious—to kill the one and satisfy our sexual desires with the
other. To make the set of our adult oedipal drama more convincing, then, we like to
recruit a third party to assist as stunt-double for our same sex parent. If you are a
man, maybe you like to bring one of your best friends around the house. Do you
sometimes, rather irrationally, imagine he and your wife are flirting? Do you secretly
enjoy your romantic "triumph" over him from time to time? These thoughts are likely to be very, very subtle, so you will have to look into your mind with a powerful
magnifying lens, such as offered through meditation practice or psychotherapy. If
you are a woman, maybe you have a competition going with your husband's sister.
Whenever she comes around, you notice yourself—very, very subtly, of course—

competing with her for his attention. Maybe you insult her a bit after she has gone, and enjoy when your husband seems to take your side against her. Look very carefully at your most meaningful relationships, Freud would suggest, and you will see all sorts of disguised oedipal triangles.

THE RIDDLE OF THE SPHINX

Now, back to our riddle of the Sphinx. "What has four legs in the morning," the Sphinx asked Oedipus, "two legs in the afternoon and three in the evening?" Oedipus' answer: man. Man crawls as an infant, walks in the middle of life, and uses a cane—the third leg—in old age. Although Oedipus solved this riddle, he failed to solve the real riddle, the riddle *behind* the riddle. The so-called moral behind the Sphinx's riddle is that it is important to *consciously* understand where we came from, who we are at present and where we are heading in the future. In our present context, before we can truly understand our current sexual dissatisfaction and thereby prepare the way toward increased satisfaction in the future, we have to recognize and work through our deeply repressed infantile wishes. If we are sexually dissatisfied—and to the degree that we gawk at every sexy billboard ad and grocery store customer, we are probably sexually dissatisfied—there must be old, consciously unacceptable psychological material we are still refusing to recognize. Like Oedipus, our very act of trying to flee our own psychological "prophecies" inevitably brings about unpleasant consequences. If we are to avoid repeating Oedipus' mistake and avert unwanted relationships and situations, we will have to watch ourselves very closely—learn to watch deeper and deeper layers of our mind quietly reeling by. Rather than having our hidden conflicts unexpectedly emerge and, like Oedipus, feel the occasional need to "put our eyes out," Freud would suggest we learn to consciously recognize and own up to those unacceptably sexy beasties we have stuffed in the very back of our psychological sock drawer.

Romance

Obviously, one of the reasons people have sex, or at least want to have sex, is because they are in love. I am differentiating here between "loving" someone and being "in love" with someone. In the context of romance, it is this second state of affairs that primarily concerns us. For our purposes, "in love" means having romantic feelings, engaging in a romance with someone. And what exactly are romantic feelings?

> There's a fascination frantic
> In a ruin that's romantic;
> Do you think you are sufficiently decayed?
> —W. S. GILBERT, *THE MIKADO*, ACT 2

Due to the very nature of romance, it is pretty much impossible to define romantic feelings. Still, we have some clues. Ideas about romance, similar to those expressed above, tend to recur over and over—particularly in art, literature, folktales, and so on. Apparently, such mediums continually remind us, the "fascination frantic" of romance seems to require "ruin" and "decay." Moreover, the genuineness of something seems to be somehow obscured when we speak of it too romantically. This isn't quite getting at the *feel* of the thing, though. This is a job, I think, best left to Hollywood—arguably the current "expert" on romance.

To see how Hollywood—and thereby popular culture at large—conceptualizes romance, we need only trace the required plot for the mainstream romantic movie. (1) Our lovers meet, they "fall" in love. Usually, this happens more or less unexpectedly, suddenly and somewhat chaotically, not unlike Humpty Dumpty's "great fall." She drops something—an earring, let us suppose. Both our would-be lovers stoop to pick it up. Squatting there on the floor, their hands touch for the first time, their eyes meet, the violins swell and whirl. From this moment on, our lovers are lost in a gooey fog of one sort or another. They are dizzy with romance, consumed with thoughts of the romantic other. In the words of Irving Berlin, it's all "moonlight and music and love and romance"[12] at this point. (2) The plot thickens. Enter ruin and decay. There is usually a misunderstanding of one sort or another, a tragic disagreement maybe, and someone, or something, comes undone. The romance has gone sour. The violins are replaced, for the time being, with cellos and dissonant piano chords. (3) At this point, we have two options: (3a) The Romantic Comedy. After anguishing nights of loneliness, just-missed phone calls, and a few late night bar scenes, the understanding gets resolved. Romance is romance once again, violins newly swollen and whirling. What happens next? Well, we don't really know. Things tend to get resolved in about the last five minutes or so, and we are left to our imaginations as the credits roll. And let's face it: Who really wants to see the happy couple a few months later arguing about who puts away the socks on laundry day? (3b) The Romantic Tragedy. This is the decidedly less popular option. Things go from bad to worse. Maybe romantic anguish evolves into a chronic sickness of some variety—polio, let's say. He becomes a cripple, she becomes an alcoholic mother of three by a man she has never "truly" loved. They accidentally meet years later, our original lovers, in their favorite park from yesteryear. They smile sadly, part ways once again—still managing to avoid the mundane reality of the sock argument, please notice. Are they still in love? Is the fire still burning after so long a time? Couples argue this point as they exit the theater, feeling slightly gypped.

THE INEVITABILITY OF SOCK ARGUMENTS

We might stop here a minute and consider why it is that we, both individually and collectively, are so fascinated with romantic movies. It seems to me that we watch romantic movies to see what is going to happen next. In our own relationships, it seems most of us are stuck in some version of the second narrative stage. We meet someone and there are cinematic sparks and wine and candlelight. We float around in a constant daze of excitement and happiness, a foot or two above the ground. Time eventually settles in for the long haul, however, and begins to poke holes in our romantic cloud and we fall back down to earth. In reality, this fall is much more in the way of pervasive sock arguments, of course, than it is dissonant pianos and bar scenes. Maybe something specific went wrong. He slept with your best friend, she shaved her head in some experimental design. More likely, however, nothing *in particular* went awry. The romance just slowly faded, as romances tend to do, and now you are in a tense relationship wondering where all that excitement and dizziness went. You begin to wonder if you are in the market for a romantic comedy or a romantic tragedy.

According to *Merriam-Webster's Collegiate Dictionary*, "romance" tends to involve something in the way of the following: (1) a medieval tale based on legend, chivalric love and adventure; (2) a prose narrative treating imaginary characters involved in events remote in time and place and usually heroic, adventurous or mysterious; (3) a love story; (4) something that lacks basis in fact. The last one seems to say it all, doesn't it? Where there is romance, there is likely to be some kind of kooky story that lacks basis in fact. When we experience romantic feelings, we suddenly turn into some "imaginary character involved in events remote in time and place." We tend to lose track of our "real" lives for a while, that is. Sooner or later, however, reality reels us back in and we flop up on shore kicking and screaming. Turns out there was a hook inside the candy heart after all.

THE INVENTION OF ROMANCE

When we look at history, it seems that romance hasn't always been around—not in its current form, at least. Many scholars assert that, until medieval times, people got married for strategic purposes of politics and finance. As the poet, Mary Leapor, wrote, "In spite of all romantic poets sing,/This gold, my dearest, is an [sic] useful thing."[13] Sex would happen, inside—and often outside—the relationship because, well, as says evolutionary psychology, sex *needed* to happen. Gooey feelings of romantic love, being not all that practically "useful," simply weren't part of the deal. Around the 11th century, however, a new idea—new to the West, at least—of "pure desire" began to show up.

Alan Watts discusses this phenomenon of pure desire at some length in *Nature, Man and Woman*. A curious practice was spreading among the 11th-century Christians, Watts tells us, which involved the forming of odd relationships between virgin Christian girls and devout Christian men. Such relationships went so far as to allow caressing and sleeping with one another, but strictly disallowed orgasm for both parties. Why? The idea was to "store up" enough sexual energy so that a highly passionate relationship could be sustained. The virgin woman became a model of the divine. In his devoted worshipping of her, an act meant to ultimately redirect his passion toward the divine, the Christian man never allowed his desire to be satisfied or dissipated in sexual climax.

A little later, Watts says, the same idea showed up in the form of "courtly love." Here, young knights involved themselves with wives of feudal princes in a practice known as *donnoi*. Like the Christians, the practitioners of donnoi tried to create an atmosphere of "pure," or romantic, desire. Sexual energy was translated into gentlemanly and chivalrous behaviors—not to mention ambiguous, naked caressing. To actually satisfy the sexual desire directly would dirty the romance, diminish the passionate feelings of courtly love. Watts quotes a troubadour poet of the period: "He knows nothing of donnoi who wants fully to possess his lady."[14] Or, as the songwriter, Dorothy Fields wrote as recently as 1936, "A fine romance with no kisses./A fine romance, my friend, this is."[15] And so we see the continuing Western notion of romantic love being invented, or at least refined into a science, by the Christians and the knights-errant.

FANTASY, FRUSTRATION, AND WITHHOLDING

Odd as it may seem, these rather bizarre origins of romantic love significantly affect our romantic relationships to this day. As I remarked earlier, lasting romance seems to be one of those things that everyone is after but no one is finding—not for long, that is. Like the donnoi were saying, it is that *lasting* part of the romance that seems to be the tricky part. As soon as you satisfy your romantic desire, you are, quite simply, not feeling all that romantic anymore. We are not so interested in desert once we have already stuffed our bellies. This built-in paradox of romance has led us to form some pretty confusing ideas about relationships. I will outline a few of the most potentially hazardous.

To start with, there is the whole "not based in actual fact" element. We have learned to idealize our romantic partners, mentally shape him or her into whoever we want that person to be. We even go so far as to deliberately ignore contrary evidence. "He's not insensitive and disrespectful," we tell ourselves, "he just *brings a lot of passion* into his anger." "She's not really flirting with all of my friends, she's just *a very outgoing person*." We all know people who absolutely refuse to see their partner for who he or she really is.

Our cozily romantic tales tend to play out easily enough for a while, then the actual facts of the situation start to become more and more distracting. As often as not, we confuse ourselves into thinking our romantic partner must have changed somehow. "You *used to be* so passionate . . . You *used to be* so outgoing . . . What's *happened* to you?" Meanwhile, our friends are shaking their heads saying, "We've been telling you and telling you. . ." Suddenly, our lover is no longer the excitingly outlawed wife of some feudal prince, nor is she any longer some elusive goddess virgin. We have forever sullied one another by getting to know the facts, and wine and moonlight get traded in for sock folding and disputes regarding the television remote control.

Then there is the equally confusing matter of a kind of necessary frustration. If we satisfy all of our desires, we won't have the pleasure of desire anymore, right? We want to be rich, sure, but we also happen to enjoy this whole pickpocket routine immensely. So, following in the footsteps of the pioneering donnoi, we create all sorts of distance between our partner and ourselves. Maybe, like our romantic innovators, we avoid actually having sex with our partner. Truth be told, don't most of us feel a little depressed just after orgasm? We learn to avoid boredom and depression, then, by making sure those stuffed pockets remain just out of reach. Or maybe we have sex but create distance in other ways. Maybe we fight, lie, spend more time at the office, etc. After all, many a couple has often said that the best sex happens just after a fight. For that matter, we have all heard the one about absence making the heart grow fonder. So we've learned to engage in a constant push and pull of desire and satisfaction. Compulsively, we do our best to keep telling and re-telling, obsessively editing, embellishing, and revising, that same old "heroic, adventurous, or mysterious" love story—which is necessarily a tale, at some level, of deep frustration, a story of inevitable "ruin" and "decay."

On the opposite side of the coin, there is the strategy of withholding, not our own pleasure, but that of our partners. If I allow her to achieve satisfaction—through orgasm, through money-spending, a luxurious vacation, etc.—will she still be so "full of passion" for me? We learn to constantly dangle some ever-elusive prize before our romantic partners, strategically snatching it away at just the right time. It doesn't have to be directly about sex, of course. It could be something seemingly "harmless." I say I'm going to take out the trash, promise to take out the trash, but do I take out the trash? Sometimes yes, sometimes no. The "sometimes no's" are carefully timed, of course, to insure that my partner is most advantageously frustrated. Or maybe she is most likely to want sex when I'm not all that interested in it. For her to simply "give in" at the height of my sexual desire would surely be too satisfying to sustain any sort of romance. We learn to cooperate with one another, then, in this bizarre, Alice in Wonderland sort of tea party. The violins soar, the cellos groan, hands touch in the candlelight, calls are barely missed, socks lie tragically unfolded. . .

Asceticism

When it comes to sex, the ascetic motto is pretty much the same as the recent American anti-drug motto: Just Say No. If, due to unavoidable circumstances, however, you absolutely *have to* say yes, then—for God's sake—at least have the decency not to *enjoy* it! In Paul's letter to the church at Corinth, we have a more or less typical statement of this ascetic sexual strategy: "It is good for a man not to marry. . . . But if they cannot control themselves, they should marry, for it is better to marry than to burn with passion. . . . What I mean, brothers, is that the time is short. From now on those who have wives should live as if they had none" (1 Cor. 7:1–29).

This sort of thinking—sex is bad, a compelling distraction, but at least it beats burning in hell—is intricately entangled, in one way or another, with each of the world's religions. Which isn't to suggest that the most "unreligious" among us aren't also deeply affected by this ancient ascetic ideal. Regardless how we may feel about organized religion, the so-called highest values of any belief system—moral, cultural, artistic, vocational, etc.—tend to have their deepest roots in this pervasive institution. Whether we believe in a specific god, each of us wants to bring something transcendentally beautiful, something divine and "not of this earth" into our daily lives. And wherever we have people trying to bring a bit of God down to earth, bring a bit of holiness into their wordly lives, we are going to see evidence of an ascetic strategy. This strategy, unfortunately—although adaptive and useful in certain aspects—often tends toward the extreme. It can be thought of in terms of three closely interrelated elements: focus, self-restraint, and control.

Focus

The prizefighter doesn't have sex before the big fight. He believes he has only got a certain amount of energy and doesn't want to give any of it away, doesn't want to waste it. He is saving his energy for the fight, focusing all of his physical, mental, and emotional drive into this one act. To have sex before the fight would simply be making an impulsive mistake, getting distracted from the higher, or more long-term goal. In the same way, traditional Jewish culture expressly forbade the "spilling" of seed unless it was intended for the divinely sanctioned act of procreation. Proverbs 31:3 advises us, "do not spend your strength on women." In this same vein, a talented artist friend of mine tells me that it is more difficult for him to paint when he is in a sexually satisfying relationship. When he "spends" his passion in the act of sex, he asserts, there is less energy or motivation left for the artistic creation. We might see such an individual's life—whether devoted to athletics, art, or spirituality—in terms of an ongoing struggle, then, between art and sex, the mental and the physical, the spiritual and the worldly.

Although skillful focus is absolutely essential to the spiritual path, it is an idea—or a method—that is easily abused. As I have emphasized in previous chapters, skillful focus is not the same thing as *fearful avoidance*. A good many of us, due to various habitual fears, have simply yet to be altogether *on* this earth. As even the story of Christ's crucifixion suggests, before we can be truly "saved," we must fall even further, participate even more deeply in the messy and often painful ways of the material universe. The goal of concentration practice, for instance, is to cultivate a precise, laser beam like presence that can be fixed on any internal working or external task we wish to better understand or more efficiently pursue. From the practical perspective, however, such refined concentration can be used for harm just as easily as for good. Rather than deal with our many psychological tensions, for example, we can learn to simply ignore them, focusing on our breath, etc., in moments of discomfort. Although useful to a degree, such ascetic methods can be quite confusing and disadvantageous—ways of anxiously detaching us from this earth rather than genuinely helping us to transcend its innate physical limitations.

In the context of sexuality, the neurotic isn't truly focusing on higher things when he or she avoids sex. Rather, such an individual is simply disguising emotional and psychological conflicts in spiritual language, adding yet another unconscious defense to the ego's arsenal—making him or herself, ironically enough, more and more *of* the very earth he or she would transcend.

Beating the Slave, My Body

In the third chapter of Colossians, Apostle Paul lays out the "Rules for Holy Living." In essence, these rules involve this ascetic avoidance of earthly, so-called distractions in favor of our holy goal: "Set your minds on things above, not on earthly things. For you died, and your life is now hidden with Christ in God. . . . Put to death, therefore, whatever belongs to your earthly nature: sexual immorality, impurity, lust, evil desires and greed, which is idolatry" (Col. 3:2, 3:5).

We have died, then, from our original state of purity into our current state of impurity, "fallen" from grace. Unlike Jesus, we have become distracted by the woman and the snake and gone for the easy apple. The Buddha said, "The deluded, imagining trivial things to be vital to life, follow their vain fancies and never attain the highest knowledge. But the wise, knowing what is trivial and what is vital, set their thoughts on the supreme goal and attain highest knowledge."[16] The deluded among us—which is the vast majority of us, Buddha would claim—have become so far stuck in the impure earth, that we have forgotten all about our divine origins. Currently, our divinity is "hidden with Christ in God," and it is our job to find it as quickly as possible. Like Paul said, "the time is short."

Later in Corinthians, Paul uses a metaphor of a race: "I do not run like a man running aimlessly. I do not fight like a man beating the air. No I beat my body and make it my slave so that after I have preached to others, I myself will not be disqualified for the prize" (1 Cor. 9:26–27). Similarly, Buddha also instructs us how to "run": "Don't run after pleasure and neglect the practice of meditation. If you forget the goal of life and get caught in the pleasures of the world, you will come to envy those who put meditation first."[17]

Although there is obvious merit in remembering our true goal as sentient beings—the goal of ultimate self-liberation or enlightenment, that is to say—this idea of "beating our bodies" is easily taken to unhealthy extremes. The vast majority of us would do better to simply learn to enjoy our natural physical desires, learn to relax and open up in the sexual act, for instance, than we would to overly engage ourselves in Paul's "race." Unfortunately, however, as outmoded ascetic ideas habitually plague Western notions of sexuality, our collective tendencies are toward self-abuse and unnatural distancing in this arena.

To complicate things further, the majority of us don't think of ourselves as ascetics. It may not seem like we are exactly "beating our bodies" to get the prize—we may not even think we are running a race at all. When you look at the lives of most Westerners, however, particularly where our attitudes toward sexuality are concerned, we seem to be carefully avoiding concrete "lower" pleasures in pursuit of some vague "higher" goal.

Let's say you have an opposite sex co-worker with whom you are friendly. What happens when you find yourself getting "distracted" by sexual thoughts about this person from time to time? You feel somehow guilty, most likely—assuming you are even able to consciously own up to these fantasies in the first place—and feel like you are somehow disrespecting this person.

Ironically, we apply this same self-restraining, self-abusing strategy the most forcefully, and most automatically, when it comes to our own spouse, or intimate romantic partner. When we first met him or her, the sex was very passionate, but now it has somehow fizzled. We likely find ourselves entertaining fantasies of some new and exciting person, someone more of a stranger to us. It's okay to dirty these other, less intimate relationships with sexual passion, say our ascetic tendencies. It's a relatively small gamble to make. To regard my own spouse with primitive sexual lust, however—well that's just not very nice, somehow not very proper, certainly not spiritual. To do such is to confuse heaven and earth, we think, to dangerously mingle love and lust.

Due to these deeply ingrained, and mostly unconscious, ascetic leanings, we have learned to focus—more like bully, in this situation—our entirely natural, healthy sexual attraction to even our most appropriate partners into strictly "spiritual" feelings. We don't get distracted by lust, falling from the garden, because we are staying firmly glued to higher feelings of love and friendly affection. Here enters our habitual feelings of sexual dissatisfaction, a lack of true passion in our relationships. Rather than making use of genuine skillful focus in such circumstances, we are simply applying a phony self-discipline, an ignorant, self-defeating restriction to our own deserved, and much needed, pleasure.

This same unconscious ascetic strategy also plays out in ways that are less directly sexual, of course. For the ascetic, remember, *all* things earthly, which means all things physical, are distractions. On the one hand, we all want more physical pleasure in our lives—more food, sex, more stuff. On the other hand, we are also after things of a much airier sort—more knowledge, understanding, and respect. Consequently, many of us are much less likely to spend that $200 bonus on a "ridiculously" expensive meal than we are a new suit for work. The new suit is much more practical, of course, which means that it is helping us along toward a seemingly higher goal. "Maybe one day when I've taken care of all the higher goals in life," we often tell ourselves, "when I've finally retired and read all the great works of literature and mastered origami, *then* maybe I can afford to properly pursue sex and food and so forth. As for right now, no one is going to catch *me* 'beating at the air.'" Whether or not we consciously recognize it, most of us have learned to think of the body, with all its clumsy desires, as a sort of pesky husk that tends to slow us down in our race for Buddha's "supreme goal" of "highest knowledge."

CONTROL

Then there is our idea of control, intricately related as it is to our habits of defensive avoidance and timid self-restraint. That is one of the most obnoxious things about that pesky husk of a body, of course—it's not so easy to control. Wherever you find an undisciplined body, ascetic thinking goes, you are obviously going to find a morally loose person attached. Alan Watts discusses our fear of loss of control in *Nature, Man and Woman*. He relates a quotation in which St. Augustine describes a time of "pure" sexuality, before the disastrous "fall" of Adam and Eve. According to St. Augustine, our sexual organs worked rather differently back then. Males got erections by their conscious intention to impregnate their mates, not due to the heat of passion, and the whole act was an innocent matter of the human body being commanded to do what it was meant to do.

> Those members, like the rest, would be moved by the command of his will, and the husband would be mingled with the loins of the wife without the seductive stimulus of passion, with calmness of mind and with no corruption of the innocence of the body. . . . Because the wild heat of passion would not activate those parts of the body, but, as would be proper, a voluntary control would employ them. Thus it would then have been possible to inject the semen into the womb through the female genitalia as innocently as the menstrual flow is now ejected.[18]

It is okay to have an erection, apparently, as long as we have consciously *decided* to do so. It is okay to have sex—to inject the semen into the womb through the female genitalia—as long as we are being properly calm about it. As soon as we let the act become corrupted by the heat of passion, however, we might as well be wild beasties. Things are obviously no longer strictly immaterial, no longer pure spirit, at such an impassioned point. Now there are messy physical "things" with minds and feelings of their own—in short, our so-called higher selves are no longer in control.

We try to avoid, at all costs, such reminders that we are never really the owners of our bodies, never really the all-powerful CEO's of our physical corporations. In some deeply unconscious way, we are hoping that if we simply ignore the fact that our body is just as much "I" as is our mind, maybe it won't be able to betray us in the end with the ultimate act of biological freewill—death.

We apply this strategy of control most energetically when it comes to our most intimate sexual relationships. This is why many married couples complain of a lack of spontaneity in their sex lives. Sex has become part of a safe and scheduled routine, another tidy item on the program. By contrast, our most spontaneous sexual experiences have been with "flings" of one sort or another, people that, truth be told, we probably never knew all that well. With someone we barely know, after all, there is always going to be a certain degree of performance or artificiality to the act. This artificiality puts a comfortable boundary between us, allows us to remain somewhat detached so that we can play a part, assume a dramatic role. As soon as we do start to really know someone, however, to genuinely and organically connect to someone with whom we are involved in a passionate sexual relationship, it tends to make us uncomfortable. Anything approaching true intimacy—which we habitually interpret as a lack of proper ego camouflage—tends to ruin the passion all too quickly. We most likely break off the relationship for flimsy reasons and head for cover rather than be burdened by the incredible guilt and shame our spontaneous sexual natures will likely cost us.

Simply put: I control my body—or at least *imagine* that I do—to insure that my identity will remain manageable. To lose that control is, essentially, to lose my self. It is not sufficient that there always remains a self of some variety—a kind of infinitely dynamic being known more accurately as the Self—I want to make sure I own *my* self, a necessarily little self, even when this owning dramatically limits my experience as a living organism. Because even a misbehaving stomach that growls in public embarrasses me considerably, I draw a clean, neat circle around myself and sit calmly at its center, imagining that the center somehow controls the rest. From time to time, my various "members" may misbehave, but around here, *we have ways* of dealing with outlaw members. Jesus said, when speaking of lust, "And if your right hand causes you to sin, cut if off and throw it away. It is better for you to lose one part of your body than for your whole body to go into hell" (Matt. 5:30). If one of our bodies' "employees" misbehaves, that is to say, we simply fire it. If our tooth aches, we yank it out. Open the utility closet in most intimate relationships, and we are likely to find a whole heap of such dutifully severed members.

Tantra

To establish a context for understanding the specifics of Tantric Buddhism, it is useful to get a general idea of how it compares to the other Buddhist schools of Theravada, Mahayana, and Dzogchen. All these schools agree on the self-evident fact that desire is the root of suffering, but one of the fundamental ways in which these schools differ is in their particular approach to working with desire.

In the Theravada and Mahayana teachings, desire is basically a hot potato. Theravada is known as the "Path of Renunciation" because the practitioner systematically renounces, or gives up, negative habits and tendencies. For this reason, there are all sorts of rules and regulating vows in the sutras (scriptures based on the Buddha's teaching), making it a rather ascetic path.

Tantra, or the Vajrayana teachings, on the other hand, isn't quite so scared of the hot potato. Instead, Tantra believes the hot potato to be the very means to liberation itself—it just needs to be cooled down a bit before handling. Tantra works directly with our desires, encouraging them, even—although it aims to transmute them, turn the profane into the sacred. Like the alchemist, who tries to transform led into gold, the Tantric practitioner seeks to transform "impure" sexual desire into a "pure" longing to merge with the divine. For this reason, sexuality plays a crucial role in the highest Tantric practices.

In Dzogchen, the hot potato is handled *just as it is*. It is neither avoided nor cooled down. The desires are not purified in Dzogchen, they are simply allowed to run their natural course and "self-liberate." Unlike in the other Buddhist schools, there is nothing to reject or transform in Dzogchen, no formal vows or commitments required of the practitioner. Sex is not particularly utilized for spiritual purposes—nor is it particularly avoided.

SEX YOGA

In the context of this discussion, Tantra is uniquely interesting because of the emphasis it places on sexual union. Before you run out and sign up with your local Tantric master, however, you should know that there is a lot more to it than you might hope. The classic Tantric text, *Tsongkhapa's Six Yogas of Naropa*, strongly emphasizes that not just anyone should perform Tantric sexual practices. "Those wishing to engage physically in the sexual yogas should be qualified. To practice on any other basis presents great dangers. One should understand this well."[19] Now what exactly, you ask, qualifies one for the sexual yogas? To give just a sample of the required resume, both the practitioner and his or her *karmamudra* (sexual partner) should "be skilled in the *sadhana* of the mandala cycle, and mature in practicing four daily sessions of yoga. . . . they should be skilled in the sixty-four ways of sexual play as described in The Treatise on Bliss. . . . be experienced in the techniques for inducing the four blisses in general and the innate wisdom awareness in particular. . . ."[20] And the list goes on. Okay, what does that mean in English?

In the preliminary and generation stages of Tantra, the practitioner involves him or herself in all sorts of incredibly complex visualizations and guru yoga exercises. These include numerous recitations of lengthy mantras, meticulous mandala meditations, and other such intensely concentrative devotional offerings. The goal here is to begin to awaken the divine aspect within the practitioner, begin to transform his or her own body into the body of the deity.

From this point, the practitioner moves on to the completion stage yogas. The most important of these, as described in length in Lama Yeshe's *The Bliss of Inner Fire: Heart Practice of the Six Yogas of Naropa*, is the highly complex practice of *tummo*, or "inner fire." The practitioner learns to withdraw his or her energies into the central channel—the core of the subtle, or astral body, running parallel to the spine, which connects the various chakras—thereby increasing his or her store of kundalini.

Once the practitioner has learned to control these energies expertly, which is far from easy, he or she is finally ready to try out the actual sexual practice. In doing so, it is essential, according to Tsongkhapa, that the practitioner "be able to control the melted drops and prevent them from escaping outside."[21] Put simply, this means that neither practitioner has what most of us consider a normal, outwardly-directed orgasm. Instead, the orgasm is directed back into the central channel, increasing rather than depleting, the subtle body's store of sexual energy. Tantric sex yoga requires that the male practitioner doesn't ejaculate—ideally, from the perspective of Tantric writings, not ever.

TANTRA AS CONTINUITY

Tantra means, literally, "continuity." This continuity refers to an ongoing flow of a kind of universal kundalini energy. Whereas the sutras of Theravada and Mahayana are scriptures recording the verbal teachings of the historical Buddha, the Tantric teachings typically take a much less tangible form. They manifest spontaneously on the astral plane, and are then conveyed by highly-evolved individuals who are able to read them there. Similarly, sexual union is considered a continuation of this same divinely energetic flow. Tantra teaches us that sexual desire, once properly transmuted, is the desire for spiritual evolution—the very same energy that manifests as teachings on the inner, or astral planes. The more sexual desire the practitioner is able to skillfully work with, then, converting it back into its original form—which is dharma, or spiritual teaching—the more he or she is able to unify the "father bliss" and the "mother wisdom."[22] This joining of essential male and female energies is achieved, quite literally, in an ideal sexual union of Tantric practitioners.

In case it's not already obvious, what most of us mean by "sex" is very, very different from what the Tantric folk mean by "sex." Although Tantra doesn't exactly judge typical sexuality as immoral, it does caution against it. Tantra's goal is to increase sexual pleasure to its ultimate state—which is no longer exactly *sexual* at such a point—through realizing the "bliss of the inner fire," but this can only be done after years of dedicated and highly-disciplined practice. Despite its rather infamous reputation, true Tantra, like most spiritual systems, clearly distinguishes between sacred sex and profane sex, selfless desire versus selfish desire.

Just Because

Hogen, a Chinese Zen teacher, lived alone in a small temple in the country. One day four traveling monks appeared and asked if they might make a fire in his yard to warm themselves.

While they were building the fire, Hogen heard them arguing about subjectivity and objectivity. He joined them and said: "There is a big stone. Do you consider it to be inside or outside your mind?"

One of the monks replied: "From the Buddhist viewpoint everything is an objectification of mind, so I would say that the stone is inside my mind."

"Your head must feel very heavy," observed Hogen, "if you are carrying around a stone like that in your mind."[23]

This story reminds us of a rather obvious flaw with all of the preceding views of sexuality: They make our heads heavy. One of the fundamental differences between the Just Because school and all the rest, is that it doesn't try to claim sex serves any function other than, well, sex. We have sex *just because*. Of course we are all fascinated, asserts this commonsense, Zen-like perspective, by naked and semi-naked bodies of all varieties. Of course we all have "sex on the brain" eight days of the week. All the above schools, we might assert, tend to miss the whole point. They take the *sex* out of sex. They confuse "sexy" with useful, strategic, or—worse yet—simply *necessary*. As the Zen teacher was reminding the monks, however, a big stone is, first and foremost, simply a big stone.

On one level, of course, we are absolutely right. To say we have sex to resolve our oedipal complexes or even to merge with the Divine Self fails to differentiate sex from psychotherapy or meditation. As we all know, sex isn't therapy, it isn't meditation—it's sex. Still, if things were really this simple, would all of us have our various sexual hang-ups, our intricate and childish wishes, our incredibly complicated—and often quite irrational—patterns of thinking and behaving when it comes to physically intimate relationships? As I suggested at this chapter's outset, so long as we are being perfectly honest, most of us are dissatisfied with our sex life to some degree or another. If sex is really all there is to sex, then why all the confusion and resentment? Why all the guilt, anxiety, and power struggles? The Zen master's big stone isn't too hung up on being a big stone, after all. It is not sitting around feeling guilty about not being big enough, and it's not exactly trying to resist its natural desire to just sort of sit there and *be* a stone. When it comes to sex, however, it seems that most of us find it very difficult to simply let it be.

The "X" in Sex

Part of the problem is this: We tend to think of sexual desire—not to mention desire in general—dualistically. To some degree or another, each of the viewpoints we have explored describes a supposedly good way to go about sex and a supposedly bad way to go about sex. For the evolutionary psychologist, for example, good sex involves strategic sexual selection and the successful passing along of genes. For the ascetic, the best sex is no sex. Sex that involves ejaculation, is quite obviously bad sex, so far as the Tantric practitioner is concerned, and so on and so forth. Follow such and such a formula of sexual behavior, each of these schools suggests—and many of these are quite subtle and relatively holistic—and you will, without a doubt, be sexually satisfied.

None of us is exactly buying that one—not really. There is clearly something missing in each of the above discussions of sexuality. Sex, like the spiritual path, is really about relationship—how lovers relate to each other, the sacred to the profane, the wanting to the getting—and is, therefore, necessarily a rather dangerous and messy affair. As long as we are working with desire of any sort, in fact, we are going to encounter paradox after paradox.

We all know the cartoon scene where a guy walks in a room and spots the jug marked "XXX," or better yet, "DO NOT DRINK OR ELSE!" Well, what does the cartoon guy do, each and every time? He makes a beeline for the jug, of course, and chugs its contents down. Each of the preceding viewpoints is essentially trying to change the label on the alluring sex jug, or—in the case of asceticism—to get rid of the jug altogether. What the cartoon guy knows, however, is that the contents of that jug just wouldn't taste as sweet with some other label. Like the spiritual seeker, he likes the mystery, the danger, the recklessness of the illogical and paradoxical journey. To clearly mark the sex jug is, essentially, to ruin its contents.

Alongside good and bad methods of handling desire, let's add a much more elusive, well, *something*. Rather than trying to reduce sex—which is simply one conceptual way of discussing the phenomenon of all relationship, the total path of self-realization, the beginning, middle, and end of *being* itself—down to some intellectually graspable process, behavior or system, let's do our best to honor its incredibly rich mystery. The funny thing about mystery, if you can really talk about it, hold it out in the light and get a good look at it, is it was never really *mysterious* in the first place. The most exciting trapeze acts are, after all, performed without a safety net. As soon as we pour out the contents of the sex jug to have a peek, they lose their flavor. It's like trying to see what shape water has once you take it out of the bathtub. A true mystery, that is, can never be properly solved.

The best I can say at this point is this: In the same way we like to complicate the natural female form with lingerie, we like to ornament sexuality with various obstacles—as we do with all life, all relationship, all spiritual realization. Part of the problem is that there *is* no problem. Paradoxically, sexual frustration, uncertainty, and confusion seem to be the ultimate sexual fetishes, the most enticing trimmings on that impossibly mysterious and alluring tree. At the same time, however, sexual frustration and confusion are, quite simply, *frustrating* and *confusing*. That big stone is in your head, not in your head and, truth be told, probably not even a big stone in the first place. Whatever satisfying sex is, whatever true spirituality is, it manifests as something like yes, no, and maybe all at once—the Tao within the Tao within the Tao. In what follows, we will continue to solve this riddle of what I call the Bermuda Love Triangle by, well, not solving it.

THE BERMUDA LOVE
TRIANGLE

*Tzu-ch'i and Tzu-yu were discussing the sounds of the winds in the mountain
forests. Tzu-ch'i described this sound, what he calls the "piping of the earth," as
follows:*

*"In the high mountain forests there are huge trees—a hundred feet around—
ringed with cavities, holes like noses, mouths, ears. . . . When a breeze comes up
they call, 'Hooo,' and as the breezes pass they cry, 'Yoooo.' Small cold breezes
make small harmonies; whirlwinds make great harmonies. And when the great
winds pass, all the cavities and holes are filled with emptiness again. Have you
alone not heard it, not seen things wavering, quivering, only to return to rest
again?"*

*Tzu-yu said, "So the piping of the earth comes from its many holes, just as
the pipes and flutes we play come from varieties of bamboo. But may I be so bold
as to inquire about the piping of the heavens?"*

*Tzu-ch'i said, "It blows upon the ten thousand things, yet blows upon no two
the same. It permits each to become itself, each choosing to be itself. But from
whom, such a breath?"[1]*

Like all things along the path, this book ends as it began: with a riddle. We
each arise from the same source, the One Self, which nurtures each of us
from moment to moment, makes its music through us. Even so, each of us
gradually becomes himself or herself along the path, uniquely chooses to be
Who I Am. There is oneness—yet there is individuality. All of life, all of experience,
the entire spiritual journey itself, begins and ends with the play of these two energies,
the incredibly beautiful piping of their push and pull. But where does this one original source of awareness and being come from? What nurtures this original Self? Like
Tzu-ch'i asked, "But from whom, such a breath?" Such is the eternal mystery.

Even as each of us has "seen things wavering, quivering, only to return to rest again," so does our riddle come full circle. Who am I? How does this bizarre dance called life work? How am I ever going to get the goose out of the jar without breaking the jar, without harming the goose?

Who can say? Not me—certainly not the goose or the bottle, not even Chuang Tzu. Either way, it's out. For whatever reason, by whatever means, *here we are*—you and I—enjoying the piping of the heavens as the Self shapes us and molds us, as each of us shapes and molds the Self.

Round and Round the Circle

Buddhism speaks of interdependence, the self-evident truth that all things are intimately connected and related to one another. Without you, there is no me. Without the shrubs in my front yard, there is no God. Without God, there is no you, no shrubs in my front yard. Like every Zen koan, it is a logically impossible circle— yet one that even the smallest child intuitively grasps. This is the essence of love, the fundamental, self-perfected secret of IS-ness.

As I suggested at this book's outset, the most important thing as we all go round and round this paradoxical circle of being, is not "figuring it all out"—it is simply, well, going round and round the circle. As we do so, we necessarily explore relationship, an infinitely dynamic exploration that, by definition, has no ultimate end. As I come to know you, you come to know me, we come to know the Self. And just then, in that perfect moment of oneness, that singular moment of silent harmony and stillness—for no *rational* reason whatsoever—that wind starts up through the mountain forests once again, the "piping of the earth," which is also the piping of the heavens, and you and I are individuals once again, simultaneously the seeker and the sought, going round and round and round. . .

Without a doubt, the existential journey of being, the journey of I AM-ness, is a unique, indefinable one, strange beyond the furthest limits of rationality. It is at times beautiful, full of divine creativity and truth, at times frustratingly difficult and seemingly without meaning. Being as such, as we explore this ongoing circle of relating, we would do best to hold the following words of Apostle Paul steady in our hearts. Such is the deeply intuitive, universal message that holds—just barely, at times—the whole crazy dance together: "If I speak in the tongues of men and of angels, but have not love, I am only a resounding gong or a clanging symbol. If I have the gift of prophecy and can fathom all mystery and all knowledge, and if I have a faith that can move mountains, but have not love, I am nothing"(1 Cor. 13:2).

The Word Became Flesh

In the beginning was the Word, and the Word was with God, and the Word was God." So begins the Gospel of John, metaphorically retelling the creation story of Genesis, reminding us how "The Word Became Flesh." The accompanying notes in *The New International Version Study Bible* tell us that the Greeks and the Jews disagreed about what exactly *Word* meant. The Greeks used *Word* to refer to the rational principle that governs the universe—what the Taoists would call the Tao, what the philosophers like to call *logos*. The Jews, however, used *Word* to refer directly to God, to Yahweh. This is more or less where the study notes leave us—as if they have somehow clarified things.

The question that immediately arises is: What exactly is the difference between God and the rational principle that governs the universe? For that matter, John then goes on to emphasize the divinity of Jesus: "The word became flesh and made his dwelling among us. We have seen his [presumably Jesus'] glory, the glory of the One and Only, who came from the Father, full of grace and truth" (John 1:14). Regardless what the study notes might have to say on this subject, things seem to be pretty confusing. It is similar to the above situation of Tzu-ch'i's "piping of the heavens." On the one hand, we have oneness, the "One and Only." On the other hand, we have separateness—the Word, Jesus, and the Father, somehow distinct from one another. Presumably, the opening line of the Gospel of John is referencing the Holy Trinity in one way or another—Father, Son, Holy Ghost. As soon as we try to get specific and sort things out logically, however, we run into problems. Is Jesus, for example, the Word? Is he God? Is he the Word *with* God?

Whatever any Biblical scholars might want to say otherwise, this fundamental existential situation, like the content of the previous chapter's sex jug, is unclear—and necessarily so. Still, it seems safe enough to assert that John is somehow trying to call attention to the simultaneous oneness and distinctness within the Divine Being. I would suggest that this scripture is best understood as a way of describing all relationships, the relationship of the Holy Trinity included. It is not just the Holy Trinity that John is describing, that is, but the entire universe *in relation to* itself. As such, this simply isn't going to be a very logical relationship. Rather, it is one of those situations where, in Huston Smith's words, "reality can be too strange for logic to comprehend."[2] It may not be logical, but it is simple—so simple and self-evident, in fact, that we are going to find it very difficult to put into language. In the context of Plato, it's like trying to describe the color red without referencing anything red.

THE PERVASIVE PARADOX OF THREE

We could make things a little more immediate, at least, by thinking of our own ordinary relationships. On the one hand, I know I am a separate being, a person distinct from the other beings around me. Even when I am alone, that is to say, I'm still undeniably me. This is the first way of being John describes—the way of "the Word." Then there is the "withness" aspect, the way in which I can only experience myself *in relation to* other individuals. For example, I can't really fully appreciate my capacity for kindness or anger when I am all by myself, right? This is the second way of being John describes—the way in which the Word is "with" God. Lastly, and perhaps most confusing, I sometimes experience my core unity with other beings. These are the moments of true intimacy, moments in which we share a feeling or an experience with someone to the degree where each of us temporarily forgets ourself. Interestingly, such moments tend to remind us of the abstract act of relating itself, the strange space you and I would call "us." This is the third way of being that John describes—the way in which the Word "is" God. We might rephrase John's opening like this, then: In the beginning was Bob, and Bob was with Sue, and Bob was Sue. Once again, it's not so much that we have three distinct things here, so much as three distinct ways, or modes, of being.

Not surprisingly, then, when we stop a minute to consider how our minds tend to break the world down into categories, we notice we unconsciously favor groupings of three. Good, bad, neutral . . . yes, no, maybe . . . height, length, width . . . proton, electron, neutron . . . past, present, future . . . he, she, it . . . father, mother, child . . . As the opening of John suggests, we find this same tendency to understand things in triads at the core of most spiritual systems. In addition to the Christian's core idea of Father, Son, and Holy Ghost, for example, we also have Jesus, Mary, and Joseph receiving gifts from the three wise men, Jesus resurrecting on the third day, Jonah three days in the belly of the whale, and so forth. The Buddhist's have their Three Great Vehicles (Theravada, Mahayana, and Tantra), and their Three Jewels (the Buddha, the dharma, and the sangha). Toltecs have their first, second, and third attentions, their three ways of working with the known, the unknown, and the unknowable. The Hindus have their three perfections of Shiva, their three rivers of the subtle body, their three phases of the mind. I could go on, but the point is clear enough: Three seems to be a very important universal idea or structure—what Jungian psychologists might call an archetype—at the core of religion and mysticism.

The *Tao Te Ching* tells us that the "three begot the ten thousand things."[3] Okay, but what exactly are these three? Call them what you want to—Father, Son, Holy Ghost or mind, body, spirit—the names aren't so important. There are three ways of being, an elusive triangle of relationship. And we all know what can happen in certain triangles, right? How about love triangles or, better yet, the Bermuda Triangle? In such triangles, people tend to go in but don't come out. They get lost—or worse. Whether or not we typically recognize it, every time we intimately involve ourselves with someone, we are traveling inside just such a risky triangle. This is why so many of us seem to fear intimate relationships of this or that variety. Someone or something starts to get uncomfortably close to us and we ask,

"What happens when my navigation instruments fail me? What happens when my plane takes a sudden nosedive?"

From Whom, Such a Breath?

There is a certain mystical experience the Buddhists call *sunyata*. This experience tends to be realized through meditation or dream yoga, but can also be spontaneously realized through sexual intercourse, extreme pain, or any other unusually intense experience. To experience sunyata is to experience a temporary loss of self. The individual, all his or her restless desires and needs momentarily calmed, totally surrenders his or her individuality, not by consciously choosing, exactly, but because this is just what happens when all restless desire and need is momentarily calmed. When he or she "wakes up" from such a direct experience of no-thingness, back in his or her ordinary body, personality, etc., the question automatically arises: How did I end up *here* again? It is a truly wonderful and miraculous "accident," to be sure, this realization of sunyata—"but from whom, such a breath?"

Although we can't answer the "from whom" question, we can answer the "how" part. Sunyata aside, How did I end up here? How did I end up a person in a body, aware of internal and external experience? Each of us intuitively knows the answer already: Love, Truth, Awareness—such is the infinitely creative energy that spontaneously remakes us from the clear light of emptiness we dissolve into each night in deep sleep, the unseen hand that rebuilds us each morning exactly as we already are. This is the very same force that binds the proton, neutron, and electron, the same force that keeps the earth spinning on its axis, the organizing energy that motivates the very next beat of your heart, the unthinking blink of your eye. For this reason, and only this reason, you embark on the authentic spiritual path—or rather, when the time is right, this force *calls* you to the path as the sunlight calls the seedling to maturity.

To summarize our exploration so far, let's plant our awareness in three distinct vantage points, the three points of the Bermuda Love Triangle, and see what we can see.

I Am

I am a nice person . . . I am a talented mathematician . . . As we have been examining, these ready-made ways in which we tend to define ourselves are essentially statements of comparison. They have meaning only when measured against people who aren't nice, people who aren't talented mathematicians, etc. You are unlikely to respond to the question, "Who are you?" by answering, "I am an upright mammal with a very large brain." Why not? Well, although this statement does distinguish you from the rest of the animal kingdom, it fails to define you as an individual human. We have learned, rightly or wrongly, that the measure of our individuality comes from countless comparisons to other individuals.

In our triangle metaphor, this sort of relative definition is expected. You can't have a triangle with just one angle, after all. In order for that angle to have *meaning*, you have to place it in the context of two other angles. This means, mathematically speaking, that you can define any one angle by measuring the other two, right? This is more or less what we are doing when we make comparative statements about ourselves. We are trying to give our own, personal angle of awareness geometric meaning by establishing a context that involves the other two—in this case, the angles of He/She Is and We Are.

On one level, this sort of relating is just fine. You can observe how easily it jumps the tracks, though, and becomes a compulsive train wreck waiting to happen over and over again. Let's reconsider the sexual act, for example. How much energy do we spend in comparison to others? The woman has sex and there is a little tape playing in the back of her head saying, "I wonder if *he* thinks I'm as beautiful as that woman in *Playboy* magazine? I wonder if *we're* still in love?" And the man, of course, is no different. His tape loop is also spinning out of control. "Am I as good a lover as her last lover? Does *she* find me as attractive as her co-worker, Bentley? Are *we* truly passionate lovers?" Such is this constant insecurity of the I Am angle playing out, anxiously clawing about for the safety of the He/She Is and We Are angles.

When you begin to really pay attention, when you settle down—through meditation, psychotherapy, or any other means of bringing more awareness to the very subtle workings of your mental apparatus—and can watch your mind twisting and turning throughout the sexual act, you will probably be amazed at how relentless this sort of thing is. It can be absolutely exhausting. No wonder so many of us are dissatisfied with our sex lives. We are so busy comparing, so uncomfortable with the solitude and quietness of the space of pure I AM-ness, we have very little space left to simply *be ourselves* in sex.

THE WORD AS OM

If we are to truly adopt the perspective of John's "Word," however, we would assume there is some way to approach experience without all this compulsive comparison. There should be some way to simply be Who I Am without dragging in all these distractions. As John implied, the "Word" already contains everything else, every person, place, and thing of our everyday experience, so why all the anxiety and fear of aloneness? As I have emphasized time and again, we mistrust the sanctity of our own, ordinary self because we have forgotten how to truly connect to it in its entirety. We fear nothing so much as solitude, the utterly calm space of no distraction, because we are used to fragmenting ourselves into good and bad parts and identifying with some fractured aspect of ourselves. Left alone with only this internal war to occupy us, we feel as if we are losing our minds. If we are to let go of all this insecure comparing, then, we are going to have to find some way to reconnect to our whole selves.

In *Foundations of Tibetan Mysticism*, Lama Govinda discusses the sacred seed syllable OM (AH-UH-MM). In certain mystical systems, says Govinda, this sound "opens every solemn utterance, every formula of worship, every meditation."[4] For such a system, this is, literally, the original Word. What does this seed syllable mean? It means, quite simply, OM. As Lama Govinda describes it, "OM is the primordial sound of timeless reality, which vibrates within us from the beginningless past and which reverberates in us. . . . It is the transcendental sound of the inborn law of all things, the eternal rhythm of all that moves, a rhythm, in which law becomes the expression of perfect freedom."[5] OM is the totality of the Self, your own self in all its fullness. Before OM does you much good, of course, you have to be able to hear it.

If you have yet to work with the mantra OM, I would suggest you try out an experiment. Find somewhere calm and quiet and make yourself comfortable. Take a few deep breaths and relax. Sound this mantra externally a few times, however feels most natural to you. After you have really got the sound of it, the physical vibration of it, allow it to sound internally, or mentally. It's not really something that you have to make happen—it's already happening. Like Lama Govinda said, this sound has been vibrating within us from the "beginningless past." If you can calm your mind enough to really listen deeply, go in past all your various worries and compulsive anxieties, you can hear OM turning over and over at your center of awareness. It is a definite sound, but it is also a kind of feeling, a kind of mysterious movement within space.

As you begin to hear this inner, energetic vibration more and more clearly, turn your attention outward once again. As you listen to the wind outside, cars passing along the streets, children playing, you start to recognize OM in those sounds as well. Each and every one of those sounds, you begin to notice, is really composed of tiny little beads of OM strung together in various intricate ways. If you can really hear it, you can also start to *see* it. Watch the sunlight through the blinds, the flicker of a candle, and it's the same thing all over again. Sound and movement are one— wave upon wave of the original "inborn" Word.

LOSING YOURSELF TO GAIN YOURSELF

When asked to define himself, God said simply, "I AM that I AM." We could abbreviate this even further to simply, "I AM." Say this over and over like a mantra and you will notice it begins to sound a lot like OM. Coincidence? Once again, listen deeply, deeply within the heart of any moment and you will hear every cell and thought of your person vibrating with this original Word of OM-ness or I AM-ness. This Word is God, is your own, moment-to-moment awareness. Listen at the moment of orgasm, the moment when you awake each morning, the moment of your most intense anger or joy, and you will hear it arising out of nothing, returning to nothing.

In addition to working with the mantra OM, you can try out another very simple exercise. Take a few moments each day and try to see yourself in the world around you. Notice how both your friends and enemies reflect aspects of your own personality. Assume that those qualities you most admire in others, along with those characteristics that most annoy you, are simply external manifestations of your own internal state. Similarly, the natural world is a vast mirror reflecting your own nature. Drops of rain trickling down a window pane, a summer breeze—these are, quite literally, the movements of your own mind. Even an ordinary chair, as it turns out, is truly still only when your mind is truly still. Learn to look deeply, past all the surface constructions and concepts we fasten to the external world like guardrails and see if this is true. Relax your gaze into that ordinary chair and watch its subtle wobble, watch it breathing along with you. To truly be yourself is, quite simply, to be the entire universe experiencing itself from the unique vantage point of your individual self.

As you learn to better recognize yourself in everything internal and external, you begin to appreciate a beautiful, ongoing process of merging and separating—the very rhythm of life itself. In those moments where you hear yourself or see yourself most clearly, even the process of hearing and seeing becomes a manifestation of OM. In such moments you truly lose self-consciousness and you merge, dissolve back into the One. It happens countless times in every minute if you can only learn to recognize it. And at the same time, there is an ongoing process of separating. You begin to notice, and appreciate the exotic uniqueness of, those moments in which you fail to recognize yourself in your infinite internal and external form. Rather than needing to chastise yourself for losing "presence," however, you enjoy such moments equally. In reality, you come to realize that you are just as present in these moments as you are in any other. It is like the artist who becomes so engrossed in painting that, if asked, couldn't tell you the color of the shirt he was wearing in that moment, or even what color he was just using.

He/She Is

Whereas in the previous section I encouraged you to connect to the totality of the Self through the vantage point of the "Word," here I will emphasize the vantage point of the Word "is" God. Bob is no longer just Bob, and he is not simply with Sue—he is Sue. We've just had a go at connecting to the ways in which Bob necessarily contains Sue—the ways in which you somehow contain every aspect of your external experience—so now we will flip this vantage point upside down, take a look at the ways in which Sue contains Bob. We are going to connect to the whole through the unique perspective of the so-called other guy—the angle of He Is, She Is. This journey can be a little trickier, of course, as each of us feels less directly attuned to He Is-ness or She Is-ness than we do I Am-ness. Such is the nature of being an individual, after all. To illustrate the peculiar dilemma of this angle of exploration, we can turn to the 17th century's father of modern philosophy, René Descartes.

THE CARTESIAN DILEMMA: CAN WE EVER REALLY KNOW SOMEONE ELSE?

In Descartes' *Meditation on First Philosophy*, he sets out to distinguish between knowledge that is "completely certain and indubitable," and knowledge that is "in some respects doubtful."[6] Descartes begins with the observation that everything he knows, or *thinks* he knows, seems to be "received either from the senses or through the senses."[7] So it goes with our friends Bob and Sue. What does Bob know about Sue? Well, he knows she is a brunette, for one thing, and he also knows she is a very caring person. *How* does Bob know? Simple. By using his physical senses. His vision tells him that Sue is, quite obviously, a brunette. Similarly, he knows her to be caring because he has seen and heard her manifesting nurturing behaviors. In this sense, "Bob is Sue" means that Sue is merely an object with which Bob interacts in his own mind. Because Bob's senses happen in his mind, and because everything Bob knows about Sue comes from his senses, Sue is really more "in here" from where Bob sits, than she is "out there."

Already, Descartes says, we have got a bit of a problem. Knowledge that comes from the senses is, by definition, open to doubt because the senses themselves are imperfectly reliable. He offers three primary criticisms of sensory knowledge. First, we know our senses can deceive us. Descartes offers the example of a stick appearing bent in water when, in reality, it is actually straight. For that matter, how about the "objects in mirror are closer than they appear" phenomenon? Simple daily observation confirms that our senses, quite often, misreport certain features of the material world.

Second, Descartes says, we could be dreaming. Even if my senses are reporting accurately, how can I know that they are not simply describing some invention of my own imagination? Just because I can seemingly test the world around me with my five senses in no way disproves I'm simply sleeping, interacting with my own unconscious. That is what *makes* it the unconscious in the first place, after all—the fact that it remains fundamentally hidden from me. Philosophers call this criticism the argument from illusion objection (see page 191).

Third, in a slight variation of this argument from illusion objection, Descartes offers the idea of an "evil deceiver." Put simply, Descartes' brain might be wired wrong, some evil deceiver may have created him with malicious intent. Every time Descartes thinks he is seeing red, for instance, he may actually be seeing green. The fact that he can confirm some object's "redness" by comparing his observations with those of other individuals proves nothing. These other individuals might simply be the product of Descartes' own malfunctioning brain.

Descartes' conclusion, then, is that everything he thought he has known so far has actually been based on doubtful observations. So far as Bob can tell, there may not be a "real" Sue out there anywhere at all. So far as Bob only knows Sue through his senses, at least, Sue may very well be a product Bob's own fertile imagination. For that matter, even if there is a real Sue, Bob can never be certain he is accurately perceiving her. Every time he turns his back, for instance, seemingly kind Sue may be sharpening her favorite kitchen knife with a villainous smile on her lips.

TESTING, TESTING...

Before we are too quick to say, "Yeah, *but* . . . " meaning, okay, but for all *practical* purposes, Bob obviously knows Sue is real—we should pause a minute. I would suggest that some of the most recurrent problems in any relationship stem from this same fact of the basic uncertainty of our senses. We fear, in a very deep way, that the other person isn't really "out there." Fearing we may be all alone, and are merely dreaming up the entire external world to distract us from this feeling of intense loneliness, we keep running various sorts of tests. We keep running misguided experiments, albeit unconsciously, hoping to prove the external reality of the other person. One of the most ironic of these tests is what I call the "provoking contrary behavior" test.

The reasoning behind this test goes like this: If I am somehow inventing Sue in my own mind, I would expect her to behave only as I would wish her to, right? I know that I don't want anyone screaming insults at me, for instance, so to the degree that Sue does this, I can be confident of her own, individual or concrete reality. To the degree that she behaves contrary to my own wants, then, I paradoxically feel more secure in our relationship. This would offer some insight into the compulsive patterns we play out with other people. The more intimate we become with someone, the more we start to panic, fearing we have somehow been misled by Descartes' evil deceiver and are simply interacting with our own mental fantasies. What do we do? We start to provoke this other person, try to manipulate him or her into behaving exactly opposite the way we think we would have that individual behave.

This never works, of course. We only need to observe our own bodies for a day or so to see where this strategy goes wrong. My stomach, for instance, is very much a part of me. In the same way that Sue is Bob, my stomach is me. Can I correctly assume, then, that my stomach will only behave as I want it to? Obviously, no. How many times does your stomach decide to manifest a so-called contrary behavior and growl at the most inopportune times? Does this prove your stomach, then, is somehow a separate entity "out there?" Obviously, just because Sue acts against my will, then, it doesn't prove that she is separate from me. It simply suggests that she may very well be a part of me, like my stomach, of which I don't yet have full awareness or conscious control.

Another test we like to run is what I call the "fixed characteristic" test. We have seen how our imagination works—in dreams, fantasies, and creative activities—so we know it tends to be a very fluid instrument. Mental images and ideas, stuff that is strictly "in here," tend to shift seamlessly into one another like the colors and shapes of a kaleidoscope. For this reason, we like the other person in our relationships to manifest certain characteristics in a very stable way. The more he or she changes, particularly in some abrupt and unpredictable manner, the more we fear he or she lacks concrete, material substance. Bob doesn't want Sue to suddenly gain fifty pounds. Is this simply because Bob is a jerk? Maybe. More likely, however, Bob is simply insecure. He wants Sue to stay *reliably* Sue. Similarly, Sue wants Bob to hug her every day when he gets home from work. Is Sue simply needy? Possibly. On a deeper level, however, she is probably seeking proof of Bob's fundamental "Bob-ness." She wants Bob to remain, in some objectively measurable respects, a fixed point of reference "out there" so she can be certain that she is not simply dreaming him.

Needless to say, this one doesn't work either. People inevitably change—such is one of the ways in which we can tell the difference between a person and a mannequin. At the very least, even for that rare person who doesn't look a day older at 60 than at 20, he or she is still going to change to the degree that his or her body simply no longer functions. This is, of course, the fundamental change which so disturbs most of us. Consequently, when those close to us die, we begin to question the meaning of It All, reconsider the fundamental nature of reality. "Is there *really* a God, or is that simply an idea in my own head?" we anxiously ponder. "Is life just some dirty trick being played on me? Am I going absolutely crazy?"

THE CERTAINTY OF SUCHNESS

If everything we know about someone comes through our imperfect senses, and if our strategies to test for reality outside of those senses necessarily fail us, can we really ever *know* a person? Descartes offers an example that would suggest we can. He asks us to consider a piece of wax just taken from the honeycomb. Our senses tell us that this wax is hard and cold with a lingering flavor of honey. As we melt this wax, however, it becomes warm and liquid, and the honey flavor disappears. In short, all of the original sensory information about the wax has changed. We might say that the old wax has physically "died." Even so, I know somehow that the same wax still remains. "So what was there in the wax," asks Descartes, "that was so distinctly grasped?"[8] There seems to be some sort of knowable essence of a thing, what the Zen folks call "suchness" or "thusness," outside of its sensory particulars, but what is it exactly? Sue can get tattooed, drunk, shave her head, and lose a limb, but she is still, undeniably, recognizably Sue. But how?

This is where the famous Cartesian *cogito* makes its dramatic entrance: "I think, therefore I am."[9] Descartes says it a little differently in his *Meditations on First Philosophy*: "Thus, after everything has been most carefully weighed, it must finally be established that this pronouncement 'I am, I exist' is necessarily true every time I utter it or conceive it in my mind."[10] In our context, we might say that Descartes is recognizing the original Word present in himself. He is essentially commenting to his own undeniable OM-ness or I Am-ness. After all, even if he is being deceived by his senses, he is still *being* either way. This knowledge of I Am-ness, says Descartes, is not a sensory knowledge. Rather, it is a "clear and distinct" understanding given Descartes by the "light of nature."[11] Sound familiar? It is more of a deep feeling or intuition than it is a sensory experience, claims Descartes—what the Tibetans call "the clear light of the natural mind."

Okay, but what about Sue? Bob can be certain Bob exists, but how can he be certain Sue also exists? This is where Descartes applies a kind of circular logic for which he is often criticized. He concludes, more or less, that since this undeniable feeling of the "light of nature" is present alongside the undeniable fact of his existence, *anywhere* this clear feeling is present, there must be some undeniable truth. For Descartes, this undeniable feeling is equally present when he considers the Am-ness of God, so God must be real. We are not going to worry so much about God just now, however, as we are still working on Sue. How can Bob experience this same indubitable feeling of OM-ness in Sue?

The answer is quite simple: love. Sue becomes unquestionably real to the degree that Bob loves her. In this Cartesian context, I don't mean exactly the same thing most of us usually mean when we use the word "love." The sort of love I am talking about goes much deeper—the total empathy that you sometimes feel for another person that makes you forget all about your own concerns, complaints, accomplishments, etc. Momentarily, you so connect to that person's unique vantage point in the universe that you literally see things through his or her eyes. What perfect love or empathy really is, then, is the ability to let go of your own rigid boundaries so that you can essentially feel the other person's I Am-ness from his or her own perspective. Ironically, the more you connect to another individual's I Am-ness, the more you realize it's not really different from your own I Am-ness. For that matter, you begin to appreciate God's I Am-ness is no different from my own daily awareness.

EXERCISES IN OTHERNESS

Obviously, we are not contemplating an intellectual phenomenon here. It's a core, existential process that is deeply intuitive and emotive. As such, you can only authentically understand the angle of He Is or She Is through direct experience. To this end, I offer two simple exercises.

■ *Remembering the Other:* Think of someone close to you. Recall some past interaction with this person, the more intense the better. As you recall this interaction, you will no doubt get distracted by all your own feelings and thoughts surrounding this situation. Although these are perfectly legitimate, they are simply not within your current focus. You are after the vantage point of He Is or She Is, remember—

not I Am. Setting your own experience aside, then, you can try to tune into this person's experience.

Using his or her body language, personal history and verbal communication as pointers, you can dive in deep to this recollection and try to really feel this individual from the *inside*. The more you do so, no doubt, the more persistent your own feelings will arise as distractions. Once again, you can gently set these aside and return to your object of focus—just as in concentration practice. When you have truly connected to this person's experience, you will know. When your focus has been intense enough, you will arrive at the place in which you understand the feeling of I Am-ness doesn't belong to anyone in particular. We all share it equally, regardless of our intelligence, so-called moral standing, or any other individual characteristics.

Being the Other

Using this same person, or some other person that you are close to, focus on his or her experience as intense situations arise in the present. Whether this person's feelings manifest as happiness about some recent accomplishment or good news, or even anger toward you personally, try to meet him or her in this inner space. Once again, your own experience will repeatedly distract you, so keep returning to your focus. Interestingly, once you have legitimately sat where that person sits, even this individual's feelings of anger toward you will no longer disturb you. Experienced from the inside out, that is to say, such feelings don't really *feel* aggressive. Rather, once you can truly see beyond yourself, you recognize these feelings to be nothing other than the universal fire of I Am-ness, Descartes' "light of nature," burning brightly like a flame in a colored glass.

Do unto Sue

The preceding exercises will readily call attention to your habits of judgment and competition. As long as you have a list of rules or expectations about how another person *should* be, you begin to recognize that you are simply not going to be able to experience his or her own "light of nature" so directly. This is the difference between conditional and unconditional love. As you give up your right to demand this or that behavior of another person, you come to experience that person as he or she truly is—which means you come to experience your own self as you truly are. Since Bob is Sue, the more limits he places on who Sue is allowed to be, the more limits he is placing on his own being. He is simply limiting the ways in which he is willing to experience himself, refusing to look at his own face in certain mirrors of awareness.

We Are

Here is where things really start to get sticky. In the beginning there was Bob, and Bob was with Sue . . . It is this whole "with-ness" aspect of being that tends to make this vantage point seem much more unsettled than the other two. In the first perspective we examined, the angle of I Am, our ultimate goal is rather clear: to see ourselves in everyone and everything. Similarly, the angle of He Is or She Is, points in a relatively clear direction. We are learning, through our cultivation of selfless love and empathy, to see everyone in ourselves. Both of these paths, or angles of approach, then, provide us with a relatively clear map of progress. In one way or another, we are logically proceeding from a restricted place of awareness, a place of selfishness we could say, to a much larger experience of being, a realization of one-ness. We could graphically depict this relatively logical journey as follows:

BOB
I AM

(progress)

BOB IS SUE,
HE/SHE IS

It may not be an easy journey, but it appears to be a clearly mapped one. Wherever we find ourselves along this path, we glimpse our destination in the distance and understand our basic travel route..

The problem here is that what we are really after isn't a straight line—we are after a triangle. As soon as we add in this element of "withness," this angle of We Are, our journey gets much more confusing. It is no longer a linear journey at all, in fact. Now, in the words of Chuang Tzu, we are going two ways at once. We are still heading for oneness, sure, but now we are also heading for individuality, distinction. Apparently, if any of these angles are to have complete geometric meaning, they must all stand in relation to one another.

This third way of being, the way of "withness," is, by definition, quite difficult to describe. No graphic or logic of any sort can really capture the essence of this perspective. Even so, in the hopes that we may be able to point a finger at what is already there in each of us individual awareness, we can look at some other familiar triads, see how this third angle provides a new context for the whole paradoxical journey. As we shall see, every triad contains a sort of "odd man out," which both confuses matters and supplies that triad's fundamental meaning. The Russian mystic, Gurdjieff, called this strange phenomenon—a process in which "the higher blends with the lower in order to actualize the middle"—the "Law of Three."[12] The following are examples of this paradoxical law.

SEXUALITY: THE NECESSARY FRUSTRATION OF PASSION

Furthering the last chapter's discourse, we can explore the triad of being implied by the sex act. Each time we have sex, we set out from the point of being relatively disinterested in sex, point A, and gradually arrive—ideally, at least—at the point of orgasm, point B, the point of satisfaction. In and of themselves, point A and point B don't cause us that much grief. They make perfect sense to our logical, progress-oriented minds. Somewhere along the way, however, we always encounter that frustrating point C. Maybe in the middle of sex we think, "If only, just this once he would. . . " Or maybe we disapprovingly notice those few extra pounds she has gained. Maybe, for a moment here and there, we feel guilty, ashamed, self-conscious, angry, bored, physically strained—pick your favorite distraction. Ironically, I would suggest that if the act of sex moves perfectly smoothly from start to finish, progresses orderly without various "tangents," it's not really sex at all. It's more like reading a travel brochure than a novel, that is to say, more like watching a Christmas tree than a movie. Like Woody Allen said, it's not good sex if it's not dirty.

To better understand how this aspect of necessary frustration comes into play, we can consider the circumstances in which we first begin to develop sexual feelings. As Freud noted, both male and female children show obvious physiological signs of arousal when they begin breastfeeding. He calls this phase of sexual development the oral erotogenic stage. At this stage, Freud says, the child naturally associates sexual desire with the desire for oral consumption. Obviously, this same association, albeit more or less unconscious, follows us into adulthood. How often, for instance, have we heard someone say, "I love you so much I want to eat you up?" For that matter, how often do we find ourselves substituting food for sex or affection? On some level, we quite literally want to eat our sexual partners up. This is where the frustration comes in. We have a primitive desire to somehow consume our lover alongside a more mature desire to be *with* him or her. Obviously, it has got to be one or the other. Once again, we are faced with the familiar "can't have your cake and eat it too" situation.

As with all triads of being, to engage in lovemaking in a truly and deeply passionate way, then, involves a kind of desperation, a kind of impossible desire. We have to urgently want that person without ever really "having" him or her. We are simultaneously heading in opposite directions from the start, racing along our opposing roads of progress toward oneness and we-ness at exactly the same rate. Not only are we simultaneously heading for two different destinations, as it turns out, we are never really going to reach either of them. To paraphrase Ramana Maharshi, when speaking of the spiritual journey, there is no path, no liberation.

You can't set someone free if he is not already in prison, right? We like to pretend we are in jail, spiritually or sexually speaking, simply because we enjoy it. Once again, we dance this amazing and strangely beautiful dance of gradual "liberation" because we are, first and foremost, dancers. Each and every one of us is an artist, a director, and we keep playing our movie over and over, tinkering with endless variations and permutations.

Even so, there are those among us who have worked out the many kinks of this dance to the point where they simply don't need to engage themselves in this sort of ambivalence anymore. Having fully accepted the necessary frustration of sex and every other manifestation of that elusive point C, they have learned to so completely dissolve their egos into this mysterious third force that they are beyond such notions as progress, frustration, etc. At such a point, sex is no longer of particular interest to these individuals—nor is any other situation or activity in particular. Rather, such a person simply *is* from moment to moment, perfectly peaceful and content with the indescribable suchness of existence.

STORY: THE AESTHETIC OF CONFLICT

This is the beginning, middle, and end triad. Every story, after all, is supposed to have each of these three elements. The beginning and end are easy enough for our conceptual minds to grasp, implying as they do a more or less linear journey. If there is to be a proper story at all, however, we have got to have a conflict somewhere along the way—most typically, in and around that slippery narrative twilight called "the middle." Even if this conflict gets resolved perfectly in the end, there is simply no way around the inevitable experience of frustration present in the middle. Moreover, to judge the middle strictly from the viewpoint of the end isn't really fair—it makes for a rather boring story, at the very least, like rereading a murder mystery. A compelling story, that is to say, requires a convincing tug-of-war between tension and release. In this context, to really *be* in the middle, means to be frustrated. To be truly *in the middle of things*—genuinely and openly invested in this or that outcome, that is, despite the many obstacles and general messiness whatever story has naturally accumulated—means that we don't yet appreciate that there is a tidy resolution on the way. In that singularly tense moment—Will she leave me? Did I pass the exam? Is the boss about to fire me?—we hope, we hold our breath, we grip the edge of our seats. . . . We are, quite simply, fully alive and participating in the organic universe.

The sex act is one version of this familiar story—as is the spiritual path. If we are going to truly enjoy these journeys, if we are going to really put our whole being into the existential game, we have simply got to learn to appreciate the artistic merits of frustration. It is not that we learn to adopt some sort of self-punishing attitude, of course, but that we learn to more fully and courageously appreciate the story of life, the bizarre tale of being. We discover ourselves in conflict after conflict throughout this tale, many of them quite exotic and intricate, because we enjoy the inimitable thrill of resolution, the joy of release. Once again, we love this story of being—not despite its inherent conflict—but because of it.

At the same time, certainly highly evolved individuals have transcended the need for conflict altogether. The entirety of the so-called story is present at every narrative twist and turn for such individuals. As such, they are beyond time, beyond the ordinary plots of the everyday struggle of being. They no longer require that obstacles be encountered, nor do they need to get any dilemmas "worked out." They are not exactly opposed to such things, nor do they describe them as unpleasant, they simply no longer require the emotional drama that so compels the majority of us. They have realized the state of constant satisfaction, the state of peaceful stability, which no longer defines itself in terms of change, no longer relies upon the push and pull of having and not having.

PREFERENCE: THE PARADOX OF THE UNDESIRABLE

In this much-beloved triangle of being, we see the world primarily in terms of its relation to our wants and needs. We perceive the world as a collection of more or less stagnant things—kind of like a cosmic shopping mall—which we desire on a continuum from "very much" to "not at all." Depending on how easily these various things are obtained, and how pleasantly we experience their immediate effects, we rank them as good, neutral, or bad.

Take a minute to mentally list items belonging to each of these categories for you personally, and you will notice a certain structure or pattern holding the whole cosmic shopping mall together. On the most automatic, knee jerk level, your lists will verify, good means things that are relatively rare or particularly hard won. You work and you work and *finally* you receive that promotion at work. If you got one every day, notice, it wouldn't be such a grand affair any longer, no longer a cause for celebration. That promotion is so rare because it is expensive, meaning it requires a substantial investment of time, energy and emotion. Similarly, let's suppose you win the lottery. It probably didn't exactly require an enormous amount of effort on your part, but such a feat is so incredibly rare—almost to the point of logical impossibility—that it is highly valued, nonetheless. The so-called best things in life, then, are those things we most strongly prefer and, due to their expense, rarity, etc., most infrequently get.

Neutral things happen, quite simply, because they *need* to happen. For most of us, going to the toilet or drinking a glass of water would be a neutral activity, as would be breathing, sleeping, etc. By definition, neutral things happen all the time, and require little investment on our part. They are not exactly newsworthy, such events, but they involve little conflict. If a feeling of great satisfaction accompanies the realization of good things, a simple recognition of functionality seems to accompany the fulfilling of neutral wants and needs. As such, we tend to think of neutral activities, experiences, and situations as means to more or less pass the time between more obviously good things. They are so pervasive, in fact, happening everyday anywhere and everywhere around us, that we tend to overlook them.

Bad things, however, seem to reside in a category all their own. They represent the exact negation, in fact, of our wants, wishes, and needs. If good things are enthusiastically desired, neutral things are dutifully tolerated. We can appreciate the necessity of good and neutral aspects of our lives easily enough. We tend to think of our lives as a linear journey, an accumulation of better and better things, slowed only by our necessary trafficking of, well, necessary things. Bad things, however, seem to throw a nasty wrench into the works. An obnoxious boss, rain on our wedding day, the flu, a serial killer—these are all bad because they complicate things, get in the way of our habitual goals and desires. Unlike neutral things, which seem to merely slow us down in the pursuit of our goals, bad things have a tendency to turn those very goals on their heads. As such, bad things hang out around that pesky point C in our triangle. They remain dark, mysterious, unpredictable, likely to pop up at any moment and frustrate our would-be orderly progress from point A to point B. Our cognitive habit of preference, then, is simply our belief that the primary goal of experience is a logical one: to collect good things, tolerate neutral things and avoid bad things.

At the same time, however, good, bad, and neutral naturally interpenetrate one another. We all recognize that good things are best appreciated when we have been stuck in a particularly bad situation, right? For example, for whom is winning the lottery a greater good: a rich man or someone living in abject poverty? As I have emphasized again and again, our experience of good necessarily arises from our experience of bad. Our pervasive tendencies to prefer this over that, him over her, me over you, is fundamentally misguided. We can think of bad experiences as the incredibly fertile soil from whence good things grow. The ultimate pursuit of happiness and satisfaction necessarily includes the pursuit, or at least sincere acceptance of, unhappiness and frustration. Ironically, it is nothing other than our deeply entrenched preferences that keep us from realizing this ultimate pursuit.

Individual preferences aside, without this constant juggling of opposites, life would simply be lukewarm, a necessary trip to the bathroom. Moreover, once we begin to truly appreciate this paradox, even those routine trips to the bathroom start to seem more and more interesting. Herein lies the inimitable mystery of point C, the ever-elusive and subtle craft of so-called tangents. Venture deeply enough, and fearlessly enough, into the unknown realms of point C, and you realize there are really no such existential creatures as good, bad, or neutral—a state of affairs which is good, which is not so good, which is well beyond, beneath, and within concepts such as good and not so good.

Desire

At this point, we could represent our situation like this:

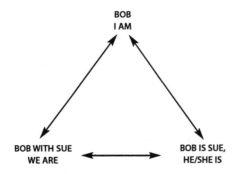

Now every point of our triangle is connected to every other point by two-way arrows. These arrows no longer exactly represent progress, however, as it is not entirely clear anymore where Bob and Sue are heading. There is still movement, to be sure, only this movement has some other, less easily definable motivation. We could call the force that propels Bob and Sue from one point to another love, desire, compassion, frustration, emptiness, desirelessness—just about anything will do. All these names fall short, however, as this motivating force is the Tao itself, which defies all labels and categories.

Even so, as I have been emphasizing the role of desire throughout these pages, we can consider the force that propels Bob and Sue along, the essential glue that makes the triangle a triangle, to be this paradoxical phenomenon. Because of this pervasive energy of wanting, Bob and Sue are all over the place, their triangle never sitting still for a single moment. Ram Dass' silent teacher was describing this same pervasive force when he wrote the following on his teaching slate: "Desire is a trap. Desire-lessness is Moksha (liberation). Desire is the creator. Desire is the destroyer. Desire is the universe."[13]

As a summary, in consideration of this singular force, which is at the core of all relationship, which both creates the spiritual path and distracts us from it, I would like to suggest two seemingly contrary methods of harnessing desire: skillfully restricting it and fully embracing it.

SKILLFULLY RESTRICTING DESIRE

To better understand desire by skillfully restricting it, you can begin by choosing one behavior that you would like to change. Let's say you overeat. You simply decide to not overeat as a kind of concentration practice. Every time you notice the desire to overeat, you return to your object of focus: eating healthily. In one way or another, this restriction of desire tends to be the preferred method of most spiritual systems, as well as civilization in general. If you can employ this method with sufficient focus, you will notice a couple of quite interesting things.

First, you can't really get *rid* of desire; you can only displace it onto something else. You resist your urge to overeat, but what do you do instead? Could be anything—drink a glass of water, read a book, whatever. No matter what you do instead, there is still *desire* doing its thing. Maybe you are more comfortable with some manifestations of desire than others. There is nothing wrong with that, of course—so long as you understand that your attachment to not overeating is, well, your *attachment*. In and of itself, that is to say, there is nothing more "spiritual" about not overeating than there is overeating. The more you work with desire the more you appreciate this ironic fact. Eventually, you reach a point where you simply do what you do—not because you think you are exactly "getting somewhere," not because you are doing spiritual practice—just because that is what *you* do. That's what desire does. It is both an infinite "creator" and a "trap."

Second—and this is one of the craziest aspects of the whole dance—you are simply not going to "give up" certain desires until you *desire* to. Can you see how this works? As we examined in the first chapter, your very attempts to give up desire necessarily create more desire! Even so, if you have decided to quit overeating—or to restrict the manifestation of your habitual desires in any other skillful way—there is still a valuable lesson to be learned in resisting your desire to overeat. This is the only way, after all, you can really begin to appreciate how beautiful, ridiculous, sacred, frustrating, etc., desire is. You create a little friction. You struggle and struggle to resist this and that desire and then it hits you: Why bother working so hard? Desire is desire is desire, so why not just sit back and let myself happen? If you understand this self-evident existential fact, you understand it. If you don't, then you are going to have to learn to work with your desire by "limiting" it sooner or later.

FULLY EMBRACING DESIRE

Ironically, the more difficult—and ultimately more effective—way to work with desire is by fully embracing it. Simply decide, for example, that you intend to do anything and everything you want today. Anything that crosses your mind, however whimsical, immoral, etc., you intend to act on. As with the above practice, if you can pursue this one with sufficient focus, you will notice a couple of interesting things.

First, every desire has a kind of counter-desire. Let's say you have a thought flash through your head: I want to kill my boss. Well, immediately thereafter, you are going to have another thought flash through your head: I also want to be a good person, and good people don't kill their bosses. So which desire wins out? Whichever one is stronger, quite simply. Once you can really see desire for what it is, you realize that you don't somehow get extra points for doing the so-called right thing—that is just your thing, after all, your attachment. What really makes any given behavior right for you, is your ability to pursue it from a space of direct perception, a place of liberated awareness that verifies your actions are no better or worse, no more or less sacred than those of any other being. This is the state of harmony, the state where you happen, your life happens, but there is no central command tower struggling to make all the right decisions.

Second, the moment you have truly committed yourself to acting on your every passing desire, you realize that you have already been doing this all along. You have never shoplifted, for instance, but why not? Well, as we examined in the counter-desire, you probably have never—by definition—really wanted to. There are people who really want to shoplift, of course. For such individuals, this desire to shoplift simply wins out over its accompanying anti-shoplifting desire. Once you can truly comprehend this situation, you no longer fear "letting yourself go," because you recognize that you have already *gone*. Like every other being in the world, each of us does exactly as he or she wants to—or, to be more "spiritual" about it, exactly as the Self wants each of us to. To genuinely recognize and accept this essential truth is to transcend self-importance, to go beyond selfishness. It is all the one Tao relating to the one Tao, after all—which is what we have really been examining through our Bermuda Love Triangle metaphor all along.

No Corners

The perfect square has no corners. . . .
The greatest form has no shape.[14]

As you become increasingly skilled at working with desire through either of the desire-working paths, you begin to recognize the ultimate irony more fully: They are the same path. Limiting desire, embracing desire—these are just two names for the same process. What is this process? You can call it living, loving, being, creating—none of these words really says anything other than, "I do what I do, you do what you do." The more each of us can see Who We Really Are, the safer we feel meeting one another in this shared, sacred space in which ranking simply doesn't apply. As it turns out, there are no winners or losers, spiritually speaking—there are just dancers doing whatever dance they have to do, get to do, just now.

Try to keep an open mind when dealing with these seemingly conflicting approaches to understanding desire. Rather than jumping to conceptual or theoretical conclusions, try out one of the practices I've described and see for yourself. Learn to watch how your own mind works with desire on a day-to-day basis, observe it coming and going from one form into the next, continually emerging and dissolving into one behavior after another. In those moments when you can see desire for what it is, fully accept your own desires—just as they already are—as well as those of other individuals, along with the natural and seemingly unnatural laws of the world around you, a curious thing happens: the Bermuda Love Triangle mysteriously disappears—it swallows itself. Words like desire, love, and relationship no longer mean anything. Being everywhere and in everything, they become redundant. In such moments, the Bermuda Love Triangle takes it true form, which is beyond the grasp of the conceptual mind.

A Zen Love Story

A monk told the Zen master: "I have just entered the monastery. Please teach me."

"Have you eaten your rice porridge?" the Zen master asked.

"I've eaten it," the monk replied.

The Zen master said: "Then you had better wash your bowl."

And at that moment the monk was enlightened.[15]

The spiritual path, like your daily life, can often seem overwhelming. There is so much to do, it often seems, so much to think about, so much to understand. But take heart: Always and in every situation, the truth is in plain view—and tends to be much, much simpler than you think.

APPENDIX OF
DEVOTIONAL PRAYERS

FOLLOWING ARE TRADITIONAL EXAMPLES of formal prayers used in guru yoga:

BODHISATTVA VOWS

1. I resolve to become enlightened for the sake of all living beings.
2. I will cut the roots of all delusive passions.
3. I will penetrate the farthest gates of Dharma.
4. I will realize the supreme way of Buddha.[1]

THE FOUR IMMEASURABLE THOUGHTS

May all sentient being have happiness and the causes of happiness;

May all sentient beings be free from suffering and the causes of suffering;

May all sentient beings never be separated from the happiness that knows no suffering;

May all sentient beings abide in equanimity, free from attachment and anger that hold some close and others distant.[2]

INNER MANDALA

The objects of my attachment, aversion and ignorance—friends, enemies and strangers—

My body, wealth and enjoyments;

Without any sense of loss I offer this collection.

Please accept it with pleasure

And bless me with freedom from the three poisons [attachment, dislike, ignorance].

I send forth this jeweled mandala to you precious gurus.[3]

THE LORD'S PRAYER (MATT. 6: 9-13)

Father,
hallowed be your name,
your kingdom come
as on earth as it is in heaven.
Give us each day our daily bread.
Forgive us our sins,
for we also forgive everyone who has sinned against us.
And lead us not into temptation.
Amen.

PSALM 23

The Lord is my shepherd, I shall not be in want.
He makes me lie down in green pastures,
he leads me beside quiet waters,
he restores my soul.
He guides me in paths of righteousness for his name's sake.
Even though I walk through the valley of the shadow of death,
I will fear no evil, for you are with me;
Your rod and your staff, they comfort me.
You prepare a table before me in the presence of my enemies.
You anoint my head with oil; my cup overflows.
Surely goodness and love will follow me all the days of my life,
and I will dwell in the house of the Lord forever.
Amen.

Notes

CHAPTER 1 NOTES

1. Sigmund Freud, *Civilization and Its Discontents* (1930), in Peter Gay, ed., *The Freud Reader* (New York: Norton, 1989), p. 754.
2. Freud, *Civilization and Its Discontents*, in Gay, *Freud Reader,* p. 763.
3. Freud, *Civilization and Its Discontents,* in Gay, *Freud Reader*, p. 755.
4. Charles Darwin, *On the Origin of Species* (Boston: Harvard University Press, 1975), ch. 3.
5. Emily Dickinson, "Because I Could Not Stop for Death" (1863), in Gerald DeWitt Sanders, John Herbert Nelson, and M. L. Rosenthal, eds., *Chief Modern Poets of England and America, Volume II: The American Poets* (Toronto: Macmillan, 1929), p. 21.
6. Sam Hamill, trans. and J. P. Seaton, ed., *The Essential Chuang Tzu* (Boston: Shambhala, 1998), p. 12.
7. Alan Watts, *The Book on the Taboo Against Knowing Who You Are* (New York: Vintage, 1989), p. 87.
8. Gia-fu Feng and Jane English, trans., *Tao Te Ching* (New York: Vintage, 1997), Chapter 32.
9. John Lennon and Paul McCartney, "I Am the Walrus," on *Magical Mystery Tour* (EMI Records, Ltd., 1967).
10. Henry David Thoreau, *Walden* (1854), in Joseph Wood Krutch, ed., *Walden and Other Writings by Henry David Thoreau* (New York: Bantam, 1962), p. 122.
11. Eknath Easwaran, trans., *The Dhammapada* (Tomales, CA: Nilgiri Press, 1985), p. 26.
12. Easwaran, *The Dhammapada*, pp. 29, 30
13. Easwaran, *The Dhammapada*, p. 30.
14. Easwaran, *The Dhammapada*, 31.
15. Ibid.
16. Quoted in Easwaran, *The Dhammapada*, 31.
17. Freud, *Civilization and Its Discontents*, in Gay, *Freud Reader*, p. 729.
18. Easwaran, *The Dhammapada*, p. 45. My italics.
19. Easwaran, *The Dhammapada*, p. 46.
20. Feng and English, *Tao Te Ching*, Chapter 1.
21. This and further biblical references (except where noted) come from *The NIV Study Bible*, Kenneth L. Barker, ed. (Grand Rapids, MI: Zondervan, 1995).
22. Feng and English, *Tao Te Ching*, Chapter 46.
23. David Godman, ed., *Be as You Are: The Teachings of Sri Ramana Maharshi* (London: Penguin, 1985), p. 118.

CHAPTER 2 NOTES

1. Quoted in Eknath Easwaran, trans., *The Dhammapada* (Tomales, CA: Nilgiri Press, 1985), p. 14.
2. Ken Wilber, Jack Engler, and Daniel Brown, eds., *Transformations of Consciousness: Conventional and Contemplative Perspectives on Development* (Boston: Shambhala, 1984), pp. 191, 213.
3. Jiddu Krishnamurti, *Penguin Krishnamurti Reader* (London: Penguin, 1970), "Questions and Answers."
4. Jimi Hendrix, "An Infinity of Jimi's," *Life* magazine, October 3, 1969.
5. Angelus Silesius, quoted in Huston Smith, *The World's Religions* (New York: HarperCollins, 1958), p. 262.
6. Sigmund Freud, *An Autobiographical Study* (1925), in Peter Gay, ed., *The Freud Reader* (New York: Norton, 1989), p. 24.
7. Friedrich Nietzsche, *The Gay Science,* Walter Kaufman, trans. (New York: Vintage, 1974), p. 228.

8. Henry David Thoreau, *Walden*, in Jospeh Wood Krutch, ed., *Walden and Other Writings by Henry David Thoreau* (New York: Bantam, 1962), p. 345.

9. Thomas Cleary, ed., *The Pocket Zen Reader* (Boston: Shambhala, 1999), p. 102.

10. Kenneth K. S. Ch'en, *Buddhism in China: A Historical Survey* (Princeton: Princeton University Press, 1964), p. 358.

11. Easwaran, *The Dhammapada*, p. 44.

12. Jiddu Krishnamurti, *Total Freedom: The Essential Krishnamurti* (New York: HarperCollins, 1996), p. 1.

13. Groucho Marx, *Groucho and Me* (Cambridge, MA: Da Capo Press, 1995).

14. Krishnamurti, *Total Freedom*, p. xiv.

15. William Gemmell, trans., *The Diamond Sutra* (Berwick, ME: Ibis Press, 2003), pp. 17–18.

16. Gia-fu Feng and Jane English, trans., *Tao Te Ching* (New York: Vintage Books, 1997), Chapter 14.

17. Sam Hamill, trans., and J. P. Seaton, ed., *The Essential Chuang Tzu* (Boston: Shambhala, 1998), pp. 14, 29.

18. Easwaran, *The Dhammapda*, p. 94.

19. Satguru Sivaya Subramuniyaswami, *Merging with Siva: Hinduism's Contemporary Metaphysics* (Kapaa, Hawaii: Himalayan Academy, 1999), p. 577.

20. Subramuniyaswami, *Merging with Siva*, p. 5.

21. From the *Udana* (Solemn Utterances), in *The Minor Anthologies of the Pali Canon, Part II: Udana: Verses of Uplift and Itivuttaka: As It Is Said*, F. L. Woodward, trans. (Oxford: Oxford University Press, 1948), ch. 8, sect. 3.

22. Hamill and Seaton, *The Essential Chuang Tzu*, p. 10.

23. Paul Simon, "Gumboots," on *Graceland* (Warner Brothers Records, 1986).

24. Feng and English, *Tao Te Ching*, Chapter 48.

25. Feng and English, *Tao Te Ching*, Chapter 8.

26. Ibid.

27. John Lennon and Paul McCartney, "I Am the Walrus," *Magical Mystery Tour* (London: EMI Records, 1967).

28. Alan Watts, *This Is It*, (New York: Vintage Books, 1958), p. 31.

29. Smith, *The World's Religions*, p. 71.

30. Hamill and Seaton, trans., *The Essential Chuang Tzu*, pp. 12–13.

CHAPTER 3 NOTES

1. David Godman, ed., *Be as You Are: The Teachings of Sri Ramana Maharshi* (London: Penguin, 1985), p. 96.

2. James Boswell, *The Life of Samuel Johnson* (New York: Knopf, 1993).

3. Thomas Cleary, ed., *The Pocket Zen Reader* (Boston and London: Shambhala, 1999), p. 10.

4. Godman, *Be as You Are*, p. 100.

5. Ram Dass, comp., *Miracle of Love: Stories about Neem Karoli Baba* (Santa Fe: Hanuman Foundation, 1979), p. 399.

6. Steve Newmark, comp., *Maharajji's Darshan* (Hanuman Tape Library).

7. Paul Reps and Nyogen Senzaki, comps., *Zen Flesh Zen Bones: A Collection of Zen and Pre-Zen Writings* (Boston: Tuttle Publishing, 1998), p. 72.

8. Godman, *Be as You Are*, pp. 83–84.

9. Carlos Castañeda is the author of a series of books (*The Teachings of don Juan, A Separate Reality,* and *Journey to Ixtlan* are among the most popular) about his apprenticeship with don Juan, a Mexican Yaqui Indian sorcerer to whom Castañeda originally went to study psychotrophic substances, particularly jimson weed, psilocybin, and peyote, as part of his anthropological studies.

10. Ram Dass, *Be Here Now*, p. 8.

11. Godman, *Be as You Are*, p. 12.

CHAPTER 4 NOTES

1. Adapted from Paul Reps and Nyogen Senzaki, *Zen Flesh, Zen Bones: A Collection of Zen and Pre-Zen Writings* (Boston: Tuttle, 1989), pp. 33–34.
2. Gia-fu Feng and Jane English, trans., *Tao Te Ching* (New York: Vintage, 1997), Chapter 19.
3. Jorge Luis Borges, *Labyrinths: Selected Stories & Other Writings* (New York: New Directions, 1964), p. 99.
4. Borges, *Labyrinths*, p. 98.
5. Feng and English, *Tao Te Ching*, Chapter 2.
6. Feng and English, *Tao Te Ching*, Chapter 28.
7. Thomas Robert Malthus, *An Essay on the Principle of Population* (New York: Penguin, 1983). Originally published in 1798.
8. Feng and English, *Tao Te Ching*, Chapter 28.
9. David Godman, ed., *Be as You Are: The Teachings of Sri Ramana Maharshi* (London: Penguin, 1985), p. 215.
10. Friedrich Nietzsche, *The Gay Science*, Walter Kaufman, trans. (New York: Vintage, 1974), p. 175.
11. Feng and English, *Tao Te Ching*, Chapter 20.
12. Friedrich Nietzsche, *Twilight of the Idols* (1888), in Steven M. Cahn, ed., *Classics of Western Philosophy* (Indianapolis: Hackett, 1977), p. 996.
13. Feng and English, *Tao Te Ching*, Chapter 41.
14. Edward Lorenz, *The Essence of Chaos* (Seattle: University of Washington Press, 1993), p. 4.
15. Claude E. Shannon, "A Mathematical Theory of Information," *Bell System Technical Journal* 27 (1948): 379–423, 623–656.
16. N. Katherine Hayles, *Chaos Band: Orderly Disorder in Contemporary Literature and Science* (Ithaca, NY: Cornell University Press, 1990), pp. 94–96.
17. Ilya Prigogine and Isabelle Stengers, *Order Out of Chaos: Man's New Dialogue with Nature* (New York: Bantam, 1984).
18. Feng and English, *Tao Te Ching*, Chapter 67.
19. Feng and English, *Tao Te Ching*, Chapter 74.
20. Jaroslav Pelikan, trans., *Sacred Writings: Buddhism: The Dhammapada* (New York: Book-of-the-Month Club, 1992), p. 13.
21. Godman, *Be as You Are*, p. 210.

CHAPTER 5 NOTES

1 In Thomas Cleary, trans., *The Taoist Classics: The Collected Translations*, vol. III (Boston: Shambhala, 2000), p. 114.
2. John H. Clark, *A Map of Mental States*, quoted in Georg Feuerstein, Ph.D., *The Yoga Tradition: Its History, Literature, Philosophy and Practice* (Prescott, Arizona: Hohm Press, 1998), p. 334.
3. Lama Anagarika Govinda, *Foundations of Tibetan Mysticism* (York Beach, ME: Weiser, 1969), 17.
4. Ram Dass, *Be Here Now* (Kingsport, TN: Hanuman Foundation, 1978), p. 84.
5. David Lee Roth, "Shy Boy," on *Eat 'em and Smile* (New York: Warner, 1986).
6. Carlos Castañeda, *The Fire from Within* (New York: Washington Square Press, 1984), pp. 183–202.

CHAPTER 6 NOTES

1. Alan Watts, *The Wisdom of Insecurity: A Message for an Age of Anxiety* (New York: Vintage, 1951), p. 34.
2. Tenzin Wangyal, *Wonders of the Natural Mind: The Essence of Dzogchen in the Native Bon Tradition of Tibet* (Barrytown, NY: Station Hill, 1993), p. 139.
3. Wangyal, *Wonders of the Natural Mind*, p. 138.
4. Michael Eigen, the *Psychoanalytic Mystic* (New York: ESF Publishers and Free Association Books, 1998), ch. 10.

5. Gia-fu Feng and Jane English, trans., *Tao Te Ching* (New York: Vintage, 1997), Chapter 42.
6. Feng and English, *Tao Te Ching*, Chapter 34.
7. Ram Dass, comp., *Miracle of Love: Stories about Neem Karoli Baba* (Santa Fe: Hanuman Foundation, 1979), p. 345.
8. Feng and English, *Tao Te Ching*, Chapter 2.
9. Nancy McWilliams, *Psychoanalytic Diagnosis: Understanding Personality Structure in the Clinical Process* (New York: Guilford Press, 1994), p. 97.
10. McWilliams, *Psychoanalytic Diagnosis*, p. 118.
11. Feng and English, *Tao Te Ching*, Chapter 11.
12. Thomas Cleary, ed., *The Pocket Zen Reader* (Boston: Shambhala, 1999), p. 95.

CHAPTER 7 NOTES

1. Chogyal Namkhai Norbu, *Dzogchen: The Self-Perfected State* (Ithaca, NY: Snow Lion, 1989), p. 60.
2. Sam Hamill, trans. and J.P. Seaton, ed., *The Essential Chuang Tzu* (Boston: Shambhala, 1998), p. 123.
3. Alan Watts, *This Is It: And other Essays on Zen and Spiritual Experience* (New York: Vintage, 1973), p. 29.
4. In John Myrdhin Reynolds, trans., *The Golden Letters* (Ithaca, NY: Snow Lion, 1996), p. 39.
5. "The Recorded Conversations of Zen Master I-Hsüan,: in Wing-Tsit Chan, trans., *A Source Book in Chinese Philosophy* (Princeton: Princeton University Press, 1969), ch. 26, section C, par. 5.
6. Tenzin Wangyal, *Wonders of the Natural Mind: The Essence of Dzogchen in the Native Bon Tradition of Tibet* (Barrytown, NY: Station Hill, 1993), p. 91.
7. Gia-fu Feng and Jane English, trans., *Tao Te Ching* (New York: Vintage, 1997), Chapter 18.
9. Wangyal, *Wonders of the Natural Mind*, p. 96.
10. Wangyal, *Wonders of the Natural Mind*, p. 94.
11. Wangyal, *Wonders of the Natural Mind*, pp. 94–95.
12. Wangyal, *Wonders of the Natural Mind*, p. 95.
13. Wangyal, *Wonders of the Natural Mind*, p. 126.
14. Ibid.

CHAPTER 8 NOTES

1. P. D. Ouspensky, *In Search of the Miraculous: Fragments of an Unknown Teaching* (New York: Harcourt Brace, 1974), p. 30.
2. Masao Abe, "The Self in Jung and Zen," in Anthony Molino, ed., *The Couch and the Tree: Dialogues in Psychoanalysis and Buddhism* (New York: North Point Press, 1998), p. 183.
3. Jack Engler, "Therapeutic Aims in Psychotherapy and Meditation: Developmental Stages in the Representation of the Self," in Ken Wilber, Jack Engler, and Daniel Brown, eds., *Transformations of Consciousness: Conventional and Contemplative Perspectives on Human Development* (Boston: Shambhala, 1984), p. 23.
4. Engler, "Therapeutic Aims in Psychotherapy and Meditation," p. 24.
5. Jeffrey B. Rubin, *Psychotherapy and Buddhism: Toward an Integration* (New York: Plenum Press, 1996), p. 60.
6. Sigmund Freud, *The Ego and the Id* (1923), in Peter Gay, ed., *The Freud Reader* (New York: Norton, 1989), p. 630.
7. Carl Jung, *Aion: Researches into the Phenomenology of the Self, Collected Works of C. G. Jung*, vol. 9ii, R. F. C. Hull, trans. Bollingen Series XX (Princeton: Princeton University Press, 1968), ¶ 1–42.
8. Nancy McWilliams, *Psychoanalytic Diagnosis: Understanding Personality Structure in the Clinical Process* (New York: The Guilford Press, 1994), p. 73.
9. Quoted in McWilliams, *Psychoanalytic Diagnosis*, p. 230.
10. Burness E. Moore, M.D., and Bernard D. Fine, M.D., eds., *Psychoanalytic Terms and Concepts* (New Haven: Yale University Press, 1990), p. 53.
11. McWilliams, *Psychoanalytic Diagnosis*, p. 231.

12. Moore and Fine, *Psychoanalytic Terms and Concepts*, p. 90.
13. Moore and Fine, *Psychoanalytic Terms and Concepts*, p. 132.
14. Ibid.
15. McWilliams, *Psychoanalytic Diagnosis*, p. 281.
16. McWilliams, *Psychoanalytic Diagnosis*, p. 282.
17. Moore and Fine, *Psychoanalytic Terms and Concepts*, p. 116.
18. Ibid.
19. McWilliams, *Psychoanalytic Diagnosis*, p. 263.
20. McWilliams, *Psychoanalytic Diagnosis*, p. 168.
21. Otto Kernberg, "Borderline Personality Organization," *Journal of the American Psychology Association* 15 (1967): 641–685.
22. Moore and Fine, *Psychoanalytic Terms and Concepts*, p. 171.
23. Ibid.
24. McWilliams, *Psychoanalytic Diagnosis*, p. 191.
25. McWilliams, *Psychoanalytic Diagnosis*, p. 195.
26. McWilliams, *Psychoanalytic Diagnosis*, p. 248.
27. Moore and Fine, *Psychoanalytic Terms and Concepts*, p. 114.
28. Eknath Easwaran, trans., *The Dhammapada* (Tomales, CA: Nilgiri Press, 1986), pp. 163, 198-199.
29. Walpola Rahula, *What the Buddha Taught,* (New York: Grove Press, 1969), p. 51.
30. Jack Engler, "Therapeutic Aims in Psychotherapy and Meditation," p. 41.
31. Jack Engler, "Therapeutic Aims in Psychotherapy and Meditation," pp. 42-43.
32. Jack Kornfield, *A Path with Heart: A Guide Through the Perils and Promises of Spiritual Life* (New York: Bantam, 1993), p. 245.
33. Kornfield, *A Path with Heart*, p. 246.
34. Kornfield, *A Path with Heart*, p. 244.

Chapter 9 Notes

1. John Lennon and Paul McCartney, "Strawberry Fields Forever," on *The Magical Mystery Tour* (London: EMI Records, 1967).
2. Sigmund Freud, *The Ego and the Id* (1923), in Peter Gay, ed., *The Freud Reader* (New York: Norton, 1989), p. 657.
3. Ibid.
4. Sam Hamill, trans.and J. P. Seaton, ed., *The Essential Chuang Tzu* (Boston: Shambhala, 1999), p. 18.
5. Alfred North Whitehead, *Process and Reality* (New York: The Free Press, 1979), pt. 2, ch. 1.
6. Stephen LaBerge, *Lucid Dreaming: The Power of Being Awake and Aware in Your Dreams* (New York: Ballantine, 1985), pp. 48–49. See also Nathaniel Kleitman, *Sleep and Wakefulness* (Chicago: University of Chicago Press, 1987).
7. LaBerge, *Lucid Dreaming*, pp. 203–206.
8. See Michael Katz's Introduction in Namkhai Norbu, *Dream Yoga and the Practice of Natural Light* (Ithaca, NY: Snow Lion, 1992), p. 21.
9. Stephen LaBerge and Howard Rheingold, *Exploring the World of Lucid Dreaming* (New York: Ballantine, 1990), chapters 2 and 3.
10. Sigmund Freud, *The Interpretation of Dreams* (1909), second ed. (Oxford and New York: Oxford Univerity Press, 2000), ch. 7, sect. E.
11. Sigmund Freud, "The Unconscious" (1915), in Gay, *The Freud Reader*, p. 578.
12. Carl Jung, "The Concept of the Collective Unconscious" (1936), *The Archetypes and the Collective Unconscious, Collected Works of C. G. Jung*, vol. 9i, in Joseph Campbell, ed., *The Portable Jung* (New York: Viking, 1971), p. 60.
13. Ibid.
14. Campbell, *The Portable Jung*, p. 45
15. Hamill and Seaton, *The Essential Chuang Tzu*, 17.
16. Norbu, *Dream Yoga*, pp. 108–109.

17. The Bible, King James Version.
18. Glenn Mullin, trans. and ed., *Tsongchapa's Six Yogas of Naropa* (Ithaca, NY: Snow Lion, 1997).

CHAPTER 10 NOTES

1. Carlos Castañeda, *The Art of Dreaming* (New York: HarperCollins, 1993), p. viii.
2. Namkhai Norbu, *Dream Yoga and the Practice of Natural Light* (Ithaca, NY: Snow Lion, 1992), p. 39.
3. Tenzin Wangyal Rinpoche, *The Tibetan Yogas of Dream and Sleep* (Ithaca, NY: Snow Lion, 1998), p. 62.
4. Norbu, *Dream Yoga*, p. 40.
5. Wangyal, *The Tibetan Yogas of Dream and Sleep*, p. 62.
6. Wangyal, *The Tibetan Yogas of Dream and Sleep*, p. 63.
7. Wangyal, *The Tibetan Yogas of Dream and Sleep*, p. 214.
8. Norbu, *Dream Yoga*, p. 40.
9. John Lennon and Paul McCartney, "Strawberry Fields Forever," on *Magical Mystery Tour* (EMI Records, Ltd., 1967).
10. Wangyal, *The Tibetan Yogas of Dream and Sleep*, p. 64.
11. Namkhai Norbu., *Dzogchen: The Self-Perfected State* (Ithaca, NY: Snow Lion, 1996), pp. 68–69.

CHAPTER 11 NOTES

1. In Francisco J. Varela, ed. and narrator, *Sleeping, Dreaming and Dying: An Exploration of Consciousness with the Dalai Lama* (Boston: Wisdom, 1997), p. 129.
2. Glenn H. Mullin, trans. and ed., *Tsongchapa's Six Yogas of Naropa* (Ithaca, NY: Snow Lion, 1996), p. 177.
3. Mullin, *Six Yogas*, p. 178.
4. Frederick S. Perls, *Gestalt Therapy Verbatim* (New York: The Gestalt Journal, 1969), pp. 103–105.
5. Mullin, *Six Yogas*, p. 181.
6. Carlos Castañeda, *The Art of Dreaming* (New York: HarperCollins, 1993), ch. 2.
7. Mullin, *Six Yogas*, p. 179.
8. Stephen LaBerge and Howard Rheingold, *Exploring the World of Lucid Dreaming* (New York: Ballantine, 1990), ch. 2.
9. Mullin, *Six Yogas*, pp. 179–180.
10. Mullin, *Six Yogas*, p. 180.
11. Ibid.
12. Mullin, *Six Yogas*, p. 205.
13. Mullin, *Six Yogas*, p. 181.
14. Ibid.
15. Ibid.
16. Mullin, *Six Yogas*, p. 182.
17. Mullin, *Six Yogas*, p. 183.

CHAPTER 12 NOTES

1. Ram Dass, comp., *Miracle of Love: Stories about Neem Karoli Baba* (Santa Fe: Hanuman Foundation, 1979), p. 189.
2. Alan Ayckbourn, *Bedroom Farce* (1978), act 2.
3. Sigmund Freud, *Civilization and Its Discontents* (1930), in Peter Gay, ed., *The Freud Reader* (New York: Norton, 1989), p. 747.
4. Gia-fu Feng and Jane English, trans., *Tao Te Ching* (New York: Vintage, 1997), Chapter 2.
5. Feng and English, *Tao Te Ching*, Chapter 15.
6. David M. Buss, *The Evolution of Desire: Strategies of Human Mating* (New York: Basic Books, 1994), p. 5.

7. Carrie Fisher, *Surrender the Pink* (New York: Simon & Schuster, 1990).

8. Charles Darwin, *On the Origin of Species* (Boston: Harvard University Press, 1975), ch. 14.

9. Devendra Singh, "Adaptive Significance of Waist-to-Hip Ratio and Female Physical Attractiveness," *Journal of Personality and Social Psychology* 65 (1993): 293–307.

10. Sigmund Freud, *Three Essays on the Theory of Sexuality* (1924), in Gay, *The Freud Reader*, p. 285.

11. Sigmund Freud, *A Special Type of Choice of Object Made by Men* (1918), in Gay, *The Freud Reader*, p. 392.

12. Irving Berlin, "Let's Face the Music and Dance," 1936, in the movie, *Follow the Fleet.*

13. Mary Leapor, "Mira to Octavia," in Richard Greene, *Mary Leapor: A Study in Eighteenth-Century Women's Poetry* (Oxford and New York: Oxford University Press, 1994).

14. Alan Watts, *Nature, Man and Woman* (New York: Vintage Books, 1991), p. 172.

15. Dorothy Fields, "A Fine Romance."

16. Eknath Easwaran, trans., *The Dhammapada* (Tomales, CA: Nilgiri Press, 1985), p. 79.

17. Easwaran, *The Dhammapada*, p. 143.

18. St. Augustine, *De Civitate Dei,* quoted in Watts, *Nature, Man and Woman*, p. 149.

19. Glenn H. Mullin, trans. & ed., *Tsongchapa's Six Yogas of Naropa* (Ithaca, NY: Snow Lion, 1996), p. 165.

20. Ibid.

21. Ibid.

22. Lama Thubten Yeshe, *The Bliss of Inner Fire: Heart Practice of the Six Yogas of Naropa* (Boston: Wisdom Publications, 1998), p. 182.

23. Paul Reps and Nyogen Senzaki, comp., *Zen Flesh Zen Bones: A Collection of Zen and Pre-Zen Writings* (Boston: Tuttle Publishing 1998), p. 87.

CHAPTER 13 NOTES

1. Sam Hamill, trans. and J. P. Seaton, ed., *The Essential Chuang Tzu* (Boston: Shambhala, 1999), p. 9.

2. Huston Smith, *The World's Religions* (San Francisco: Harper, 1991), p. 127.

3. Gia-fu Feng and Jane English, trans., *Tao Te Ching* (New York: Vintage, 1997), Chapter 42.

4. Lama Anagarika Govinda, *Foundations of Tibetan Mysticism* (York Beach, ME: Weiser, 1967), p. 46.

5. Govinda, *Foundations of Tibetan Mysticism*, p. 47.

6. René Descartes, *Meditations on First Philosophy*, in Steven M. Cahn, ed., *Classics of Western Philosophy* (Indianapolis: Hackett, 1999), pp. 351, 353.

7. René Descartes, *Meditations on First Philosophy*, in Cahn, *Classics of Western Philosophy*, p. 351.

8. René Descartes, *Meditations on First Philosophy*, in Cahn, *Classics of Western Philosophy*, p. 356.

9. René Descartes, *Discourse on Method and Related Writings*, Desmond M. Clarke, trans. (New York: Penguin USA, 2000), pt. 4.

10. René Descartes, *Meditations on First Philosophy*, in Cahn, *Classics of Western Philosophy*, p. 354.

11. René Descartes, *Meditations on First Philosophy*, in Cahn, *Classics of Western Philosophy*, p. 349.

12. G. I. Gurdjieff, *Beelzebub's Tales to His Grandson: An Objectively Impartial Criticism of the Life of Man, All and Everything*, First Series (London: Arkana, 1992), p. 763.

13. Ram Dass, *Be Here Now* (Kingsport, TN: Hanuman Foundation, 1978), p. 34.

14. Feng and English, *Tao Te Ching*, Chapter 41.

15. From "The Gateless Gate," (*Mumonkan*) in Paul Reps and Nyogen Senzaki, comp., *Zen Flesh, Zen Bones: A Collection of Zen and Pre-Zen Writings* (Boston: Tuttle Publishing, 1998), p. 123.

APPENDIX NOTES

1. Ram Dass, *Be Here Now* (Kingsport, Tennessee: Hanuman Foundation, 1978), p. 7.

2. Kathleen McDonald, *How to Meditate: A Practical Guide* (Boston: Wisdom Publications, 1984), p. 147.

3. McDonald, *How to Meditate*, p. 146.

Suggestions for Further Reading

In addition to the books listed in the bibliography, I recommend the following for further study:

BUDDHISM AND GENERAL SPIRITUALITY

Dass, Ram. *The Only Dance there Is: Talks at the Menninger Foundation, 1970, and Spring Grove Hospital, 1972*. New York: Doubleday, 1974. (Originally published by the Transpersonal Institute, 1970, 1971, and 1973.)

Dass, Ram with Stephen Levine. *Grist for the Mill*. Berkeley, CA: Celestial Arts, 1987. (Originally published by Unity Press in 1976.)

Easwaran, Eknath, trans. *Classics of Indian Spirituality*. Tomales, CA: Nilgiri Press, 1989. A boxed set that includes *The Bhagavad Gita, The Upanishads*, and *The Dhammapada;* each volume is also sold individually.

Kornfield, Jack. *A Path with Heart: A Guide through the Perils and Promises of Spiritual Life*. New York: Bantam, 1993.

Levine, Stephen and Ondrea. *Embracing the Beloved: Relationship as a Path of Awakening*. New York: Doubleday, 1995.

Osho. *Autobiography of a Spiritually Incorrect Mystic*. New York: St. Martin's Griffin, 2000.

GURUS

Dass, Ram. *Miracle of Love: Stories about Neem Karoli Baba*. Santa Fe: Hanuman Foundation, 1979.

Murphet, Howard. *Sai Baba: Man of Miracles*. York Beach, ME: Weiser, 1977.

Osborne, Arthur. *Ramana Maharshi and the Path of Self-Knowledge*. York Beach, ME: Weiser, 1995.

Yogananda, Paramahansa. *Autobiography of a Yogi*. Los Angeles: Self-Realization Fellowship, 1979.

MEDITATION AND DEVOTIONAL PRACTICES

Dass, Ram. *Journey of Awakening: A Meditator's Guidebook*. New York: Bantam, 1978.

Gunaratana, Henepola. *Mindfulness in Plain English*. Boston: Wisdom Publications, 1991.

PHILOSOPHY

Emerson, Ralph Waldo. *Emerson's Essays: First and Second Series Complete in One Volume*. Introduced by Irwin Edman. New York: Harper Colophon Books.

Originally published by Thomas Y. Crowell Company. 1926. (Particularly recommended: *Self-Reliance*, *The Over-Soul*, and *Circles*.)

James, William. *The Varieties of Religious Experience: A Study in Human Nature*. Edited with an introduction by Martin E. Marty. New York: Viking Penguin, 1982.

Kaufman, Walter, trans. and ed. *Basic Writings of Nietzsche*. New York: Random House, Modem Library Giant, 1968. (Particularly recommended: *Beyond Good and Evil* and *On the Genealogy of Morals* [co-edited by R. J. Hollingdale].)

Wilber, Ken. *A Brief History of Everything*. Boston: Shambhala, 1996.

———. *The Spectrum of Consciousness*. Wheaton, Illinois: Quest Books, 1977.

PSYCHOLOGY

Epstein, Mark. *Going to Pieces without Falling Apart: A Buddhist Perspective on Wholeness*. New York: Broadway Books, 1998.

———. *Thoughts without a Thinker. Psychotherapy from a Buddhist Perspective*. New York: Basic Books, 1995.

TIBETAN STUDIES: DZOGCHEN AND TANTRA

Gyatso, Geshe Kelsang. *Tantric Grounds and Paths. How to Enter, Progress on, and Complete the Vajrayana Path*. London: Tharpa Publications, 1994.

Norbu, Namkhai. *The Crystal and the Way of Light: Sutra, Tantra, and Dzogchen*. Compiled and edited by John Shane. Ithaca, NY: Snow Lion, 2000.

———. *The Mirror: Advice on the Presence of Awareness*. Translated from Tibetan into Italian and edited by Adriano Clemente. Translated from Italian by Andrew Lukianowicz. Barrytown, NY: Station Hill Openings, 1983.

Wangyal Rinpoche, Tenzin. *Wonders of the Natural Mind: The Essence of Dzogchen in the Native Bon Tradition of Tibet*. Barrytown, NY: Station Hill, 1993.

Yehse, Lama. *Introduction to Tantra: A Vision of Totality*. Compiled and edited by Jonathan Landlaw. Boston: Wisdom Publications, 1987.

———. *The Tantric Path of Purification: The Yoga Method of Heruka Vajrasattva*. Compiled and edited by Nicholas Ribush. Boston: Wisdom Publications, 1995.

TOLTEC STUDIES AND DREAM PRACTICE

Abelar, Taisha. *The Sorcerer's Crossing: A Woman's Journey*. Foreword by Carlos Castañeda. New York: Penguin USA, 1993.

Castaneda, Carlos. *Journey to Ixtlan: The Lessons of don Juan*. New York: Pocket Books, 1975.

———. *A Separate Reality: Further Conversations with don Juan*. New York: Pocket Books, 1972.

————. *Tales of Power.* New York: Pocket Books, 1975.

————. *The Teachings of don Juan: A Yaqui Way of Knowledge.* New York: Pocket Books, 1974.

Donner, Florinda. *Being-in-Dreaming: An Initiation into the Sorcerer's World.* San Francisco: HarperSanFrancisco. 1992.

————. *The Witch's Dream: A Healer's Way of Knowledge.* New York: Simon and Schuster, 1985.

Eagle Feather, Ken. *A Toltec Path: A User's Guide to the Teachings of don Juan Matus, Carlos Castaneda, and Other Toltec Seers.* Charlottesville, VA: Hampton Roads, 1995.

————. *Tracking Freedom: A Guide for Personal Evolution.* Charlottesville, VA: Hampton Roads. 1998.

————. *Traveling with Power: The Exploration and Development of Perception.* Charlottesville, VA: Hampton Roads. 1992.

Kleitman, Nathaniel. *Sleep and Wakefulness.* Chicago: University of Chicago Press, 1987.

LaBerge, Steven and Howard Rheingold, *Exploring the World of Lucid Dreaming.* New York: Ballantine, 1990.

Monroe, Robert. *Ultimate Journey.* New York: Main Street Books, 1996.

Wangyal Rinpoche, Tenzin. *The Tibetan Yogas of Dream and Sleep.* Ithaca, NY: Snow Lion, 1998.

ZEN AND TAOISM

Masunaga, Reiho, trans. *A Primer of Soto Zen: A Translation of Dogen 's Shobogenzo Zuimonki.* Honolulu: University of Hawaii Press, 1971.

Sekida, Katsuki. *Zen Training: Methods and Philosophy.* New York and Tokyo: Weatherhill, 1975.

Watts, Alan and Al Chung-Liang Huang. *Tao: The Watercourse Way.* New York: Random House, 1977.

Bibliography

Abe, Masao. "The Self in Jung and Zen." In Anthony Molino, ed. *The Couch and the Tree: Dialogues in Psychoanalysis and Buddhism*. New York: North Point Press, 1998.

Barker, Kenneth L., ed. *The NIV Study Bible*. Grand Rapids, MI: Zondervan, 1995.

Bible, The. King James Version.

Borges, Jorge Luis. *Labyrinths: Selected Stories & Other Writings*. New York: New Directions, 1964.

Boswell, James. *The Life of Samuel Johnson*. New York: Knopf, 1993.

Buss, David M. *The Evolution of Desire: Strategies of Human Mating*. New York: Basic Books, 1994.

Campbell, Joseph, ed. *The Portable Jung*. New York: Penguin Books, 1971.

Castañeda, Carlos. *The Art of Dreaming*. New York: HarperCollins, 1993.

———. *Fire from Within*. New York: Washington Square Books, 1984.

Cahn, Steven M. ed., *Classics of Western Philosophy*. Indianapolis: Hackett Publishing, 1999.

Chan, Wing-Tsit. *A Source Book in Chinese Philosophy*. Princeton: Princeton University Press, 1969.

Ch'en, Kenneth K. S. *Buddhism in China: A Historical Survey*. Princeton: Princeton University Press, 1964.

Cleary, Thomas, ed. *The Pocket Zen Reader*. Boston and London: Shambhala, 1999.

———. *The Taoist Classics: The Collected Translations*. Vol. III. Boston: Shambhala. 2000.

Darwin, Charles. *On the Origin of Species*. Boston: Harvard University Press, 1975.

Dalai Lama, H. H., *Dzogchen: The Heart Essence of the Great Perfection: Teachings Given in the West*. (Ithaca, NY: Snow Lion Publications, 2001.

Dass, Ram. *Be Here Now*. Kingsport, TN: Hanuman Foundation, 1978.

Dass, Ram, comp. *Miracle of Love: Stories about Neem Karoli Baba*. Santa Fe: Hanuman Foundation, 1979.

Descartes, René. *Discourse on Method and Related Writings*. Desmond M. Clarke, trans. New York: Penguin USA, 2000.

Descartes, René. *Meditations on First Philosophy*. In Steven M. Cahn, ed., *Classics of Western Philosophy*. Indianapolis: Hackett Publishing, 1999.

Dickinson, Emily. "Because I Could Not Stop for Death" (1863). In Gerald DeWitt Sanders, Nelson, John Herbert and M. L. Rosenthal, eds., *Chief Modern Poets of England and America, Volume II: The American Poets*. Toronto: Macmillan, 1929.

Easwaran, Eknath, trans. *The Dhammapada*. Tomales, CA: Nilgiri Press, 1985.

Eigen, Michael. *The Psychoanalytic Mystic*. New York: ESF Publishers and Free Association Books, 1998.

Engler, Jack. "Therapeutic Aims in Psychotherapy and Meditation: Developmental Stages in the Representation of the Self." In Ken Wilber, Jack Engler, and Daniel Brown, eds., *Transformations of Consciousness: Conventional and Contemplative Perspectives on Human Development*. Boston: Shambhala, 1984.

Feng, Gia-fu and Jane English, trans., *Tao Te Ching*. New York: Vintage, 1997.

Feuerstein, Ph.D., Georg. *The Yoga Tradition: Its History, Literature, Philosophy and Practice*. Prescott, AZ: Hohm Press, 1998.

Fisher, Carrie. *Surrender the Pink*. New York: Simon & Schuster, 1990.

Freud, Sigmund. *An Autobiographical Study* (1925). In Peter Gay, ed., *The Freud Reader* New York: Norton, 1989.

———. *Civilization and Its Discontents* (1930). In Peter Gay, ed., *The Freud Reader*. New York: Norton, 1989.

———. *The Ego and the Id* (1923). In Peter Gay, ed., *The Freud Reader*. New York: Norton, 1989.

———. *The Interpretation of Dreams* (1909). Second edition. Oxford and New York: Oxford Univerity Press, 2000.

———. *A Special Type of Choice of Object Made by Men* (1918). In Gay, *The Freud Reader*. New York: Norton, 1989.

———. *Three Essays on the Theory of Sexuality* (1924). In Gay, *The Freud Reader*. New York: Norton, 1989.

———. "The Unconscious" (1915). In Gay, *The Freud Reader*. New York: Norton, 1989.

Gemmell, William, trans. *The Diamond Sutra*. Berwick, ME: Ibis Press, 2003.

Godman, David, ed. *Be as You Are: The Teachings of Sri Ramana Maharshi*. London: Penguin, 1985.

Govinda, Lama Anagarika. *Foundations of Tibetan Mysticism*. York Beach, ME: Weiser, 1967.

Gay, Peter, ed. *The Freud Reader* New York: Norton, 1989.

Greene, Richard. *Mary Leapor: A Study in Eighteenth-Century Women's Poetry*. Oxford & New York: Oxford University Press, 1994.

G. I. Gurdjieff, *Beelzebub's Tales to His Grandson: An Objectively Impartial Criticism of the Life of Man, All and Everything*. London: Arkana, 1992.

Hamill, Sam, trans. and J. P. Seaton, ed. *The Essential Chuang Tzu*. Boston: Shambhala, 1998.

Hayles, N. Katherine. *Chaos Band: Orderly Disorder in Contemporary Literature and Science* Ithaca, NY: Cornell University Press, 1990.

Hendrix, Harville. *Getting the Love You Want: A Guide for Couples.* New York: HarperPerennial Library, 1990.

Hendrix, Jimi. "An Infinity of Jimi's." *Life* magazine, October 3, 1969.

Jung, Carl. *Aion: Phenomenology of the Self, Collected Works of C. G. Jung,* vol. 9ii. Princeton: Princeton University Press, 1968. In Joseph Campbell, ed. *The Portable Jung.* New York: Penguin Books, 1971.

———. "The Concept of the Collective Unconscious" (1936). *The Archetypes and the Collective Unconscious, Collected Works of C. G. Jung,* vol. 9i. In Joseph Campbell, ed., *The Portable Jung.* New York: Viking, 1971.

Kernberg, Otto. "Borderline Personality Organization," *Journal of the American Psychology Association* 15 (1967): 641–685.

Kornfield, Jack. *A Path with Heart: A Guide through the Perils and Promises of Spiritual Life.* New York: Bantam, 1993.

Krishnamurti, Jiddu. *Penguin Krishnamurti Reader.* London: Penguin, 1970.

———. *Total Freedom: The Essential Krishnamurti.* New York: HarperCollins, 1996.

Krutch, Joseph Wood, ed. *Walden and Other Writings by Henry David Thoreau.* New York: Bantam, 1962.

LaBerge, Steven. *Lucid Dreaming: The Power of Being Awake and Aware in Your Dreams.* New York: Ballantine, 1985.

LaBerge, Steven and Howard Rheingold, *Exploring the World of Lucid Dreaming.* New York: Ballantine, 1990.

Leapor, Mary. "Mira to Octavia." In Richard Greene, *Mary Leapor: A Study in Eighteenth-Century Women's Poetry.* Oxford & New York: Oxford University Press, 1994.

Lennon, John and Paul McCartney. "I Am the Walrus." *Magical Mystery Tour.* EMI Records, Ltd., 1967.

———. "Strawberry Fields Forever." *Magical Mystery Tour.* EMI Records, Ltd., 1967.

Lorenz, Edward. *The Essence of Chaos.* Seattle: University of Washington Press, 1993.

Malthus, Thomas Robert *An Essay on the Principle of Population* (1798). New York: Penguin, 1983.

Marx, Groucho. *Groucho and Me.* Cambridge, MA: Da Capo Press, 1995.

McDonald., Kathleen. *How to Meditate: A Practical Guide.* Boston: Wisdom Publications, 1984.

McWilliams, Nancy. *Psychoanalytic Diagnosis: Understanding Personality Structure in the Clinical Process.* New York: Guilford Press, 1994.

Molino, Anthony, ed. *The Couch and the Tree: Dialogues in Psychoanalysis and Buddhism.* New York: North Point Press, 1998.

Monroe, Robert. *Ultimate Journey.* New York: Main Street Books, 1996.

Moore, Burness E., M.D., and Bernard D. Fine, M.D., eds. *Psychoanalytic Terms and Concepts.* New Haven: Yale University Press, 1990.

Morehouse, David A. *Psychic Warrior.* New York: St. Martin's Press, 1998.

Mullin, Glenn H. trans. and ed. *Tsongchapa's Six Yogas of Naropa.* Ithaca, NY: Snow Lion, 1996.

Newmark, Steve, comp. *Maharajji's Darshan.* Hanuman Tape Library.

Nietzsche, Friedrich. *The Gay Science.* Walter Kaufman, trans. New York: Vintage, 1974.

———. *Twilight of the Idols* (1888). In Steven M. Cahn, ed., *Classics of Western Philosophy.* Indianapolis: Hackett, 1977.

Norbu, Namkhai. *Dream Yoga and the Practice of Natural Light.* Ithaca, New York: Snow Lion, 1992.

———. *Dzogchen: The Self-Perfected State.* Ithaca, NY: Snow Lion, 1989), p. 60.

Ouspensky, P. D. *In Search of the Miraculous: Fragments of an Unknown Teaching.* New York: Harcourt Brace, 1974.

Pelikan, Jaroslav, trans. *Sacred Writings: Buddhism: The Dhammapada.* New York: Book-of-the-Month Club, 1992.

Perls, Frederick S. *Gestalt Therapy Verbatim.* New York: The Gestalt Journal, 1969.

Plato. *Meno.* G. M. A. Grube, trans. Indianapolis: Hackett Publishing. 1976.

Plato. *The Republic.* G. M. A. Grube, trans. Revised by C. D. C. Reeve. Indianapolis: Hackett Publishing. 1992.

Prigogine, Ilya and Isabelle Stengers. *Order Out of Chaos: Man's New Dialogue with Nature.* New York: Bantam, 1984.

Rahula, Walpola. *What the Buddha Taught.* New York: Grove Press, 1969.

Reps, Paul and Nyogen Senzaki, comp. *Zen Flesh Zen Bones: A Collection of Zen and Pre-Zen Writings.* Boston: Tuttle Publishing 1998.

Reynolds, John Myrdhin trans. *The Golden Letters.* Ithaca, NY: Snow Lion, 1996.

Roth, David Lee. "Shy Boy." On *Eat 'em and Smile.* New York: Warner, 1986.

Rubin, Jeffrey B. *Psychotherapy and Buddhism: Toward an Integration.* New York: Plenum Press, 1996.

Sanders, Gerald DeWitt, John Herbert Nelson, and M. L. Rosenthal, eds., *Chief Modern Poets of England and America, Volume II: The American Poets.* Toronto: Macmillan, 1929.

Shannon, Claude. "A Mathematical Theory of Information." *Bell System Technical Journal* 27 (1948): 379–423, 623–656.

Simon, Paul. "Gumboots." On *Graceland.* New York: Warner Brothers Records.

Singh, Devendra. "Adaptive Significance of Waist-to-Hip Ratio and Female Physical Attractiveness," *Journal of Personality and Social Psychology* 65, 1993.

Smith, Huston. *The World's Religions.* New York: HarperCollins, 1958.

Subramuniyaswami, Satguru Sivaya. *Merging with Siva: Hinduism's Contemporary Metaphysics.* Kapaa, Hawaii: Himalayan Academy, 1999.

Thoreau, Henry David. *Walden* (1854). In Joseph Wood Krutch, ed., *Walden and Other Writings by Henry David Thoreau.* New York: Bantam, 1962.

Varela, Francisco J. *Sleeping, Dreaming and Dying: An Exploration of Consciousness with the Dalai Lama.* Boston: Wisdom Publications, 1997.

Wangyal Rinpoche, Tenzin. *The Tibetan Yogas of Dream and Sleep*. Ithaca, NY: Snow Lion, 1998.

———. *Wonders of the Natural Mind: The Essence of Dzogchen in the Native Bon Tradition of Tibet*. Barrytown, NY: Station Hill, 1993.

Watts, Alan. *The Book on the Taboo Against Knowing Who You Are*. New York: Vintage, 1989.

———. *Nature, Man and Woman*. New York: Vintage Books, 1991.

———. *This Is It: And other Essays on Zen and Spiritual Experience*. New York: Vintage, 1973.

———. *The Wisdom of Insecurity: A Message for an Age of Anxiety*. New York: Vintage, 1951.

Whitehead, Alfred North. *Process and Reality*. New York: The Free Press, 1979.

Wilber, Ken, Jack Engler, and Daniel Brown, eds. *Transformations of Consciousness: Conventional and Contemplative Perspectives on Development*. Boston: Shambhala, 1984.

Wilson, Colin. *From Atlantis to the Sphinx*. New York: Fromm International, 1997.

Woodward, F. L., *The Minor Anthologies of the Pali Canon, Part II: Udana: Verses of Uplift and Itivuttaka: As It Is Said*. Oxford: Oxford University Press, 1948.

Yeshe, Lama Thubten. *The Bliss of Inner Fire: Heart Practice of the Six Yogas of Naropa*. Boston: Wisdom Publications, 1998.

Index